Frommer's®

W9-CBK-875

Santa Fe, Taos & Albuquerque

10th Edition

by Lesley King

WILEY
Wiley Publishing, Inc.

About the Author

Lesley S. King grew up on a ranch in northern New Mexico where she still returns on weekends to help work cattle. She's a freelance writer and photographer, and a columnist for *New Mexico* magazine—as well as an avid kayaker and skier. Formerly the managing editor for *The Santa Fean,* she has written about food and restaurants for *The New York Times,* the Ancestral Puebloans (Anasazi) culture for United Airline's *Hemispheres* magazine, and the environment for *Audubon.* She is the author of *Frommer's New Mexico, Frommer's Great Outdoor Guide to Arizona & New Mexico,* and *New Mexico For Dummies.* She's also the co-author of *Frommer's American Southwest.*

Published by:

Wiley Publishing, Inc.

111 River St.
Hoboken, NJ 07030-5774

ISBN 0-7645-7306-3

Editor: Kitty Wilson Jarrett
Production Editor: M. Faunette Johnston
Cartographer: Nicholas Trotter
Photo Editor: Richard Fox
Production by Wiley Indianapolis Composition Services

For information on our other products and services or to obtain technical support, please contact our Customer Care Department within the U.S. at 800/762-2974, outside the U.S. at 317/572-3993 or fax 317/572-4002.

Wiley also publishes its books in a variety of electronic formats. Some content that appears in print may not be available in electronic formats.

Manufactured in the United States of America

5 4 3 2

Contents

List of Maps

An Invitation to the Reader

In researching this book, we discovered many wonderful places—hotels, restaurants, shops, and more. We're sure you'll find others. Please tell us about them, so we can share the information with your fellow travelers in upcoming editions. If you were disappointed with a recommendation, we'd love to know that, too. Please write to:

Frommer's Santa Fe, Taos & Albuquerque, 10th Edition
Wiley Publishing, Inc. • 111 River St. • Hoboken, NJ 07030-5774

An Additional Note

Please be advised that travel information is subject to change at any time—and this is especially true of prices. We therefore suggest that you write or call ahead for confirmation when making your travel plans. The authors, editors, and publisher cannot be held responsible for the experiences of readers while traveling. Your safety is important to us, however, so we encourage you to stay alert and be aware of your surroundings. Keep a close eye on cameras, purses, and wallets, all favorite targets of thieves and pickpockets.

Other Great Guides for Your Trip:

Frommer's New Mexico
Frommer's American Southwest
Frommer's National Parks of the American West

Frommer's Star Ratings, Icons & Abbreviations

Every hotel, restaurant, and attraction listing in this guide has been ranked for quality, value, service, amenities, and special features using a **star-rating system.** In country, state, and regional guides, we also rate towns and regions to help you narrow down your choices and budget your time accordingly. Hotels and restaurants are rated on a scale of zero (recommended) to three stars (exceptional). Attractions, shopping, nightlife, towns, and regions are rated according to the following scale: zero stars (recommended), one star (highly recommended), two stars (very highly recommended), and three stars (must-see).

In addition to the star-rating system, we also use **eight feature icons** that point you to the great deals, in-the-know advice, and unique experiences that separate travelers from tourists. Throughout the book, look for:

Finds	Special finds—those places only insiders know about
Fun Fact	Fun facts—details that make travelers more informed and their trips more fun
Kids	Best bets for kids and advice for the whole family
Moments	Special moments—those experiences that memories are made of
Overrated	Places or experiences not worth your time or money
Tips	Insider tips—great ways to save time and money
Value	Great values—where to get the best deals
Warning	Warning—traveler's advisories

The following **abbreviations** are used for credit cards:

AE	American Express	DISC	Discover	V	Visa
DC	Diners Club	MC	MasterCard		

Frommers.com

Now that you have the guidebook to a great trip, visit our website at **www.frommers.com** for travel information on more than 3,000 destinations. With features updated regularly, we give you instant access to the most current trip-planning information available. At Frommers.com, you'll also find the best prices on airfares, accommodations, and car rentals—and you can even book travel online through our travel booking partners. At Frommers.com, you'll also find the following:

- Online updates to our most popular guidebooks
- Vacation sweepstakes and contest giveaways
- Newsletter highlighting the hottest travel trends
- Online travel message boards with featured travel discussions

What's New in Northern New Mexico

Northern New Mexico has come by its *"mañana"* reputation honestly. Usually change happens . . . tomorrow. But there are some lively additions in the region well worth exploring.

GETTING TO KNOW SANTA FE Visitors now have their own health service, just blocks from the Plaza. **Ultimed,** 707 Paseo de Peralta (© 505/989-8707), a new urgent-care facility, offers comprehensive health care.

WHERE TO STAY IN SANTA FE Along historic Barrio de Analco in the center of downtown, the **Inn of the Five Graces,** 150 E. de Vargas St. (© 505/992-0957; www.fivegraces. com), Santa Fe's newest and best-kept secret, offers a lovely melding of the Orient and the Old West, with elaborately decorated suites with kilim rugs, ornately carved beds, and mosaic tile work in the bathrooms. The notable spa **Ten Thousand Waves,** 3451 Hyde Park Rd. (© 505/982-9304; www.tenthousandwaves.com), nestled in piñon trees just outside town, now offers accommodations. There are minimalist Japanese-adobe rooms and casitas for those seeking silence and solitude. New to this book is the **Don Gaspar Inn,** 623 Don Gaspar (© 888/986-8664 or 505/986-8664; www. dongaspar.com), a quiet and elegant place nestled in a historic neighborhood, for those who want to feel like they live in Santa Fe. See chapter 5 for details.

WHERE TO DINE IN SANTA FE Melding many flavors from Old Mexico in a cozy, intimate setting, the new **Los Mayas,** 409 W. Water St. (© 505/986-9930), is a fun addition to the Santa Fe dining scene. Santa Fe's most happening moderately priced new restaurant, the **Santa Fe Railyard Restaurant & Bar,** 530 S. Guadalupe (© 505/989-8363), offers imaginative new American food in a historic railyard building. Rated by local media as the best new inexpensive restaurant in town, **Bumble Bee's Baja Grill,** 301 Jefferson St. (© 505/820-2862), offers fast and healthy Old Mexico tacos and other spicy delights. See chapter 6 for details.

WHAT TO SEE & DO IN SANTA FE The newest news from the "City Different" is a **performance gazebo** erected on the plaza in 2004. While the structure was being built, Native American and other artifacts were found, prompting an excavation that at press time is still under way. Visitors can observe archaeologists as they brush away dirt and time, revealing pot shards, tools, and other finds. See p. 116.

EXCURSIONS FROM SANTA FE Tesuque Pueblo (9 miles north of Santa Fe on US 84/285) has a new church. The **San Diego Church,** a three-story structure, replaces an older church that burned in 1988. The **Castillo Gallery** (a mile into the village of Cordova on the High Road to

Taos; (② **505/351-4067**) has moved next door, into a brighter and more expansive space, still operated by a fine husband-and-wife artist team. See chapter 10 for details.

WHERE TO STAY IN TAOS The biggest news in the region is the opening of **El Monte Sagrado,** 317 Kit Carson Rd. (② **800/828-TAOS** or 505/758-3502; www.elmontesagrado. com). This eco-resort offers impeccable, imaginative accommodations surrounding a "Sacred Circle," an open grassy area. The resort also offers fine food and spa treatments. Taos is celebrating finally having a good hotel on its plaza. **Hotel La Fonda de Taos,** 108 South Plaza (② **800/833-2211** or 505/758-2211; www.hotellafonda. com), provides comfortable, smartly decorated rooms with a dash of history. **The Bavarian Lodge,** above Taos Ski Valley (② **888/205-8020** or 505/776-8020; www.thebavarian. com), offers its guests first access to the back bowls as well as Bavarian-style rooms in an authentic log cabin. Also at Taos Ski Valley, the **Edelweiss Lodge & Spa,** 106 Sutton Place (② **800/I-LUV-SKI** or 505/776-2301; www.edelweisslodgeandspa.com), has been rebuilt into an upscale condo-hotel, with luxury rooms and a complete spa. The owners are especially intent on attracting summer spa guests. For more details, see chapter 12.

WHERE TO DINE IN TAOS Located at El Monte Sagrado, the new **De La Tierra,** 317 Kit Carson Rd. (② **800/828-TAOS** or 505/758-3502), offers regional American food in a refined atmosphere. Diners feast on food ranging from venison medallions to rosemary-skewered shrimp. For a while Taos was without **Joseph's Table;** this fine restaurant closed. But it has reopened in an even larger space in the Hotel La Fonda on the plaza, and it still serves some of the most imaginative food in the Southwest. It's

located at 108-A South Taos Plaza (② **505/751-4512;** www.josephstable. com). Worth the trip to Taos Ski Valley even if you're not going to strap on the boards, **The Bavarian Restaurant,** above Taos Ski Valley (② **888/205-8020** or 505/776-8020), serves up delicious Bavarian-style fare such as goulash and sauerbraten in an old-world log cabin nestled in high alpine forest. Take the shuttle from the ski area up. In the quaint Arroyo Seco village, en route to the ski area, **Gypsy 360°,** 480 NM 150, Seco Plaza (② **505/776-3166**), could just be the region's best new casual spot. Serving Asian and American dishes ranging from pad Thai to Angus burgers, the place serves recipes as fresh as the ingredients in them. See chapter 13 for details.

WHAT TO SEE & DO IN TAOS A sad change has come to the **Taos Historic Museums** (② **505/758-0505**): The Kit Carson Home has passed out of their hands. Exhibits from the museum will be moved to the Martinez Hacienda (Lower Ranchitos Rd., Hwy. 240; ② **505/758-1000**). The Kit Carson Home owners plan to open their own museum. Another big change in the Taos museum scene is the shifting of the **Taos Art Museum** (② **505/758-2690**) collection from the Van Vechten Lineberry Museum (now closed) to the Fechin House, 227 Paseo del Pueblo Norte. Though the museum lost some space, it gained a lovely venue. A new hot spot for those who like to browse little villages is **Arroyo Seco,** on NM 150, about 5 miles north of town en route to Taos Ski Valley. Arroyo Seco has Gypsy 360° (see above) and fun shops and amazing mountain views. See chapter 14 for details.

TAOS AFTER DARK Nights will never be the same in Taos now that the **Anaconda Bar,** 317 Kit Carson Rd.

(© **505/758-3502**), has opened at El Monte Sagrado resort. A contemporary feel, accented by a giant anaconda snake sculpture, as well as tasty tapas and live music draw the hippest Taoseños and visitors to the spot. See p. 223.

WHERE TO DINE IN ALBU-QUERQUE Albuquerque's most happening new dining spot, **Zinc Wine Bar and Bistro,** 3009 Central Ave. NE (© **505/254-ZINC**), offers inventive meals such as blackened sliced flank steak over a Greek salad, with interesting deals, such as "wine flights," which allow diners to sample a variety of wines from a particular region, all within a moody, urban atmosphere. Almost across the street from Zinc, noted chef Jennifer James has opened a more reasonably priced sister restaurant to her namesake one. **Graze,** 3128 Central Ave. SE (© **505/268-4729**), offers small plates of new American cuisine with such interesting flavor spins that you reel delightfully. The penne with goat cheese and chorizo is delectable. See chapter 15 for details.

WHAT TO SEE & DO IN ALBU-QUERQUE Head through a tunnel with turquoise embedded in the walls, and you'll find yourself in one of Albuquerque's most colorful museums, the **Turquoise Museum,** 2107 Central Ave. NW (© **505/247-8650**), west of Old Town. It lays claim to the world's largest collection of the blue stone. Within the same district has moved ¡**Explora! Science Center and Children's Museum,** 1701 Mountain Rd. (© **505/224-8300**). The museum features hands-on scientific exhibits for kids of all ages, even 40-something ones like me. See chapter 15.

EXPLORING NEARBY PUEBLOS AND MONUMENTS If you make your way north on the Jemez Mountain Trail, make reservations at the **Cañon del Rio–Riverside Inn,** 16445 Scenic Hwy. 4, Jemez Springs (© **505/829-4377;** www.canondelrio. com). Formerly the Riverdancer, this inn near the Jemez River has been refurbished by new owners. See p. 275.

1

The Best of Northern New Mexico

New Mexico's Pueblo tribes have one character that stands out among many as a symbol of the spirit of this state: the fun-maker, called by a variety of names, most notably Koshare. Within the Native American dances, this black-and-white-striped character has many powers. He can cure some diseases, make rain fall, and increase fertility. Above all, the irreverent joker exposes our deepest foibles.

As you travel throughout northern New Mexico, you may see evidence of the Koshare-like powers in the land's magical beauty and in the tender relationships between cultures. This place has witnessed immense geologic upheavals, from volcanic explosions to cataclysmic ground shifts. It has seen tragedy in the clash between Spanish, Native American, and Anglo cultures. And yet, with its Koshare nature, it has transformed those experiences into immeasurable richness. Today, it is a land of stunning expanses, immense cultural diversity, and creativity—a place where people very much pursue their own paths.

The center of the region is Santa Fe, a hip, artsy city that wears its 400-year-old mores on its sleeve. Not far away is upstart **Taos,** the little arts town and ski center of just 5,000 people that lies wedged between the 13,000-foot **Sangre de Cristo Mountains** and the 700-foot-deep **Rio Grande Gorge. Albuquerque** is the big city, New Mexico style, where people from all over the state come to trade. Not far from these three cities are the 19 settlements and numerous ruins of the Native American Pueblo culture, an incredible testament to the resilience of a proud people. And through it all weave the **Manzano, Sandia, Sangre de Cristo,** and **Jemez mountains,** multimillion-year-old reminders of the recent arrival of humans in this vast and unique landscape.

From skiing to art galleries, you have a wealth of choices in front of you when planning a trip to northern New Mexico. To help you get started, here are some of my favorite things to do, places to stay, and places to eat in and around Santa Fe, Taos, and Albuquerque.

1 Frommer's Favorite Northern New Mexico Experiences

- **High Road to Taos:** This spectacular 80-mile route into the mountains between Santa Fe and Taos takes you through red painted deserts, villages bordered by apple and peach orchards, and the foothills of 13,000-foot peaks. You can stop in Cordova, known for its woodcarvers, or Chimayo, known for its weavers. At the fabled **Santuario de Chimayo,** you can rub healing dust between your fingers. See "Along the High Road to Taos" in chapter 10.

- **Pueblo dances:** These native dances, related to the changing cycles of the earth, offer a unique chance to see how an indigenous culture worships and rejoices. Throughout the year, the pueblos' people participate in ceremonies ranging from harvest and deer

Northern New Mexico

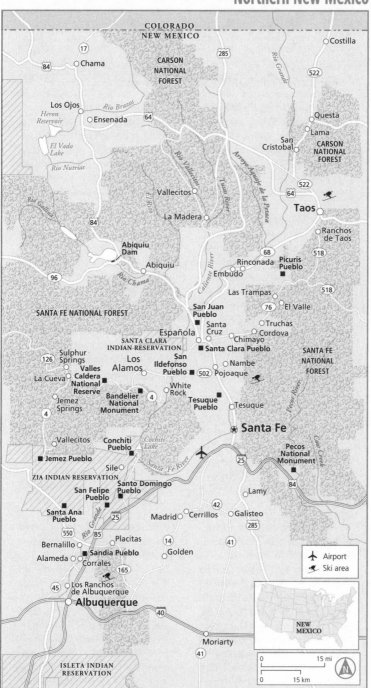

dances to those commemorating the feast days of their particular saints—all in the mystical light of the northern New Mexico sun. See chapter 10 for more information on visiting pueblos.

- **Santa Fe Opera:** One of the finest opera companies in the United States has called Santa Fe home for nearly 50 years. Performances are held during the summer months in a hilltop, open-air amphitheater. Highlights for 2005 include Osvaldo Golijov's *Ainadamar,* based on the life of poet and playwright Federico García Lorca, and Puccini's *Turandot.* See p. 139.

- **Taos Ski Valley:** World renowned for its difficult runs and the ridge where skiers hike for up to 2 hours to ski fresh powder, Taos has long been a pilgrimage site for extreme skiers. Over the years, the ski area has opened up new bowls to accommodate intermediate and beginning skiers, too. See p. 210.

- **Museum of International Folk Art:** Santa Fe's perpetually expanding collection of folk art is the largest in the world, with thousands of objects from more than 100 countries. You'll find an amazing array of imaginative works, ranging from Hispanic folk art *santos* (carved saints) to Indonesian textiles and African sculptures. See p. 108.

- **Sandia Peak Tramway:** The world's longest tramway ferries passengers 2¾ miles, from Albuquerque's city limits to the summit of the 10,378-foot Sandia Peak. On the way, you'll likely see rare Rocky Mountain bighorn sheep and birds of prey. Go in the evening to watch the sun set, then enjoy the glimmering city lights on your way down. See p. 254.

- **Albuquerque International Balloon Fiesta:** The world's largest balloon rally assembles some 750 colorful balloons and includes races and contests. Highlights are the mass ascension at sunrise and the special shapes rodeo, in which balloons in all sorts of whimsical forms, from liquor bottles to cows, rise into the sky. See "Northern New Mexico Calendar of Events," in chapter 2.

- **Bandelier National Monument:** These ruins provide a spectacular peek into the lives of the ancestral Puebloan culture, which reached its peak in this area around 1100 A.D. Less than 15 miles south of Los Alamos, the ruins spread across a peaceful canyon. You'll probably see deer and rabbits as you make your way through the canyon to the most dramatic site, a kiva and dwelling in a cave 140 feet above the canyon floor. See p. 153.

- **Northern New Mexican Enchiladas:** There are few things more New Mexican than the enchilada. You can order red or green chile, or "Christmas"—half and half. Sauces are rich, seasoned with *ajo* (garlic) and oregano. New Mexican cuisine isn't smothered in cheese and sour cream, so the flavors of the chiles, corn, and meats can really be savored. Enchiladas are often served with *frijoles* (beans), *posole* (hominy), and *sopaipillas* (fried bread). See "Chiles, *Sopaipillas* & Other New Mexican Specialties" in the appendix.

- **The Galleries Along Canyon Road:** Originally a Pueblo Indian route over the mountains and later an artists' community, Santa Fe's Canyon Road is now gallery central—the arts capital of the Southwest. The narrow one-way street is lined with more than 100 galleries, in addition to restaurants and private residences. Artwork ranges from the beautiful to the bizarre. You can step into artists' simple studio galleries as well as refined galleries showing world-renowned artists' works, such as paintings by Georgia O'Keeffe and sculptures by Frederic Remington. Be sure to stop for lunch at one of the streetside cafes. See "Walking Tour 2: Barrio de Analco & Canyon Road," in chapter 7.

- **Rio Grande Gorge:** A hike into this dramatic gorge is unforgettable. You'll first see it as you come over a rise heading toward Taos, a colossal slice in the earth formed 130 million years ago. Drive about 35 miles north of Taos, near the village of Cerro, to the Rio Grande Wild River Area. From the lip of the canyon, you descend through millions of years of geologic history on land inhabited by Indians since 16,000 B.C. When you reach the river, you can dip your toes in the fabled *rio*. If you're visiting during spring and early summer, and you like an adrenaline rush, be sure to hook up with a professional guide and raft the Taos Box, a 17-mile stretch of class IV whitewater rapids. See chapter 14.

- **María Benitez Teatro Flamenco:** Flamenco dancing originated in Spain, strongly influenced by the Moors; it is a cultural expression held sacred by Spanish gypsies. Intricate toe and heel clicking, sinuous arm and hand gestures, expressive guitar solos, and *cante hondo,* or "deep song," characterize the passionate dance. A native

New Mexican, María Benitez was trained in Spain, to which she returns each year to find dancers and prepare her show. This world-class dancer and her troupe perform at the Radisson Hotel in Santa Fe from late June to early September. See p. 141.

- **Old Town:** Albuquerque's commercial center until about 1880, Old Town still gives a remarkable sense of what life was once like in a Southwestern village. You can meander down crooked streets and narrow alleys and rest in the cottonwood-shaded plaza. Though many of the shops are now very touristy, you can still happen upon some interesting shopping and dining finds here. Native Americans sell jewelry, pottery, and weavings under a portal on the plaza. See p. 252.

- **Taos Pueblo:** Possibly the original home of Pueblo-style architecture, this bold structure where 200 residents still live much as their ancestors did a thousand years ago is awe-inspiring. Rooms built of mud are poetically stacked to echo the shape of Taos Mountain behind them. As you explore the pueblo, you can visit the residents' studios, munch on bread baked in an *horno* (a beehive-shaped oven), and wander past the fascinating ruins of the old church and cemetery. See p. 206.

2 Best Bed-and-Breakfast Inns

- **Hacienda Antigua** (Albuquerque): This 200-year-old adobe inn was the first stagecoach stop out of Old Town in Albuquerque and now offers a glimpse of those old days with refreshing modern touches. The guest rooms surround a quiet courtyard, and a pool and hot tub are tucked away.

The place sings of old New Mexico, with history evident in places such as La Capilla, the home's former chapel, which is now a guest room. See p. 238.

- **Dos Casas Viejas** (Santa Fe): These two old houses *(dos casas viejas)* offer the kind of luxury accommodations you'd expect from a fine hotel. The rooms, each with a patio and private entrance, are finely renovated and richly decorated, all with Mexican-tile floors and kiva fireplaces. Enjoy your breakfast alongside the elegant lap pool or on your private patio. Treat yourself to the in-room spa treatments. See p. 74.

- **Casa de las Chimeneas** (Taos): This 80-year-old adobe home has been a model of Southwestern elegance since its opening in 1988. The inn has a spa with a small fitness room and sauna, as well as complete massage and facial treatments. Rooms range from newer units with heated Saltillo tile floors, gas kiva fireplaces, and jetted tubs to more traditional ones with an antique feel. See p. 184.

3 Best Historic Hotels

- **La Posada de Albuquerque** (Albuquerque): Built in 1939 by Conrad Hilton as the famed hotelier's first inn in his home state of New Mexico, this hostelry on the National Register of Historic Places feels like old Spain. An elaborate Moorish brass-and-mosaic fountain stands in the center of the tiled lobby floor, and old-fashioned tin chandeliers hang from the two-story ceiling. All guest-room furniture is handcrafted. There are spacious rooms with big windows looking out across the city and toward the mountains. See p. 236.

- **The Bishop's Lodge** (Santa Fe): More than a century ago, Bishop Jean-Baptiste Lamy often escaped clerical politics by hiking into a valley north of town called Little Tesuque. He built a retreat and chapel that years later have become The Bishop's Lodge. All rooms are spacious and feature handcrafted furniture and local artwork. Activities include horseback riding, hiking, tennis, and swimming. See p. 69.

- **La Fonda** (Santa Fe): Though other hotels far surpass this one in terms of swank, this place still reigns for its old Santa Fe charm. The La Fonda was the inn at the end of the Santa Fe Trail; it saw trappers, traders, and merchants, as well as notables such as President Rutherford B. Hayes and General Ulysses S. Grant. A great place to wander through, have lunch, and even go dancing, its rooms vary broadly, all with the crookedness and originality of a historical place. If you have deep pockets, try the newer deluxe suites, which are a very refined choice. See p. 64.

- **The Historic Taos Inn** (Taos): This inn occupies a number of 19th-century Southwestern homes. Dr. Thomas Paul Martin purchased the complex in 1895; after his death his widow, Helen, turned it into a hotel. All rooms are unique and comfortable, decorated with Spanish colonial art, Taos-style furniture, and other interesting touches; though some have quirks that don't appeal to modern travelers. See p. 178.

4 Best Resorts

- **Hyatt Regency Tamaya Resort and Spa** (Albuquerque): Situated on Santa Ana Pueblo land, this grand resort has all a human might need to get away from the world. Three swimming pools, a 16,000-square-foot full-service spa and fitness center, the 18-hole

Twin Warriors Championship Golf Course designed by Gary Panks, and views of the Sandia Mountains make for plenty to do. Meanwhile, spacious rooms offer quiet for those who'd rather do nothing. It's only 15 minutes from Albuquerque and 45 minutes from Santa Fe. See p. 240.

* **La Posada de Santa Fe Resort and Spa** (Santa Fe): With the feel of a meandering adobe village but the service of a fine hotel, this has become one of New Mexico's premier resorts. It has a Zen-Southwestern-style spa and pool and

spacious spa rooms. Most rooms don't have views but have outdoor patios, and most are tucked back into the quiet compound. See p. 64.

* **El Monte Sagrado** (Taos): With guest rooms and casitas set around a grassy "Sacred Circle," this new eco-resort is the quintessence of refinement. Every detail, from the waterfalls and chemical-free pool and hot tubs to the authentic theme decor in the rooms, has been created with conscious care. See p. 176.

5 Best Places to Dine

* **Jennifer James** (Albuquerque): This French bistro-style restaurant serves contemporary American cuisine with plenty of panache. You might feast on pan-seared pork with apple bread pudding or grilled quail over endive and radicchio. See p. 246.
* **The Compound** (Santa Fe): This reincarnation of one of Santa Fe's classic restaurants serves daring contemporary American food in a soulful setting. Such delicacies as monkfish chorizo with watercress or grilled beef tenderloin with Italian potatoes will please sophisticated palates—and probably simpler ones too. See p. 82.
* **Santacafé** (Santa Fe): The food here borrows from an international menu of preparations and offerings. The minimalist decor accentuates the beautiful architecture of the 18th-century Padre Gallegos House. One of my favorite dishes is the Alaskan halibut with English peas and saffron couscous. See p. 87.
* **The Shed** (Santa Fe): The Shed, a Santa Fe luncheon institution

since 1953, occupies several rooms in part of a rambling hacienda that was built in 1692. The sauces here have been refined over the years, creating amazing flavors in basic dishes like enchiladas, burritos, and stuffed *sopaipillas.* The mocha cake is renowned. See p. 95. Sister restaurant **La Choza** is just as good, with a similar menu. See p. 94.

* **De La Tierra** (Taos): Located at the new eco-resort El Monte Sagrado, this elegant restaurant serves imaginative regional American food and other delights such as wild game. The venison medallions with garlic mashed potatoes is excellent, as is the rosemary skewered shrimp with corn polenta. An expansive wine list completes the experience. See p. 194.
* **Joseph's Table** (Taos): Now in new digs on Taos Plaza, this font of creativity serves delightful dishes with plenty of flair. Try the steak au poivre over mashed potatoes with a wild mushroom salad. Delectable. See p. 194.

2

Planning Your Trip to Northern New Mexico

As with any trip, a little preparation is essential before you start your journey to northern New Mexico. This chapter provides a variety of planning tools, including information on when to go and how to get there.

1 Visitor Information

Numerous agencies can assist you with planning your trip. The Visitors Information Center for the **New Mexico Department of Tourism** is located at 491 Old Santa Fe Trail, Santa Fe, NM 87501 (© **800/545-2070** or 505/827-7336). You can also find general New Mexico information on the Department of Tourism's website at **www.newmexico.org**. Santa Fe, Taos, and Albuquerque each have their own information service for visitors (see the "Orientation" sections in chapters 4, 11, and 15, respectively).

A valuable resource for information on outdoor recreation is the **Public Lands Information Center,** located on the south side of town at 1474 Rodeo Rd., Santa Fe, NM 87505 (© **877/276-9404** or 505/438-7542).

Here, adventurers can find out what's available on lands administered by the National Forest Service, the Bureau of Land Management, the Fish and Wildlife Service, the National Park Service, the New Mexico Department of Game and Fish (which sells hunting and fishing licenses), and the New Mexico State Parks Division. The Information Center collaborates with the New Mexico Department of Tourism. Log on to the website at **www.publiclands.org**, and you'll also be able to access links to 261 separate sites, which can be found by looking up either a particular activity or agency.

For Internet addresses of individual cities' visitor centers, see chapters 4, 11, and 15.

2 Money

If you come from a major city such as New York or London, you may find northern New Mexico overall fairly inexpensive, although Santa Fe will be closer in price to what you're accustomed to. In Taos and Albuquerque you can still get good accommodations and meals without even wincing. Santa Fe, however, may hurt a bit, especially if you hit the hottest spots in town, which cater to sophisticated tastes.

ATMs

As in most U.S. destinations, ATMs (automated teller machines) are ubiquitous in the cities of northern New Mexico. However, in the small mountain towns, they're scarce. ATMs are linked to a network that most likely includes your bank at home. **Cirrus** (© **800/424-7787**; www.mastercard.com) and **PLUS** (© **800/843-7587**; www.visa.com) are the two most popular networks in the U.S. and in this

What Things Cost in Santa Fe	US$	Euro €	UK£
Double room in high season at La Posada de Santa Fe Resort & Spa	279	243	151
Double room in high season at Santa Fe Motel and Inn	114	99	62
Dinner for two at Geronimo, without drinks, tax, or tip	105	91	57
Dinner for two at La Choza, without drinks, tax, or tip	25	22	14
An imported Mexican beer at the Dragon Room	3.50	3	2
One-hour massage at Ten Thousand Waves Japanese Health Spa	80	70	43
Adult admission to the Museum of International Folk Art	7	6	4

region; call or check online for ATM locations at your destination.

TRAVELER'S CHECKS

Traveler's checks are something of an anachronism from the days before the ATM made cash accessible at any time. These days, traveler's checks seem less necessary because most cities have 24-hour ATMs that allow you to withdraw small amounts of cash as needed. However, if you do decide to use them, you can still purchase traveler's checks at any bank in a variety of denominations.

CREDIT CARDS

Credit cards are invaluable when you're traveling. They are a safe way to carry money and provide a convenient record of all your expenses. You can also withdraw cash advances from your credit cards at any bank (though you'll start paying hefty interest on the advance the moment you receive the cash). At most banks, you don't even need to go to a teller; you can get a cash advance at the ATM if you know your PIN. If you've forgotten yours or didn't even know you had one, call the number on the back of your credit card and ask the bank to send it to you (it usually takes 5–7 business days).

The most common credit cards accepted in northern New Mexico are American Express, Diners Club, Discover, MasterCard, and Visa.

3 When to Go

Forget any preconceptions you may have about the New Mexico "desert." The high desert climate of this part of the world is generally dry but not always warm. Santa Fe and Taos, at 7,000 feet above sea level, have midsummer highs in the 90s (30s Celsius) and lows in the 50s (teens Celsius). This is the busiest time of year in New Mexico, when most cultural activities are in full swing and prices and temperatures rise. You'll want to make hotel reservations in advance.

Spring and fall are some of New Mexico's most pleasant seasons, with highs in the 60s (teens Celsius), and lows in the 30s (−1°C and below). Spring can be windy, but the skiing can be excellent, with sunny days and the season's accumulated deep snow. Fall is a particularly big draw because the aspens turn golden in the mountains. In both spring and fall, tourist traffic is sparse and room rates are lower.

Winter can be delightful in northern New Mexico, when typical daytime temperatures are in the low 40s (single digits Celsius), and overnight lows are in the teens (–8°C and below). The snowy days here are some of the prettiest you'll ever see, and during a good snow year (as much as 300 in. at Taos Ski Valley), skiers can really enjoy the region. However, during holidays, the slopes can get crowded. During all the seasons, temperatures in Albuquerque, at 5,300 feet, often run about 10° warmer than elsewhere in the northern region.

Average Temperatures (High/Low) and Annual Rainfall (Inches)

		Jan	Apr	July	Oct	Rainfall
Albuquerque	Temp (°F)	46/28	69/42	91/66	71/45	8.9
	Temp (°C)	8/–2	21/6	33/19	22/7	
Santa Fe	Temp (°F)	42/18	62/33	85/56	65/38	14.0
	Temp (°C)	6/–8	17/1	29/13	18/3	
Taos	Temp (°F)	40/10	64/29	87/50	67/32	12.1
	Temp (°C)	4/–12	18/–2	31/10	19/0	

NORTHERN NEW MEXICO CALENDAR OF EVENTS

January

New Year's Day. Transfer of canes to new officials and various dances at most pueblos. Turtle Dance at Taos Pueblo (no photography allowed). Call ✆ **800/793-4955** for more information. January 1.

Winter Wine Festival. A variety of wine offerings and food tastings prepared by local chefs take place in the Taos Ski Valley. Call ✆ **505/776-2291** for details. Mid-January.

February

Candelaria Day Celebration, Picuris Pueblo. Traditional dances. Call ✆ **505/587-2519** for more information. February 2.

Mt. Taylor Winter Quadrathlon. Hundreds of athletes come from all over the West to bicycle, run, cross-country ski, and snowshoe up and down this mountain. For information, call ✆ **800/748-2142.** Mid-February.

Just Desserts Eat and Ski. Cross-country skiers skate from point to point on the Enchanted Forest course near Red River, tasting decadent desserts supplied by area restaurants. Call ✆ **505/754-2374.** Late February.

March

National Fiery Foods/Barbecue Show. Here's your chance to taste the hottest of the hot and plenty of milder flavors, too. Some 10,000 general public attendees show up to taste sauces, salsas, candies, and more, and to see cooking demonstrations at the Albuquerque Convention Center. For information call ✆ **505/873-8680** or go to **www.fiery-foods.com**. Early March.

Rio Grande Arts and Crafts Festival. A juried show featuring 200 artists and craftspeople from around the country takes place at the State Fairgrounds in Albuquerque. Call ✆ **505/292-7457** for more information, or visit **www.riograndefestivals.com**. Second week of March.

Chimayo Pilgrimage. On Good Friday, thousands of pilgrims trek on foot to the Santuario de Chimayo, a small church north of Santa Fe that's believed to aid in miracles. For information, call ✆ **505/351-4889.**

April

Easter Weekend Celebration. Celebrations include Masses, parades, corn dances, and other dances, such as the bow and arrow dance at Nambe. Call ✆ **800/793-4955** for information.

American Indian Week, Indian Pueblo Cultural Center, Albuquerque. A celebration of Native American traditions and culture. For dates and information, call ✆ **505/843-7270.**

Gathering of Nations Powwow, University Arena, Albuquerque. Dance competitions, arts-and-crafts exhibitions, and Miss Indian World contest. Call ✆ **505/836-2810,** or visit **www.gatheringofnations. com**. Late April.

May

Taste of Santa Fe. Sample Santa Fe's best chefs' recipes, including appetizers, entrees, and desserts at Santa Fe's Sweeney Center. For information call ✆ **505/983-4823.** First Tuesday in May.

Taos Spring Arts Festival. Contemporary visual, performing, and literary arts are highlighted during 2 weeks of gallery openings, studio tours, performances by visiting theatrical and dance troupes, live musical events, traditional ethnic entertainment, literary readings, and more.

Events are held at venues throughout Taos and Taos County. For dates and ticket info contact the Taos County Chamber of Commerce, P.O. Drawer I, Taos, NM 87571 (✆ **800/732-TAOS** or 505/758-3873; www.taoschamber.com). All month.

June

San Antonio Feast Day. Corn dances at many of the pueblos. For information, call ✆ **505/843-7270.** June 13.

Rodeo de Santa Fe. This 4-day event features a Western parade, a rodeo dance, and five rodeo performances. It attracts hundreds of cowboys and cowgirls from all over the Southwest who compete for sizable purses in such events as Brahma bull and bronco riding, calf roping, steer wrestling, barrel racing, trick riding, and clown and animal acts.

The rodeo grounds are at 3237 Rodeo Rd., off Cerrillos Road, 5½ miles south of the plaza. Performances are in the evening Wednesday to Saturday; and on Saturday afternoon. For tickets and information, call ✆ **505/471-4300** or visit **www.rodeodesantafe.org**. It takes place sometime around the third weekend in June.

Rodeo de Taos, County Fairgrounds, Taos. A fun event featuring local and regional participants. For information, call ✆ **505/758-5700** or, in mid- to late June call ✆ **505/758-3974.** Third or fourth weekend in June.

Taos Solar Music Festival, Kit Carson Municipal Park, Taos. Sit out on the grass, under the sun, and listen to major players at this event celebrating the summer solstice. A tribute to solar energy, the event has a stage powered by a solar generator and educational displays within a "Solar Village." For information, call ✆ **505/758-9191.** Late June.

New Mexico Arts and Crafts Fair. A tradition for 41 years, this juried show offers work from more than 200 New Mexico artisans, accompanied by nonstop entertainment for the whole family. This can be a good place to find Hispanic arts and crafts.

The fair is held at the State Fairgrounds in Albuquerque. Admission cost varies. For information, call ✆ **505/884-9043** or check online at **www.nmartsandcrafts fair.org**. Last full weekend in June.

July

Fourth of July celebrations (including fireworks displays) are held all over New Mexico. Call the chambers of commerce in specific towns and cities for information.

Pancake Breakfast on the Plaza. Rub elbows with Santa Fe residents at this locals' event on the plaza. For information call ✆ **505/982-2002.** July 4.

Taos Pueblo Powwow. Intertribal competition in traditional and contemporary dances. Call ✆ **505/ 758-1028** for more information. Second weekend in July.

Eight Northern Pueblos Artist and Craftsman Show. More than 600 Native American artists exhibit their work at the eight northern pueblos. Traditional dances and food booths; location varies. Call ✆ **505/747-1593** for location and exact dates. Third weekend in July.

Fiestas de Santiago y Santa Ana. The celebration begins with a Friday-night Mass at one of the three Taos-area parishes, where the fiesta queen is crowned. During the weekend there are candlelight processions, special Masses, music, dancing, parades, crafts, and food booths.

Taos Plaza hosts many events and most are free. For information, contact the Taos Fiesta Council, P.O. Box 3300, Taos, NM 87571 (✆ **800/732-8267;** www.fiestasde taos.com). Third weekend in July.

Spanish Market. More than 300 Hispanic artists from New Mexico and southern Colorado exhibit and sell their work in this lively community event. Artists are featured in special demonstrations, while an entertaining mix of traditional Hispanic music, dance, foods, and pageantry creates the ambience of a village celebration. Artwork for sale includes *santos* (painted and carved saints), textiles, tinwork, furniture, straw appliqué, and metalwork.

The markets are found at Santa Fe Plaza in Santa Fe. For information, contact the Spanish Colonial Arts Society, P.O. Box 5378, Santa Fe, NM 87502 (✆ **505/982-2226;** www.spanishcolonial.org). Last full weekend in July.

August

San Lorenzo Feast Day, Picuris Pueblo. Traditional dances and foot races. Call ✆ **505/587-2519** or visit **www.santaana.org/calendar. htm** for details. August 10.

The Indian Market. This is the largest all–Native American market in the country. About 1,000 artisans display their baskets and blankets, jewelry, pottery, woodcarvings, rugs, sand paintings, and sculptures at rows of booths around Santa Fe Plaza, surrounding streets, and de Vargas Mall. Sales are brisk. Costumed tribal dancing and crafts demonstrations are scheduled in the afternoon.

The market is free, but hotels are booked months in advance. For information, contact the **Southwestern Association for Indian Arts,** P.O. Box 969, Santa Fe, NM 87504-0969 (✆ **505/983-5220;** www.swaia.org). Third weekend in August.

Music from Angel Fire. World-class musicians gather in Angel Fire to perform classical and chamber music. For information and schedules, call ✆ **505/377-3233** or go to **www.angelfirenm.com.** Mid-August to the first week in September.

September

New Mexico Wine Festival. New Mexico wines are showcased at this annual event in Bernalillo, near Albuquerque, which features wine tastings, an art show, and live entertainment. For a schedule of events, call ℂ **505/867-3311.** Labor Day weekend.

La Fiesta de Santa Fe. An exuberant combination of spirit, history, and general merrymaking, La Fiesta is the oldest community celebration in the United States. The first fiesta was celebrated in 1712, 20 years after the peaceful resettlement of New Mexico by Spanish conquistadors in 1692. La Conquistadora, a carved Madonna credited with the victory, is the focus of the celebration, which includes Masses, a parade for children and their pets, a historical/hysterical parade, mariachi concerts, dances, food, and arts, as well as local entertainment on the plaza. Zozobra, "Old Man Gloom," a 40-foot-tall effigy made of wood, canvas, and paper, is burned at dusk on Thursday to revitalize the community.

Zozobra kicks off La Fiesta. For information call ℂ **505/988-7575.** Weekend following Labor Day.

Enchanted Circle Century Bike Tour. About 500 cyclists turn out to ride 100 miles of scenic mountain roads, starting and ending in Red River. All levels of riders are welcome, though not everyone completes this test of endurance. Call ℂ **505/754-2366.** Weekend following Labor Day.

New Mexico State Fair and Rodeo. This is one of America's top state fairs; it features parimutuel horse racing, a nationally acclaimed rodeo, entertainment by top country artists, Native American and Spanish villages, the requisite midway, livestock shows, and arts and crafts.

The fair and rodeo, which last 17 days, are held at the State Fairgrounds in Albuquerque. Advance tickets can be ordered by calling ℂ **505/265-1791** or visiting www.nmstatefair.com. Early September.

Taos Trade Fair, La Hacienda de los Martinez, Lower Ranchitos Road, Taos. This 2-day affair reenacts Spanish colonial life of the mid-1820s and features Hispanic and Native American music, weaving and crafts demonstrations, traditional foods, dancing, and visits by mountain men. Call ℂ **505/758-0505.** Last full weekend in September.

San Geronimo Vespers Sundown Dance and Trade Fair, Taos Pueblo. This event features a Mass and procession; traditional corn, buffalo, and Comanche dances; an arts-and-crafts fair; foot races; and pole climbs by clowns. Call ℂ **505/758-1028** for details. Last weekend in September.

Santa Fe Wine & Chile Fiesta. This lively celebration boasts 5 days of wine and food events, including seminars, guest chef demonstrations and luncheons, tours, a grand tasting and reserve tasting, an auction, and a golf tournament. It takes place at many venues in downtown Santa Fe with the big event on the last Saturday. Tickets go on sale in early July and sell out quickly. For information call ℂ **505/438-8060** or visit **www.santafewineandchile.org**. Last Wednesday through Sunday in September.

Taos Fall Arts Festival. Highlights include arts-and-crafts exhibitions and competitions, studio tours, gallery openings, lectures, concerts, dances, and stage plays. Simultaneous events include the **Old Taos Trade Fair,** the **Wool Festival,** and **San Geronimo Day** at Taos Pueblo.

The festival is held throughout Taos and Taos County Events, schedules, and tickets (where required) can be obtained from the **Taos County Chamber of Commerce,** P.O. Drawer I, Taos, NM 87571 (℗ **800/732-8267** or 505/758-3873; www.taoschamber.com). Mid-September (or the third weekend) to the first week in October.

October

Albuquerque International Balloon Fiesta. The world's largest balloon rally, this 9-day festival brings together more than 750 colorful balloons and includes races and contests. There are mass ascensions at sunrise, "balloon glows" in the evening, and balloon rides for those desiring a little lift. Various special events are staged all week.

Balloons lift off at Balloon Fiesta Park (at I-25 and Alameda NE) on Albuquerque's northern city limits. For information, call ℗ **800/733-9918** or visit **www.balloonfiesta. com**. Second week in October.

Taos Mountain Balloon Rally. The Albuquerque fiesta's "little brother" offers mass dawn ascensions, tethered balloon rides for the public, and a Saturday parade of balloon baskets (in pickup trucks) from Kit Carson Park around the plaza. Call ℗ **800/732-8267** for more information. Last weekend of October.

November

Dixon Art Studio Tour. Northern New Mexico's most notable village studio tour. Walk Dixon's main street that winds through hills planted with fruit trees, and wander into artists' homes and studios, where you're likely to see some excellent arts-and-crafts finds. For more details, call ℗ **505/579-4363.** You can find information about this and other area art studio tours at **www.artnewmexico.com**. First weekend in November.

Weems Artfest. Approximately 260 artisans, who work in a variety of media, come from throughout the world to attend this 3-day fair, held at the State Fairgrounds in Albuquerque. It's one of the top 100 arts-and-crafts fairs in the country. For details, call ℗ **505/293-6133.** Early November.

Festival of the Cranes. People come from all over the world to attend this bird-watching event just an hour and a half south of Albuquerque at Bosque del Apache National Wildlife Refuge, near Socorro. Call ℗ **505/835-1828.** Weekend before Thanksgiving.

Yuletide in Taos. This holiday event emphasizes northern New Mexican traditions, cultures, and arts, with carols, festive classical music, Hispanic and Native American songs and dances, historic walking tours, art exhibitions, dance performances, candlelight dinners, and more.

Events are staged by the **Taos County Chamber of Commerce,** P.O. Drawer I, Taos, NM 87571 (℗ **800/732-8267;** www.taos chamber.com). From Thanksgiving through New Years Day.

December

Winter Spanish Market, Sweeney Convention Center, Santa Fe. Approximately 150 artists show their wares at this little sister to July's major event. See the Spanish Market in July (above) for more information. Call ℗ **505/982-2226.** First full weekend in December.

Christmas in Madrid Open House. Even if you never get out of your car, it's worth going to see the spectacular lights display in this village between Albuquerque and Santa Fe on the Turquoise Trail. You'll also find entertainment, refreshments in shops, and Santa

Claus. For additional information call ✆ **505/471-1054.** First two weekends in December.

Canyon Road Farolito Walk, Santa Fe. Locals and visitors bundle up and stroll Canyon Road, where streets and rooftops are lined with *farolitos* (candle lamps). Musicians play and carolers sing around *luminarias* (little fires). Though it's not responsible for the event, the **Santa Fe Convention and Visitors Bureau** (✆ **505/955-6200**) can help direct you there; or ask your hotel concierge. Christmas Eve at dusk.

Dance of the Matachines and Other Dances. Many pueblos celebrate the Christmas holiday with dances. The Dance of the Matachines takes place at Picuris and San Juan pueblos on Christmas day. Contact ✆ **505/852-5265** for dance schedules for these and other pueblos. Christmas Eve through Christmas Day.

Torchlight Procession, Taos Ski Valley. Bold skiers carve down a steep run named Snakedance in the dark while carrying golden fire. For information call ✆ **800/992-7669** or 505/776-2291, or visit **www.ski taos.org**. December 31.

4 Insurance, Health & Safety

TRAVEL INSURANCE AT A GLANCE

Check your existing insurance policies before you buy travel insurance to cover trip cancellation, lost luggage, medical expenses, or car-rental insurance. You're likely to have partial or complete coverage. But if you need some, ask your travel agent about a comprehensive package. The cost of travel insurance varies widely, depending on the cost and length of your trip, your age and overall health, and the type of trip you're taking, but expect to pay between 5% and 8% of the vacation itself.

TRIP-CANCELLATION INSURANCE (TCI)

Trip-cancellation insurance helps you get your money back if you have to back out of a trip, if you have to go home early, or if your travel supplier goes bankrupt. Allowed reasons for cancellation can range from sickness to natural disasters to the State Department declaring your destination unsafe for travel. (Insurers usually won't cover vague fears, though, as many travelers discovered when they tried to cancel their trips in Oct 2001 because they were wary of flying.) In

this unstable world, trip-cancellation insurance is a good buy if you're getting tickets well in advance; who knows what the state of the world, or of your airline, will be in 9 months? Insurance policy details vary, so read the fine print—and make sure that your airline is on the list of carriers covered in case of bankruptcy. A good resource is **"Travel Guard Alerts,"** a list of companies considered high risk by Travel Guard International (see website below). Protect yourself further by paying for the insurance with a credit card; by law, consumers can get their money back on goods and services not received if they report the loss within 60 days after the charge is listed on their credit card statement.

Note: Many tour operators, particularly those offering trips to remote or high-risk areas, include insurance in the cost of the trip or can arrange insurance policies through a partnering provider; this is a convenient and often cost-effective way for the traveler to obtain insurance. Make sure the tour company is a reputable one, however: Some experts suggest you avoid buying insurance from the tour company you're traveling with, saying it's better to buy from a "third party" insurer than to put all your money in one place.

For more information, contact one of the following recommended insurers: **Access America** (© 866/807-3982; www.accessamerica.com); **Travel Guard International** (© 800/826-4919; www.travelguard.com); **Travel Insured International** (© 800/243-3174; www.travelinsured.com); or **Travelex Insurance Services** (© 888/457-4602; www.travelex-insurance.com).

MEDICAL INSURANCE

Most health insurance policies cover you if you get sick away from home—but check, particularly if you're insured by an HMO. Members of **Blue Cross/Blue Shield** can now use their cards at select hospitals in most major cities worldwide (© **800/810-BLUE** or www.bluecares.com for a list of hospitals).

Some credit card companies (American Express and certain Visa and MasterCards, for example) offer automatic flight insurance against death or dismemberment in case of an airplane crash if you paid for your ticket with their card.

If you require additional medical insurance, try **MEDEX Assistance** (© 410/453-6300; www.medexassist.com) or **Travel Assistance International** (© **800/821-2828;** www.travelassistance.com; for general information on services, call the company's Worldwide Assistance Services, Inc., at © **800/777-8710**).

The cost of medical travel insurance varies widely. Check your existing policies before you buy additional coverage. Also, check to see if your medical insurance covers you for emergency medical evacuation: If you have to buy a one-way same-day ticket home and forfeit your nonrefundable round-trip ticket, you may be out big bucks.

LOST-LUGGAGE INSURANCE

On domestic flights, checked baggage is covered up to $2,500 per ticketed passenger. If you plan to check items more valuable than the standard liability, see if your valuables are covered by your homeowner's policy, get baggage insurance as part of your comprehensive travel-insurance package, or buy Travel Guard's "BagTrak" product. Don't buy insurance at the airport, as it's usually overpriced. Be sure to take any valuables or irreplaceable items with you in your carry-on luggage, as many valuables (including books, money, and electronics) aren't covered by airline policies.

If your luggage is lost, immediately file a lost-luggage claim at the airport, detailing the luggage contents. For most airlines, you must report delayed, damaged, or lost baggage within 4 hours of arrival. The airlines are required to deliver luggage, once found, directly to your house or destination free of charge.

CAR-RENTAL INSURANCE (LOSS/DAMAGE WAIVER OR COLLISION DAMAGE WAIVER)

If you hold a private auto insurance policy, you probably are covered in the U.S. for loss or damage to the car, and for liability in case a passenger is injured. The credit card you used to rent the car also may provide some coverage.

Car-rental insurance probably does not cover liability if you caused the accident. Check your own auto insurance policy, the rental company policy, and your credit card coverage for the extent of coverage: Is your destination covered? Are other drivers covered? How much liability is covered if a passenger is injured? (If you rely on your credit card for coverage, you may want to bring a second credit card with you, as damages may be charged to your card and you may find your-self stranded with no money.)

Car-rental insurance costs about $20 a day.

THE HEALTHY TRAVELER

One thing that sets New Mexico apart from most other states is its elevation. Santa Fe and Taos are about 7,000 feet above sea level; Albuquerque is more than 5,000 feet above sea level. The reduced oxygen and humidity can pre-cipitate some unique problems, not the least of which is acute mountain sickness. In its early stages, you might experience headaches, shortness of breath, loss of appetite and/or nausea, tingling in the fingers or toes, lethargy, and insomnia. The condition can usu-ally be treated by taking aspirin as well as getting plenty of rest, avoiding large meals, and drinking lots of nonalco-holic fluids (especially water). If it per-sists or worsens, you must return to a lower altitude. Other dangers of higher elevations include hypothermia and sun exposure, and these should be taken seriously. To avoid dehydration, drink water as often as possible.

Limit your exposure to the sun, especially during the first few days of your trip and, thereafter, between 11am and 2pm. Liberally apply sun-screen with a high protection factor. Remember that children need more protection than adults do.

It is important to monitor your children's health while in New Mex-ico. They are just as susceptible to mountain sickness, hypothermia, sun-burn, and dehydration as you are.

Other things to be wary of are arroyos, or creek beds in the desert where flash floods can occur without warning. If water is flowing across a road, *do not* try to drive through it because chances are the water is deeper and flowing faster than you think. Just wait it out. Arroyo floods don't last long.

Finally, if you're an outdoorsperson, be on the lookout for snakes—partic-ularly rattlers. Avoid them. Don't even get close enough to take a picture (unless you have a very good zoom lens).

The most reliable hospitals in the area are **St. Vincent's Hospital,** 455 St. Michaels Dr. in Santa Fe (℃ **505/ 820-5250**), and **Presbyterian Hospi-tal,** 1100 Central Ave. SE in Albu-querque (℃ **505/841-1234,** or 505/ 841-1111 for emergency service).

WHAT TO DO IF YOU GET SICK AWAY FROM HOME

If you worry about getting sick away from home, consider purchasing **med-ical travel insurance** and carry your ID card in your purse or wallet. In most cases, your existing health plan will provide the coverage you need. See "Medical Insurance," above, for more information.

If you suffer from a chronic illness, consult your doctor before your departure. For conditions like epilepsy, diabetes, or heart problems, wear a **MedicAlert Identification Tag** (℃ **800/825-3785;** www.medicalert. org), which will immediately alert doctors to your condition and give them access to your records through MedicAlert's 24-hour hot line.

Pack **prescription medications** in your carry-on luggage, and carry them in their original containers. Also bring along copies of your prescriptions in case you lose your pills or run out. And don't forget **sunglasses** and an extra pair of **contact lenses** or **pre-scription glasses.**

THE SAFE TRAVELER

Tourist areas as a rule are safe, but, despite recent reports of decreases in violent crime in Santa Fe, it would be wise to check with the tourist offices in Santa Fe, Taos, and Albuquerque if you are in doubt about which neighbor-hoods are safe. (See the "Orientation"

Fire, Water & Golf

Over the past few years, national news programs have run vivid stories with the banner headline "New Mexico is Burning." Though the state has witnessed some major wildfires, including the Cerro Grande in Los Alamos in 2000, which trespassed into the city leveling some 400 dwellings, New Mexico has never been "on fire." Forests in the West will always burn—it's a natural part of their cycles. However, the state's forests are drier than they've been in many years, which may be leading to more fires.

A more apt headline for the state's recent problems is "New Mexico is Drying Up." Blame global warming or simply weather cycles; the state has received scant rain and snowfall in recent years. For a few years running, Santa Fe residents have been forced to abide by water-use restrictions, limiting how much they can water their gardens and wash their cars.

The drought has led to a focused assessment of water use throughout the region, and golf courses have emerged as the big black hat. And yet, more continue to be built. Area pueblos are scrambling to take advantage of the income golf can bring in. Santa Ana Pueblo has installed two 18-hole courses, and Pojoaque and Santa Clara have each installed 18 holes.

With longstanding water rights in hand, the pueblos believe they are entitled to use the water. All this presupposes a well that can't run dry, but with Rio Grande flows at their lowest in years, the future looks grim. How does this affect the traveler? You can be relatively sure you won't burn up during your visit, you may have to *ask* for a glass of water when you dine at a restaurant, and, well, you might want to bring along your clubs—while the water lasts.

sections in chapters 4, 11, and 15 for the names and addresses of the specific tourist bureaus.)

Remember that hotels are open to the public, and in a large hotel, security may not be able to screen everyone who enters. Always lock your room door; don't assume that once inside your hotel you are automatically safe and no longer need to be aware of your surroundings.

Be aware that New Mexico has a higher-than-average reported incidence of rape. Women should not walk alone in isolated places, particularly at night.

5 Tips for Travelers with Special Needs

TRAVELERS WITH DISABILITIES

Most disabilities shouldn't stop anyone from traveling. There are more options and resources out there than ever before. Throughout the state of New Mexico, measures have been taken to provide access for travelers with disabilities. Several bed-and-breakfasts have made one or more of their rooms completely wheelchair accessible. The **Information Center for New Mexicans with Disabilities** (© **800/552-8195** in New Mexico, or 505/272-8549 outside the state) accesses a database with lists of services ranging from restaurants and hotels to wheelchair rentals. It's a service of the **Developmental Disabilities Planning Council** (℡ 505/827-7590). The *Access New Mexico* guide lists accessible hotels, attractions, and restaurants throughout the state. For more information, contact the **Governor's Committee on Concerns of the Handicapped,** 491 Old Santa Fe Trail, Lamy Building Room 117, Santa Fe, NM 87503 (℡ 505/827-6465; www.state.nm.us/gcch/access nm.htm). The chambers of commerce in Santa Fe and Taos will answer questions regarding accessibility in their areas. It is advisable to call hotels, restaurants, and attractions in advance to be sure that they are fully accessible.

ORGANIZATIONS

- **The MossRehab Hospital** (℡ 215/456-9603; www.moss resourcenet.org) provides friendly, helpful phone assistance through its **Travel Information Service.**

- **The Society for Accessible Travel & Hospitality** (℡ 212/447-7284; fax 212/725-8253; www. sath.org) offers a wealth of travel resources for all types of disabilities and informed recommendations on destinations, access guides, travel agents, tour operators, vehicle rentals, and companion services. Annual membership costs $45 for adults, $30 for seniors and students.

- **The American Foundation for the Blind** (℡ 800/232-5463; www.afb.org) provides information on traveling with Seeing Eye dogs.

PUBLICATIONS

- **Mobility International USA** (℡ 541/343-1284; www.miusa. org) publishes *A World of Options,* a 658-page book of resources, covering everything from biking trips to scuba outfitters, and a biannual newsletter, *MIUSA'S Global Impact.* Minimum donation $35.

- **Twin Peaks Press** (℡ 360/694-2462) publishes travel-related books for travelers with special needs.

- *Open World for Disability and Mature Travel* magazine, published by the Society for Accessible Travel & Hospitality (see above), is full of good resources and information. A year's subscription is $13 ($21 outside the U.S.).

GAY & LESBIAN TRAVELERS
Common Bond (℡ 505/891-3647) provides information and outreach services for Albuquerque's gay and lesbian community as well as referrals for other New Mexico cities. A recorded message on this phone line gives lists of bars and clubs, businesses, and publications, as well as health and crisis information and a calendar of events. Volunteers are on hand (generally in the evenings) to answer questions. Another good resource is **www.gay nm.com**, a website that provides news, resources, and lists of events.

The **International Gay and Lesbian Travel Association** (IGLTA; ℡ 800/448-8550 or 954/776-2626; fax 954/776-3303; www.iglta.org) links travelers up with gay-friendly hoteliers, tour operators, and airline and cruise-line representatives. It offers monthly newsletters, marketing mailings, and a membership directory that's updated once a year. Membership is $200 yearly, plus a $100 administration fee for new members.

PUBLICATIONS

- *Out & About* (℡ 800/929-2268 or 415/644-8044; www.outand about.com) offers guidebooks and a newsletter 10 times a year that is packed with solid information on the global gay and lesbian scene.

- *Spartacus International Gay Guide* and *Odysseus* are good, annual guidebooks focused on gay men, with some information for lesbians. You can get them from most gay and lesbian bookstores, or order them from **Giovanni's Room,** 1145 Pine St., Philadelphia, PA 19107 (© **215/923-2960;** www.giovannisroom.com).

- *Gay Travel A to Z: The World of Gay & Lesbian Travel Options at Your Fingertips,* by Marianne Ferrari (Ferrari Publications), is a very good gay and lesbian guidebook series.

SENIOR TRAVEL

Mention the fact that you're a senior when you make your travel reservations. Although all of the major U.S. airlines except America West have canceled their senior discount and coupon book programs, many hotels still offer discounts for seniors. In most cities, people over the age of 60 qualify for reduced admission to theaters, museums, and other attractions, as well as discounted fares on public transportation.

Members of **AARP** (formerly known as the American Association of Retired Persons), 601 E St. NW, Washington, DC 20049 (© **888/687-2277;** www.aarp.org), get discounts on hotels, airfares, and car rentals. AARP offers members a wide range of benefits, including *AARP: The Magazine* and a monthly newsletter. Anyone over 50 can join.

Alliance for Retired Americans, 888 16th St. NW, Suite 520, Washington, DC 20006 (© **800/333-7212;** www.retiredamericans.org), offers a newsletter six times a year and discounts on hotel and auto rentals.

Many reliable agencies and organizations target the 50-plus market. **Elderhostel** (© **877/426-8056;** www.elderhostel.org) arranges study programs for those ages 55 and over (and a spouse or companion of any age) in the U.S. and in more than 80 countries around the world, with 13 sites within New Mexico. Most courses last 5 to 7 days in the U.S. (2–4 weeks abroad), and many include airfare, accommodations in university dormitories or modest inns, meals, and tuition. **ElderTreks** (© **800/741-7956;** www.eldertreks.com) offers small-group tours to off-the-beaten-path or adventure-travel locations, restricted to travelers 50 and older.

PUBLICATIONS

- The Albuquerque-based monthly tabloid *Prime Time,* (© **505/880-0470**) publishes a variety of articles aimed at New Mexicans 50 years and older.
- *101 Tips for Mature Travelers,* available from Grand Circle Travel (© **800/221-2610** or 617/350-7500; www.gct.com).
- *The 50+ Traveler's Guidebook* (St. Martin's Press).
- *Travel Unlimited: Uncommon Adventures for the Mature Traveler* (Avalon).
- *Unbelievably Good Deals and Great Adventures That You Absolutely Can't Get Unless You're Over 50* (McGraw-Hill), by Joann Rattner Heilman.

FAMILY TRAVEL

If you have enough trouble getting your kids out of the house in the morning, dragging them thousands of

---

(*Warning*   **A Note About Health**

Senior travelers are often more susceptible than others to changes in elevation and may experience heart or respiratory problems. Consult your physician before your trip.

miles away may seem like an insurmountable challenge. But family travel can be immensely rewarding, giving you new ways of seeing the world through smaller pairs of eyes.

Be aware that family travel in northern New Mexico may be a little different from what you're accustomed to. You'll find few huge Disney-like attractions here. Instead, the draws are culture and the outdoors. Rather than spending time in theme parks, you may go whitewater rafting down the Rio Grande, skiing at one of the many family-friendly areas, climbing a wooden ladder up to a cliff dwelling, or trekking through the wilderness with a llama.

If your brood is not very adventurous, don't worry. Some of the hotels and resorts listed in this book have inviting pools to laze around or on-site activities planned especially for kids. Whatever your choice, northern New Mexico will definitely offer your children a new perspective on the United States by exposing them to ancient ruins, Southwestern cuisine, and Hispanic and Native American cultures that they may not experience elsewhere.

To locate those accommodations, restaurants, and attractions that are particularly kid friendly, refer to the "Kids" icon throughout this guide.

Familyhostel (☏ **800/733-9753;** www.learn.unh.edu/familyhostel) takes the whole family, including kids ages 8 to 15, on moderately priced domestic and international learning vacations. Lectures, fields trips, and sightseeing are guided by a team of academics.

PUBLICATIONS

- The Santa Fe quarterly *Tumbleweeds* (☏ **505/984-3171**) offers useful articles on family-oriented subjects in the Santa Fe area and a quarterly day-by-day calendar of family events. Free in locations all over Santa Fe or by mail for $15.
- Lynnell Diamond's *New Mexico for Kids* (Otter Be Reading

Books), a learning activity guidebook for young people, is available online at **Amazon.com**.
- *How to Take Great Trips with Your Kids* (The Harvard Common Press) is full of good general advice that can apply to travel anywhere.

WEBSITES

- **Family Travel Files** (www.thefamilytravelfiles.com) offers an online magazine and a directory of off-the-beaten-path tours and tour operators for families.
- **Family Travel Forum** (www.familytravelforum.com) is a comprehensive site that offers customized trip planning.
- **Family Travel Network** (www.familytravelnetwork.com) offers travel tips and reviews of family-friendly destinations, vacation deals, and thoughtful features such as "What to Do When Your Kids Are Afraid to Travel" and "Kid-Style Camping."
- **Traveling Internationally with Your Kids** (www.travelwithyourkids.com) is a comprehensive site that offers sound advice for traveling with children.

STUDENT TRAVEL

Always carry your student identification with you. Tourist attractions, transportation systems, and other services may offer discounts if you have appropriate proof of your student status. Don't be afraid to ask. A high school or college ID card or International Student Card will suffice.

Student-oriented activities abound on and around college campuses, especially at the University of New Mexico in Albuquerque. In Santa Fe, there are two small 4-year colleges: the College of Santa Fe and the liberal arts school St. John's College. Santa Fe Community College is a 2-year college offering various associate degrees.

STA Travel (© 800/781-4040; www.sta.com or www.statravel.com) is the biggest student-travel agency in the world, although its bargain-basement prices are available to people of all ages. (*Note:* In 2002, STA Travel bought competitors **Council Travel** and **USIT Campus** after they went bankrupt. It's still operating some offices under the Council name, but they are owned by STA.) **Travel CUTS** (© 800/667-2887 or 416/614-2887; www.travelcuts.com) offers similar services for both Canadians and U.S. residents. Irish students may prefer to turn to **USIT** (© 01/602-1600; www.usitnow.ie), an Ireland-based specialist in student, youth, and independent travel.

6 Getting There

BY PLANE

The gateway to Santa Fe, Taos, and other northern New Mexico communities is the **Albuquerque International Sunport** (© 505/842-4366 for the administrative offices; www.cabq.gov/airport; call the individual airlines for flight information).

Airlines serving Albuquerque include **American** (© 800/433-7300), **America West** (© 800/235-9292), **Continental** (© 800/523-3273), **Delta** (© 800/221-1212), **Frontier** (© 800/432-1359), **Mesa** (© 800/637-2247), **Northwest** (© 800/225-2525), **Southwest** (© 800/435-9792), **TWA** (© 800/221-2000), and **United** (© 800/241-6522).

In conjunction with United Airlines, **United Express** (© 800/241-6522) offers commuter flights to and from **Santa Fe Municipal Airport** (© 505/955-2900) via Denver. In addition, **America West** serves Santa Fe from Phoenix. Flying into Santa Fe will save you time but will cost more than flying into Albuquerque.

GETTING THROUGH THE AIRPORT

With the federalization of airport security, security procedures at U.S. airports are more stable and consistent than ever before. Generally, you'll be fine if you arrive at the airport **1 hour** before a domestic flight; if you show up late, tell an airline employee, and she'll probably whisk you to the front of the line.

Bring a **current, government-issued photo ID** such as a driver's license or passport. Keep your ID at the ready to show at check-in, the security checkpoint, and sometimes even the gate. (Children under 18 do not need government-issued photo IDs for domestic flights.)

In 2003, the TSA phased out **gate check-in** at all U.S. airports. And **e-tickets** have made paper tickets nearly obsolete. Passengers with e-tickets can beat the ticket-counter lines by using airport **electronic kiosks** or even **online check-in** from home computers. Online check-in involves logging on to your airlines' website, accessing your reservation, and printing out your boarding pass—and the airline may even offer you bonus miles to do so! If you're using a kiosk at the airport, bring the credit card you used to book the ticket or your frequent-flier card. Print out your boarding pass from the kiosk and simply proceed to the security checkpoint with your pass and a photo ID. If you're checking bags or looking to snag an exit-row seat, you will be able to do so using most airline kiosks. Even the smaller airlines are employing the kiosk system, but always call your airline to make sure these alternatives are available. **Curbside check-in** is also a good way to avoid lines, although a few airlines still ban curbside check-in; call before you go.

Security checkpoint lines are getting shorter than they were during

> **Tips Don't Stow It—Ship It**
>
> If ease of travel is your main concern and money is no object, you can ship your luggage and sports equipment with one of the growing number of luggage-service companies that pick up, track, and deliver your luggage (often through couriers such as Federal Express) with minimum hassle for you. Traveling luggage-free may be ultra-convenient, but it's not cheap: One-way overnight shipping can cost from $100 to $200, depending on what you're sending. Still, for some people, especially the elderly or the infirm, it's a sensible solution to lugging heavy baggage. Specialists in door-to-door luggage delivery are **Virtual Bellhop** (www.virtualbellhop. com), **SkyCap International** (wwww.skycapinternational.com), **Luggage Express** (www.usxpluggageexpress.com), and **Sports Express** (www.sports express.com).

2001 and 2002, but some doozies remain. If you have trouble standing for long periods of time, tell an airline employee; the airline will provide a wheelchair. Speed up security by **not wearing metal objects** such as big belt buckles. If you've got metallic body parts, a note from your doctor can prevent a long chat with the security screeners. Keep in mind that only **ticketed passengers** are allowed past security, except for folks escorting children or travelers with disabilities.

Federalization has stabilized **what you can carry on** and **what you can't.** The general rule is that sharp things are out, nail clippers are okay, and food and beverages must be passed through the X-ray machine—but that security screeners can't make you drink from your coffee cup. Bring food in your carry-on rather than checking it, as explosive-detection machines used on checked luggage have been known to mistake food (especially chocolate, for some reason) for bombs. Travelers in the U.S. are allowed one carry-on bag, plus a "personal item" such as a purse, briefcase, or laptop bag. Carry-on hoarders can stuff all sorts of things into a laptop bag; as long as it has a laptop in it, it's still considered a personal item. The **Transportation Security Administration (TSA)** has issued a list of restricted items; check its website (www.tsa.gov) for details.

Airport screeners may decide that your checked luggage needs to be searched by hand. You can now purchase luggage locks that allow screeners to open and relock a checked bag if hand-searching is necessary. Look for Travel Sentry certified locks at luggage or travel shops and Brookstone stores (you can buy them online at www.brookstone.com). These locks, approved by the TSA, can be opened by luggage inspectors with a special code or key. For more information on the locks, visit www.travelsentry.org. If you use something other than TSA-approved locks, your lock will be cut off your suitcase if a TSA agent needs to hand-search your luggage.

GETTING INTO TOWN FROM THE AIRPORT

Most hotels have courtesy vans to meet their guests and take them to their respective destinations. In addition, **Checker Airport Express** (© 505/765-1234) in Albuquerque runs vans to and from city hotels. Find Checker's booth near the baggage claim area. In Santa Fe, **Roadrunner Shuttle** (© 505/424-3367) meets every flight and takes visitors anywhere in Santa Fe.

FLYING FOR LESS: TIPS FOR GETTING THE BEST AIRFARE

Passengers sharing the same airplane cabin rarely pay the same fare. Travelers who need to purchase tickets at the last minute, change their itinerary at a moment's notice, or fly one-way often get stuck paying the premium rate. Here are some ways to keep your airfare costs down:

- Passengers who can book their ticket **far in advance,** who can **stay over Saturday night,** or who **fly midweek** or **at less-trafficked hours** may pay a fraction of the full fare. If your schedule is flexible, say so, and ask if you can secure a cheaper fare by changing your flight plans.

- You can also save on airfares by keeping an eye out in local newspapers for **promotional specials** or **fare wars,** when airlines lower prices on their most popular routes. You rarely see fare wars offered for peak travel times, but if you can travel in the off-months, you may snag a bargain.

- Search **the Internet** for cheap fares (see "Planning Your Trip Online," below).

- Join **frequent-flier clubs.** Accrue enough miles, and you'll be rewarded with free flights and elite status. It's free, and you'll get the best choice of seats, faster response to phone inquiries, and prompter

service if your luggage is stolen, if your flight is canceled or delayed, or if you want to change your seat. You don't need to fly to build frequent-flier miles—**frequent-flier credit cards** can provide thousands of miles for doing your everyday shopping.

- For many more tips about air travel, including a rundown of the major frequent-flier credit cards, pick up a copy of *Frommer's Fly Safe, Fly Smart* (Wiley Publishing, Inc.).

BY CAR

Albuquerque is at the crossroads of two major interstate highways. I-40 runs from Wilmington, North Carolina (1,870 miles east) to Barstow, California (580 miles west). I-25 extends from Buffalo, Wyoming (850 miles north), to El Paso, Texas (265 miles south). I-25 skims past Santa Fe's southern city limits. To reach Taos, you have to leave I-25 at Santa Fe and travel north 74 miles via US 84/285 and NM 68, or exit I-25 9 miles south of Raton, near the Colorado border, and proceed 100 miles west on US 64.

Parking is quite available and reasonably priced throughout the region both at meters and in city parking garages.

The following table shows the approximate mileage to Santa Fe from various cities around the United States.

Tips Travel in the Age of Bankruptcy

Airlines go bankrupt, so protect yourself by **buying your tickets with a credit card,** as the Fair Credit Billing Act guarantees that you can get your money back from the credit card company if a travel supplier goes under (and if you request the refund within 60 days of the bankruptcy). **Travel insurance** can also help, but make sure it covers against "carrier default" for your specific travel provider. And be aware that if a U.S. airline goes bust midtrip, a 2001 federal law requires other carriers to take you to your destination (albeit on a space-available basis) for a fee of no more than $25, provided that you rebook within 60 days of the cancellation.

Distances to Santa Fe (in Miles)

From	Distance	From	Distance
Atlanta	1,417	Minneapolis	1,199
Boston	2,190	New Orleans	1,181
Chicago	1,293	New York	1,971
Cleveland	1,558	Oklahoma City	533
Dallas	663	Phoenix	595
Denver	391	St. Louis	993
Detroit	1,514	Salt Lake City	634
Houston	900	San Francisco	1,149
Los Angeles	860	Seattle	1,477
Miami	2,011	Washington, D.C.	1,825

BY BUS

Because Santa Fe is only about 58 miles northeast of Albuquerque via I-40, most visitors to Santa Fe take the bus directly from the Albuquerque airport, at a cost of about $20 to $25 one-way. **Sandia Shuttle Express** buses (© **888/775-5696**) make the 70-minute run between the airport and Santa Fe hotels 10 times daily each way (from Albuquerque to Santa Fe 6:30am–6pm; from Santa Fe to Albuquerque 8:45am–8:20pm). Reservations are required, ideally 48 hours in advance. **Santa Fe Shuttle** (© **888/ 833-2300**) offers eight trips daily (from Albuquerque to Santa Fe 6:30am–10:45pm; from Santa Fe to Albuquerque 5:05am–8pm). Reservations are required. Two other bus services shuttle between Albuquerque and Taos (via Santa Fe) for $20 to $35 one-way: **Faust's Transportation** (© **888/ 830-3410** or 505/758-3410), and **Twin Heart Express & Transportation** (© **800/654-9456** or 505/751-1201).

The **public bus depot** in Albuquerque is located on 2nd Street at Lead (300 2nd St. SW). Contact **Texas, New Mexico, and Oklahoma** (TNM&O; © **505/242-4998**) for information and schedules. Fares run about $11 to Santa Fe and $22 to Taos. However, the **bus stations** in Santa Fe (858 St. Michael's Dr.; © **505/471-0008**) and Taos (5 miles south of the plaza at 1386 Paseo del Pueblo Sur; © **505/758-1144**) are several miles south of each city center. Because additional taxi or shuttle service is needed to reach most accommodations, travelers usually find it more convenient to pay a few extra dollars for an airport-to-hotel shuttle.

BY TRAIN

Amtrak (© **800/USA-RAIL** or 505/ 842-9650; www.amtrak.com) passes through northern New Mexico twice daily. The *Southwest Chief,* which runs between Chicago and Los Angeles, stops once eastbound and once westbound in Gallup, Albuquerque, Lamy (for Santa Fe), Las Vegas, and Raton. The Albuquerque train station is in the center of downtown, with easy access to hotels. A spur runs on a limited schedule from Lamy approximately 20 miles to downtown Santa Fe, walking distance to the plaza.

You can get a copy of Amtrak's National Timetable from any Amtrak station, from travel agents, or by writing Amtrak, 400 N. Capitol St. NW, Washington, DC 20001. You can also check Amtrak timetables online, at **www.amtrak.com**. A photo ID is required for check-in.

7 Escorted Tours, Package Deals & Special-Interest Vacations

Before you start your search for the lowest airfare, you may want to consider booking your flight as part of a travel package such as an escorted tour or a package tour. What you lose in adventure, you'll gain in time and money saved when you book accommodations, and maybe even food and entertainment, along with your flight.

PACKAGE TOURS FOR INDEPENDENT TRAVELERS

Package tours are not the same thing as escorted tours. With a package tour, you travel independently but pay a group rate. Packages usually include airfare, a choice of hotels, and car rentals, and packagers often offer several options at different prices. In many cases, a package that includes airfare, hotel, and transportation to and from the airport will cost you less than just the hotel alone would have, had you booked it yourself. That's because packages are sold in bulk to tour operators—who resell them to the public at a cost that drastically undercuts standard rates.

RECOMMENDED PACKAGE TOUR OPERATORS

One good source of package deals is the airlines and train companies themselves. Try **Southwest Airlines Vacations** (© 800/243-8372; www.swavacations.com) and **Amtrak Vacations** (© 800/654-5748; www.amtrakvacations.com).

 Vacation Together (© 800/839-9851; www.vacationtogether.com) allows you to search for and book packages offered by a number of tour operators and airlines. The **United States Tour Operators Association**'s website (www.ustoa.com) has a search engine that allows you to look for operators that offer packages to a specific destination. Travel packages are also listed in the travel section of your local Sunday newspaper. **Liberty Travel** (© 888/271-1584; www.libertytravel.com), one of the biggest packagers in the Northeast, often runs full-page ads in Sunday papers. Or check ads in the national travel magazines, such as *Arthur Frommer's Budget Travel Magazine, Travel & Leisure, National Geographic Traveler,* and *Condé Nast Traveler.*

PROS & CONS OF PACKAGE TOURS

Packages can save you money because they are sold in bulk to tour operators, who sell them to the public. They offer group prices but allow for independent travel. The disadvantages are that you're usually required to make a large payment up front, you may end up on a charter flight, and you have to deal with your own luggage and with transfers between your hotel and the airport, if transfers are not included in the package price. Packages often don't allow for complete flexibility or a wide range of choices. For instance, you may prefer a quiet inn but have to settle for a popular chain hotel instead. Your choice of travel days may be limited as well.

ESCORTED TOURS (TRIPS WITH GUIDES)

Escorted tours are structured group tours, with a group leader. The price usually includes everything from airfare to hotels, meals, tours, admission costs, and local transportation.

RECOMMENDED ESCORTED TOUR OPERATORS

Not many escorted tours are offered in New Mexico. The tour companies I spoke to said most visitors to New Mexico have such disparate interests it's difficult to create packages to please them. Still, a few tour companies can help you arrange a variety of day trips during your visit and can also secure lodging. **Tauck World Discovery** (☏ **800/788-7885;** www.tauck. com), 10 Norden Place, Norwalk, CT 06855, offers weeklong cultural trips to northern New Mexico. **Destination Southwest, Inc.,** 20 First Plaza Galeria, Suite 212, Albuquerque, NM 87102 (☏ **800/999-3109** or 505/ 766-9068; www.destinationsouthwest. com), offers an escorted tour to the Albuquerque International Balloon Fiesta. **Rojotours & Services,** P.O. Box 15744, Santa Fe, NM 87506-5744 (☏ **505/474-8333**), can help with a variety of day trips during your visit.

8 Planning Your Trip Online

SURFING FOR AIRFARES

The "big three" online travel agencies, **Expedia.com, Travelocity,** and **Orbitz,** sell most of the air tickets bought on the Internet. (Canadian travelers should try expedia.ca and Travelocity. ca; U.K. residents can go to www. expedia.co.uk and www.opodo.co.uk.) Each has different business deals with the airlines and may offer different fares on the same flights, so it's wise to shop around. Expedia and Travelocity will also send you **e-mail notification** when a cheap fare becomes available to your favorite destination. Of the smaller travel agency websites, **SideStep** (www.sidestep.com) has gotten the best reviews from Frommer's authors. It's a browser add-on that purports to "search 140 sites at once," but in reality it only beats competitors' fares as often as other sites do.

Also remember to check **airline websites,** especially those for low-fare carriers such as Southwest, JetBlue, AirTran, WestJet, or Ryanair, whose fares are often misreported or simply missing from travel agency websites. Even with major airlines, you can often shave a few bucks from a fare by booking directly through the airline and avoiding a travel agency's transaction fee. But you'll get these discounts only by **booking online:** Most airlines now offer online-only fares that even their phone agents know nothing about.

Great **last-minute deals** are available through free weekly e-mail services provided directly by the airlines. Most of these are announced on Tuesday or Wednesday and must be purchased online. Most are only valid for travel that weekend, but some (such as Southwest's) can be booked weeks or months in advance. Sign up for weekly e-mail alerts at airline websites or check mega-sites that compile comprehensive lists of last-minute specials, such as **Smarter Living** (www.smarterliving. com). For last-minute trips, **site59. com** and **lastminutetravel.com** in the U.S. and **lastminute.com** in Europe often have better air-and-hotel package deals than the major-label sites. A website listing numerous bargain sites and airlines around the world is iTravelnet (**www.itravelnet.com**).

If you're willing to give up some control over your flight details, use what is called an **"opaque" fare service** such as **Priceline** (www.priceline. com; www.priceline.co.uk for Europeans) or its competitor **Hotwire** (www.hotwire.com). Both offer rockbottom prices in exchange for travel on a "mystery airline" at a mysterious time of day, often with a mysterious change of planes en route. The mystery airlines are all major, well-known carriers—and the possibility of being sent from Philadelphia to Chicago via Tampa is remote; the airlines' routing computers have gotten a lot better than they used to be. But your chances of getting a 6am or 11pm flight are pretty high. Hotwire tells you flight prices before you buy; Priceline usually has better deals than Hotwire, but you have to play their "name our price" game. The helpful folks at **BiddingForTravel** (www.biddingfortravel.com) do a good job of demystifying Priceline's prices and strategies. Priceline and Hotwire are great for flights within North America and between the U.S. and Europe. But for flights to other parts of the world, consolidators will almost always beat their fares. *Note:* In 2004 Priceline added non-opaque service to its roster. You now have the option to pick exact flights, times, and airlines from a list of offers—or opt to bid on opaque fares.

For much more about airfares and savvy air-travel tips and advice, pick up a copy of *Frommer's Fly Safe, Fly Smart* (Wiley Publishing, Inc.).

SURFING FOR HOTELS

Shopping online for hotels is generally done one of two ways: by booking through the hotel's own website or through an independent booking agency (or a fare-service agency like Priceline; see below). These Internet hotel agencies have multiplied in mind-boggling numbers of late, competing for the business of millions of consumers surfing for accommodations around the world. This competitiveness can be a boon to consumers who have the patience and time to shop and compare the online sites for good deals—but shop they must, for prices can vary considerably from site to site. And keep in mind that hotels at the top of a site's listing may be there for no other reason than that they paid money to get the placement.

Of the "big three" sites, **Expedia** offers a long list of special deals and "virtual tours" or photos of available rooms so you can see what you're paying for (a feature that helps counter the claims that the best rooms are often held back from bargain-booking websites). **Travelocity** posts unvarnished customer reviews and ranks its properties according to the AAA rating system. Also reliable are **Hotels.com** and **Quikbook.com**. An excellent free

program, **TravelAxe** (www.travelaxe. net), can help you search multiple hotel sites at once, even ones you may never have heard of—and conveniently lists the total price of a room, including the taxes and service charges. Another booking site, **Travelweb** (www.travelweb.com), is partly owned by the hotels it represents (including the Hilton, Hyatt, and Starwood chains) and is therefore plugged directly into the hotels' reservations systems—unlike independent online agencies, which have to fax or e-mail reservation requests to the hotel, a good portion of which get misplaced in the shuffle. More than once, travelers have arrived at the hotel, only to be told that they have no reservation. To be fair, many of the major sites are undergoing improvements in service and ease of use, and Expedia will soon be able to plug directly into the reservations systems of many hotel chains—none of which can be bad news for consumers. In the meantime, it's a good idea to **get a confirmation number** and **make a printout** of any online booking transaction.

In the opaque website category, **Priceline** and **Hotwire** are even better for hotels than for airfares; with both, you're allowed to pick the neighborhood and quality level of your hotel before offering up your money. Priceline's hotel product is much better at getting five-star lodging for three-star prices than at finding anything at the bottom of the scale. On the down side, many hotels stick Priceline guests in their least desirable rooms. Be sure to go to the BiddingForTravel website (see above) before bidding on a hotel room on Priceline; it features a fairly up-to-date list of hotels that Priceline uses in major cities. For both Priceline and Hotwire, you pay upfront, and the fee is nonrefundable. *Note:* Some hotels do not provide loyalty program credits or points or other frequent-stay

Frommers.com: The Complete Travel Resource

For an excellent travel-planning resource, we highly recommend **Frommers.com** (www.frommers.com), voted Best Travel Site by *PC Magazine*. We're a little biased, of course, but we guarantee that you'll find the travel tips, reviews, monthly vacation giveaways, bookstore, and online-booking capabilities thoroughly indispensable. Among the special features are our popular **Destinations** section, where you'll get expert travel tips, hotel and dining recommendations, and advice on the sights to see for more than 3,500 destinations around the globe; the **Frommers.com Newsletter,** with the latest deals, travel trends, and money-saving secrets; our **Community** area featuring **Message Boards,** where Frommer's readers post queries and share advice (sometimes even our authors show up to answer questions); and our **Photo Center,** where you can post and share vacation tips. When your research is done, the **Online Reservations System** (www.frommers.com/book_a_trip) takes you to Frommer's preferred online partners for booking your vacation at affordable prices.

amenities when you book a room through an opaque online service.

SURFING FOR RENTAL CARS

For booking rental cars online, the best deals are usually found at **rental-car company websites,** although all the major online travel agencies also offer rental-car reservations services. **Priceline** and **Hotwire** work well for rental cars, too; the only "mystery" is which major rental company you get, and for most travelers the difference between Hertz, Avis, and Budget is negligible.

9 Getting Around Northern New Mexico

BY CAR

The most convenient way to get around northern New Mexico is by private car. Auto and RV rentals are widely available for those who arrive without their own transportation, either at the Albuquerque airport or at locations around each city.

I have received good rates and service from **Avis** at the Albuquerque airport (© 800/831-2847, 505/842-4080, or 505/471-5892 in Santa Fe); **Thrifty,** 2039 Yale Blvd. SE, Albuquerque (© 800/367-2277 or 505/842-8733); **Hertz,** Albuquerque International Airport (© 800/654-3131 or 505/842-4235); **Dollar,** Albuquerque International Airport (© 800/369-4226); **Budget,** Albuquerque International Airport (© 505/247-3443); **Alamo,** 2601 Yale SE, Albuquerque (© 800/327-9633); and **Rent-A-Wreck** of Albuquerque, 504 Yale SE (© 800/247-9556 or 505/232-7552).

Drivers who need wheelchair-accessible transportation should call **Wheelchair Getaways of New Mexico,** 1015 Tramway Lane NE, Albuquerque (© 800/408-2626 or 505/247-2626; www.wheelchairgetaways.com); the company rents vans by the day, week, or month.

BY PLANE

If you don't have a car and don't want to rent one, your options for getting around New Mexico are very limited. Two airlines fly between a selected number of cities and towns: **Rio Grande Air** (© 877/435-9742; www. riograndeair.com) flies between Albuquerque, Santa Fe, Farmington, Ruidoso, and Taos; and **Mesa Airlines** (© 800/637-2247; www.mesa-air. com) flies between Albuquerque,

Farmington, Carlsbad, Clovis, Roswell, and Hobbs.

BY TRAIN

Railway routes are extremely limited around the region. **Amtrak** (© 800/USA-RAIL or 505/842-9650; www. amtrak.com) runs from Albuquerque to Lamy, with a small spur railroad running to Santa Fe.

10 The 21st-Century Traveler

INTERNET ACCESS AWAY FROM HOME

Travelers have any number of ways to check their e-mail and access the Internet on the road. Of course, using your own laptop—or even a PDA (personal digital assistant) or electronic organizer with a modem—gives you the most flexibility. But even if you don't have a computer, you can still access your e-mail and even your office computer from cybercafes.

WITHOUT YOUR OWN COMPUTER

It's hard nowadays to find a city that *doesn't* have a few cybercafes. Although there's no definitive directory for cybercafes—these are independent businesses, after all—two places to start looking are at **www.cybercaptive. com** and **www.cybercafe.com**.

Aside from formal cybercafes, most **youth hostels** nowadays have at least one computer you can get to the Internet on. And most **public libraries** across the world offer Internet access free or for a small charge. Avoid **hotel business centers** unless you're willing to pay exorbitant rates.

Most major airports now have **Internet kiosks** scattered throughout their gates. These kiosks, which you'll also see in shopping malls, hotel lobbies, and tourist information offices around the world, give you basic Web access for a per-minute fee that's usually higher than cybercafe prices. The kiosks' clunkiness and high price

mean they should be avoided whenever possible.

To retrieve your e-mail, ask your **Internet service provider (ISP)** if it has a Web-based interface tied to your existing e-mail account. If your ISP doesn't have such an interface, you can use the free **mail2web** service (www. mail2web.com) to view and reply to your home e-mail. For more flexibility, you may want to open a free, Web-based e-mail account with **Yahoo! Mail** (www.mail.yahoo.com). (Microsoft's Hotmail is another popular option, but Hotmail has severe spam problems.) Your home ISP may be able to forward your e-mail to the Web-based account automatically.

If you need to access files on your office computer, look into a service called **GoToMyPC** (www.gotomypc. com). The service provides a Web-based interface for you to access and manipulate a distant PC from anywhere—even a cybercafe—provided that your "target" PC is on and has an always-on connection to the Internet (such as with a cable modem or DSL). The service offers top-quality security, but if you're worried about hackers, use your own laptop rather than a cybercafe computer to access the GoToMyPC system.

WITH YOUR OWN COMPUTER

Wi-fi (wireless fidelity) is the buzzword in computer access, and more and more hotels, cafes, and retailers are signing on as wireless "hotspots" from where you can get high-speed connection without cable wires, networking hardware, or a phone line (see below). You can get wi-fi connection one of several ways. Many laptops sold in the past year have built-in wi-fi capability (an 802.11b wireless Ethernet connection). Mac owners have their own networking technology, Apple AirPort. For those with older computers, an 802.11b/**Wi-fi card** (around $50) can be plugged into your laptop. You sign up for wireless access service much as you do cellphone service, through a plan offered by one of several commercial companies that have made wireless service available in airports, hotel lobbies, and coffee shops, primarily in the U.S. (followed by the U.K. and Japan). **T-Mobile Hotspot** (www.t-mobile.com/hotspot) serves up wireless connections at more than 1,000 Starbucks coffee shops nationwide. **Boingo** (www.boingo.com) and **Wayport** (www.wayport.com) have set up networks in airports and high-class hotel lobbies. **iPass** providers (see below) also give you access to a few hundred wireless hotel lobby setups. Best of all, you don't need to be staying at the Four Seasons to use the hotel's network; just set yourself up on a nice couch in the lobby. The companies' pricing policies can be byzantine, with a variety of monthly, per-connection, and per-minute plans, but in general you pay around $30 a month for limited access—and as more and more companies jump on the wireless bandwagon, prices are likely to get even more competitive.

There are also places that provide **free wireless networks** in cities around the world. To locate these free hotspots, go to **www.personaltelco.net/index.cgi/WirelessCommunities**.

Most business-class hotels throughout the world offer dataports for laptop modems, and a few thousand hotels in the U.S. and Europe now offer free high-speed Internet access using an Ethernet network cable. You can bring your own cables, but most hotels rent them for around $10. **Call your hotel in advance** to see what your options are.

In addition, major ISPs have **local access numbers** around the world, allowing you to go online by simply placing a local call. Check your ISP's

Digital Photography on the Road

Many travelers are going digital these days when it comes to taking vacation photographs. Not only are digital cameras left relatively unscathed by airport X-rays, but with digital equipment, you don't need to lug armloads of film with you as you travel. In fact, nowadays you don't even need to carry your laptop to download the day's images to make room for more. With a **media storage card,** sold by all major camera dealers and many electronics stores, you can store hundreds of images in your camera. These "memory" cards come in different configurations—from memory sticks to flash cards to secure digital cards—and different storage capacities (the more megabytes of memory, the more images a card can hold) and range in price from $30 to over $200. (**Note:** Each camera model works with a specific type of card, so you'll need to determine which storage card is compatible with your camera.) When you get home, you can print the images out on your own color printer or take the storage card to a camera store, drugstore, or chain retailer. Or you can have the images developed online with a service like **Snapfish** (www.snapfish.com) for something like 25¢ a shot.

Online Traveler's Toolbox

Veteran travelers usually carry some essential items to make their trips easier. Following is a selection of handy online tools to bookmark and use.

- **New Mexico Travel.** Your best bets for finding maps, deals, transport information, tours, and calendars are the **New Mexico Department of Tourism** website (www.newmexico.org) and the **Santa Fe Department of Tourism** site (www.santafe.org). The latter also gives current weather conditions. Two generic sites that list similar information are **Info.com** (www.info.com) and **Tripadvisor.com** (www.tripadvisor.com). Plug in the city you'll be visiting, and see what comes up.

- **New Mexico Tickets.** To find out who's playing, whether it be instruments or sports, log on to the **Ticketmaster** website (www.ticketmaster.com), plug in the city where you're staying, and see what comes up.

- **Indian Pueblos.** Although it's still refining its site, the **Indian Pueblo Cultural Center** (www.indianpueblo.org/ipcc) has links to New Mexico pueblos, as well as a calendar of dances and other events.

- **Airplane Seating and Food.** Find out which seats to reserve and which to avoid (and more) on all major domestic airlines at www.seatguru.com. And check out the type of meal (with photos) you'll likely be served on airlines around the world at www.airlinemeals.com.

- **Intellicast** (www.intellicast.com) and **Weather.com** (www.weather.com). Give weather forecasts for all 50 states and for cities around the world.

- **Mapquest** (www.mapquest.com). This best of the mapping sites lets you choose a specific address or destination, and in seconds, it will return a map and detailed directions.

- **Time and Date** (www.timeanddate.com). See what time (and day) it is anywhere in the world.

- **Travel Warnings** (http://travel.state.gov, www.fco.gov.uk/travel, www.voyage.gc.ca, www.dfat.gov.au/consular/advice). These sites report on places where health concerns or unrest might threaten American, British, Canadian, and Australian travelers. Generally, U.S. warnings are the most paranoid; Australian warnings are the most relaxed.

- **Universal Currency Converter** (www.xe.com/ucc). See what your dollar, euro, or pound is worth in more than 100 other countries.

- **Visa ATM Locator** (www.visa.com), for locations of PLUS ATMs worldwide, or **MasterCard ATM Locator** (www.mastercard.com), for locations of Cirrus ATMs worldwide.

website or call its toll-free number and ask how you can use your current account away from home and how much it will cost.

If you're traveling outside the reach of your ISP, you may be able to use the **iPass** network, which has dial-up numbers in most countries. You'll have to sign up with an iPass provider, which will then tell you how to set up your computer for your destination(s). For a list of iPass providers, go to www.ipass.com and click on "Individuals Buy Now." One solid provider is **i2roam** (www.i2roam.com; © **866/ 811-6209** or 920/235-0475).

Wherever you go, bring a **connection kit** of the right power and phone adapters, a spare phone cord, and a spare Ethernet network cable—or find out whether your hotel supplies them to guests.

USING A CELLPHONE

Just because your cellphone works at home doesn't mean it'll work elsewhere in the country (thanks to the fragmented U.S. cellphone system). It's a good bet that your phone will work in major cities. But take a look at your wireless company's coverage map on its website before heading out—T-Mobile, Sprint, and Nextel are particularly weak in rural areas. If you need to stay in touch at a destination where you know your phone won't work, **rent** a phone that does from **InTouch Global** (© **800/872-7626;** www.in touchglobal.com) or a rental-car location, but beware that you'll pay $1 a minute or more for airtime.

If you're venturing deep into national parks, you may want to consider renting a **satellite phone ("satphone"),** which is different from a cellphone in that it connects to

satellites rather than ground-based towers. A satphone is more costly than a cellphone but works where there are no cellular signals and no towers. Unfortunately, you'll pay at least $2 per minute to use a satphone, and it only works where you can see the horizon (i.e., usually not indoors). In North America, you can rent Iridium satphones from **Roadpost** (© **888/ 290-1606;** www.roadpost.com). **In-Touch Global** (see above) offers a wider range of satphones but at higher rates.

If you're not from the U.S., you'll be appalled at the poor reach of our **GSM (Global System for Mobiles) wireless network,** which is used by much of the rest of the world (see below). Your phone will probably work in most major U.S. cities; it definitely won't work in many rural areas. (To see where GSM phones work in the U.S., check out www.t-mobile. com/coverage/national_popup.asp.) And you may or may not be able to send SMS (text messaging) home—something Americans tend not to do anyway, for various cultural and technological reasons. (International budget travelers like to send text messages home because it's much cheaper than making international calls.) Assume nothing—call your wireless provider and get the full scoop. In a worst-case scenario, you can always rent a phone; InTouch Global delivers to hotels.

11 Recommended Reading

Many well-known writers have made their homes in northern New Mexico in the 20th century. In the 1920s, the most celebrated were **D. H. Lawrence** and **Willa Cather,** both short-term Taos residents. Lawrence, the romantic and controversial English novelist, spent time here between 1922 and 1925; he reflected on his sojourn in *Mornings in Mexico* and *Etruscan Places.* Lawrence's Taos period is

described in *Lorenzo in Taos,* which his patron, Mabel Dodge Luhan, wrote. Cather, a Pulitzer-prize winner famous for her depictions of the pioneer spirit, penned *Death Comes for the Archbishop,* among other works. This fictionalized account of the 19th-century Santa Fe bishop, Jean-Baptiste Lamy, grew out of her stay in the region.

Many contemporary authors also live in and write about New Mexico.

John Nichols, of Taos, whose *Milagro Beanfield War* was made into a Robert Redford movie in 1987, writes insightfully about the problems of poor Hispanic farming communities. Albuquerque's Tony Hillerman has for 2 decades woven mysteries around Navajo tribal police in books such as *Listening Woman* and *A Thief of Time.* (Robert Redford, this time as director, is making a movie version of each of Hillerman's novels that feature the character Jim Chee for PBS.) In recent years, Sarah Lovett has joined his ranks with a series of gripping mysteries, most notably *Dangerous Attachments.* The Hispanic novelist Rudolfo Anaya's *Bless Me, Ultima* and Pueblo writer Leslie Marmon Silko's *Ceremony* capture the lifestyles of their respective peoples. A coming-of-age story, Richard Bradford's *Red Sky at Morning* juxtaposes the various cultures of New Mexico. Edward Abbey wrote of the desert environment and politics; his *Fire on the Mountain,* set in New Mexico, was one of his most powerful works.

Excellent works about Native Americans of New Mexico include *The Pueblo Indians of North America* (Holt, Rinehart & Winston, 1970) by Edward P. Dozier and *Living the Sky: The Cosmos of the American Indian* (University of Oklahoma Press, 1987) by Ray A. Williamson. Also look for *American Indian Literature 1979–1994* (Ballantine, 1996), an anthology edited by Paula Gunn Allen.

For general histories of the state, try Myra Ellen Jenkins and Albert H. Schroeder's *A Brief History of New Mexico* (University of New Mexico Press, 1974) and Marc Simmons's *New Mexico: An Interpretive History* (University of New Mexico Press, 1988). In addition, Claire Morrill's *A Taos Mosaic: Portrait of a New Mexico Village* (University of New Mexico Press, 1973) does an excellent job of portraying the history of that small New Mexican town. I have also enjoyed Tony Hillerman's (ed.) *The Spell of New Mexico* (University of New Mexico Press, 1976) and John Nichols and William Davis's *If Mountains Die: A New Mexico Memoir* (Alfred A. Knopf, 1979). *Talking Ground* (University of New Mexico Press, 1996), by Santa Fe author Douglas Preston, tells of a contemporary horseback trip through Navajoland, exploring the native mythology. One of my favorite texts is *Enchantment and Exploitation* (University of New Mexico Press, 1985) by William deBuys. A new, very extensive book that attempts to capture the multiplicity of the region is *Legends of the American Southwest* (Alfred A. Knopf, 1997) by Alex Shoumatoff.

Enduring Visions: 1,000 Years of Southwestern Indian Art, by the Aspen Center for the Visual Arts (Publishing Center for Cultural Resources, 1969), and Roland F. Dickey's *New Mexico Village Arts* (University of New Mexico Press, 1990) are both excellent resources for those interested in Native American art. If you become intrigued with Spanish art during your visit to New Mexico, you'll find E. Boyd's *Popular Arts of Spanish New Mexico* (Museum of New Mexico Press, 1974) to be quite informative.

3

For International Visitors

Howling coyotes and parched cow skulls, dusty cowboys and noble Native Americans—you've seen them in the movies, along with dreamy sunsets and pastel earth hues. Though the denizens and landscapes of the southwestern United States may seem familiar, for most the reality is quite different. This chapter will help you prepare for some of the uniquely American situations you are likely to encounter.

1 Preparing for Your Trip

ENTRY REQUIREMENTS

Check at any U.S. embassy or consulate for current information and requirements. You can also obtain a visa application and other information online at the **U.S. State Department**'s website, at **www.travel.state.gov**.

VISAS The U.S. State Department has a **Visa Waiver Program** that allows citizens of certain countries to enter the United States without visas for stays of up to 90 days. At press time these included Andorra, Australia, Austria, Belgium, Brunei, Denmark, Finland, France, Germany, Iceland, Ireland, Italy, Japan, Liechtenstein, Luxembourg, Monaco, the Netherlands, New Zealand, Norway, Portugal, San Marino, Singapore, Slovenia, Spain, Sweden, Switzerland, and the United Kingdom. Citizens of these countries need only a valid passport and a round-trip air or cruise ticket in their possession upon arrival. If they first enter the United States, they may also visit Mexico, Canada, Bermuda, and/or the Caribbean islands and return to the United States without a visa. Further information is available from any U.S. embassy or consulate. Canadian citizens may enter the United States without visas; they need only proof of residence.

Citizens of all other countries must have (1) a valid passport that expires at least 6 months later than the scheduled end of their visit to the United States, and (2) a tourist visa, which may be obtained without charge from any U.S. consulate.

To obtain a visa, the traveler must submit a completed application form (either in person or by mail) with a 1½-inch-square photo, and must demonstrate binding ties to a residence abroad. Usually you can obtain a visa at once or within 24 hours, but it may take longer during the summer rush from June through August. If you cannot go in person, contact the nearest U.S. embassy or consulate for directions on applying by mail. Your travel agent or airline office may also be able to provide you with visa applications and instructions. The U.S. consulate or embassy that issues your visa will determine whether you will be issued a multiple- or single-entry visa and any restrictions regarding the length of your stay.

British subjects can obtain up-to-date passport and visa information by calling the **U.S. Embassy Visa Information Line** (℡ 0891/200-290) or the **London Passport Office** (℡ 0990/210-410 for recorded information), or they can find the visa information on the **U.S. Embassy Great Britain** website (www.passport.gov.uk).

Irish citizens can obtain up-to-date passport and visa information through the **Embassy of USA Dublin,** 42 Elgin Rd., Dublin 4, Ireland (℃ 353/1-668-8777; http://dublin.usembassy.gov).

Australian citizens can obtain up-to-date passport and visa information by calling the **U.S. Embassy Canberra,** Moonah Place, Yarralumla, ACT 2600 (℃ 02/6214-5600; http://canberra.usembassy.gov) or by checking the **U.S. Diplomatic Mission**'s website, at http://usembassy-australia.state.gov/consular.

Citizens of **New Zealand** can obtain up-to-date passport and visa information by calling the **U.S. Embassy New Zealand,** 29 Fitzherbert Terrace, Thorndon, Wellington, New Zealand (℃ 644/462-6000), or get the information directly from the "Services to New Zealanders" section of the website **http://usembassy.org.nz**.

Canadians need only show proof of residence to enter the United States, but often showing a passport is the easiest and most convenient way to do this. You can pick up a passport application at any of 28 regional passport offices or at most travel agencies. Applications, which must be accompanied by two identical passport-size photographs and proof of Canadian citizenship, are available at travel agencies throughout Canada or from the central **Passport Office, Department of Foreign Affairs and International Trade,** Ottawa, ON K1A 0G3 (℃ 800/567-6868; www.dfait-maeci.gc.ca/passport). Processing takes 5 to 10 days if you apply in person or about 3 weeks by mail.

MEDICAL REQUIREMENTS

Unless you're arriving from an area known to be suffering from an epidemic (particularly cholera or yellow fever), inoculations or vaccinations are not required for entry into the United States. If you have a medical condition that requires **syringe-administered medications,** carry a valid signed prescription from your physician; the Federal Aviation Administration (FAA) no longer allows airline passengers to pack syringes in their carry-on baggage without documented proof of medical need. If you have a disease that requires treatment with **narcotics,** you should also carry documented proof with you—smuggling narcotics aboard a plane is a serious offense that carries severe penalties in the U.S.

For **HIV-positive visitors,** requirements for entering the United States are somewhat vague and change frequently. According to the latest publication of *HIV and Immigrants: A Manual for AIDS Service Providers,* the Immigration and Naturalization Service (INS) doesn't require a medical exam for entry into the United States, but INS officials may stop individuals because they look sick or because they are carrying AIDS/HIV medicine.

If an HIV-positive noncitizen applies for a non-immigrant visa, the question on the application regarding communicable diseases is tricky no matter which way it's answered. If the applicant checks "no," INS may deny the visa on the grounds that the applicant committed fraud. If the applicant checks "yes" or if INS suspects the person is HIV-positive, it will deny the visa unless the applicant asks for a special waiver for visitors. This waiver is for people visiting the United States for a short time—for instance, to attend a conference, to visit close relatives, or to receive medical treatment. It can be a confusing situation. For up-to-the-minute information, contact **AIDSinfo** (℃ 800/448-0440, or 301/519-6616 outside the U.S.; www.aidsinfo.nih.gov) or the **Gay Men's Health Crisis** (℃ 212/367-1000; www.gmhc.org).

DRIVER'S LICENSES   Foreign driver's licenses are mostly recognized in the U.S., although you may want to get an international driver's license if your home license is not written in English.

CUSTOMS

WHAT YOU CAN BRING IN

Every visitor over 21 years of age may bring in, free of duty, the following: (1) 1 liter of wine or hard liquor; (2) 200 cigarettes, 100 cigars (but not from Cuba), or 3 pounds of smoking tobacco; and (3) $100 worth of gifts. These exemptions are offered to travelers who spend at least 72 hours in the United States and who have not claimed them within the preceding 6 months. It is altogether forbidden to bring into the country foodstuffs (particularly fruit, cooked meats, and canned goods) and plants (vegetables, seeds, tropical plants, and the like). Foreign tourists may bring in or take out up to $10,000 in U.S. or foreign currency with no formalities; larger sums must be declared to U.S. Customs on entering or leaving, which includes filing form CM 4790. For more specific information regarding U.S. Customs and Border Protection, contact your nearest U.S. embassy or consulate, or the **U.S. Customs** office (© **202/927-1770;** www.customs.us treas.gov).

WHAT YOU CAN TAKE HOME

U.K. citizens returning from a non-E.U. country have a Customs allowance of: 200 cigarettes; 50 cigars; 250 grams of smoking tobacco; 2 liters of still table wine; 1 liter of spirits or strong liqueurs (over 22% volume); 2 liters of fortified wine, sparkling wine, or other liqueurs; 60cc (ml) of perfume; 250cc (ml) of toilet water; and £145 worth of all other goods, including gifts and souvenirs. People under 17 cannot have the tobacco or alcohol allowance. For more information, contact **HM Customs & Excise** at © **0845/010-9000** (from outside the U.K., 020/8929-0152), or visit www.hmce.gov.uk.

For a clear summary of **Canadian** rules, request the booklet *I Declare,* issued by the **Canada Revenue Agency** (© **800/461-9999** in Canada, or 204/983-3500; www.ccra-adrc.gc. ca). Canada allows its citizens a C$750 exemption, and you're allowed to bring back duty-free 1 carton of cigarettes, 1 can of tobacco, 40 imperial ounces of liquor, and 50 cigars. In addition, you're allowed to mail to Canada gifts valued at less than C$60 a day, provided they're unsolicited and don't contain alcohol or tobacco (write on the package, "Unsolicited gift, under $60 value"). All valuables should be declared on the Y-38 form before departure from Canada, including serial numbers of valuables you already own, such as expensive foreign cameras. *Note:* The C$750 exemption can be used only once a year and only after an absence of 7 days.

The duty-free allowance in **Australia** is A$400 or, for those under 18, A$200. Citizens ages 18 and over can bring in 250 cigarettes or 250 grams of loose tobacco, and 1,125 milliliters of alcohol. If you're returning with valuables you already own, such as foreign-made cameras, you should file form B263. A helpful brochure available from Australian consulates or Customs offices is *Know Before You Go.* For more information, call the **Australian Customs Service** at © **1300/363-263** or visit www.customs.gov.au.

The duty-free allowance for **New Zealand** is NZ$700. Citizens over 17 can bring in 200 cigarettes, 50 cigars, or 250 grams of tobacco (or a mixture of all three if their combined weight doesn't exceed 250g), plus 4.5 liters of wine and beer or 1.125 liters of liquor. New Zealand currency does not carry import or export restrictions. Fill out a certificate of export, listing the valuables you are taking out of the country; that way, you can bring them back without paying duty. Most questions are answered in a free pamphlet available at New Zealand consulates and Customs offices: *New Zealand Customs Guide for Travellers, Notice no. 4.* For more information, contact **New Zealand Customs Service,** The Customhouse, 17–21 Whitmore St., Box 2218, Wellington (© **0800/428-786** or 04/473-6099; www.customs.govt.nz).

HEALTH INSURANCE

Although it's not required of travelers, health insurance is highly recommended. Unlike many European countries, the United States does not usually offer free or low-cost medical care to its citizens or visitors. Doctors and hospitals are expensive, and in most cases they require advance payment or proof of coverage before they render their services. Insurance policies can cover everything from the loss or theft of your baggage and trip cancellation to the guarantee of bail in case you're arrested. Good policies will also cover the costs of an accident, repatriation, or death. See "Insurance, Health & Safety," in chapter 2 for more information. Packages such as **Europ Assistance's "Worldwide Healthcare Plan"** are sold by European automobile clubs and travel agencies at attractive rates. **Worldwide Assistance Services, Inc.** (© **800/821-2828;** www.worldwide assistance.com) is the agent for Europ Assistance in the United States.

Although lack of health insurance may prevent you from being admitted to a hospital in nonemergencies, don't worry about being left on a street corner to die: The American way is to fix you now and bill the living daylights out of you later.

INSURANCE FOR BRITISH TRAVELERS Most big travel agents offer their own insurance and will probably try to sell you their package when you book a holiday. Think before you sign. **Britain's Consumers'**

Association recommends that you insist on seeing the policy and reading the fine print before buying travel insurance. **The Association of British Insurers** (© **020/7600-3333;** www.abi.org.uk) gives advice by phone and publishes *Holiday Insurance,* a free guide to policy provisions and prices. You might also shop around for better deals: Try **Columbus Direct** (© **0845/330-8518;** www.columbusdirect.net).

INSURANCE FOR CANADIAN TRAVELERS Canadians should check with their provincial health plan offices or call **Health Canada** (© **613/957-2991;** www.hc-sc.gc.ca) to find out the extent of their coverage and what documentation and receipts they must take home in case they are treated in the United States.

MONEY

CURRENCY The U.S. monetary system is very simple: The most common **bills** are the $1 (colloquially, a "buck"), $5, $10, and $20 denominations. There are also $2 bills (seldom encountered), $50 bills, and $100 bills (the last two are usually not welcome as payment for small purchases). The paper money was recently redesigned, making the famous faces adorning them disproportionately large. The old-style bills are still legal tender.

There are seven denominations of coins: 1¢ (1 cent, or a penny); 5¢ (5 cents, or a nickel); 10¢ (10 cents, or a dime); 25¢ (25 cents, or a quarter); 50¢ (50 cents, or a half dollar); the gold-colored "Sacagawea" coin worth $1; and, prized by collectors, the rare, older silver dollar.

Note: The "foreign-exchange bureaus" so common in Europe are rare even at airports in the United States and nonexistent outside major cities. It's best not to change foreign money (or traveler's checks denominated in a currency other than U.S. dollars) at a small-town bank or even a branch in a big city; in fact, leave any

---

Tips Travel Tip

Be sure to keep a copy of all your travel papers separate from your wallet or purse, and leave a copy with someone at home should you need it faxed in an emergency.

---

currency other than U.S. dollars at home—it may prove a greater nuisance to you than it's worth.

TRAVELER'S CHECKS Though traveler's checks are widely accepted, make sure that they're denominated in U.S. dollars, as foreign-currency checks are often difficult to exchange. The three traveler's checks that are most widely recognized—and least likely to be denied—are **Visa, American Express,** and **Thomas Cook.** Be sure to record the numbers of the checks, and keep that information in a separate place in case they get lost or stolen. Most businesses are pretty good about taking traveler's checks, but you're better off cashing them in at a bank (in small amounts, of course) and paying in cash. Remember: You'll need identification, such as a driver's license or passport, to change a traveler's check.

CREDIT CARDS & ATMs Credit cards are the most widely used form of payment in the United States: **Visa** (Barclaycard in Britain), **MasterCard** (Eurocard in Europe, Access in Britain, Chargex in Canada), **American Express, Diners Club, Discover,** and **Carte Blanche.** There are, however, a handful of stores and restaurants that do not take credit cards, so be sure to ask in advance. Most businesses display a sticker near their entrance to let you know which cards they accept. *Note:* Businesses may require a minimum purchase, usually around $10, to use a credit card.

It is strongly recommended that you bring at least one major credit card. You must have a credit or charge card to rent a car. Hotels usually require a credit-card imprint as a deposit against expenses, and in an emergency, a credit card can be priceless.

You'll find **automated teller machines (ATMs)** on just about every block—at least in almost every town—across the country. Some ATMs will allow you to draw U.S. currency against your bank and credit cards. Check with your bank before leaving home, and remember that you will need your personal identification number (PIN) to do so. Most accept Visa, MasterCard, and American Express, as well as ATM cards from other U.S. banks. Expect to be charged up to $3 per transaction, however, if you're not using your own bank's ATM.

ATM cards with major credit card backing, known as **"debit cards,"** are now a commonly acceptable form of payment in most stores and restaurants. Debit cards draw money directly from your checking account. Some stores enable you to receive "cash back" on your debit-card purchases. This is one way around ATM fees.

SAFETY

GENERAL SUGGESTIONS Tourist areas as a rule are safe, but, despite recent reports of decreases in violent crime in many cities, it would be wise to check with the tourist offices in Santa Fe, Taos, and Albuquerque if you are in doubt about which neighborhoods are safe. (See the "Orientation" sections in chapters 4, 11, and 15 for the names and addresses of the specific tourist bureaus.)

Remember that hotels are open to the public, and in a large hotel, security may not be able to screen everyone

SIZE CONVERSION CHART

Women's Clothing

American	4	6	8	10	12	14	16
French	34	36	38	40	42	44	46
British	6	8	10	12	14	16	18

Women's Shoes

American	5	6	7	8	9	10
French	36	37	38	39	40	41
British	4	5	6	7	8	9

Men's Suits

American	34	36	38	40	42	44	46	48
French	44	46	48	50	52	54	56	58
British	34	36	38	40	42	44	46	48

Men's Shirts

American	14 ½	15	15 ½	16	16 ½	17	17½
French	37	38	39	41	42	43	44
British	14 ½	15	15 ½	16	16 ½	17	17½

Men's Shoes

American	7	8	9	10	11	12	13
French	39½	41	42	43	44½	46	47
British	6	7	8	9	10	11	12

who enters. Always lock your room door; don't assume that once inside your hotel you are automatically safe and no longer need to be aware of your surroundings.

Be aware that New Mexico has a fairly high reported incidence of rape. Women should not walk alone in isolated places, particularly at night.

DRIVING SAFETY   Question your rental agency about personal safety, or ask for a brochure of traveler safety tips when you pick up your car. Obtain written directions, or a map with the route clearly marked, from the agency to show you how to get to your destination. (Many agencies now offer the option of renting a cellphone for the duration of your car rental; check with the rental agent when you pick up the car. Otherwise, contact **InTouch USA** at ✆ **800/872-7626** or www.intouch usa.com for short-term cellphone

rental.) And, if possible, arrive and depart during daylight hours.

In recent years, carjacking, a crime that targets both cars and drivers, has been on the rise in all U.S. cities. If you exit a highway into a questionable neighborhood, leave the area as quickly as possible. If you have an accident, even on the highway, stay in your car with the doors locked until you are able to assess the situation or until the police arrive. If you are involved in a minor accident with no injuries and the situation appears to be suspicious, motion to the other driver to follow you to the nearest police precinct or well-lit service station.

If you see someone on the road who indicates a need for help, do not stop. Take note of the location, drive to a well-lighted area, and telephone the police by dialing ✆ **911.**

Also, make sure that you have enough gasoline in your tank to reach your intended destination, so that you're not forced to look for a service station in an unfamiliar and possibly unsafe neighborhood—especially at night.

2 Getting to the U.S.

AIRLINE DISCOUNTS The smart traveler can find numerable ways to reduce the price of a plane ticket simply by taking time to shop around. For example, travelers from overseas can take advantage of the **APEX** (Advance-Purchase Excursion) fares offered by all the major international carriers. British travelers should check out **British Airways** (© 0845/ 77-333-77 in the U.K., or 800/247-9297 in the U.S.), which offers direct flights from London to New York and to Los Angeles, as does **Virgin Atlantic Airways** (© 0870/380-2007 in the U.K., or 800/862-8621 in the U.S.). Canadian readers might book flights on **Air Canada** (© 888/247-2262), which offers service from Toronto, Montreal, and Calgary to New York and to Los Angeles. In addition, many other international carriers serve the New York and Los Angeles airports, including **Air France** (© 800/ 237-2747), **Alitalia** (© 800/223-5730), **Japan Airlines** (© 800/525-3663), **Lufthansa** (© 800/645-3880), and **Qantas** (© 300/650-729 in Australia, or 800/227-4500 in the U.S.). **SAS** (© 800/221-2350) serves New York, Chicago, and Seattle, but not Los Angeles. Connecting flights to New Mexico can be obtained at the major U.S. airports mentioned above. For more money-saving airline advice, see "Getting There," in chapter 2.

IMMIGRATION AND CUSTOMS CLEARANCE Visitors arriving by air, no matter what the port of entry, should cultivate patience and resignation before setting foot on U.S. soil. Getting through immigration control can take as long as 2 hours on some days, especially on summer weekends, so be sure to carry this guidebook or something else to read. This is especially true in the aftermath of the September 11, 2001, terrorist attacks; security clearances have been considerably beefed up at U.S. airports.

People traveling by air from Canada, Bermuda, and certain countries in the Caribbean can sometimes clear Customs and Immigration at the point of departure, which is much quicker.

Travelers arriving by car or by rail from Canada will find that the border-crossing formalities are more streamlined.

For further information about transportation to Santa Fe, Taos, and Albuquerque, see "Orientation," in chapters 4, 11, and 15, respectively.

Tips Prepare to Be Fingerprinted

Starting in January 2004, many international visitors traveling on visas to the United States will be photographed and fingerprinted at Customs in a new program created by the Department of Homeland Security called **US-VISIT**. Non–U.S. citizens arriving at airports and on cruise ships must undergo an instant background check as part of the government's ongoing efforts to deter terrorism by verifying the identity of incoming and outgoing visitors. Exempt from the extra scrutiny are visitors entering by land or those from 28 countries (mostly in Europe) that don't require visas for short-term visits. For more information, go to the **Department of Homeland Security** website, at **www.dhs.gov/dhspublic**.

3 Getting Around the U.S.

BY PLANE Some large airlines (for example, Northwest and Delta) offer travelers on their transatlantic or transpacific flights special discount tickets under the name **Visit USA,** allowing mostly one-way travel from one U.S. destination to another at very low prices. These discount tickets are not on sale in the United States and must be purchased abroad in conjunction with your international ticket. This system is the best, easiest, and fastest way to see the United States at low cost. You should obtain information well in advance from your travel agent or the office of the airline concerned because the conditions attached to these discount tickets can be changed without advance notice.

BY TRAIN International visitors (excluding those from Canada) can also buy a **USA Rail Pass,** good for 15 or 30 days of unlimited travel on **Amtrak** (© **800/USA-RAIL;** www. amtrak.com). The pass is available through many overseas travel agents. Prices in 2004 for a 15-day pass were $295 off-peak, $440 peak; a 30-day pass costs $385 off-peak, $550 peak. With a foreign passport, you can also buy passes at some Amtrak offices in the United States, including locations in San Francisco, Los Angeles, Chicago, New York, Miami, Boston, and Washington, D.C. Reservations are generally required and should be made for each part of your trip as early as possible. Regional rail passes are also available.

BY BUS Although bus travel can be an economical form of public transit for short hops between U.S. cities, it can also be slow and uncomfortable— certainly not an option for everyone (particularly when Amtrak, which is far more luxurious, offers similar rates). **Greyhound/Trailways** (© **800/231-2222;** www.greyhound.com), the sole nationwide bus line, offers an **International Ameripass** that must be purchased before coming to the United States, or by phone through the Greyhound International Office at the Port Authority Bus Terminal in New York City (© **212/971-0492**). The pass can be obtained from foreign travel agents or through Greyhound's website (order at least 21 days before your departure to the U.S.) and costs less than the domestic version. 2004 passes cost as follows: $160 for 4 days, $219 for 7 days, $269 for 10 days, $329 for 15 days, $379 for 21 days, $439 for 30 days, $489 for 45 days, and $599 for 60 days. You can get more info about the pass at the website or by calling © **402/330-8552.** In addition, special rates are available for seniors and students.

BY CAR Unless you plan to spend the bulk of your vacation time in a city where walking is the best and easiest way to get around (i.e., New York City or New Orleans), the most cost-effective, convenient, and comfortable way to travel around the United States is by car. The interstate highway system connects cities and towns all over the country; in addition to these high-speed, limited-access roadways, there's an extensive network of federal, state, and local highways and roads. Some of the national car-rental companies include **Alamo** (© 800/462-5266; www.alamo.com), **Avis** (© 800/230-4898; www.avis.com), **Budget** (© 800/527-0700; www.budget.com), **Dollar** (© 800/800-3665; www. dollar.com), **Hertz** (© 800/654-3131; www.hertz.com), **National** (© 800/ 227-7368; www.nationalcar.com), and **Thrifty** (© 800/847-4389; www. thrifty.com).

If you plan to rent a car in the United States, you probably won't need the services of an additional automobile organization. If you're planning to buy or borrow a car, automobile-association membership is recommended. **AAA, the American Automobile Association** (© 800/ 222-4357), is the country's largest auto club and supplies its members with maps, insurance, and, most importantly, emergency road service. The cost of joining runs from $63 for singles to $87 for two members, but if you're a member of a foreign auto club

with reciprocal arrangements, you can enjoy free AAA service in America.

For information on renting cars in the United States, see "Automobile Organizations" and "Automobile Rentals" in "Fast Facts: For the International Traveler," below; "By Car" in "Getting There," in chapter 2; and "By Car" in "Getting Around," in chapters 4, 11, and 15.

FAST FACTS: For the International Traveler

Automobile Organizations Auto clubs supply maps, suggested routes, guidebooks, accident and bail-bond insurance, and emergency road service. The **American Automobile Association (AAA)** is the major auto club in the United States. If you belong to an auto club in your home country, inquire about AAA reciprocity before you leave. You may be able to join AAA even if you're not a member of a reciprocal club; to inquire, call AAA (© **800/222-4357**). AAA is actually an organization of regional auto clubs; so look under "AAA Automobile Club" in the White Pages of the telephone directory. AAA has a nationwide emergency road service telephone number: © **800/AAA-HELP.**

In addition, some automobile-rental agencies now provide many of these same services. Inquire about their availability when you rent a car.

Automobile Rentals To rent a car you need a major credit card and a valid driver's license. In addition, you usually need to be at least 25 years old (some companies do rent to younger people but add a daily surcharge). Be sure to return your car with the same amount of gas you started with; rental companies charge excessive prices for gasoline. See "By Car" in "Getting Around," in chapters 4, 11, and 15, for the phone numbers of car-rental companies in Santa Fe, Taos, and Albuquerque, respectively.

Business Hours See "Fast Facts," in chapters 4, 11, and 15.

Climate See "When to Go," in chapter 2.

Currency Exchange You'll find currency-exchange services at major airports with international service. Elsewhere, they may be quite difficult to come by. In the United States, a very reliable choice is **Thomas Cook Currency Services, Inc.** It sells commission-free foreign and U.S. traveler's checks, drafts, and wire transfers. Its rates are competitive, and the service is excellent. Thomas Cook maintains several offices in New York City, including one at 511 Madison Ave. For the locations and hours of offices nationwide, call © **800/287-7362.**

For Santa Fe, Taos, and Albuquerque banks that handle foreign-currency exchange, see the "Fast Facts" sections in chapters 4, 11, and 15, respectively.

Drinking Laws The legal age for purchase and consumption of alcoholic beverages is 21; proof of age is required and often requested at bars, nightclubs, and restaurants, so it's always a good idea to bring ID when you go out. Beer and wine often can be purchased in supermarkets, but liquor laws vary from state to state. In New Mexico, major supermarkets and liquor stores sell beer, wine, and liquor.

Do not carry open containers of alcohol in your car or any public area that isn't zoned for alcohol consumption. The police can fine you on the spot. And nothing will ruin your trip faster than getting a citation for DUI ("driving under the influence"), so don't even think about driving while intoxicated.

Electricity Like Canada, the United States uses 110–120 volts AC (60 cycles), compared to 220–240 volts AC (50 cycles) in most of Europe, Australia, and New Zealand. If your small appliances use 220–240 volts, you'll need a 110-volt transformer and a plug adapter with two flat parallel pins to operate them here. Downward converters that change 220–240 volts to 110–120 volts are difficult to find in the United States, so bring one with you.

Embassies & Consulates All embassies are located in the nation's capital, Washington, D.C. Some consulates are located in major U.S. cities, and most nations have missions to the United Nations in New York City. If your country isn't listed below, call for directory information in Washington, D.C. (© **202/555-1212**) or visit **www.embassy.org/embassies**.

The embassy of **Australia** is at 1601 Massachusetts Ave. NW, Washington, DC 20036 (© **202/797-3000**; www.austemb.org). There are consulates in New York, Honolulu, Houston, Los Angeles, and San Francisco.

The embassy of **Canada** is at 501 Pennsylvania Ave. NW, Washington, DC 20001 (© **202/682-1740**; www.canadianembassy.org). Other Canadian consulates are in Buffalo, Detroit, Los Angeles, New York, and Seattle.

The embassy of **Ireland** is at 2234 Massachusetts Ave. NW, Washington, DC 20008 (© **202/462-3939**; www.irelandemb.org). Irish consulates are in Boston, Chicago, New York, and San Francisco.

The embassy of **Japan** is at 2520 Massachusetts Ave. NW, Washington, DC 20008 (© **202/238-6700**; www.embjapan.org). Japanese consulates are located in many cities, including Atlanta, Boston, Detroit, New York, San Francisco, and Seattle.

The embassy of **New Zealand** is at 37 Observatory Circle NW, Washington, DC 20008 (© **202/328-4800**; www.nzemb.org). New Zealand consulates are in Los Angeles, Salt Lake City, San Francisco, and Seattle.

The embassy of the **United Kingdom** is at 3100 Massachusetts Ave. NW, Washington, DC 20008 (© **202/462-1340**; www.britainusa.com). Other British consulates are in Atlanta, Boston, Chicago, Cleveland, Houston, Los Angeles, New York, San Francisco, and Seattle.

Emergencies Call © **911** to report a fire, call the police, or get an ambulance anywhere in the United States. This is a toll-free call. (No coins are required at public telephones.)

If you encounter serious problems, contact the **Travelers Aid International** (© **202/546-1127**; www.travelersaid.org) to help direct you to a local branch. This nationwide, nonprofit, social-service organization geared to helping travelers in difficult straits offers services that might include reuniting families separated while traveling, providing food and/or shelter to people stranded without cash, or even emotional counseling. If you're in trouble, seek out Travelers Aid.

Gasoline (Petrol) Petrol is known as gasoline (or simply "gas") in the United States, and petrol stations are known as both gas stations and service stations. Taxes are already included in the printed price of gas. One U.S. gallon equals 3.8 liters or 0.83 imperial gallons. There are usually several grades (and price levels) of gasoline available at most gas stations, and their names change from company to company. Unleaded gas with the highest octane ratings is the most expensive; however, most rental cars take the least expensive—"regular" unleaded gas.

Most gas stations are essentially self-service, although some offer higher-priced full service as well. Late- or all-night stations are usually self-service only.

Holidays Banks, government offices, post offices, and many stores, restaurants, and museums are closed on the following legal national holidays: January 1 (New Year's Day), the third Monday in January (Martin Luther King, Jr., Day), the third Monday in February (Presidents' Day, Washington's Birthday), the last Monday in May (Memorial Day), July 4 (Independence Day), the first Monday in September (Labor Day), the second Monday in October (Columbus Day), November 11 (Veterans' Day/Armistice Day), the fourth Thursday in November (Thanksgiving Day), and December 25 (Christmas). Also, the Tuesday following the first Monday in November is Election Day and is a federal government holiday in presidential-election years (held every 4 years, and next in 2008).

Internet Access Most city libraries in New Mexico have computers on which visitors can access the Internet for a small fee. In a few cities you'll find cybercafes and other businesses that offer service for a fee. See the "Fast Facts" sections in chapters 4, 11, and 15.

Legal Aid If you are "pulled over" for a minor infraction (such as speeding), never attempt to pay the fine directly to a police officer; this could be construed as attempted bribery, which is a serious crime. Pay fines by mail or directly into the hands of the clerk of the court. If you're accused of a serious offense, say and do nothing before consulting a lawyer. In the U.S. the burden is on the state to prove a person's guilt beyond a reasonable doubt, and everyone has the right to remain silent, whether he or she is suspected of a crime or actually arrested. Once arrested, a person can make one telephone call to a party of his or her choice. Call your embassy or consulate.

Mail If you aren't sure what your address will be in the United States, mail can be sent to you, in your name, **c/o General Delivery** at the main post office of the city or region where you expect to be. (Call ✆ **800/275-8777** in the U.S. for information on the nearest post office.) The addressee must pick up mail in person and must produce proof of identity (driver's license, passport, etc.). Most post offices will hold your mail for up to 1 month and are open Monday to Friday from 8am to 6pm and Saturday from 9am to 3pm.

Generally found at intersections, **mailboxes** are blue with a red-and-white stripe and carry the inscription "U.S. MAIL." If your mail is addressed to a U.S. destination, don't forget to include the five-digit **postal code** (or zip code) after the two-letter abbreviation of the state to which the mail is addressed. This is essential for prompt delivery.

At press time, domestic **postage rates** were 23¢ for a postcard and 37¢ for a letter. For international mail, a first-class letter of up to ½ ounce costs 80¢ (60¢ to Canada and Mexico); a first-class postcard costs 70¢ (50¢ to Canada and Mexico); and a preprinted postal aerogramme costs 70¢.

Measurements　See the chart on the inside front cover of this book for details on converting metric measurements to U.S. equivalents.

Newspapers & Magazines　National newspapers include the *New York Times, USA Today,* and the *Wall Street Journal.* National news weeklies include *Newsweek, Time,* and *U.S. News and World Report.* In large cities, most newsstands offer a small selection of the most popular foreign periodicals and newspapers, such as the *Economist* and *Le Monde.* For information on local publications, see the "Fast Facts" sections in chapters 4, 11, and 15.

Radio & Television　Audiovisual media, with six coast-to-coast networks—ABC, CBS, NBC, Fox, the Public Broadcasting System (PBS), and the cable network CNN—play a major part in American life. In big cities, viewers have a choice of several dozen channels (including basic cable), most of them transmitting 24 hours a day, not counting the pay-TV channels that show recent movies or sports events. All options are usually indicated on your hotel TV set. You'll also find a wide choice of local radio stations, both AM and FM, each broadcasting particular kinds of talk shows and/or music—classical, country, jazz, pop, gospel—punctuated by news broadcasts and frequent commercials. For information on local stations, see the "Fast Facts" sections in chapters 4, 11, and 15.

Safety　See "Safety" in "Preparing for Your Trip," earlier in this chapter.

Taxes　The United States has no value-added tax (VAT) or other indirect tax at the national level. Every state, county, and city has the right to levy its own local tax on all purchases, including hotel and restaurant checks, airline tickets, and so on. For information on taxes in Santa Fe, Taos, and Albuquerque, see the "Fast Facts" sections in chapters 4, 11, and 15.

Telephone, Telegraph, Telex & Fax　The telephone system in the United States is run by private corporations, so rates, especially for long-distance service and operator-assisted calls, can vary widely. Generally, hotel surcharges on long-distance and local calls are astronomical, so you're usually better off using a **public pay telephone,** which you'll find clearly marked in most public buildings and private establishments as well as on the street. Convenience grocery stores and gas stations always have them. Many convenience groceries and packaging services sell **prepaid calling cards** in denominations up to $50; using these can be the least expensive way to call home. Many public phones at airports and other locations now accept American Express, MasterCard, and Visa credit cards. **Local calls** made from public pay phones in most locales cost either 25¢ or 35¢. Pay phones do not accept pennies, and few will take anything larger than a quarter.

You may want to look into leasing a cellphone for the duration of your trip. For information, see "Using a Cellphone" under "The 21st-Century Traveler," in chapter 2.

Most long-distance and international calls can be dialed directly from any phone. **For calls within the United States and to Canada,** dial 1 followed by the area code and the seven-digit number. **For other international calls,** dial 011 followed by the country code, city code, and the telephone number of the person you are calling.

Calls to area codes **800, 888, 877,** and **866** are toll-free. However, calls to numbers in area codes **700** and **900** (chat lines, bulletin boards, "dating" services, and so on) can be very expensive—usually a charge of 95¢ to $3 or more per minute, and they sometimes have minimum charges that can run as high as $15 or more.

For **reversed-charge or collect calls,** and for person-to-person calls, dial 0 (zero, not the letter O) followed by the area code and number you want; an operator will then come on the line, and you should specify that you are calling collect, or person-to-person, or both. If your operator-assisted call is international, ask for the overseas operator.

For **local directory assistance** ("information"), dial ✆ **411;** for **long-distance information,** dial 1, then the appropriate area code and 555-1212.

Telegraph and telex services are provided primarily by Western Union. You can bring your telegram into the nearest Western Union office (there are hundreds across the country) or dictate it over the phone (✆ **800/325-6000**). You can also telegraph money, or have it telegraphed to you, very quickly over the Western Union system, but this service can cost as much as 15% to 20% of the amount sent.

Most hotels have **fax machines** available for guest use (be sure to ask about the charge to use it). Many hotel rooms are even wired for guests' fax machines. A less expensive way to send and receive faxes may be at stores such as **The UPS Store** (formerly Mail Boxes Etc.), a national chain of retail packing service shops. (Look in the Yellow Pages directory under "Packing Services.")

There are two kinds of telephone directories in the United States. The so-called **White Pages** list private households and business subscribers in alphabetical order. The inside front cover lists emergency numbers for police, fire, ambulance, the Coast Guard, poison-control center, crime-victims hot line, and so on. The first few pages tell you how to make long-distance and international calls, complete with country codes and area codes. Government numbers are usually printed on blue paper within the White Pages. Printed on yellow paper, the so-called **Yellow Pages** list all local services, businesses, industries, and houses of worship, according to activity, with an index at the front or back. (Drugstores/pharmacies and restaurants are also generally listed by geographic location.) The Yellow Pages also include city plans or detailed area maps, postal zip codes, and public transportation routes.

Time The continental United States is divided into **four time zones:** Eastern Standard Time (EST), Central Standard Time (CST), Mountain Standard Time (MST), and Pacific Standard Time (PST). Alaska and Hawaii have their own zones. For example, noon in New York City (EST) is 11am in Chicago (CST), 10am in Santa Fe (MST), 9am in Los Angeles (PST), 8am in Anchorage (AST), and 7am in Honolulu (HST).

New Mexico is on Mountain Standard Time (MST), 7 hours behind Greenwich Mean Time. **Daylight saving time** is in effect from the first

Sunday in April through the last Saturday in October (actually, the change is made at 2am on Sun), except in parts of Arizona (the Navajo reservation *does* observe daylight saving time; the rest of the state does not), Hawaii, part of Indiana, and Puerto Rico. Daylight saving time moves the clock 1 hour ahead of standard time. (Americans use the adage "Spring forward, fall back" to remember which way to change their clocks and watches.)

Tipping Tips are a very important part of certain workers' income, and gratuities are the standard way of showing appreciation for services provided. Tipping is so ingrained in the American way of life that the annual income tax of tip-earning service personnel is based on how much they should have received in light of their employers' gross revenues. Accordingly, they may have to pay tax on a tip you didn't actually give them. (Tipping is certainly not compulsory if the service is poor!)

Here are some rules of thumb: In hotels, tip **bellhops** at least $1 per bag ($2–$3 if you have a lot of luggage) and tip the **chamber staff** $1 to $2 per day (more if you've left a disaster area for him or her to clean up). Tip the **doorman** or **concierge** only if he or she has provided you with some specific service (for example, calling a cab for you or obtaining difficult-to-get theater tickets). Tip the **valet-parking attendant** $1 every time you get your car.

In restaurants, bars, and nightclubs, tip **service staff** 15% to 20% of the check, tip **bartenders** 10% to 15%, tip **checkroom attendants** $1 per garment, and tip **valet-parking attendants** $1 per vehicle.

As for other service personnel, tip **cab drivers** 15% of the fare; tip **skycaps** at airports at least $1 per bag ($2–$3 if you have a lot of luggage); and tip **hairdressers** and **barbers** 15% to 20%.

Tipping ushers at movies and theaters, and gas-station attendants, is not expected.

Toilets You won't find public toilets, or "restrooms," on the streets in most U.S. cities, but they can be found in hotel lobbies, bars, restaurants, museums, department stores, railway and bus stations, and service stations. Large hotels and fast-food restaurants are probably the best bet for good, clean facilities. If possible, avoid the toilets at parks and beaches, which tend to be dirty; some may be unsafe. Restaurants and bars in resorts or heavily visited areas may reserve their restrooms for patrons. Some establishments display a notice indicating this. You can ignore this sign or, better yet, avoid arguments by paying for a cup of coffee or a soft drink, which will qualify you as a patron. Along major highways are "rest stops," many with restroom facilities.

4

Getting to Know Santa Fe

After visiting Santa Fe, Will Rogers reportedly once said, "Whoever designed this town did so while riding on a jackass backwards and drunk." You, too, may find yourself perplexed when maneuvering through this, the oldest capital city in the United States. The meandering lanes and one-way streets can frustrate your best intentions. The best way to get a feel for the idiosyncrasies of the place is to see it on foot.

Like most cities of Hispanic origin, Santa Fe contains a **plaza** in the center of the city. Here, you'll find tall shade trees and lots of grass. The area is full of restaurants, shops, art galleries, and museums, many within centuries-old buildings, and is dominated by the beautiful **St. Francis Cathedral,** a French Romanesque structure.

On the plaza, you'll see Native Americans selling jewelry under the portal of the **Palace of the Governors,** teenagers in souped-up low-riders cruising along, and people young and old hanging out in the ice-cream parlor. Such diversity, coupled with the variety of architecture, prompted the tourism department here to begin calling this city of 65,000 residents the "City Different."

Not far away is **Canyon Road,** a narrow, mostly one-way street packed with galleries and shops. Once it was the home of many artists, and today you'll still find some who work within gallery studios. There are a number of fine restaurants in this district as well.

Farther to the east slopes the rugged **Sangre de Cristo** range. Locals spend a lot of time in these mountains, picnicking, hiking, and skiing. When you look up at the mountains, you see the peak of **Santa Fe Baldy** (with an elevation of over 12,600 ft.). Back in town, to the south of the plaza, is the Santa Fe River, a tiny tributary of the Rio Grande that is little more than a trickle for much of the year.

North is the **Española Valley,** and beyond that, the village of Taos, about 66 miles away. South of the city are ancient Native American **turquoise mines** in the Cerrillos Hills, and to the southwest is metropolitan Albuquerque, some 58 miles away. To the west, across the Caja del Rio Plateau, is the **Rio Grande,** and beyond that, the 11,000-foot **Jemez Mountains** and **Valle Grande**—an ancient and massive volcanic caldera. Pueblos dot the entire Rio Grande Valley, within an hour's drive in any direction.

1 Orientation

ARRIVING

BY PLANE Many people choose to fly into the Albuquerque International Sunport. However, if you want to save time and don't mind paying a bit more, you can fly into the **Santa Fe Municipal Airport** (© 505/955-2900), just outside the southwestern city limits on Airport Road. In conjunction with United Airlines, commuter flights are offered via Denver, Colorado, by **United Express**

Santa Fe Orientation

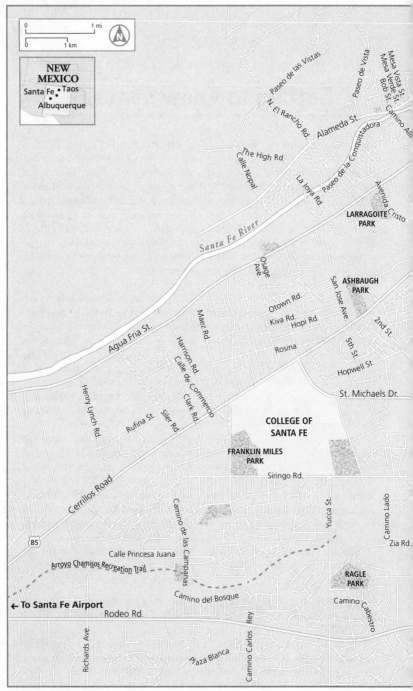

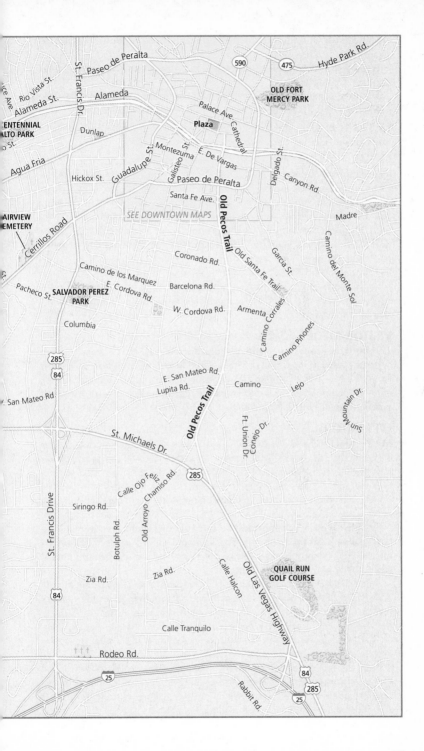

SEE DOWNTOWN MAPS

(© 800/241-6522), which is operated by **Great Lakes Aviation** (© 800/473-4118).

If you do fly into Albuquerque, you can rent a car or take one of the bus services. See "Getting There," in chapter 2, for details.

From the Santa Fe Municipal Airport, **Roadrunner Shuttle** (© 505/424-3367) meets every flight and takes visitors anywhere in Santa Fe.

BY TRAIN & BUS For detailed information about train and bus service to Santa Fe, see "Getting There," in chapter 2.

BY CAR I-25 skims past Santa Fe's southern city limits, connecting it along one continuous highway from Billings, Montana, to El Paso, Texas. I-40, the state's major east–west thoroughfare, which bisects Albuquerque, affords coast-to-coast access to Santa Fe. (From the west, motorists leave I-40 in Albuquerque and take I-25 north; from the east, travelers exit I-40 at Clines Corners and continue 52 miles to Santa Fe on US 285. *Note:* Diesel is scarce on US 285, so be sure to fill up before you leave Clines Corners.) For those coming from the northwest, the most direct route is via Durango, Colorado, on US 160, entering Santa Fe on US 84.

For information on car rentals in Albuquerque, see "Getting Around Northern New Mexico," in chapter 2; for agencies in Santa Fe, see "Getting Around," later in this chapter.

VISITOR INFORMATION
The **Santa Fe Convention and Visitors Bureau** is at 201 W. Marcy St., in Sweeney Center at the corner of Grant Street downtown (P.O. Box 909), Santa Fe, NM 87504-0909 (© 800/777-CITY or 505/955-6200). You can also log on to the bureau's website, at **www.santafe.org**. You might also try **www.visit santafe.com** for more information.

CITY LAYOUT
MAIN ARTERIES & STREETS The limits of downtown Santa Fe are demarcated on three sides by the horseshoe-shaped Paseo de Peralta and on the west by St. Francis Drive, otherwise known as US 84/285. Alameda Street follows the north side of the Santa Fe River through downtown, with the State Capitol and other government buildings on the south side of the river, and most buildings of historic and tourist interest on the north, east of Guadalupe Street.

The plaza is Santa Fe's universally accepted point of orientation. Its four diagonal walkways meet at a central fountain, around which a strange and wonderful assortment of people of all ages, nationalities, and lifestyles can be found at nearly any hour of the day or night.

If you stand in the center of the plaza looking north, you'll be gazing directly at the Palace of the Governors. In front of you is Palace Avenue; behind you, San Francisco Street. To your left is Lincoln Avenue, and to your right is Washington Avenue, which divides the downtown avenues into east and west. St. Francis Cathedral is the massive Romanesque structure a block east, down San Francisco Street. Alameda Street is 2 full blocks behind you.

Near the intersection of Alameda Street and Paseo de Peralta, you'll find Canyon Road running east toward the mountains. Much of this street is one-way. The best way to see it is to walk up or down, taking time to explore shops and galleries and even have lunch or dinner.

Running to the southwest from the downtown area, beginning opposite the state office buildings on Galisteo Avenue, is Cerrillos Road. Once the main north–south highway connecting New Mexico's state capital with its largest city, it is now a 6-mile-long motel and fast-food strip. St. Francis Drive, which crosses Cerrillos Road 3 blocks south of Guadalupe Street, is a far less tawdry byway, linking Santa Fe with I-25, located 4 miles southwest of downtown. The Old Pecos Trail, on the east side of the city, also joins downtown and the freeway. St. Michael's Drive connects the three arteries.

FINDING AN ADDRESS   The city's layout makes it difficult to know exactly where to look for a particular address. It's best to call ahead for directions.

MAPS   Free city and state maps can be obtained at tourist information offices. An excellent state highway map is published by the **New Mexico Department of Tourism,** 491 Old Santa Fe Trail, Lamy Building, Santa Fe, NM 87503 (© **800/ 733-6396** or 505/827-7307; to receive a tourism guide call © **800/777-CITY**). There's also a Santa Fe visitor center in the same building. More specific county and city maps are available from the **State Highway and Transportation Department,** 1120 Cerrillos Rd., Santa Fe, NM 87504 (© **505/827-5100**). Members of the **American Automobile Association,** 1644 St. Michael's Dr. (© **505/471-6620**), can obtain free maps from the AAA office. Other good regional maps can be purchased at area bookstores.

2 Getting Around

The best way to see downtown Santa Fe is on foot. Free **walking-tour maps** are available at the **tourist information center** in Sweeney Center, 201 W. Marcy St. (© **800/777-CITY** or 505/984-6760), and several guided walking tours, as well as two self-guided tours, are included in chapter 7.

BY BUS

In 1993, Santa Fe opened **Santa Fe Trails** (© **505/955-2001**), its first public bus system. There are seven routes, and visitors can pick up a map from the Convention and Visitors Bureau. Some buses operate Monday to Friday 6am to 11pm and Saturday 8am to 8pm. There is some service on Sunday, and there is no service on holidays. Call for a current schedule and fare information.

BY CAR

Cars can be rented from any of the following firms in Santa Fe: **Avis,** Santa Fe Airport (© **505/471-5892**); **Budget,** 1946 Cerrillos Rd. (© **505/984-1596**); **Enterprise,** 2641A Cerrillos Rd., 4450 Cerrillos Rd. (at the Auto Park), and Santa Fe Hilton, 100 Sandoval St. (© **505/473-3600**); and **Hertz,** Santa Fe Airport (© **505/471-7189**).

If Santa Fe is merely your base for an extended driving exploration of New Mexico, be sure to give the vehicle you rent a thorough road check before starting out. There are a lot of wide-open desert and wilderness spaces here, so if you break down, you could be stranded for hours before someone passes by, and cellphones don't tend to work in these remote areas.

Make sure your driver's license and auto club membership (if you have one) are valid before you leave home. Check with your auto-insurance company to make sure you're covered when out of state and/or when driving a rental car.

Note: In 2002, the Santa Fe City Council imposed a law prohibiting use of cellphones while driving within the city limits, with strict fines imposed. If you need to make a call, be sure to pull off the road.

Street parking is difficult to find during summer months. There's a metered parking lot near the federal courthouse, 2 blocks north of the plaza; a city lot

---

(*Warning*   **Driving Warning**

New Mexico has one of the highest per-capita rates of traffic deaths in the nation; although the number has actually been dropping in recent years, it's still a good idea to drive extra carefully!

---

behind Santa Fe Village, a block south of the plaza; and a another city lot at Water and Sandoval streets. If you stop by the Santa Fe Convention and Visitors Bureau, at the corner of Grant and Marcy streets, you can pick up a wallet-size guide to Santa Fe parking areas. The map shows both street and lot parking.

Unless otherwise posted, the speed limit on freeways is 75 mph; on most other two-lane open roads it's 60 to 65 mph. The minimum age for drivers is 16. Seat belts are required for drivers and all passengers ages 5 and over; children under 5 must use approved child seats.

Since Native American reservations enjoy a measure of self-rule, they can legally enforce certain designated laws. For instance, on the Navajo reservation, it is forbidden to transport alcoholic beverages, leave established roadways, or go without a seat belt. Motorcyclists must wear helmets. If you are caught breaking reservation laws, you are subject to reservation punishment—often stiff fines and, in some instances, detainment.

The **State Highway and Transportation Department** has a toll-free hot line (© **800/432-4269**) that provides up-to-the-hour information on road closures and conditions.

BY TAXI

Cabs are difficult to flag from the street, but you can call for one. Expect to pay a standard fee of $2.40 for the service and an average of about $2.35 per mile. **Capital City Cab** (© **505/438-0000**) is the main company in Santa Fe.

BY BICYCLE

Riding a bicycle is an excellent way to get around town. Check with **Sun Mountain Bike Company,** 102 E. Water St. (inside El Centro) (© **505/982-8986**); **Bike-N-Sport,** 1829 Cerillos Rd. (© **505/820-0809**); or **Santa Fe Mountain Sports,** 607 Cerillos Rd. (© **505/988-3337**) for rentals.

FAST FACTS: **Santa Fe**

Airport   See "Orientation," above.

Area Code   All of New Mexico is in area code **505**. However, at press time the state was initiating moves to add another area code, which may affect Santa Fe.

ATM Networks   As in most U.S. destinations, ATMs are ubiquitous in the cities of northern New Mexico. However, in the small mountain towns, they're scarce. ATMs are linked to a network that most likely includes your bank at home. **Cirrus** (© **800/424-7787**; www.mastercard.com) and **PLUS** (© **800/843-7587**; www.visa.com) are the two most popular networks in the U.S. and in this region.

Babysitters Most hotels can arrange for sitters on request. Alternatively, call professional, licensed sitters **Ida Rajotte** (© **505/471-6875**) or **Linda Iverson** (© **505/982-9327**).

Business Hours **Offices** and **stores** are generally open Monday to Friday, 9am to 5pm, with many stores also open Friday night, Saturday, and Sunday in the summer season. Most **banks** are open Monday to Thursday, 9am to 5pm, and Friday, 9am to 6pm. Some may also be open Saturday morning. Most branches have ATMs available 24 hours. Call establishments for specific hours.

Car Rentals See "Getting Around Northern New Mexico," in chapter 2, or "Getting Around," above.

Climate See "When to Go," in chapter 2.

Currency Exchange You can exchange foreign currency at **Bank of America,** 1234 St. Michael's Dr. (© **505/473-8211**).

Dentists **Dr. Gilman Stenzhorn** (© **505/982-4317** or 505/983-4491) offers emergency service. He's located at 1496 St. Francis Dr., in the St. Francis Professional Center.

Doctors **The Lovelace Clinic,** 440 St. Michaels Dr. (© **505/995-2400**), is open Monday to Thursday, 8am to 6pm; Fridays, 8am to 5pm; and Saturdays, 8am to 3pm. For physician and surgeon referral and information services, call the **American Board of Medical Specialties** (© **866/275-2267**).

Embassies & Consulates See "Fast Facts: For the International Traveler," in chapter 3.

Emergencies For police, fire, or ambulance emergencies, dial © **911.**

Etiquette & Customs Certain rules of etiquette should be observed when visiting the pueblos. See chapter 10 for details.

Hospitals **St. Vincent Hospital,** 455 St. Michaels Dr. (© **505/983-3361,** or 505/995-3934 for emergency services), is a 248-bed regional health center. Patient services include urgent and emergency-room care and ambulatory surgery. Health services are also available at the **Women's Health Services Family Care and Counseling Center** (© **505/988-8869**). **Ultimed,** 707 Paseo de Peralta (© **505/989-8707**), a new urgent care facility near the plaza, offers comprehensive health care.

Hot Lines The following hot lines are available in Santa Fe: **battered families** (© **505/473-5200**), **poison control** (© **800/432-6866**), **psychiatric emergencies** (© **888/920-6333** or 505/820-6333), and **sexual assault** (© **505/986-9111**).

Information See "Visitor Information," under "Orientation," above.

Internet Access Head to the **Santa Fe Public Library** at 145 Washington Ave. (© **505/955-6780**), or retrieve your e-mail at **FedEx Kinko's,** 301 N. Guadalupe (© **505/982-6311**).

Libraries **The Santa Fe Public Library** is half a block from the plaza, at 145 Washington Ave. (© **505/955-6780**). There are branch libraries at Villa Linda Mall and at 1730 Llano St., just off St. Michaels Drive. **The New Mexico State Library** is at 1209 Camino Carlos Rey (© **505/476-9700**). Specialty libraries include the **Archives of New Mexico,** 1205 Camino Carlos Rey, and the **New Mexico History Library,** 120 Washington Ave.

Liquor Laws The legal drinking age is 21 throughout New Mexico. Bars may remain open until 2am Monday to Saturday and until midnight on Sunday. Wine, beer, and spirits are sold at licensed supermarkets and liquor stores, but there are no package sales on election days until after 7pm, and on Sundays before noon. It is illegal to transport liquor through most Native American reservations.

Lost Property Contact the **city police** at ⓒ 505/955-5030.

Newspapers & Magazines The **New Mexican**—Santa Fe's daily paper—is the oldest newspaper in the West. Its offices are at 202 E. Marcy St. (ⓒ 505/983-3303; www.santafenewmexican.com). The weekly **Santa Fe Reporter,** 132 E. Marcy St. (ⓒ 505/988-5541; www.sfreporter.com), published on Wednesday and available free at stands all over town, is often more willing to be controversial, and its entertainment listings are excellent. Regional magazines published locally are **New Mexico** magazine (monthly, statewide interest; www.nmmagazine.com) and the **Santa Fean** magazine (10 times a year, Southwestern lifestyles; www.santafean.com).

Pharmacies **Del Norte Pharmacy,** at 1691 Galisteo St. (ⓒ 505/988-9797), is open Monday to Friday, 8:30am to 6pm, and Saturday, 9am to noon. Emergency and delivery service are available.

Police In case of emergency, dial ⓒ **911.** For all other inquiries, call the **Santa Fe Police Department,** 2515 Camino Entrada (ⓒ 505/428-3710). The **Santa Fe County Sheriff,** with jurisdiction outside the city limits, is located at 35 Camino Justicia (ⓒ 505/986-2400).

Post Offices The **main post office** is at 120 S. Federal Place (ⓒ 505/988-6351), 2 blocks north and 1 block west of the plaza. It's open from 7:30am to 5:30pm. The **Coronado Station branch** is at 2071 S. Pacheco St. (ⓒ 505/438-8452), and is open Monday to Friday, 8am to 6pm, and Saturday 9am to 1pm. Some of the major hotels have stamp machines and mailboxes with twice-daily pickup. The zip code for central Santa Fe is 87501.

Radio Local radio stations are **BLU** (102.9), which plays contemporary jazz, and **KBAC** (98.1), which plays alternative rock and folk music.

Safety Although the tourist district appears very safe, Santa Fe is not on the whole a safe city; theft and the number of reported rapes have risen. The good news is that Santa Fe's overall crime statistics do appear to be falling. Still, when walking the city streets, guard your purse carefully because there are many bag-grab thefts, particularly during the summer tourist months. Also, be as aware of your surroundings as you would in any other major city.

Taxes A tax of 6.43% is added to all purchases, with an additional 5% added to lodging bills.

Taxis See "Getting Around," above.

Television There are five Albuquerque network affiliates: **KOB-TV** (Channel 4, NBC), **KOAT-TV** (Channel 7, ABC), **KQRE-TV** (Channel 13, CBS), **KASA-TV** (Channel 2, FOX), and **KNME-TV** (Channel 5, PBS).

Time Zone New Mexico is on **Mountain Standard Time**, 1 hour ahead of the West Coast and 2 hours behind the East Coast. When it's 10am in Santa Fe, it's noon in New York, 11am in Chicago, and 9am in San Francisco. Daylight saving time is in effect from early April to late October.

Useful Telephone Numbers Information on **road conditions** in the Santa Fe area can be obtained by calling the State Highway and Transportation Department (© **800/432-4269**). For **time and temperature,** call © **505/473-2211.**

Weather For **weather forecasts,** call © **505/988-5151.**

5

Where to Stay in Santa Fe

It's difficult to find a bad place to stay in Santa Fe. From downtown hotels to Cerrillos Road motels, ranch-style resorts to quaint bed-and-breakfasts, the standard of accommodations is almost universally high.

You should be aware of the seasonal nature of the tourist industry in Santa Fe. Accommodations are often booked solid through the summer months, and most places raise their prices accordingly. Rates increase even more during Indian Market, the third weekend of August. During these periods it's essential to make reservations well in advance.

Still, there seems to be little agreement on what constitutes the tourist season; one hotel may raise its rates July 1 and lower them again in mid-September, while another may raise its rates from May to November. Some hotels recognize a shoulder season, so it pays to shop around during the in-between seasons of May through June and September through October.

No matter the season, discounts are often available to seniors, affiliated groups, corporate employees, and others. If you have any questions about your eligibility for these lower rates, be sure to ask.

A combined city-state tax of about 11.5% is added to every hotel bill in Santa Fe. And unless otherwise indicated, all recommended accommodations come with a private bathroom.

RESERVATIONS SERVICES Year-round reservation assistance is available from **Santa Fe Central Reservations** (✆ 800/745-9910), the **Accommodation Hot Line** (✆ 800/338-6877), **All Santa Fe Reservations** (✆ 877/737-7366), and **Santa Fe Stay,** which specializes in casitas (✆ 800/995-2272). **Emergency Lodging Assistance** is available free after 4pm daily (✆ 505/986-0038). All of the above are private companies and may have biases toward certain properties. Do your own research before calling.

1 Downtown

Everything within the horseshoe-shaped Paseo de Peralta and east a few blocks along either side of the Santa Fe River is considered downtown Santa Fe. All these accommodations are within walking distance of the plaza.

VERY EXPENSIVE

Eldorado Hotel ★★ Since its opening in 1986, the Eldorado has been a model new hotel for the city. In a large structure, the architects managed to meld Pueblo Revival style with an interesting cathedral feel, inside and out. The lobby is grand, with a high ceiling that continues into the court area and the cafe, all adorned with well over a million dollars' worth of Southwestern art. The spacious, quiet rooms continue the artistic motif, with a warm feel created by the kiva fireplaces in many as well as the custom-made furniture. You'll find families, businesspeople, and conference-goers staying here. Most of the rooms have

Downtown Santa Fe Accommodations

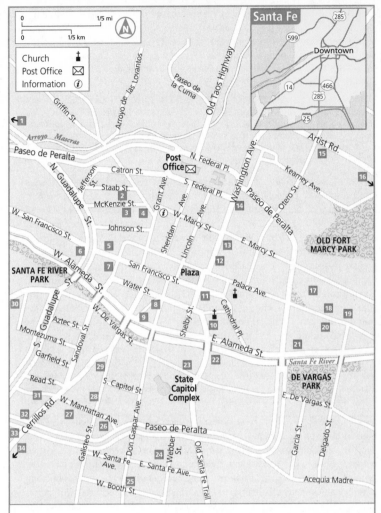

Santa Fe
Downtown

Church	✝
Post Office	✉
Information	ⓘ

Adobe Abode **2**
Alexander's Inn **19**
Don Gaspar Inn **25**
Dos Casas Viejas **30**
Eldorado Hotel **5**
El Farolito **28**
El Paradero **27**
Four Kachinas Inn **24**
Garrett's Desert Inn **22**
Grant Corner Inn **4**
Hacienda Nicholas **17**
Hilton of Santa Fe **7**

Hotel Plaza Real **13**
Hotel St. Francis **8**
Hotel Santa Fe **32**
Inn and Spa at Loretto **10**
Inn of the Anasazi **12**
Inn of the Five Graces **23**
Inn of the Governors **9**
Inn on the Alameda **21**
La Fonda **11**
La Posada de Santa Fe
  Resort and Spa **20**
The Madeleine **18**

Old Santa Fe Inn **29**
Pueblo Bonito **26**
Radisson Hotel Santa Fe **1**
Santa Fe Accommodations **15**
Santa Fe Budget Inn **34**
Santa Fe Motel and Inn **31**
Santa Fe Plaza Travelodge **33**
Spencer House
  Bed & Breakfast Inn **3**
Ten Thousand Waves **16**
Territorial Inn **14**
Water Street Inn **6**

views of downtown Santa Fe, many from balconies. If you're really indulging, join the ranks of Mick Jagger, Geena Davis, and King Juan Carlos of Spain and try the penthouse five-room presidential suite. The Eldorado also manages the nearby Zona Rosa condominiums, which are two-, three-, and four-bedroom suites with full kitchens. The innovative and elegant restaurant The Old House serves creative American cuisine (see chapter 6).

309 W. San Francisco St., Santa Fe, NM 87501. ☏ **800/286-6755** or 505/988-4455. Fax 505/995-4544. www. eldoradohotel.com. 219 units. High season $279–$1,500 double; low season $169–$900 double. Ski and other package rates are available. AE, DC, DISC, MC, V. Valet parking $16 per night. Pets accepted. **Amenities:** 2 restaurants; bar; heated rooftop pool; medium-size health club (with a view); Jacuzzi; his-and-hers saunas; concierge; business center; salon; room service; massage; laundry service; dry cleaning. *In room:* A/C, TV, dataport, minibar, coffeemaker, hair dryer, iron, safe.

Hilton of Santa Fe ⭐   With its landmark bell tower, the Hilton encompasses a full city block (1 block from the plaza) and incorporates most of the historic landholdings of the 350-year-old Ortiz family estate. It's built around a lovely courtyard pool and patio area, and it's a fine blend of ancient and modern styles. A renovation late in 2004 has brought more style to the rooms and common areas, with handcrafted furnishings and hip Southwestern decor. Rooms vary slightly in size; my favorites are a little smaller than some but have balconies opening onto the courtyard. The Hilton also has the Casa Ortiz de Santa Fe, luxury casitas with kitchens situated in a 1625 coach house adjacent to the hotel. Two restaurants on the Hilton's grounds occupy the premises of the early-18th-century Casa Ortiz. The Piñon Grill serves a variety of wood-fire-grilled items in a casual atmosphere, and the Chamisa Courtyard serves breakfast.

100 Sandoval St. (P.O. Box 25104), Santa Fe, NM 87501-2131. ☏ **800/336-3676,** 800/HILTONS, or 505/988-2811. Fax 505/986-6439. www.hilton.com. 157 units. $159–$299 double; $239–$549 suite; $419–$559 casita, depending on time of year. Additional person $20. AE, DC, DISC, MC, V. Parking $10 per night. **Amenities:** 2 restaurants; bar; outdoor pool; exercise room; Jacuzzi; concierge; car-rental desk; courtesy van; business center; room service; laundry service; dry cleaning. *In room:* A/C, TV, dataport, coffeemaker, hair dryer, iron, safe.

Hotel Plaza Real   This New Orleans–meets–Santa Fe Territorial-style hotel built in 1990 provides comfortable rooms near the plaza. The construction and decor of the lobby are rustically elegant, built around a fireplace with balconies perched above. Clean and attractively decorated rooms have Southwestern-style furniture and accents such as *bancos* (adobe benches) and French doors opening onto balconies or terraces that surround a quiet courtyard decorated with *ristras* (strung chiles). Try the bar for an afternoon drink or the veranda for coffee. Service has been inconsistent since the Radisson acquired the hotel a few years ago.

125 Washington Ave., Santa Fe, NM 87501. ☏ **877/901-7666** or 505/988-4900. Fax 505/983-9322. www. hotelplazareal.com. 56 units. $149–$219 double, depending on time of year and type of room. Additional person $20. Children under 12 stay free in parent's room. AE, DC, DISC, MC, V. Parking $12 per day. **Amenities:** Lounge; nearby health-club access; laundry service; dry cleaning. *In room:* A/C, TV, dataport, coffeemaker, hair dryer, iron.

Inn & Spa at Loretto ⭐   This much-photographed hotel, just 2 blocks from the plaza, was built in 1975 to resemble Taos Pueblo. Light and shadow dance upon the five-level structure as the sun crosses the sky. With ongoing refinements, this hotel has become a comfortable and chic place to stay. Decor is a Southwest/ Montana ranch style, with faux painted walls and an interesting and cozy lobby lounge. The hotel's rooms and bathrooms are standard size, with the same decor as the rest of the hotel. Be aware that the Loretto likes convention traffic, so sometimes service lags for travelers. Overall, it is fairly quiet and has nice views—especially on the northeast side, where you'll see both the historic St. Francis Cathedral and the Loretto Chapel (with its "miraculous" spiral staircase; see "More Attractions," in chapter 7). The newly added Spa Terre offers a range of treatments, from facials to massages, in intimate, Southwest-meets-Asia rooms.

211 Old Santa Fe Trail (P.O. Box 1417), Santa Fe, NM 87501. ✆ **800/727-5531** or 505/988-5531. Fax 505/984-7988. www.hotelloretto.com. 135 units. Jan–Mar $159–$265 double; Apr–June $185–$299 double; July–Oct $215–$499 double; Nov–Dec $185–$299 double. Additional person $25. Children 17 and under stay free in parent's room. AE, DC, DISC, MC, V. Valet parking $15 per night. **Amenities:** Restaurant; lounge; outdoor pool (heated year-round); spa; concierge; business center with audiovisual conferencing equipment; room service; valet laundry. *In room:* A/C, TV, fridge, coffeemaker, hair dryer, iron.

Inn of the Anasazi ⭐⭐⭐   The designers of this fine luxury hotel have managed to create a feeling of grandness in a very limited space. Flagstone floors and vigas create a warm and welcoming ambience that evokes the feeling of an Anasazi cliff dwelling. Oversize cacti complete the look. Accents are appropriately Navajo, in a nod to the fact that the Navajo live in the area the Anasazi once inhabited. A half block off the plaza, this hotel was built in 1991 to cater to travelers who know their hotels. On the ground floor are a living room and library with oversize furniture and replicas of Anasazi pottery and Navajo rugs. A library expansion and a new exercise room were completed in 2004. Even the smallest rooms are spacious, with pearl-finished walls and decor in cream tones accented by novelties such as iron candle sconces, original art, four-poster beds, gaslit kiva fireplaces, and humidifiers. All the rooms are quiet and comfortable, though none have dramatic views. The Anasazi Restaurant (see chapter 6) serves creative Southwestern cuisine.

113 Washington Ave., Santa Fe, NM 87501. ✆ **800/688-8100** or 505/988-3030. Fax 505/988-3277. www.innoftheanasazi.com. 57 units. Jan 5–Feb 26 $205–$405; Feb 27–Apr 28 $225–$425; Apr 29–June 23 $255–$445; June 24–Jan 4 $295–$475 double. AE, DC, DISC, MC, V. Valet parking $13 per day. **Amenities:** Restaurant (p. 81); small exercise room; concierge; room service; in-room massage; laundry service; library/boardroom. *In room:* A/C, TV/VCR/DVD, coffeemaker, hair dryer, iron, safe.

Inn of the Five Graces ⭐⭐ *Finds*   Along historic Barrio de Analco in the center of downtown, this inn holds true to its stated theme: "Here the Orient and the Old West meet, surprisingly at home in each other's arms." With floral decked courtyards, elaborately decorated suites with kilim rugs, ornately carved beds, and often mosaic tile work in the bathrooms, this is truly a "sheik" place. All but a few suites are medium-size, most with small bathrooms. The lower-priced rooms are smaller. Request one of the suites in the buildings on the north side of East de Vargas Street; they're more spacious and substantially built. Travelers seeking a fine and exotic stay will like this place; it's of the caliber of Inn of the Anasazi, though with more flair and fewer amenities. All rooms have robes, stocked fridges, patios, and CD players; some have kitchenettes.

150 E. de Vargas St., Santa Fe, NM 87501. ✆ **505/992-0957.** www.fivegraces.com. 20 units. $295–$470 double, depending on the season and type of room. Price includes extended continental breakfast and afternoon treats. AE, MC, V. Free parking. Pets welcome with fee and deposit. **Amenities:** Concierge. *In room:* A/C, TV, fridge, coffeemaker, hair dryer, iron, CD player, microwave.

Inn on the Alameda ⭐   Just across the street from the bosque-shaded Santa Fe River sits the Inn on the Alameda, a cozy stop for those who like the services of a hotel with the intimacy of an inn. Built in 1986, with additions over the years, it now rambles across four buildings. There are casita suites to the west, two three-story buildings at the center, and another one-story building that contains suites. All are Pueblo-style adobe, ranging in age, but most were built in the late 1980s. The owner, Joe Schepps, appreciates traditional Southwestern style; he's used red brick in the dining area and Mexican *equipae* (wicker) furniture in the lobby, as well as thick vigas and shiny *latillas* in a sitting area set around a grand fireplace. The rooms follow a similar good taste, some with refrigerators, CD players, safes, Jacuzzi tubs, and kiva fireplaces. The newer deluxe rooms and suites in the easternmost building are in the best shape. The traditional rooms are quaint, some with interesting angled bed configurations. The trees surrounding the inn—cottonwoods and aspens—make you feel as though you're in a tree house when you step out on some of the balconies. If you're an art shopper, this is an ideal spot because it's a quick walk to Canyon Road. An elaborate continental "Breakfast of Enchantment" is served each morning in the Agoyo Room, in the outdoor courtyard, or in your own room, and there is a complimentary afternoon wine and cheese reception from 4 to 5pm. A full-service bar is open nightly.

303 E. Alameda St., Santa Fe, NM 87501. ℂ **800/289-2122** or 505/984-2121. Fax 505/986-8325. www. innonthealameda.com. 69 units. $129–$209 queen; $142–$222 king; $210–$350 suites; reduced off-season rates are available. Rates include breakfast and afternoon wine and cheese reception. AE, DC, DISC, MC, V. Free parking. Pets welcome. **Amenities:** Bar; medium-size fitness facility; 2 open-air Jacuzzis; concierge; massage; child care by arrangement; coin-op laundry; same-day dry cleaning; pet amenities and a pet-walking map. *In room:* A/C, TV, dataport, hair dryer, iron.

La Fonda 𝄐 Whether you stay in this hotel or not, it's worth strolling through just to get a sense of how Santa Fe once was—and in some ways still is. This was the inn at the end of the Santa Fe Trail; it saw trappers, traders, and merchants, as well as notables such as President Rutherford B. Hayes and General Ulysses S. Grant. The original inn was dying of old age in 1920 when it was razed and replaced by the current La Fonda. Its architecture is pueblo revival: imitation adobe with wooden balconies and beam ends protruding over the tops of windows. Inside, the lobby is rich and slightly dark, with people bustling about, sitting in the cafe, and buying jewelry from Native Americans.

The hotel has seen some renovation through the years, as well as a whole new wing recently completed to the east, where you'll find deluxe suites and new meeting spaces. If you want a feel of the real Santa Fe, this is the place to stay. Overall, however, this hotel isn't the model of refinement. For that, you'd best go to the Hotel Santa Fe or other newer places. No two rooms are the same here, and while each has its own funky touch, some are more kitsch than quaint. Some have refrigerators, fireplaces, and private balconies. A recently added spa offers a variety of treatments from massages to salt glows, as well as a sauna and Jacuzzi. The French Pastry Shop is the place to get cappuccino and crepes; La Fiesta Lounge draws many locals to its economical New Mexican food lunch buffet; and La Plazuela offers some of the best new Southwestern cuisine in town, in a skylit garden patio. The Bell Tower Bar is the highest point in downtown Santa Fe—a great place for a cocktail and a view of the city.

100 E. San Francisco St. (P.O. Box 1209), Santa Fe, NM 87501. ℂ **800/523-5002** or 505/982-5511. Fax 505/ 988-2952. www.lafondasantafe.com. 167 units. $219–$269 standard double; $239–$289 deluxe double; $349–$539 suite. Additional person $15. Children under 12 stay free in parent's room. AE, DC, DISC, MC, V. Parking $9 per day in a covered garage. **Amenities:** Restaurant; 2 bars; outdoor pool; spa; exercise room; 2 indoor Jacuzzis; concierge; tour desk; room service; massage room and in-room massage; babysitting; laundry service; dry cleaning. *In room:* A/C, TV, dataport, coffeemaker, hair dryer, iron, safe.

La Posada de Santa Fe Resort and Spa 𝄐𝄐 If you're in the mood to stay in a little New Mexico adobe village, you'll enjoy this recently renovated luxury hotel just 3 blocks from the plaza. The main building is an odd mix of architecture. The original part was a Victorian mansion built in 1882 by Abraham

Staab, a German immigrant, for his bride, Julia. Later it was adobeized—an adobe structure was literally built around it—so that now the Victorian presence is only within the charming bar and four rooms, which still maintain the origi-nal brick and high ceilings. It is said that Julia Staab, who died in 1896, contin-ues to haunt the place. Mischievous but good-natured, she is Santa Fe's best-known and most frequently witnessed ghost. If you like Victorian interiors more than Santa Fe style, these rooms are a good bet.

The rest of the hotel follows in the Pueblo-style construction and is quaint; it's especially nice in the summer, when surrounded by acres of green grass. Here, you get to experience squeaky maple floors, vigas and *latillas,* and, in many rooms, kiva fireplaces. Be aware that unless you've secured a suite, most rooms tend to be fairly small. Fortunately, the hotel benefited from a $23-million face-lift completed in 1999. Most notable are the Zen-Southwestern-style spa and pool and spacious spa rooms. Travelers who are reluctant to trust the whims of older adobe construction should reserve one of the spa rooms or any of the 40 other new rooms. The hotel attracts travelers and a fair number of families, though it is pushing for more convention business. Most rooms don't have views but have outdoor patios, and most are tucked back into the quiet compound.

330 E. Palace Ave., Santa Fe, NM 87501. (C) **800/727-5276** or 505/986-0000. Fax 505/982-6850. www. laposadadesantafe.com. 157 units. $199–$359 double; suites $289 and way up, depending on the season. Various spa packages available. AE, DC, DISC, MC, V. Valet parking $14 per day. **Amenities:** 2 restaurants; bar; outdoor pool; exercise room; spa with full treatments; Jacuzzi; bike rental; concierge; salon; room serv-ice; in-room massage; babysitting; dry cleaning. *In room:* A/C, TV, dataport, minibar, coffeemaker, hair dryer, iron, safe.

Ten Thousand Waves ⭐ *Moments* Longing for a little Zen in your life? This inn provides minimalist Japanese-adobe accommodations nestled within piñon trees below Ten Thousand Waves Japanese Health Spa (p. 127), a truly unique place renowned for its hot tubs and spa treatments. Inn guests receive compli-mentary use of communal baths. About a 10-minute drive from the plaza, the place is en route to Santa Fe Ski area. Travelers seeking to enjoy the silence of their own being seek out this place. They need to be fit because the paths con-necting the rooms with the spa have enough steps to make you gasp during your mantra. Rooms are aesthetically bare, medium-size with clean lines and with paper lamps, kimonos, and such hanging about. All have wood-burning fire-places, robes, CD players, and balconies; four have full kitchens; and most have TV/VCRs. The High Moon is the most elaborate room, with a full kitchen, two balconies, and lots of space. More spartan and small is the Zen room, decorated in minimalist decor, and with no TV.

3451 Hyde Park Rd., Santa Fe, NM 87501. (C) **505/982-9304** or 505/992-5025. Fax 505/989-5077. www.ten thousandwaves.com. 9 units. $190–$260 double. Additional person $20. Rates include use of communal baths. AE, DISC, MC, V. Free parking. One or more pets welcome, with advance notice, for $20 per night. **Amenities:** Spa with full treatments; coin-op laundry. *In room:* Fridge, coffeemaker, hair dryer, iron, CD player, microwave.

EXPENSIVE

Don Gaspar Inn ⭐⭐ *Finds* If you'd like to pretend that you live in Santa Fe during your vacation, that you're blessed with your very own Southwestern-style home, in a historic neighborhood, full of artful touches such as Native American tapestries and a kiva fireplace, this is your inn. A 10-minute walk from the plaza, the Don Gaspar occupies three homes, connected by brilliant gardens and brick walkways. Rooms vary in size, though all are plenty spacious, most with patios, some with kitchenettes, and there's even a full house for rent. Travelers looking for an adventure beyond a hotel stay, but without the close interaction of a B&B, enjoy this place. Though the rooms don't have views, all are quiet. The Courtyard Casita, with a kitchenette and a sleeper couch in its own room, is nice for a small family. The Territorial Suite, with carpet throughout and Italian marble in the bath, is perfect for a romantic getaway. All rooms have bathrobes and fireplaces. The friendly and dedicated staff serves a full breakfast such as green-chile stew with fresh baked items on the patio under a peach tree (the fruit from which they make cobbler) in the warm months and in the atrium in winter.

623 Don Gaspar, Santa Fe, NM 87505. © **888/986-8664** or 505/986-8664. Fax 505/986-0696. www.don gaspar.com. 12 units. $115–$175 double; $145–$195 suite; $165–$295 casita or house. Rates include full breakfast. AE, MC, V. Free parking. **Amenities:** Babysitting; same-day laundry service. *In room:* A/C, TV/VCR, hair dryer, iron.

Hotel St. Francis 🏵 If you long for the rich fabrics, fine antiques, and slow pace of a European hotel, this is your place. The building was first constructed in the 1880s; it became fairly dilapidated but was renovated in 1986. Now elegantly redecorated, the lobby is crowned by a Victorian fireplace with hovering cherubs, a theme repeated throughout the hotel. The rooms continue the European decor, each with its own unique bent. You'll find a fishing room, a golf room, a garden room, and a music room, with each motif evoked by the furnishings: a vintage set of golf clubs here, a sheet of music in a dry-flower arrangement there. The hotel, which attracts individual travelers as well as families and many Europeans, is well cared for by a concierge who speaks six languages. Enjoy high tea in the lobby 3 to 5:30pm daily. Request a room facing east, and you'll wake each day to a view of the mountains, seen through lovely lace. Larger rooms have coffeemakers and hair dryers.

210 Don Gaspar Ave., Santa Fe, NM 87501. © **800/529-5700** or 505/983-5700. Fax 505/989-7690. www. hotelstfrancis.com. 83 units. $92–$185 double; $205–$380 suite, depending on the season. Children under 12 stay free in parent's room. AE, DC, DISC, MC, V. Parking $5 per day. **Amenities:** Restaurant; bar; access to nearby health club; concierge; room service; laundry service; dry cleaning; library and gaming tables. *In room:* A/C, TV, fridge, safe.

Hotel Santa Fe 🏵 *Finds* About a 10-minute walk south of the plaza you'll find this newer three-story establishment, the only Native American–owned hotel in Santa Fe. It is a good choice for consistent, well-planned lodgings. Picuris Pueblo is the majority stockholder here, and part of the pleasure of staying here is the culture the Picuris bring to your visit. This is not to say that you'll get any sense of the rusticity of a pueblo in your accommodations—this sophisticated 14-year-old hotel is decorated in Southwestern style, with a few novel aspects such as an Allan Houser bronze buffalo dancer watching over the front desk and a fireplace surrounded by comfortable furniture in the lobby. The rooms are medium-size, with clean lines and comfortable beds, the decor accented with pine Taos-style furniture. Rooms on the north side get less street noise from Cerrillos Road and have better views of the mountains, but they don't have the sun shining onto their balconies. You will get a strong sense of the Native American presence on the patio during the summer, when Picuris dancers come to perform and bread bakers uncover the *horno* (oven) and prepare loaves for sale.

Opened in October 2001, The Hacienda at Hotel Santa Fe is a unique addition and features 35 luxurious rooms and suites, all with cozy fireplaces, 10-foot ceilings, handcrafted Southwestern furnishings, and plush duvets to snuggle into on chilly nights. The restaurant serves a standard breakfast, but for lunch and dinner you can dine on Native American food from all over the Americas. Expect buffalo and turkey instead of beef and chicken.

1501 Paseo de Peralta, Santa Fe, NM 87501. © 800/825-9876 or 505/982-1200. Fax 505/984-2211. www. hotelsantafe.com. 163 units. $99–$199 double; $129–$269 junior suite, depending on the season. Hacienda rooms and suites $199–$459. Additional person $10. Children 17 and under stay free in parent's room. AE, DC, DISC, MC, V. Free parking. Pets accepted with $20 fee. **Amenities:** Restaurant; outdoor pool; Jacuzzi; concierge; car-rental desk; room service; in-room massage; babysitting; coin-op laundry; dry cleaning. *In room:* A/C, TV, dataport, minibar, iron, safe.

Inn of the Governors ★   Rooms in this inn tucked 2 blocks from the plaza have the feel of a Southwestern home but come with the service and amenities of a fine hotel. The building (situated where the governor's mansion once was) is Territorial style, with a brick-trimmed roofline and distinctive portals. Built in 1965, it received a lovely remodel in 2004. The medium-size rooms have Native American accents and delightful touches such as Mexican tile in the bathrooms, robes, and comfortable beds; many have fireplaces. Rooms on the north side look toward downtown and the mountains, and many have balconies. Unlike any other downtown hotel, this one serves a complimentary full breakfast buffet in the morning and sherry and cookies in the afternoon. The Del Charro Saloon serves food until midnight, a rarity in Santa Fe.

101 W. Alameda St., Santa Fe, NM 87501. © 800/234-4534 or 505/982-4333. Fax 505/989-9149. www.inn ofthegovernors.com. 100 units. Jan–Mar $99–$269; Apr–June $159–$279; July to mid-Oct $189–$339; mid-Oct to Dec $99–$269; holidays $189–$339 double. Additional person $15. Rates include full breakfast buffet and sherry and cookies in the afternoon. Children 16 and under stay free in parent's room. AE, DC, DISC, MC, V. Free parking. **Amenities:** Restaurant; bar; outdoor pool (heated year-round); concierge; limited room service; massage; laundry service. *In room:* A/C, TV, fridge, hair dryer, iron.

MODERATE

Garrett's Desert Inn *(Value)*   Completion of this hotel in 1957 prompted the Historic Design Review Board to implement zoning restrictions throughout downtown. Apparently, residents were appalled by the huge air conditioners adorning the roof. Though they're still unsightly, the hotel makes up for them. First, with all the focus today on retro fashions, this hotel, located 3 blocks from the plaza, is totally in. It's a clean, two-story, concrete block building around a broad parking lot. The hotel underwent a complete remodel in 1994, with touch-ups through the years; it has managed to maintain some '50s touches, such as Art Deco tile in the bathrooms and plenty of space in the rooms, while being updated with larger windows and sturdy doors and wood accents. Rooms are equipped with tile vanities; minisuites have refrigerators and microwaves.

311 Old Santa Fe Trail, Santa Fe, NM 87501. © 800/888-2145 or 505/982-1851. Fax 505/989-1647. www. garrettsdesertinn.com. 83 units. $89–$165, depending on season and type of room. AE, DISC, MC, V. **Amenities:** Restaurant; bar; outdoor pool; concierge; room service; in-room massage; laundry service; dry cleaning. *In room:* A/C, TV, dataport, coffeemaker, hair dryer, iron.

Old Santa Fe Inn *(Finds)* *(Kids)*   Want to stay downtown and savor Santa Fe–style ambience without wearing out your plastic? This is your hotel. A multi-million-dollar renovation to this 1930s court motel has created a comfortable, quiet inn just a few blocks from the plaza. Rooms verge on small but are decorated with such lovely handcrafted colonial-style furniture that you probably won't mind. All have small Mexican-tiled bathrooms, each with an outer vanity; most have gas fireplaces. You have a choice of king, queen, or twin bedrooms as well as suites. Though there's no pool or hot tub to wet you down, as there are at some of the other downtown moderately priced motels, this could still be a good choice for families because it has some adjoining rooms. Breakfast is served in an atmospheric dining room next to a comfortable library.

320 Galisteo St., Santa Fe, NM 87501. (℃) **800/745-9910** or 505/995-0800. Fax 505/995-0400. www.oldsanta feinn.com. 43 units. Winter $89–$136 double, $119–$169 suite; summer $127–$149 double, $199–$249 suite. Rates include continental breakfast. AE, DC, DISC, MC, V. *In room:* A/C, TV/VCR, dataport, fridge, coffee-maker, CD player.

Santa Fe Motel and Inn If you like walking to the plaza and restaurants but don't want to pay big bucks, this little compound is a good choice. Rooms here are larger than at the nearby Budget Inn and have more personality than those at the Travelodge. Ask for one of the casitas in back—you'll pay more but get a little turn-of-the-20th-century charm, plus more quiet and privacy. Some have vigas, others have skylights, fireplaces, and patios. The main part of the motel, built in 1955, is two-story Territorial style, with upstairs rooms that open onto a portal with a bit of a view. All guest rooms are decorated with a Southwest motif and have very basic furnishings but nice, comfortable beds. Some rooms have kitchenettes, with refrigerators, microwaves, stoves, coffeemakers, and toasters. Fresh-brewed coffee is served each morning in the office, where a bulletin board lists Santa Fe activities.

510 Cerrillos Rd., Santa Fe, NM 87501. (℃) **800/930-5002** or 505/982-1039. Fax 505/986-1275. www.santa femotel.com. 23 units. $69–$139, depending on the season and type of room. Additional person $10. Rates include continental breakfast. AE, DC, MC, V. Free parking. *In room:* A/C, TV, hair dryer, iron.

INEXPENSIVE

Santa Fe Budget Inn *Value* If you're looking for a convenient, almost-down-town location at a reasonable price, this is one of your best bets. This two-story stucco adobe motel with portals is spread through three buildings and is about a 10-minute walk from the plaza. Built in 1985, it was remodeled in 1994 and has seen ongoing renovations. The rooms are plain, basic, and fairly small. Santa Fe Opera and Fiesta posters add a splash of color. The bathrooms and furniture could use some updating, but if you're a traveler who spends a lot of time out of the room, that probably won't matter to you; the motel is clean and functional, with comfortable beds and good reading lights. It's near McDonald's, and there's a small park in the back and an outdoor pool. To avoid street noise, ask for a room at the back of the property. An adjacent restaurant serves American and New Mexican food.

Kids **Family-Friendly Hotels**

The Bishop's Lodge (p. 69) Riding lessons, tennis courts with instruction, a pool with a lifeguard, a stocked trout pond just for kids, a summer daytime program, horseback trail trips, and more make this a veritable day camp for all ages.

Old Santa Fe Inn (p. 67) Although this inn doesn't have a pool or hot tub, it's a good-priced place downtown, and it has some adjoining rooms.

Residence Inn (p. 70) Spacious suites house families comfortably. An outdoor pool, fully equipped kitchens, patio grills, and a grocery-shopping service add to the appeal.

725 Cerrillos Rd., Santa Fe, NM 87501. ✆ **800/288-7600** or 505/982-5952. Fax 505/984-8879. www.santafe budgetinn.com. 160 units. $58–$72 double. Additional person $7. AE, DC, MC, V. Free parking. **Amenities:** Outdoor pool. *In room:* A/C, TV.

Santa Fe Plaza Travelodge   You can count on this motel near Hotel Santa Fe (6 blocks to the plaza) on busy Cerrillos Road for comfort, convenience, and a no-frills stay. The rooms are very clean, nicely lit, and, despite the busy location, relatively quiet. New mattresses and a pretty Southwestern ceiling border add to the comfort and decor.

646 Cerrillos Rd., Santa Fe, NM 87501. ✆ **800/578-7878** or 505/982-3551. Fax 505/983-8624. www.trav elodge.com. 48 units. May–Oct $65–$88 double; Nov–Apr $39–$69 double. AE, DC, DISC, MC, V. Free parking. **Amenities:** Outdoor pool. *In room:* A/C, TV, fridge, coffeemaker.

2 The North Side

Within easy reach of the plaza, the north side encompasses the area that lies north of the loop of Paseo de Peralta.

VERY EXPENSIVE

The Bishop's Lodge ★★ *Kids*   This resort holds special significance for me because my parents met in the lodge and were later married in the chapel. It's a place rich with history. More than a century ago, when Bishop Jean-Baptiste Lamy was the spiritual leader of northern New Mexico's Roman Catholic population, he often escaped clerical politics by hiking into this valley called Little Tesuque. He built a retreat and a humble chapel (now on the National Register of Historic Places) with high-vaulted ceilings and a hand-built altar. Today, Lamy's 1,000-acre getaway has become The Bishop's Lodge.

A recent $17-million renovation spruced up the place and added a spa and 10,000 square feet of meeting space. The guest rooms, spread through many buildings, feature handcrafted furniture and regional artwork. Standard rooms are spacious, and many have balconies, while deluxe rooms feature traditional kiva fireplaces, a combination bedroom/sitting room, and private decks or patios. The newest rooms are luxurious, and some have spectacular views of the Jemez Mountains. The Bishop's Lodge is an active resort three seasons of the year, with activities such as horseback riding, nature walks, and cookouts; in the winter, it takes on the character of a romantic country retreat. A children's program keeps kids busy for much of the day.

Bishop's Lodge Rd. (P.O. Box 2367), Santa Fe, NM 87504. ✆ **505/983-6377.** Fax 505/989-8739. www. bishopslodge.com. 111 units. Summer $299–$399 double; fall and spring $249–$349 double; midwinter $189–$269 double. Additional person $15. Children 3 and under stay free in parent's room. Ask about packages that include meals. AE, DC, DISC, MC, V. Free parking. **Amenities:** Restaurant; outdoor pool; tennis courts; spa; Jacuzzi; sauna; steam room; concierge; courtesy shuttle; room service; in-room massage; babysitting; laundry service. *In room:* A/C, TV, coffeemaker, safe.

EXPENSIVE

Santa Fe Accommodations   Santa Fe Accommodations manages **Fort Marcy Hotel Suites.** Located about an 8-minute walk from the plaza, these condominiums climb up a hill north of town and are a decent choice for those who like the amenities a condo offers. They are privately owned, so decor and upkeep vary. All have fireplaces and full kitchens, with microwave ovens, ranges, and refrigerators, and most have dishwashers. The units have plenty of space, and the grounds are well kept, with some nature trails winding about. Some of the units, however, are showing their age (built in 1975).

320 Artist Rd., Santa Fe, NM 87501. ⓒ **800/745-9910** or 505/982-6636. Fax 505/984-8682. www.santafe
hotels.com. 100 units. $49–$239 1-bedroom (up to 3 adults); $79–$299 2-bedroom (up to 5 adults);
$109–$339 2-bedroom town house (up to 5 adults); $139–$399 3-bedroom town house (up to 7 adults). Special events $319–$599. Children 18 and under stay free in parent's room. Rates include continental breakfast. AE, DC, DISC, MC, V. Free on- and off-street parking. **Amenities:** Indoor pool; business center; coin-op
laundry. *In room:* A/C, TV/DVD, kitchen, hair dryer, iron.

MODERATE

Radisson Hotel Santa Fe   Set on a hill as you head north toward the Santa
Fe Opera, this three-story hotel has recently benefited from a multi-million-dollar renovation that has made it a lovely place. I question the service, though. The
new theme here is Native American, with Anasazi-style stacked sandstone
throughout the lobby and dining room, a theme that carries into the guest
rooms. They are medium-size, decorated in earth tones with bold prints, some
with views of the mountains, others overlooking the pool. Premium rooms are
more spacious, some with large living rooms and private balconies. Each parlor
suite has a Murphy bed and kiva fireplace in the living room, a big dining area,
a wet bar and refrigerator, and a jetted bathtub. The condo units nearby come
with fully equipped kitchens, fireplaces, and private decks.

750 N. St. Francis Dr., Santa Fe, NM 87501. ⓒ **800/333-3333** or 505/992-5800. Fax 505/992-5856. www.
radisson.com. 128 units, 32 condos. $259 double; $225 suite; $309 condo. AE, DC, DISC, MC, V. Free parking.
Amenities: Outdoor pool; free shuttle service to downtown. *In room:* A/C, TV, hair dryer, iron.

3 The South Side

Santa Fe's major strip, Cerrillos Road, is US 85, the main route to and from
Albuquerque and the I-25 freeway. It's about 5¼ miles from the plaza to the Villa
Linda Mall, which marks the southern boundary of the city. Most motels are on
this strip, although several of them are to the east, closer to St. Francis Drive (US
84) or the Las Vegas Highway.

EXPENSIVE

Residence Inn ★ *(Kids)*   Designed to look like a neighborhood, this inn provides the efficient stay that you'd expect from a Marriott, its parent company. It's
located about 10 minutes from the plaza, a quiet drive through a few neighborhoods. The lobby and breakfast area are warmly decorated in red tile, with a
fireplace and Southwestern accents such as *bancos* and drums. There are three
sizes of suites, each roomy, each with a fully equipped kitchen. All rooms have
fireplaces and balconies and are decorated with Southwestern furnishings. Outside, there are plenty of amenities to keep family members happy, including barbecue grills on the patio. Most who stay here are leisure travelers, but you'll also
encounter some government workers and business travelers, all of whom benefit from free high-speed Internet access. Guests gather for complimentary hors
d'oeuvres Monday through Thursday from 5 to 6:30pm.

1698 Galisteo St., Santa Fe, NM 87505. ⓒ **800/331-3131** or 505/988-7300. Fax 505/988-3243. www.
residenceinn.com. 120 suites. $109–$199 studio suite; $119–$199 studio double suite; $129–$239 penthouse suite. Rates vary according to season and include continental breakfast and Mon–Thurs evening hors
d'oeuvres. AE, DC, DISC, MC, V. Free parking. **Amenities:** Outdoor pool; sports court; access to nearby health
club; 3 Jacuzzis; coin-op laundry; laundry service; dry cleaning; jogging trail. *In room:* A/C, TV, kitchen.

MODERATE

Best Western Inn of Santa Fe *(Value)*   This three-story pink hotel, a 15-minute
drive from the plaza, offers clean cookie-cutter-type rooms at a reasonable price.
It's a security-conscious hotel; rooms can be entered only from interior corridors,

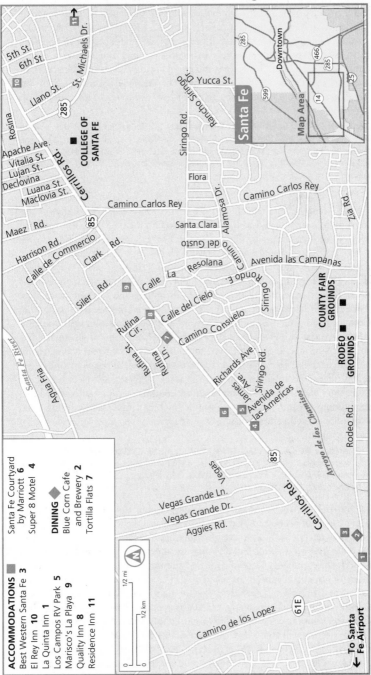

ACCOMMODATIONS ▪

Best Western Santa Fe **3**
El Rey Inn **10**
La Quinta Inn **1**
Los Campos RV Park **5**
Marisco's La Playa **9**
Quality Inn **8**
Residence Inn **11**

Santa Fe Courtyard
by Marriott **6**
Super 8 Motel **4**

DINING ◆

Blue Corn Cafe
and Brewery **2**
Tortilla Flats **7**

and there is a private safe in each room. Built in 1990, renovations are ongoing. The lobby is decorated in light pastels, with nice little tables where guests can eat their complimentary continental breakfast. The indoor Jacuzzi and pool are very clean, a good family spot to relax between outings. The somewhat narrow rooms have Aztec-motif bedspreads and blond furniture. Some doubles are more spacious, with a couch. All have fairly small but functional bathrooms. Suites are larger, some with an in-room Jacuzzi; others have two rooms, with a sleeper sofa in one.

3650 Cerrillos Rd., Santa Fe, NM 87505. ℂ 800/528-1234 or 505/438-3822. Fax 505/438-3795. www.best western.com. 97 units. $50–$100 double; $75–$145 suite, depending on the season. Children 12 and under stay free in parent's room. Rates include continental breakfast. AE, DC, DISC, MC, V. Free parking. Pets allowed with prior approval. **Amenities:** Indoor pool; Jacuzzi; laundry service. *In room:* A/C, TV, coffeemaker, hair dryer, safe.

El Rey Inn ★ *Finds*   Staying at "The King" makes you feel like you're traveling the old Route 66 through the Southwest. The white stucco buildings of this court motel are decorated with bright trim around the doors and hand-painted Mexican tiles on the walls. Opened in the 1930s, it received additions in the 1950s, and remodeling is ongoing. The lobby has vigas and tile floors, and it is decorated with Oriental rugs and dark Spanish furniture. No two rooms are alike. The oldest section, nearest the lobby, feels a bit cramped, though the rooms have style, with Art Deco tile in the bathrooms and vigas on the ceilings. Some have little patios. Be sure to request a room as far back as possible from Cerrillos Road. The two stories of suites around the Spanish colonial courtyard are the sweetest deal I've seen in all of Santa Fe. These rooms make you feel like you're at a Spanish inn, with carved furniture and cozy couches. Some rooms have kitchenettes. To the north sit 10 deluxe units around the courtyard. These rooms offer more upscale amenities and gas log fireplaces, as well as distinctive furnishings and artwork. A complimentary continental breakfast is served in a sunny room or on a terrace in the warmer months. There's also a sitting room with a library and games tables, as well as a picnic area, a playground, and an exercise room.

1862 Cerrillos Rd. (P.O. Box 4759), Santa Fe, NM 87502. ℂ 800/521-1349 or 505/982-1931. Fax 505/989-9249. www.elreyinnsantafe.com. 85 units. $95–$165 double; $120–$225 suite. Rates include continental breakfast. AE, DC, DISC, MC, V. Free parking. **Amenities:** Outdoor pool; exercise room; Jacuzzi; sauna; coin-op laundry. *In room:* A/C, TV, fridge, coffeemaker, hair dryer, iron, safe.

La Quinta Inn *Value*   Though it's a good 15-minute drive from the plaza, this is my choice of economical Cerrillos Road chain hotels. Built in 1986, it has been fully remodeled in a very comfortable and tasteful way. The rooms within the three-story white-brick buildings have an unexpectedly elegant feel, with lots of deep colors and Art Deco tile in the bathrooms. There's plenty of space in these rooms, and they're lit for mood as well as for reading. A complimentary continental breakfast is served in the intimate lobby. The outdoor kidney-shaped pool has a nice lounging area and is open and heated May to October. The hotel is just across a parking lot from the Villa Linda Mall, which shoppers and moviegoers will appreciate. The Kettle, a 24-hour coffee shop, is adjacent.

4298 Cerrillos Rd., Santa Fe, NM 87507. ℂ 800/531-5900 or 505/471-1142. Fax 505/438-7219. www.lq. com. 130 units. June to mid-Oct $89–$110 double; late Oct to May $60–$66 double. Children 18 and under stay free in parent's room. Discount for AAA members. Rates include continental breakfast. AE, DC, DISC, MC, V. Free parking. Maximum 2 pets stay free. **Amenities:** Outdoor heated pool; coin-op laundry; same-day dry cleaning; executive-level rooms. *In room:* A/C, TV, dataport, coffeemaker, hair dryer, iron.

Santa Fe Courtyard by Marriott   This is a good choice if you don't mind mixing business with pleasure. Since it caters to a lot of conference traffic, there's a definite business feel to this hotel. Built in 1986, it received a $3.5-million renovation after being acquired by Marriott. The decor is tasteful Southwestern, with rooms opening onto cavelike balconies or walkways bordered by grass. Though it's situated on busy Cerrillos Road, the rooms are placed so that they are quiet. The newly remodeled cafe serves breakfast, lunch, and dinner.

3347 Cerrillos Rd., Santa Fe, NM 87505. © **800/777-3347** or 505/473-2800. Fax 505/473-4905. www.santa fecourtyard.com. 213 units. $59–$89 double; $90–$249 suite. AE, DC, DISC, MC, V. Free parking. **Amenities:** Restaurant; indoor pool; exercise room; 2 Jacuzzis; room service; laundry service; dry cleaning; executive-level rooms; ballroom. *In room:* A/C, TV, dataport, fridge, coffeemaker, hair dryer, iron.

INEXPENSIVE

Quality Inn   This hotel on the south end of town, about a 10-minute drive from the plaza, provides good standard rooms at reasonable prices. Built in 1970, it's a two-story white stucco building with a red-tile roof. Remodeling is ongoing. Expect nothing fancy here, even with the remodeling. Rooms are fairly quiet, with big windows to let in lots of light. Request a room looking in toward the courtyard and pool, and you'll get a bit of a resort feel. The restaurant, South Side Cafe, serves Mexican food and has a full-service lounge.

3011 Cerrillos Rd., Santa Fe, NM 87507. © **877/966-2787** or 505/471-1211. Fax 505/438-9535. 99 units. www.qualityinn.com. $55–$104 double. AE, DC, DISC, MC, V. Free parking. Pets accepted. **Amenities:** Restaurant/lounge; outdoor pool. *In room:* A/C, TV, coffeemaker, hair dryer.

Super 8 Motel   It's nothing flashy, but this pink stucco, boxy motel, which has received the Pride of Super 8 award, attracts regulars who know precisely what to expect. You'll get a clean, comfortable room with double beds, a desk, and a few other amenities.

3358 Cerrillos Rd., Santa Fe, NM 87507. © **800/800-8000** or 505/471-8811. Fax 505/471-3239. www. super8.com. 96 units. $45–$80 double, depending on the season. Rates include continental breakfast. AE, DC, DISC, MC, V. Free parking. **Amenities:** Coin-op laundry. *In room:* A/C, TV, coffeemaker, safe.

4 Bed & Breakfasts

If you prefer a homey, intimate setting to the sometimes-impersonal ambience of a large hotel, one of Santa Fe's bed-and-breakfast inns may be right for you. All those listed here are located in or close to the downtown area and offer comfortable accommodations at expensive to moderate prices.

Adobe Abode ⭐   A short walk from the plaza, in the same quiet residential neighborhood as the Georgia O'Keeffe Museum, Adobe Abode is one of Santa Fe's most imaginative B&Bs. The living room is cozy, decorated with folk art. The creativity shines in each of the guest rooms as well, some located in the main house, which was built in 1907. Others, in back, are newer. The Provence Suite, decorated in sunny yellow and bright blue, offers a feel of France, while the Bronco Room is filled with cowboy paraphernalia: hats, Pendleton blankets, pioneer chests, and an entire shelf lined with children's cowboy boots. Two rooms have fireplaces, and several have private patios. Complimentary sherry, fruit, and cookies are served daily in the living room. Every morning a full breakfast of fresh fruit and a hot dish such as green-chile corn soufflé is served in the country-style kitchen.

202 Chapelle St., Santa Fe, NM 87501. © **505/983-3133.** Fax 505/983-3132. www.adobeabode.com. 6 units. $135–$185 double. Rates include breakfast and afternoon snacks. DISC, MC, V. Limited free parking. *In room:* A/C, TV, coffeemaker, hair dryer, iron.

Alexander's Inn ★★   This inn, just 6 blocks from the plaza, continues to receive outstanding recommendations from such publications as *Glamour* ("one of the most romantic inns in the Southwest") and *Travel Holiday* ("a backdrop for a fairytale"). The 1903 Victorian/New England–style house, situated in a quiet residential area, is filled with delicious antiques, bedding, and draperies. The rooms have stenciling on the walls, hooked and Oriental rugs, muted colors such as apricot and lilac, and white iron or four-poster queen-size beds (there are some king-size beds as well). Separate from the inn are cottages complete with kitchens (equipped with stove, oven, refrigerator, and swamp coolers, some with microwave) and living rooms with kiva fireplaces. Some have more Southwestern charm than others, so discuss your desires when making reservations. An extended continental breakfast of homemade baked goods is served in the dining room or on the veranda every morning, as are afternoon tea and cookies. Under the same excellent management, the **Hacienda Nicholas** ★★ (© **888/ 284-3170** or 505/992-8385; www.haciendanicholas.com), just a few blocks away, offers guests a delightful Southwestern stay in rooms gathered around a sunny patio.

529 E. Palace Ave., Santa Fe, NM 87501. © **888/321-5123** or 505/986-1431. Fax 505/982-8572. www. alexanders-inn.com. 10 units (8 with bathroom), 5 cottages. $85–$250 double. Additional person $25. Rates include breakfast and afternoon tea. AE, DISC, MC, V. Free parking. Pets accepted with $20 deposit. **Amenities:** Tennis club privileges; Jacuzzi; concierge; activities desk. *In room:* A/C, TV, dataport, hair dryer.

Dos Casas Viejas ★★★   These two old houses *(dos casas viejas)*, not far from the plaza, offer the kind of luxury accommodations you'd expect from a fine hotel. Behind an old wooden security gate is a meandering brick lane along which are the elegant guest rooms. The innkeepers, Susan and Michael Strijek, maintain the place impeccably. The grounds are manicured, and the rooms, each with a patio and private entrance, are finely renovated and richly decorated. All rooms have Mexican-tile floors and kiva fireplaces; most have diamond-finished stucco walls and embedded vigas. They're furnished with Southwestern antiques and original art. Some have canopy beds, and one has a sleigh bed; all are covered with fine linens and down comforters. Guests can use the library and dining area (where a European breakfast is served each morning) in the main building. Breakfast can also be enjoyed on the patio alongside the elegant lap pool or (after you collect it in a basket) on your private patio.

610 Agua Fría St., Santa Fe, NM 87501. © **505/983-1636.** Fax 505/983-1749. www.doscasasviejas.com. 8 units. $195–$295 double. Additional person $20. Rates include full breakfast. MC, V. Free parking. **Amenities:** Outdoor pool; concierge; same-day dry cleaning. *In room:* A/C, TV, dataport, fridge, coffeemaker, hair dryer, iron.

El Farolito ★★   The owners of this inn, which is within walking distance of the plaza, have created an authentic theme experience for guests in each room. The themes include the Native American Room, decorated with rugs and pottery; the South-of-the-Border Room, with Mexican folk art with a full-size sofa sleeper; and the elegant Santa Fe–style Opera Room, with hand-carved, lavishly upholstered furniture. A two-room suite has been added in the main building, with a queen-size iron bed and Southwestern decor. The walls of most of the rooms are rubbed with beeswax during plastering to give them a smooth, golden finish. All rooms have kiva fireplaces (except for the new suite) and private patios. The common area displays works by notable New Mexico artists. Part of the inn was built before 1912, and the rest is new, but the old-world elegance carries through. For breakfast, the focus is on healthy food with a little decadence thrown in. You'll enjoy fresh fruit and homebaked breads and pastries. Under the same stellar ownership (but a little less expensive) is the nearby **Four Kachinas Inn** ⭑ (✆ **888/634-8782** or 505/982-2550; www.fourkachinas.com), where Southwestern-style rooms sit around a sunny courtyard. A little less lavish than those at El Farolito, these rooms are sparkly clean, all with patios.

514 Galisteo St., Santa Fe, NM 87501. ✆ **888/634-8782** or 505/988-1631. Fax 505/988-4589. www.farolito. com. 8 units. $150–$280 casita. Rates include expanded continental breakfast. AE, DISC, MC, V. Free parking. **Amenities:** Babysitting by appointment; valet laundry. *In room:* A/C, TV, coffeemaker, hair dryer, iron.

El Paradero ⭑   Located about a 10-minute walk from the plaza, El Paradero ("the stopping place") provides reliable, unpretentious accommodations and good service. It began in about 1810 as a Spanish adobe farmhouse, and it doubled in size in 1878, when Territorial-style details were added. In 1912, Victorian touches were incorporated in the styling of its doors and windows. Innkeepers Ouida MacGregor and Thom Allen opened it as one of Santa Fe's first bed-and-breakfasts over 20 years ago. They're deeply involved in the city and can direct visitors to unexpected sights and activities. Nine ground-level rooms surround a central courtyard and offer a clean, white decor, hardwood or brick floors, folk art, and hand-woven textiles on the walls. Three more luxurious upstairs rooms feature tile floors and bathrooms as well as private balconies. Five rooms have fireplaces. Two suites occupying a brick 1912 coachman's house, a railroad-era Victorian building, are elegantly decorated with period antiques and provide living rooms with fireplaces, kitchen nooks, TVs, and phones. The ground floor of the main building has a parlor, a living room with a piano and fireplace, and a Mexican-style breakfast room where a full gourmet breakfast and afternoon tea are served daily.

220 W. Manhattan Ave., Santa Fe, NM 87501. ✆ **505/988-1177.** Fax 505/988-3577. www.elparadero.com. 14 units. May–Oct $85–$165 double; Nov–Dec and Mar–Apr $80–$150 double; Jan–Feb $75–$135 double. Rates include full breakfast and afternoon tea. AE, MC, V. Free parking. Pets accepted, $15 per night. **Amenities:** Concierge. *In room:* A/C.

Grant Corner Inn ⭑⭑   This early-20th-century manor, just 2 blocks west of the plaza and next door to the new Georgia O'Keeffe Museum, offers a quiet stay with a fanciful Victorian ambience. Each room is furnished with antiques, from brass or four-poster beds to armoires and quilts, and terry robes are available for those staying in rooms with shared bathrooms. All rooms have ceiling fans, and some are equipped with small refrigerators. Each room has its own character. For example, one has a hand-painted German wardrobe closet dating from 1772 and a washbasin with brass fittings in the shape of a fish; another has a private outdoor deck that catches the morning sun; another has an antique collection of dolls and stuffed animals. Two rooms have kitchenettes, and two also have laundry facilities. The inn's office doubles as a library and gift shop. In addition to the rooms mentioned above, Grant Corner Inn offers accommodations in its hacienda, located at 604 Griffin St. It's a Southwestern-style condominium with two bedrooms and a fully equipped kitchen. Breakfast, for both the inn and the hacienda, is served each morning in front of the living-room fireplace or on the front veranda in summer. The meals are so good that an enthusiastic public arrives for brunch here every Sunday (the inn is also open to the public for weekday breakfasts). Afternoon tea and snacks are also complimentary.

122 Grant Ave., Santa Fe, NM 87501. ✆ **800/964-9003** or 505/983-6678 for reservations, 505/984-9001 for guest rooms. Fax 505/983-1526. www.grantcornerinn.com. 9 units, 1 hacienda. $130–$240 double. Hacienda: $145–$165 if the guest rooms are rented separately; $270–$310 for entire house. Additional person $20.

Rates include full gourmet breakfast and afternoon tea. AE, MC, V. Free parking. Some rooms appropriate for children. **Amenities:** Restaurant (breakfast only); Jacuzzi; concierge; tour desk; in-room massage; laundry service. *In room:* A/C, TV, hair dryer, iron.

The Madeleine ★★   Lace, flowery upholstery, and stained glass surround you at this 1886 Queen Anne–style inn just 5 blocks east of the plaza. All rooms have terry robes, some offer fireplaces, and there's a Jacuzzi for all to share. Two units share a bathroom. One of my favorite rooms is the Morning Glory, with a king-size bed, a corner fireplace, and lots of sun. An adjacent cottage built in 1987 received an award for compatible architecture from the Santa Fe Historical Association. The two rooms in the cottage are larger than the other rooms, with king-size beds and bay windows. In winter, a full breakfast (which often includes quiche or waffles) is served family-style in the dining room. In summer, it's served under apricot trees, on a flagstone patio surrounded by flowers. Tea, lemonade, and cocoa, along with homemade cookies and brownies, are available throughout the day.

106 Faithway St., Santa Fe, NM 87501. © **888/877-7622** or 505/982-3465. Fax 505/982-8572. www. madeleineinn.com. 8 units (6 with bathroom), 2 cottages. $85–$110 double with shared bathroom; $130–$210 double with private bathroom. Additional person $25. Rates include full breakfast and afternoon tea. AE, DISC, MC, V. Free parking. **Amenities:** Access to nearby health club; Jacuzzi; concierge; business center. *In room:* A/C, TV/VCR, dataport, hair dryer.

Pueblo Bonito   Private courtyards and narrow flagstone paths give a look of elegance to this 19th-century adobe hacienda and stables, located a few blocks south of the Santa Fe River. This is a good choice if you like more of an inn feel rather than a home feel in a B&B. Each guest room is named for a Pueblo tribe of the surrounding countryside. Every room—decorated with Native American rugs on wood or brick floors—has a queen-size bed and a fireplace. A recent renovation added some new furniture and mirrors. Bathrooms are small but attractively tiled. Six rooms are suites, each with a fully stocked kitchen, a living/dining room with fireside seating, and a bedroom. The remainder are standard units with locally made willow headboards and couches, dining alcoves, and old Spanish-style lace curtains. Continental breakfast is served in the dining room or on the sun deck; if you prefer, you can order room service. Afternoon margaritas and wine are served daily.

138 W. Manhattan Ave., Santa Fe, NM 87501. © **800/461-4599** or 505/984-8001. Fax 505/984-3155. www. pueblobonitoinn.com. 18 units. $85–$165 double. Rates include continental breakfast and afternoon refreshments. AE, DISC, MC, V. Free parking. **Amenities:** Jacuzzi; concierge; room service; coin-op laundry. *In room:* A/C, TV, hair dryer, iron.

Spencer House Bed & Breakfast Inn ★   This inn, located near the O'Keeffe Museum, is unique among Santa Fe bed-and-breakfasts. Instead of Southwestern-style furnishings, you'll find beautiful antiques from England, Ireland, and colonial America. One guest room features an antique brass bed, and another a pencil-post bed, yet another an English panel bed; all rooms have Ralph Lauren fabrics and linens. All bathrooms are modern and very clean. In summer, a full breakfast—coffee, tea, yogurt, cereal, fresh fruit, and main course—is served on the outdoor patio. In winter, guests dine in an atrium. Afternoon tea is served in the breakfast room. In back, an 800-square-foot cottage has been split into two separate rooms, each with a private full bath and whirlpool tub, one with a full kitchen, fireplace, and private patio. Some rooms have coffeemakers, TVs, and telephones.

222 McKenzie St., Santa Fe, NM 87501. ✆ 800/647-0530 (7am–6pm) or 505/988-3024. Fax 505/984-9862. www.spencerhse-santafe.com. 6 units. $107–$175 double. Rates include full breakfast and afternoon tea. MC, V. Limited free parking. **Amenities:** Concierge; laundry service. *In room:* A/C, hair dryer, iron.

The Territorial Inn ✪   This Territorial-style building, which dates from the 1890s and is situated 1½ blocks from the plaza, has a delightful Victorian feel with plenty of amenities. Constructed of stone and adobe, with a pitched roof, it has two stories connected by a curving tiled stairway. Eighteen of its rooms, typically furnished with early American antiques, offer private bathrooms; the remaining two share a bathroom. All rooms are equipped with ceiling fans and sitting areas, and two have fireplaces. Guests enjoy an extended continental breakfast in a sophisticated common area or, in warm months, in the back garden, which is shaded by large cottonwoods. Guests can also relax in the rose garden and the gazebo-enclosed Jacuzzi.

215 Washington Ave., Santa Fe, NM 87501. ✆ 800/745-9910 or 505/989-7737. Fax 505/986-9212. www. territorialinn.com. 20 units, 18 with bathroom. $88–$170 double. Higher rates during special events. Additional person $20. Rates include extended continental breakfast. AE, DC, DISC, MC, V. Free parking. Children under 10 not accepted. **Amenities:** Jacuzzi; concierge. *In room:* A/C, TV, hair dryer.

Water Street Inn ✪✪   An award-winning adobe restoration 4 blocks from the plaza, this friendly inn features beautiful Mexican-tile bathrooms, several kiva fireplaces or wood stoves, and antique furnishings. Each room is packed with Southwestern art and books. In the afternoon, a happy hour, with quesadillas and margaritas, is offered in the living room or on the upstairs portal, where an extended continental breakfast is also served. All rooms are decorated in a Moroccan/Southwestern style. Room no. 3 provides a queen-size hideaway sofa to accommodate families. Room no. 4 features special regional touches in its decor and boasts a chaise longue, a fur rug, built-in seating, and a corner fireplace. Four new suites have elegant contemporary Southwestern furnishings and outdoor private patios with fountains. Most rooms have balconies or terraces.

427 Water St., Santa Fe, NM 87501. ✆ 800/646-6752 or 505/984-1193. Fax 505/984-6235. www.water streetinn.com. 12 units. $100–$250 double. Rates include continental breakfast and afternoon hors d'oeuvres and refreshments. AE, DISC, MC, V. Free parking. Children and pets welcome with prior approval. **Amenities:** Jacuzzi; concierge; room service. *In room:* A/C, TV/VCR, dataport, hair dryer.

5 RV Parks & Campgrounds

RV PARKS

At least four private camping areas, mainly for recreational vehicles, are located within a few minutes' drive of downtown Santa Fe. Typical rates are $28 for full RV hookups, $18 for tents. Be sure to book ahead at busy times.

Los Campos RV Resort   The resort has 95 spaces with full hookups, picnic tables, and covered pavilion for use with reservation at no charge. It's just 5 miles south of the plaza, so it's plenty convenient, but keep in mind that it is surrounded by the city.

3574 Cerrillos Rd., Santa Fe, NM 87507. ✆ 800/852-8160. Fax 505/471-9220. http://members.aol.com/ loscampossf. $28–$33 daily; $169–$206 weekly; $450 monthly/winter; $470 monthly/summer. MC, V. Pets welcome. **Amenities:** Outdoor pool; concierge; coin-op laundry; restrooms; showers; grills; vending machines; free cable TV.

Rancheros de Santa Fe Campground ✪   Tents, motor homes, and trailers requiring full hookups are welcome here. The park's 130 sites are situated on 22 acres of piñon and juniper forest. Cabins are also available. It's located about 6 miles southeast of Santa Fe and is open March 15 to October 31.

736 Old Las Vegas Hwy. (exit 290 off I-25), Santa Fe, NM 87505. ✆ **800/426-9259** or 505/466-3482. www.rancheros.com. Tent site $17–$19; RV hookup $25–$30. DISC, MC, V. **Amenities:** Outdoor pool; coin-op laundry; restrooms; showers; grills; cable TV hookups; grocery store; recreation room; tables; fireplaces; nature trails; playground; free nightly movies May–Sept; public telephones; propane.

Santa Fe KOA   This campground, about 11 miles northeast of Santa Fe, sits among the foothills of the Sangre de Cristo Mountains, an excellent place to enjoy Northern New Mexico's pine-filled high desert. It offers full hookups, pull-through sites, and tent sites.

934 Old Las Vegas Hwy. (exit 290 or 294 off I-25), Santa Fe, NM 87505. ✆ **800/KOA-1514** or 505/466-1419 for reservations. www.koa.com. Tent site $22–$25; RV hookup $26–$31. DISC, MC, V. **Amenities:** Coin-op laundry; restrooms; showers; store/gift shop; recreation room; playground; picnic tables; dataport; propane; dumping station.

CAMPGROUNDS

There are three forested sites along NM 475 on the way to Ski Santa Fe. All are open from May to October. Overnight rates start at about $12.

Hyde Memorial State Park   About 8 miles from the city, this pine-surrounded park offers a quiet retreat. Seven RV pads with electrical pedestals and an RV dumping station are available. There are nature and hiking trails and a playground as well as a small winter skating pond.

740 Hyde Park Rd., Santa Fe, NM 87501. ✆ **505/983-7175**. www.nmparks.com. **Amenities:** Shelters; water; tables; vault toilets.

Santa Fe National Forest ★★   Black Canyon campground, with 44 sites, is located just before you reach Hyde State Park. It is one of the only campgrounds in the state for which you can make a reservation; to do so you must go through a national reservation system (✆ **877/444-6777;** www.reserveusa.com). The sites sit within thick forest, with hiking trails nearby. Big Tesuque, a first-come, first-served campground with 10 newly rehabilitated sites, is about 12 miles from town. The sites here are closer to the road and sit at the edge of aspen forests. Both Black Canyon and Big Tesuque campgrounds, located along the Santa Fe Scenic Byway, NM 475, are equipped with vault toilets.

P.O. Box 1689, Santa Fe, NM 87504. ✆ **505/438-7840** or 505/753-7331. www.fs.fed.us/r3/sfe. **Amenities:** Water; vault toilets.

6

Where to Dine in Santa Fe

Santa Fe abounds in dining options, with hundreds of restaurants in all categories. Competition among them is steep, and spots are continually opening and closing. Locals watch closely to see which ones will survive. Some chefs create dishes that incorporate traditional Southwestern foods with ingredients not indigenous to the region; their restaurants are referred to in the listings as "creative Southwestern." There is also standard regional New Mexican cuisine, and beyond that, diners can opt for excellent steak and seafood, as well as Continental, European, Asian, and, of course, Mexican menus. On the south end of town, Santa Fe has the requisite chain establishments such as **Outback Steakhouse,** 2574 Camino Entrada (℃ **505/424-6800**), **Olive Garden,** 3781 Cerrillos Rd. (℃ **505/438-7109**), and **Red Lobster,** 4450 Rodeo Rd. (℃ **505/473-1610**).

Especially during peak tourist seasons, dinner reservations may be essential. Reservations are always recommended at better restaurants.

1 Restaurants by Cuisine

AMERICAN
Cafe Dominic ✦ (Downtown, $, p. 93)
Cowgirl Hall of Fame (Downtown, $$, p. 89)
Plaza Cafe ✦ (Downtown, $, p. 95)
Second Street Brewery (South Side, $, p. 100)
Tesuque Village Market (North Side, $$, p. 97)
Zia Diner (Downtown, $, p. 96)

ASIAN
Chow's ✦ (South Side, $$, p. 97)
Longevity Café ✦ (Downtown, $, p. 94)
mu du noodles ✦✦ (South Side, $$, p. 98)
Shohko Cafe ✦ (Downtown, $$, p. 92)

BARBECUE/CAJUN
Cowgirl Hall of Fame (Downtown, $$, p. 89)

BISTRO
Paul's ✦✦ (Downtown, $$, p. 91)

CONTINENTAL
Geronimo ✦✦✦ (Downtown, $$$, p. 84)
The Old House ✦✦✦ (Downtown, $$$, p. 85)
The Palace ✦✦ (Downtown, $$$, p. 86)
The Pink Adobe ✦ (Downtown, $$$, p. 86)

CREATIVE SOUTHWESTERN
Anasazi Restaurant ✦✦ (Downtown, $$$, p. 81)
Atomic Grill (Downtown, $, p. 92)
Cafe Pasqual's ✦✦ (Downtown, $$$, p. 81)
Coyote Café ✦✦ (Downtown, $$$, p. 82)
La Casa Sena ✦✦ (Downtown, $$$, p. 84)

Key to Abbreviations: $$$$ = Very Expensive $$$ = Expensive $$ = Moderate $ = Inexpensive

Santacafé ★★★ (Downtown, $$$, p. 87)

DELI/CAFE

Cafe Dominic ★ (Downtown, $, p. 93)

Carlos's Gosp'l Cafe ★ (Downtown, $, p. 93)

Plaza Cafe ★ (Downtown, $, p. 95)

Sage Bakehouse ★ (Downtown, $, p. 95)

FRENCH

Rociada ★★★ (Downtown, $$$, p. 87)

315 ★★ (Downtown, $$$, p. 88)

GREEK

Plaza Cafe ★ (Downtown, $, p. 95)

INDIAN

India Palace ★ (Downtown, $$, p. 90)

INTERNATIONAL

Zia Diner (Downtown, $, p. 96)

ITALIAN

Andiamo! ★ (Downtown, $$, p. 88)

Il Piatto Cucina Italiano ★★ (Downtown, $$, p. 90)

Osteria d'Assisi ★ (Downtown, $$, p. 91)

The Palace ★★ (Downtown, $$$, p. 86)

Pranzo Italian Grill ★★ (Downtown, $$, p. 91)

Upper Crust Pizza ★ (Downtown, $, p. 96)

LATIN

Coyote Café ★★ (Downtown, $$$, p. 82)

MEXICAN

Bumble Bee's Baja Grill ★ (Downtown, $, p. 93)

Felipe's Tacos (South Side, $, p. 98)

Los Mayas ★ (Downtown, $$, p. 90)

Marisco's La Playa (South Side, $, p. 98)

MICROBREWERY

Blue Corn Café (Downtown, $, p. 92)

Second Street Brewery (South Side, $, p. 100)

NATIVE AMERICAN

Anasazi Restaurant ★★ (Downtown, $$$, p. 81)

Cafe San Estevan ★ (Downtown, $$, p. 88)

NEW AMERICAN

Celebrations Restaurant and Bar ★ (Downtown, $$, p. 89)

The Compound ★★★ (Downtown, $$$, p 82)

O'Keeffe Café ★ (Downtown, $$$, p. 85)

The Old House ★★★ (Downtown, $$$, p. 85)

Ristra ★★ (Downtown, $$$, p. 87)

Santacafé ★★★ (Downtown, $$$, p. 87)

Santa Fe Railyard Restaurant ★ (Downtown, $$, p. 91)

NEW MEXICAN

Blue Corn Café (Downtown, $, p. 92)

Cafe San Estevan ★ (Downtown, $$, p. 88)

Guadalupe Cafe ★★ (Downtown, $, p. 93)

La Choza ★★ (Downtown, $, p. 94)

Ore House on the Plaza ★ (Downtown, $$$, p. 85)

Plaza Cafe ★ (Downtown, $, p. 95)

The Shed ★★ (Downtown, $, p. 95)

Tía Sophia's ★ (Downtown, $, p. 95)

Tomasita's Cafe ★ (Downtown, $, p. 96)

Tortilla Flats ★ (South Side, $, p. 100)

PIZZA

Upper Crust Pizza ⭐ (Downtown, $, p. 96)

SOUTHWESTERN

The Pink Adobe ⭐ (Downtown, $$$, p. 86)

Tesuque Village Market (North Side, $$, p. 97)

SPANISH

El Farol ⭐ (Downtown, $$$, p. 82)

STEAK/SEAFOOD

El Nido ⭐ (North Side, $$$, p. 96)

Marisco's La Playa (South Side, $, p. 98)

Ore House on the Plaza ⭐ (Downtown, $$$, p. 85)

Rio Chama Steakhouse ⭐⭐ (Downtown, $$$, p. 86)

Steaksmith at El Gancho ⭐ (South Side, $$, p. 98)

Vanessie of Santa Fe ⭐ (Downtown, $$$, p. 88)

2 Downtown

This area includes the circle defined by the Paseo de Peralta and St. Francis Drive, as well as Canyon Road.

EXPENSIVE

Anasazi Restaurant ⭐⭐ CREATIVE SOUTHWESTERN/NATIVE AMERICAN   This ranks as one of Santa Fe's more interesting dining experiences. It's part of the Inn of the Anasazi (see chapter 5), but it's a fine restaurant in its own right. You'll dine surrounded by diamond-finished walls decorated with petroglyph symbols. Stacked flagstone furthers the Anasazi feel of this restaurant, named for the ancient people who once inhabited the area. There's no pretension here; the waitstaff is friendly but not overbearing, and tables are spaced nicely, making it a good place for a romantic dinner. All the food is inventive, and organic meats and vegetables are used whenever available. For breakfast, try the breakfast burrito with homemade chorizo, green-chile potatoes, and refried Anasazi beans. A must with lunch or dinner is the grilled corn tortilla and lime soup. It's thick, served with tortilla strips, thinly sliced scallions, and a chile-spiced breadstick. For an entree, try cinnamon-chili-rubbed beef medallion with chipotle white cheddar mashed potatoes and mango salsa. Desserts are thrilling; try Donna's famous tiramisu. There are daily specials, as well as a nice list of wines by the glass and special wines of the day.

At the Inn of the Anasazi, 113 Washington Ave. ✆ **505/988-3236.** Reservations recommended. Main courses $7.50–$12 breakfast, $9.50–$15 lunch, $18–$33 dinner. AE, DC, DISC, MC, V. Daily 7–10:30am, 11:30am–2:30pm, and 5:30–10pm.

Cafe Pasqual's ⭐⭐ CREATIVE SOUTHWESTERN   "You have to become the food, erase the line between it as an object and you. You have to really examine its structure, its size, its color, its strength, its weakness, know who grew it, how long it's been out of the field," says Pasqual's owner Katharine Kagel. That attitude is completely apparent in this restaurant, where the walls are lined with murals depicting voluptuous villagers playing guitars, drinking, and even flying. Needless to say, it's a festive place, though it's also excellent for a romantic dinner. Service is jovial and professional. My favorite dish for breakfast or lunch is the *huevos motuleños* (two eggs over easy on blue-corn tortillas and black beans topped with sautéed bananas, feta cheese, salsa, and green chile). Soups and salads are also served for lunch, and there's a delectable grilled-salmon burrito with herbed goat cheese and cucumber salsa. The frequently changing dinner menu offers grilled meats and seafood, plus vegetarian specials. Start with the Iroquois corn tamale with roasted poblano, zucchini, and asadero cheese, and move on to the spinach, jack cheese, and red-onion enchiladas. There's a communal table for those who would like to meet new people over a meal. Pasqual's offers imported beers and wine by the bottle or glass. Try to go at an odd hour—late morning or afternoon—or make a reservation for dinner; otherwise, you'll have to wait.

121 Don Gaspar Ave. ℂ **505/983-9340.** Reservations recommended for dinner. Main courses $5.75–$13 breakfast, $6–$15 lunch, $16–$34 dinner. AE, MC, V. Mon–Sat 7am–3pm; Sun–Thurs 5:30–9:30pm; Fri–Sat 6–10pm; summer daily 6–10:30pm. Brunch Sun 8am–2pm.

The Compound ★★★ NEW AMERICAN   This reincarnation of one of Santa Fe's classic restaurants serves some of the most flavorful and daring food in town. During warm months, a broad patio shelters diners from the city bustle. With friendly, efficient service, this is an excellent place for a romantic dinner or a relaxing lunch. Chef/owner Mark Kiffin, after nearly 8 years as chef at Coyote Café (see below), lets his creativity soar. You might start off with tuna tartare topped with Osetra caviar. For an entree, a signature dish is the grilled beef tenderloin with Italian potatoes and foie gras hollandaise. For lunch, monkfish chorizo with watercress is outrageously tasty. Finish with a bittersweet chocolate torte. A carefully selected beer and wine list accompanies the menu.

653 Canyon Rd. ℂ **505/982-4353.** Reservations recommended. Main courses $12–$20 lunch, $20–$31 dinner. AE, MC, V. Mon–Fri noon–2pm; daily 6–9pm; bar opens nightly at 5pm.

Coyote Café ★★ CREATIVE SOUTHWESTERN/LATIN   World-renowned chef and cookbook author Mark Miller has been "charged with single-handedly elevating the chile to haute status." That statement from the *New York Times Magazine* sums up for me the experience of eating at this trendy nouveau Southwestern restaurant about a block from the plaza. The atmosphere is urban Southwestern, with calfskin-covered chairs and a zoo of carved animals watching from a balcony. The exhibition kitchen shows lots of brass and tile, and the waitstaff is efficient and friendly. It's the place to go for a fun night out, or you can sample the great food for lunch at a fraction of the price. Some complain that on a busy night the space is noisy, and I'm especially careful not to sit on the *banco* toward the northeastern corner next to the always-rumbling fan.

The menu changes seasonally, so the specific dishes I mention may not be available. Start your meal with Coyote cocktails that might include a Brazilian daiquiri or margarita del Maguey. Then look for delights such as chipotle tiger prawns with griddled corn cakes or a duck tamale for appetizers. Move on to a braised-ancho lamb shank or horseradish-crusted Maine haddock. You can order drinks from the full bar or wine by the glass. Smoking is not allowed.

Coyote Café has two adjunct establishments. In summer, the place to be seen is the **Rooftop Cantina,** where light Latino/Cuban fare and cocktails are served on a festively painted terrace. (Try the chicken skewers on sugar cane.) On the ground floor is a new addition called **Cottonwoods,** offering a reasonably priced menu in a new Southwestern diner ambience.

132 Water St. ℂ **505/983-1615.** Reservations highly recommended. Main courses $6–$16 (Rooftop Cantina), $19–$36 (Coyote Café), $6–$15 (Cottonwoods). AE, DC, DISC, MC, V. Rooftop Cantina: daily 11:30am–9pm. Dining room: daily 6–9:30pm; daily 5:30–9pm during opera season.

El Farol ★ SPANISH   This is the place to head for local ambience and old-fashioned flavor. El Farol (The Lantern) is the Canyon Road artists' quarter's

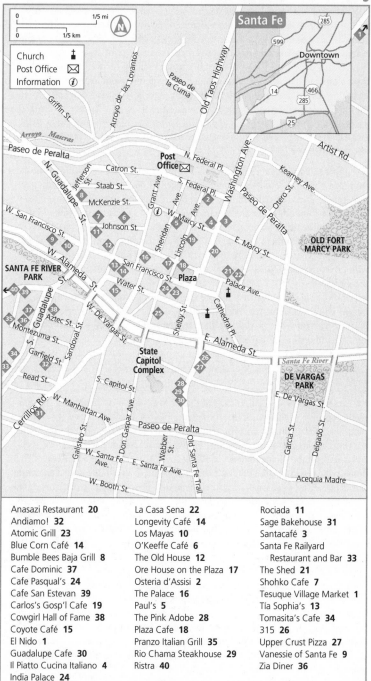

original neighborhood bar. The restaurant has cozy low ceilings and hand-smoothed adobe walls. Thirty-five varieties of tapas are offered, including such delicacies as *gambas al ajillo* (shrimp with chile, garlic, Madeira, and lime) and *conejo y vino* (stewed rabbit). You can make a meal out of two or three tapas shared with your friends or order a full dinner such as the paella or the grilled lamb chops with cranberry salsa. There is live entertainment 7 nights a week—including jazz/swing, folk, and Latin guitar music—starting at 9:30pm. In summer, two outdoor patios are open to diners.

808 Canyon Rd. ⓒ 505/983-9912. Reservations recommended. Tapas $4.50–$12; main courses $8–$15 lunch, $26–$32 dinner. DC, DISC, MC, V. Daily 11:30am–3pm and 5:30–10pm (bar is open until 1am weekdays, 2am weekends).

Geronimo ⭐⭐⭐ CONTINENTAL   This elegant restaurant offers one of Santa's Fe's most delectable dining experiences. It occupies an old adobe structure known as the Borrego House, built by Geronimo Lopez in 1756 and now completely restored, but it still retains the feel of an old Santa Fe home. I especially recommend lunch here, when you can get a taste of this complex food for a fraction of the dinner price. Reserve a spot on the porch and watch the action on Canyon Road. My favorite at lunch is the house-smoked ruby trout salad, with crimson beluga lentils, organic grains, and a sweet sesame dressing. For a dinner appetizer, try the Maryland blue crab strudel and lime-toasted pepita and red-onion salad. For an entree, the mesquite-grilled elk tenderloin with chestnut strudel is great, as is grilled Maine lobster with farmer's corn and leek compote. For dessert, you won't be disappointed by the trio of brûlées—espresso chocolate, Chambord, and orange—or the Belgian chocolate Grand Marnier cake. The menu changes seasonally, and there is an excellent wine list.

724 Canyon Rd. ⓒ 505/982-1500. Reservations recommended. Main courses $10–$19 lunch, $20–$36 dinner. AE, MC, V. Tues–Sun 11:30am–2pm; daily 6–9:30pm.

La Casa Sena ⭐⭐ CREATIVE SOUTHWESTERN   Combining alluring ambience and tasty food, this is one of Santa Fe's favorite restaurants, though the food here isn't as precise and flavorful as at Santacafé or The Old House. It sits within the Sena compound, a prime example of a Spanish hacienda, in a Territorial-style adobe house built in 1867 by Civil War hero Major José Sena. The house, which surrounds a garden courtyard, is today a veritable art gallery, with museum-quality landscapes on the walls and Taos-style handcrafted furniture. The cuisine in the main dining room might be described as northern New Mexican with a continental flair. One of my favorite lunches is the flash-fried Baja sea bass fish tacos with mango salsa. In the evening, diners might start with a salad of garden greens and grilled mushrooms, then move to a grilled lamb rack marinated with Dijon and mint and accompanied by roasted root vegetables and green peppercorn sauce.

In the adjacent **La Cantina,** waiters and waitresses sing Broadway show tunes as they carry platters from the kitchen to the table. The more moderately priced Cantina menu offers the likes of cornmeal-breaded trout and grilled stuffed pork loin with peach-onion sauce. Both restaurants have exquisite desserts; try the black-and-white bittersweet chocolate terrine with raspberry sauce. The award-winning wine list features more than 850 selections. There's patio dining in summer.

125 E. Palace Ave. ⓒ 505/988-9232. Reservations recommended. La Casa Sena main courses $8–$12 lunch, $21–$30 dinner; 5-course chef's tasting menu $42, with wine $58; La Cantina main courses $13–$23. AE, DC, DISC, MC, V. Mon–Sat 11:30am–3pm; Sunday brunch 11am–3pm; daily 5:30–10pm.

O'Keeffe Café ★ NEW AMERICAN   Following Georgia O'Keeffe's appreciation for sparse interiors, this restaurant has refined minimalist decor, with much more elaborate food. It's a place of clean lines and innovative color use. Large black-and-white photographs of O'Keeffe stirring stew and serving tea adorn the walls. This is a good place to stop in between museums or, in the warm months, to sit on the open patio and watch the summer scene pass by. The food is excellent, but for a nice dinner (in winter), the atmosphere lags behind that of places in a similar price range, such as Santacafé and Geronimo. In summer, the patio dining is superb. The menu is eclectic, with a good balance of chicken, lamb, fish, and vegetarian dishes, some in fancy salad and sandwich form (at lunch), along with more elaborate entree offerings. Most recently, I had the crab cakes with chipotle aioli, and my friend tried smoked duck breast with dried-grape risotto and almond cream—very rich. There's also a children's menu. The restaurant has a notable wine list and offers periodic wine tasting menus.

217 Johnson St. ℂ **505/946-1065**. Lunch $4–$21; dinner $6.50–$35. AE, MC, V. Mon–Sat 11am–3pm and 5:30–9:30pm (winebar 3–5:30pm); Sunday brunch 11am–3pm.

The Old House ★★★ NEW AMERICAN/CONTINENTAL   Located within the Eldorado Hotel (p. 60), this restaurant consistently rates as Santa Fe's best eatery in local publication's polls—and it's no wonder, with chef Martin Rios running the show. A native of Mexico, he worked his way up through some of Santa Fe's finest kitchens before embarking on a course at the Culinary Institute of America and returning to the City Different to turn The Old House into a nationally acclaimed restaurant, with a story running on PBS and a cover article in *Bon Appétit*. In a Southwestern atmosphere, rich with excellent Native American art, Rios serves quality meats, poultry, and seafood in refined sauces. The menu changes seasonally, with some signature dishes that remain year-round. Start with the lump crab cake, with grilled portobello and butternut squash salad. Move on to my favorite, the mustard-and-pepper–crusted lamb rack, with roasted shallot potato mash and red chile-Merlot lamb jus; or the sautéed Diver sea scallops with wild mushrooms, asparagus, and pumpkin seeds in a Xeres sherry reduction. My friend Michael says the crème brûlée here is the best dessert he's ever had, but my favorite is the warm liquid center chocolate cake. The wine list is a *Wine Spectator* award-winner.

309 W. San Francisco St. (in the Eldorado Hotel). ℂ **505/988-4455**, ext. 130. Reservations recommended. Main courses $23–$30. AE, DC, DISC, MC, V. Daily 5:30–10pm. Lounge 4:30–10pm.

Ore House on the Plaza ★ STEAK/SEAFOOD/NEW MEXICAN   The Ore House's second-story balcony, at the southwest corner of the plaza, is an ideal spot from which to watch the passing scene while you enjoy cocktails and hors d'oeuvres. In fact, it is the place to be between 4 and 6pm every afternoon. Inside, the decor is Southwestern, with plants and lanterns hanging amid white walls and booths. The menu offers fresh seafood and steaks, as well as some Nueva Latina dishes that incorporate some interesting sauces. Daily fresh fish specials include salmon and swordfish (poached, blackened, teriyaki, or lemon), rainbow trout, lobster, and shellfish. The salmon with spinach pecan pesto has become a new favorite, and you can't go wrong with the Steak Ore House (wrapped in bacon and topped with crabmeat and béarnaise sauce). The Ore House offers vegetable platters for non-carnivores.

The bar, offering live music nightly Thursday to Sunday, serves more than 65 different custom margaritas. It offers a selection of domestic and imported beers and an excellent wine list. An appetizer menu is served from 2:30 to 10pm daily, and the bar stays open until midnight or later (on Sun it closes at midnight).

50 Lincoln Ave. ℂ **505/983-8687**. Reservations recommended. Main courses $5–$13 lunch, $16–$28 dinner. AE, MC, V. 11:30am–10pm daily (bar until midnight or later).

The Palace ★★ ITALIAN/CONTINENTAL   On the site of this locals' spot, Santa Fe's 19th-century matriarch, Doña Tules, operated a thriving gambling hall and bordello. From the place's remains came a brass door knocker, half shaped like a horseshoe, and the other half like a saloon girl's stockinged leg, now the restaurant's logo. Hearkening back to those old days, The Palace serves flavorful food in a Victorian ambience with a bit of bordello flair. Under new ownership in 2004, the restaurant, to locals' relief, still has a plush and comfortable feel, but with a new elegance. The food is well prepared and imaginative, though more conservative than that at The Compound and Geronimo. The Caesar salad—prepared tableside—is always good, as are the meat dishes, such as the herb-crusted rack of lamb with mint couscous. A favorite fish dish at lunch is the Alaskan salmon scaloppini served with ratatouille. The pasta dishes are also tasty, as are the vegetarian ones and daily specials. The wine list is long and well considered. A lovely patio and a lively bar are locals' favorites. The bar has nightly entertainment including dancing on Saturday after 9pm, and its own menu from 3pm to midnight.

142 W. Palace Ave. ℂ **505/982-9891**. Reservations recommended. Lunch $7–$16; dinner $16–$34. AE, DC, DISC, MC, V. Mon–Sat 11:30am–3pm; daily 5:30–10pm. Bar: Mon–Sat 11:30am–2am; Sun 5:30pm–midnight.

The Pink Adobe ★ CONTINENTAL/SOUTHWESTERN   More show than flavor? Probably. This restaurant, located a few blocks off the plaza, offers a swirl of local old-timer gaiety and food that is more imaginative than flavorful, but The Pink Adobe has remained popular since the restaurant opened in 1944. I remember eating my first lamb curry here, and my mother ate her first blue-corn enchilada, back in the '50s, and was taken aback by the odd colors. The restaurant occupies an adobe home believed to be at least 350 years old. Guests enter through a narrow side door into a series of quaint, informal dining rooms with tile or hardwood floors. Stuccoed walls display original modern art and Priscilla Hoback pottery on built-in shelves. For lunch, I always have a chicken enchilada topped with an egg. The gypsy stew (chicken, green chile, tomatoes, and onions in sherry broth) sounds great but is on the bland side. At the dinner hour, The Pink Adobe offers the likes of escargot and shrimp rémoulade as appetizers. The local word here is that the steak Dunigan, with sautéed mushrooms and green chile, is "the thing" to order. You can't leave without trying the hot French apple pie.

Smoking is allowed only in The Dragon Room (see chapter 9), the lounge across the alleyway from the restaurant. Under the same ownership, the charming bar (a real local scene) has its own menu, offering traditional New Mexican food. Locals come to eat hearty green-chile stew.

406 Old Santa Fe Trail. ℂ **505/983-7712**. Reservations recommended. Main courses $4.75–$8.70 lunch, $14–$26 dinner. AE, DC, DISC, MC, V. Mon–Fri 11:30am–2pm; daily 5:30pm–closing. Bar: Mon–Fri 11:30am–2am; Sat 5pm–2am; Sun 5pm–midnight.

Rio Chama Steakhouse ★★ STEAK/SEAFOOD   Serving up tasty steaks in a refined ranch atmosphere, this is one of Santa Fe's best newer restaurants. It's a good spot for a business lunch or a fun-filled evening, and the patio is a bright spot during warm months. Service is efficient, and there's a full bar. My favorite for lunch is the buffalo patty, much more flavorful than beef. Lunch also brings a good selection of salads and sandwiches, as well as steaks at a reasonable price. Evenings, the prime rib is a big seller, as is the nightly seafood special. For dessert, try chocolate cake.

414 Old Santa Fe Trail. ✆ **505/955-0765.** Reservations recommended on weekend nights. Main courses $8–$22 lunch, $15–$35 dinner. AE, DC, DISC, MC, V. Daily 11am–3pm and 5–10pm; patio bar 5pm–closing.

Ristra ★★ NEW AMERICAN Restaurateur Eric Lamalle describes the food at his restaurant as "spirited," and indeed, anything you order here will likely be unique, with flavors that may startle but will certainly please you. Hearing the specials alone is like poetry: a blend of American favorites prepared with French and Southwestern accents. It's a quiet, comfortable restaurant within a century-old Victorian house minimally decorated with Native American antiques. The food is in a similar vein as Santacafé's (without the Asian influence; p. 87), but the atmosphere here is much quieter. Best of all is the patio during warm months, when you can watch the sun set. The service is completely professional but without pretense. You may want to start with black Mediterranean mussels or a beet and goat-cheese salad. For a main course, try the crispy salmon with sunchoke puree (very flavorful, with a consistency like mashed potatoes), served with sorrel, baby spinach, and a truffled vin-santo sauce; alternatively, try the mesquite-grilled filet mignon (so tender you could cut it with a fork) with horse-radish creamer potatoes, green beans, and a marrow-and-red-wine sauce. For dessert try the almond butter cake, with warm spiced apples and mascarpone caramel sauce. A long wine list covers the best wine regions of California and France; beer is also served.

548 Agua Fria St. ✆ **505/982-8608.** Reservations recommended. Main courses $19–30. AE, MC, V. Summer daily 5:30–10pm; winter Sun–Thurs 6–9pm, Fri–Sat 5:30–9:30pm.

Rociada ★★★ FRENCH Rated by *Condé Nast Traveler* as one of the world's 60 best new restaurants in 2000, Rociada continues to offer a country French dining experience with sophisticated flavors. In a classic 1883 Territorial-style building within walking distance of the plaza, the place has Nouveau-Deco decor, with clean lines, comfortable banquettes, and 1950s Thonet chairs. The menu changes seasonally. Start with a baby spinach salad with egg, crispy bacon, and red-wine mustard vinaigrette; move on to the steak frites, chargrilled and served with french fries; or try the Halibut meunière (seared with lemon butter sauce), with zucchini, capers, and a lemon confit. For dessert, try the floral trio of crème brûlées: lavender, rose, and honey. Choose from the most comprehensive French wine list in New Mexico, with 350 selections. Beer is also available.

304 Johnson St. ✆ **505/983-3800.** Reservations recommended. Main courses $15–$28. AE, MC, V. Mon–Sat 5:30–10pm.

Santacafé ★★★ *Moments* NEW AMERICAN/CREATIVE SOUTH-WESTERN When you eat at this fine restaurant, be prepared for spectacular bursts of flavor. The food combines the best of many cuisines, from Asian to Southwestern, served in an elegant setting with minimalist decor that accentuates the graceful architecture of the 18th-century Padre Gallegos House, 2 blocks from the plaza. The white walls are decorated only with deer antlers, and each room contains a fireplace. In warm months you can sit under elm trees in the charming courtyard. Beware that on busy nights the rooms are noisy. The dishes change to take advantage of seasonal specialties, each served with precision. For a starter, try the shitake and cactus spring rolls with Southwestern ponzu. One of my favorite main courses is the Alaskan halibut with English peas and saffron couscous. A heartier eater might try the bacon-wrapped black angus filet mignon with roasted-garlic mashed potatoes. There's an extensive wine list, with wine by the glass, as well. Desserts, as elegant as the rest of the food, are made in-house; try the warm chocolate upside-down cake with vanilla ice cream.

231 Washington Ave. ⓒ 505/984-1788. Reservations recommended. Main courses $9–$15 lunch, $19–$40 dinner. AE, MC, V. Mon–Sat 11:30am–2pm; daily 6–10pm. Sunday brunch served in summer, Easter Sunday, and Mother's Day.

315 ★★ FRENCH   This classy French bistro enjoyed instant success when it opened in 1995 because the food is simply excellent. The elegant atmosphere provides a perfect setting for a romantic meal, and during warm months the patio is a popular place to people-watch. The menu changes seasonally; on my last visit there, I started with a smooth and flavorful lobster bisque and moved on to lamb chops served with a tart mustard sauce and mashed potatoes. My favorite dessert here is the flourless chocolate cake: not too sweet, and luscious. Because the restaurant is so popular, reservations are an absolute must.

315 Old Santa Fe Trail. ⓒ **505/986-9190.** www.315santafe.com. Reservations highly recommended. Main courses $9–$15 lunch, $20–$29 dinner. AE, DISC, MC, V. Summer Mon–Sat 11:30am–2pm, Sun–Thurs 5:30–9:00pm, Fri–Sat 5:30–9:30pm; winter 11:30am–2pm, 5:30–9pm daily.

Vanessie of Santa Fe ★ STEAK/SEAFOOD   Vanessie is as much a piano bar as it is a restaurant. The talented musicians Doug Montgomery and Charles Tichenor hold forth at the keyboard, caressing the ivories with a repertoire that ranges from Bach to Barry Manilow. A 10-item menu, served at large, round, wooden tables beneath hanging plants in the main dining room or on a covered patio, never varies: rotisserie chicken, fresh fish, New York sirloin, filet mignon, Australian rock lobster, grilled shrimp, and rack of lamb. I especially like the rotisserie chicken. Portions are large; however, they're served a la carte, which bumps this restaurant up into the expensive category. As sides you can order fresh vegetables, sautéed mushrooms, a baked potato, or an onion loaf (my mom raves about this). For dessert, the slice of cheesecake served is large enough for three diners. There's a short wine list.

434 W. San Francisco St. (parking entrance is on Water St.). ⓒ **505/982-9966.** Reservations recommended. Dinner $15–$27. AE, DC, DISC, MC, V. Daily 5:30–10:30pm (earlier in off season).

MODERATE

Andiamo! ★ CONTEMPORARY ITALIAN   A local favorite, this neighborhood trattoria features an excellent daily-changing menu with antipasto, pasta, and excellent desserts. Though it doesn't quite have the spaciousness or the fine service of, say Pranzo, the prices are a little lower and the atmosphere is fun. In the summer you can dine on a patio. I enjoyed the Caesar salad and the penne with merguez, with a bit of musky flavor from the lamb sausage. For dessert, I'd recommend the polenta pound cake with lemon crème Anglaise. Beer and wine are served at this nonsmoking restaurant.

322 Garfield St. ⓒ **505/995-9595.** Reservations recommended. Main courses $9.50–$20. AE, DISC, MC, V. Sun–Thurs 5:30–9pm; Fri–Sat 5:30–9:30pm.

Cafe San Estevan ★ NEW MEXICAN/NATIVE AMERICAN WITH FRENCH ACCENTS   A Franciscan monk with a passion for saints, Estevan Garcia says he grew to love his art while cooking for friars and was inspired by angels to further his cooking skills. Thus was born this interesting twist on local cuisine. Though you can order a classic enchilada just as you can at so many

---

Kids Family-Friendly Restaurants

Blue Corn Café (p. 92)   A relaxed atmosphere and their own menu pleases kids, while excellent brewpub beer pleases parents.

Bumble Bee's Baja Grill (p. 93)   A casual atmosphere allows parents to relax while their kids chow down on quesadillas and burritos.

Tortilla Flats (p. 100)   Portions are gigantic, and the atmosphere is quite friendly at this southside restaurant.

Upper Crust Pizza (p. 96)   Many people feel it has the best pizza in town, and it'll deliver it to tired tots and their families at downtown hotels.

Santa Fe restaurants, here you'll find a little closer attention to sauce flavors and some innovation in food combinations. For instance, Garcia has on the menu one of my favorites, a veggie enchilada, which has calabacitas (squash cooked with corn and chile) inside. He also serves a rib-eye steak with potatoes, calabacitas, and chile caribe (red chile). If your party has varying needs, his menu can accommodate, with dishes such as *burguesa* (hamburger) or salmon served with calabacitas and salsa tropical (a salsa made with mango, jalapeno, and cilantro). The service is friendly and efficient, and the decor is casual Southwestern, a sort of hacienda feel, with vigas on the ceiling and woven tapestries on the walls. Best of all is the streetside dining, for which, during the warmer months, you might have to make a reservation. Wine (from an extensive list) and beer are served.

428 Agua Fria St. (C) 505/995-1996. Reservations recommended in evenings. Main courses $6–$10 lunch, $10–$20 dinner. AE, MC, V. Tues–Fri 11am–2pm; Sat–Sun 10am–2pm; daily 5:30–9pm.

Celebrations Restaurant and Bar ★ NEW AMERICAN   Housed in a former art gallery with artful stained-glass windows and a kiva fireplace, Celebrations boasts the ambience of a bistro and the simple charm of another era. In summer, guests can dine on a brick patio facing Canyon Road. The meals here are a delicious melding of flavors, particularly those that cook awhile, such as the étouffée and stew. Three meals are served daily, starting with breakfast—an omelet with black beans or French toast with orange syrup, for example. Lunch choices include soups, salads, pasta specials, and sandwiches. Casseroles and potpies are always available in winter. The dinner menu changes with the chef's whims, but recent specialties have included sautéed pecan trout, and my favorite, crawfish étouffée. All desserts (including the red-chile piñon ice cream) are homemade. There is a full bar, as well as a choice of beers and wines by the bottle or glass. Inquire about the early dinner special prices.

613 Canyon Rd. (C) 505/989-8904. Reservations recommended. Main courses $5–$9 breakfast and lunch, $11–$20 dinner. MC, V. Daily 8am–2pm; Wed–Sat 5pm–9pm.

Cowgirl Hall of Fame REGIONAL AMERICAN/BARBECUE/CAJUN This raucous bar/restaurant serves decent food in a festive atmosphere. The main room is a bar—a hip hangout spot, and a good place to eat as well, if you don't mind the smoke. The back room is quieter, with wood floors and tables and plenty of cowgirl memorabilia. Best of all is sitting out on a brick patio lit with strings of white lights during the warm season. The service is at times brusque, and the food varies. In winter, my favorite is a big bowl of gumbo or crawfish étoufée, and the rest of the time, I order Jamaican jerk chicken or pork tenderloin when it's a special. Careful, both can be hot. The daily blue-plate special is a real buy, especially on Tuesday nights, when it's chile rellenos. There's even a special "kid's corral" that has horseshoes, a rocking horse, a horse-shaped rubber tire swing, hay bales, and a beanbag toss. Happy hour is from 3 to 6pm. There is live music almost every night.

319 S. Guadalupe St. ℃ 505/982-2565. Reservations recommended. Main courses $5–$10 lunch, $6–$22 dinner. AE, DISC, MC, V. Mon–Fri 11am–midnight; Sat 8:30am–midnight; Sun 8am–11pm. Bar: Mon–Sat until 2am; Sun until midnight.

Il Piatto Cucina Italiano ★★ *Value* NORTHERN ITALIAN   This simple Italian cafe brings innovative flavors to thinner wallets. It's simple and elegant, with contemporary art on the walls—nice for a romantic evening. Service is efficient, though on a busy night, overworked. The menu changes seasonally, complemented by a few perennial standards. For a starter, try the grilled calamari with shaved fennel and aioli. Among entrees, my favorite is the pancetta-wrapped trout with grilled polenta and wild mushrooms, though you can't go wrong with the jumbo scampi risotto with sweet peppers. The Gorgonzola-walnut ravioli is a favorite of many, though not quite enough food to fill me up. A full wine and beer menu is available.

95 West Marcy St. ℃ 505/984-1091. Reservations recommended. Main courses $10–$14. AE, DISC, MC, V. Mon–Fri 11:30am–2pm; daily 5:30–9pm. Closed July 4th, Christmas, New Year's Day.

India Palace ★ *Value* INDIAN   Once every few weeks, I get a craving for the lamb vindaloo served at this restaurant in the center of downtown. A festive ambience, with pink walls painted with mosque shadows, makes this a nice place for a romantic meal. The service is efficient, and most of the waiters are from India, as is chef Amarjit Behal. The tandoori chicken, fish, lamb, and shrimp are rich and flavorful, as is the *baingan bhartha* (eggplant in a rich sauce). A lunch buffet provides an excellent selection of vegetarian and nonvegetarian dishes at a reasonable price. Beer and wine are available, or you might want some chai tea.

227 Don Gaspar Ave. (inside the Water St. parking compound). ℃ 505/986-5859. Reservations recommended. Main courses $9–$15; luncheon buffet $9. AE, DC, DISC, MC, V. Daily 11:30am–2:30pm and 5–10pm. Closed Super Bowl Sunday.

Los Mayas ★ *Moments* MEXICAN   If you're looking to be transported to a Mexican village cafe, this is your spot. Within easy walking distance of most downtown hotels, this little gem has three cozy, brightly painted rooms where a fire crackles in winter. In summer, there's lovely patio dining. Every night live music plays, often flamenco or Latin, to enhance the intimate ambience. The food is a refreshing alternative to New Mexican. Dishes such as enchilada banana (corn tortillas stuffed with plantains, topped with mole sauce) and nopal asado (grilled cactus, topped with squash and corn) are innovative openers reflecting the Oaxacan and Puebloan influences here. Main courses include meat, fish, poultry, and vegetarian offerings in good sauces. My favorites are the *camarones á la diabla* (shrimp in chipotle cream sauce) and the tenderloin with raspberry chipotle sauce. Most entrees come with beans and rice, which, if you find are heavy sides, can be exchanged for alternatives. Round out your meal with an agave margarita or a selection from a decent and affordable wine and beer list.

409 W. Water St. (1 block south of W. San Francisco St., just west of Guadalupe). ℃ 505/986-9930. Main courses $9–$15 lunch, $14–$20 dinner. AE, DISC, MC, V. Daily 11am–10pm.

Osteria d'Assisi ★ NORTHERN ITALIAN   Located just a couple blocks from the plaza, this restaurant offers authentic Italian food in a fun atmosphere. The place has a quaint country Italian decor with simple wooden furniture and the sound of Italian from chef Fabrezio Ventricini, of Rome, Italy, punctuating the air. For antipasto, I enjoyed the *caprese* (fresh mozzarella with tomatoes and basil, garnished with baby greens in a vinaigrette). For pasta, I recommend the lasagna, and for fish, try the delightful Italian seafood stew. All meals are served with homemade Italian bread, and there are a number of special desserts. Beer and wine are by the bottle or glass.

58 S. Federal Place. © **505/986-5858.** Main courses $6.50–$13 lunch, $12–$25 dinner. AE, DC, MC, V. Mon–Sat 11am–3pm and 5–10pm; Sun 5–10pm.

Paul's ★★ BISTRO   It would be easy to walk right by this little downtown cafe, but don't, or you'll miss one of Santa Fe's more delightful dining experiences. The lunch menu presents a nice selection of main courses, such as salad Niçoise and an incredible pumpkin bread stuffed with pine nuts, corn, green chile, red-chile sauce, queso blanco, and caramelized apples. In the evening, the lights are dimmed, and the bright Santa Fe interior (with folk art on the walls and colorfully painted screens that divide the restaurant into smaller, more intimate areas) becomes a great place for a romantic dinner. The menu might include red-chile duck wontons in soy ginger cream to start and pecan-herb-crusted baked salmon with sorrel sauce as an entree. A popular choice is the ginger sesame filet mignon served with seared asparagus. For dessert, the chocolate ganache is fantastic. Wine and beer are available. Smoking is not permitted in the restaurant.

72 W. Marcy St. © **505/982-8738.** Reservations recommended for dinner. Lunch $6–$8.50; dinner $14–$19; twilight 3-course dinner $22. AE, DC, DISC, MC, V. Mon–Sat 11:30am–2pm; daily 5:30–9pm.

Pranzo Italian Grill ★★ REGIONAL ITALIAN   Housed in a renovated warehouse and freshly decorated in warm Tuscan colors, this sister of Albuquerque's redoubtable Scalo restaurant caters to diners with a contemporary atmosphere of modern abstract art and food prepared on an open grill. Homemade soups, salads, creative thin-crust pizzas, and fresh pastas are among the less expensive menu items. *Bianchi e nere al capesante* (black-and-white linguine with bay scallops in a seafood cream sauce) and *pizza ala pesto e gamberoni* (pizza with shrimp, pesto, goat cheese, and roasted peppers) are consistent favorites. Steak, chicken, veal, and fresh seafood grills—heavy on the garlic—dominate the dinner menu. The bar offers the Southwest's largest collection of grappas, as well as a wide selection of wines and champagnes by the glass. The upstairs rooftop terrace is lovely for seasonal moon-watching over a glass of wine.

540 Montezuma St. (Sanbusco Center). © **505/984-2645.** Reservations recommended. Main courses $6–$10 lunch, $6–$24 dinner. AE, DC, DISC, MC, V. Mon–Sat 11:30am–3pm and 5pm–midnight; Sun 5–10pm.

Santa Fe Railyard Restaurant & Bar ★ *Finds* NEW AMERICAN   Santa Fe local's most talked-about new spot, the Railyard, is a fun and thoughtful addition to the restaurant scene. Set in one of the city's old railroad buildings, the place offers a comfortable ambience and imaginative food at reasonable prices. The space has clean lines, with stained concrete floors and exposed ductwork, softened with maroon booths and wooden tables. Service is friendly and knowledgeable. If you like Cajun food, start with the Chesapeake crab cakes with shrimp bisque and jicama slaw. Move on to a fish special such as one I had recently—grilled swordfish with a caper butter sauce, pasta, and a salad—or if you're really hungry, try the pork tenderloin sandwich, served with a mild "mojo" sauce that's a bit sweet and quite delectable. At dinner, a favorite is the all-day-roasted lamb shank, served with roasted-garlic mashed potatoes. Desserts are made in-house, as is the ice cream, worth sampling. Select from a carefully considered wine list or from the full bar.

530 S. Guadalupe (¼ block north of Paseo de Peralta). ✆ **505/989-8363.** Reservations recommended on weekend nights. Main courses $7.50–$10 lunch, $18–$22 dinner. Summer daily 11am–2:30pm and 5–9pm; winter Mon–Sat 11am–2:30pm, Thurs–Sat 5–9pm.

Shohko Cafe ✿ JAPANESE/SUSHI   Santa Fe's favorite sushi restaurant serves fresh fish in a 150-year-old adobe building that was once a bordello. The atmosphere is sparse and comfortable, a blending of New Mexican decor (such as ceiling vigas and Mexican tile floors) with traditional Japanese decorative touches (rice-paper screens, for instance). Up to 30 fresh varieties of raw seafood, including sushi and sashimi, are served at plain pine tables in various rooms or at the sushi bar. Request the sushi bar, where the atmosphere is coziest, and you can watch the chefs at work. My mother likes the tempura combination with veggies, shrimp, and scallops. On an odd night, I'll order the salmon teriyaki, but most nights I have sushi, particularly the *anago* and spicy tuna roll—though if you're daring, you might try the Santa Fe Roll (with green chile, shrimp tempura, and *masago*). Wine, imported beers, and hot sake are available.

321 Johnson St. ✆ **505/983-7288.** Reservations recommended. Main courses $4.25–$17 lunch, $8.50–$25 dinner. AE, DISC, MC, V. Mon–Fri 11:30am–2pm; Sun–Thurs 5:30–9pm; Fri–Sat 5:30–9:30pm.

INEXPENSIVE

Atomic Grill CREATIVE SOUTHWESTERN   A block south of the plaza, this cafe offers decent patio dining at reasonable prices. Of course, there's indoor dining as well. The whole place has a hip and comfortable feel, and the food is prepared imaginatively. This isn't my choice for downtown restaurants, but it's great if you're dining at an odd hour, particularly late at night. For breakfast try the raspberry French toast made with home-baked challah bread, served with apricot-butter and maple syrup. For lunch, the green-chile stew is tasty, although it could use more chicken habañero sausage. The fish tacos are also nice, if a little bland (ask for extra salsa), and the burgers are good. They also have wood-fired pizzas; try the grilled chicken pesto one. For dessert, the carrot cake is big enough to share and is quite tasty. Wine by the glass and 100 different beers are available. The restaurant also delivers to the downtown area from 11am to midnight.

103 E. Water St. ✆ **505/820-2866.** Most items under $9. AE, DC, DISC, MC, V. Mon–Sat 10am–3am; Sun 10am–1am.

Blue Corn Café *Kids* NEW MEXICAN/MICROBREWERY   If you're ready for a fun and inexpensive night out, eating decent New Mexican food, this is your place. Within a clean and breezy decor—wooden tables and abstract art— you'll find a raucous and buoyant atmosphere, a good place to bring kids. The overworked waitstaff may be slow, but they're friendly. I recommend sampling dishes from the combination menu. You can get two to five items served with your choice of rice, beans, or one of the best *posoles* (hominy and chile) that I've tasted. I had the chicken enchilada, which I recommend, and the chalupa, which I don't because it was soggy. You can have tacos, tamales, and rellenos, too. Kids have their own menu and crayons to keep them occupied. There are nightly specials—the shrimp fajitas were tasty, served with a nice guacamole and the usual toppings. Since this is also a brewery, you might want to sample the High Altitude Pale Ale or the Plaza Porter. My beverage choice is the prickly-pear iced tea (black tea with enough cactus juice to give it a zing). The Spanish flan is tasty and large enough to share. **The Blue Corn Cafe & Brewery** (4056 Cerrillos Rd., Suite G; ⓒ **505/438-1800**), on the south side at the corner of Cerrillos and Rodeo roads, has similar fare and atmosphere.

133 W. Water St. ⓒ **505/984-1800.** Reservations accepted for parties of 6 or more. Main courses $7–$18. AE, DC, DISC, MC, V. Daily 11am–10pm.

Bumble Bee's Baja Grill ★ *Finds* *Kids* MEXICAN   This new "beestro" offers a refreshing twist on fast food. It's actually healthy! The secret? Tacos are made Mexican style, with a tortilla folded around quality meat, fish, and poultry grilled with veggies. You pick from an array of salsas. Waist watchers can sample from a selection of salads, including one with grilled chicken and avocado. Rotisserie chicken and various burritos round out the main menu, while kids have their own options, such as the quesadillas. Diners order at a counter, and a waiter brings the food. The decor is a bit Formica-esque for my tastes, though the primary colors are fun. During warm months, I try to nab a patio table. Evenings often offer live jazz music, when folks sit back and sip beer and wine. There's also a drive-through window.

301 Jefferson (from W. San Francisco St., take Guadalupe 2 blocks north). ⓒ **505/820-2862.** Main courses $5–$11. AE, MC, V. Mon–Sat 11am–9pm.

Cafe Dominic ★ AMERICAN/DELI   This cafe offers sophisticated flavors with casual ease in a comfortable urban environment. Diners order at a counter, and a waiter brings the food. The restaurant serves a variety of breakfasts as well as soups, salads, sandwiches, New Mexican food, grilled fish and meat, and pasta. My favorite is the cobb salad, which comes with crisp bacon, grilled chicken, Gorgonzola cheese, avocado, and egg wedges. For a real City Different bargain, try the grilled salmon, served with beans, rice, salad, and grilled foccacia ($13). When dessert rolls around, you can feast on a caramel turtle cheesecake or four-layer chocolate cake.

320 South Guadalupe. ⓒ **505/982-4743.** Main courses $5–$13. AE, MC, V. Mon 7:30am–3pm; Tues–Thurs 7:30am–8:30pm; Fri 7:30am–9pm; Sat 8am–9pm; Sun 8am–5pm.

Carlos's Gosp'l Cafe ★ DELI   Imaginatively prepared soups and sandwiches, as well as good home-style breakfasts, highlight the menu at this cafe in the courtyard of the First Interstate Bank building. Definitely try the hangover stew (potato, corn, and green-chile chowder with Monterey Jack cheese, served with tasty cornbread) or the deli sandwiches. Diners order at a counter, and a waiter brings the food. Service is friendly, though at times a little absent-minded. For breakfast, try the Santa Cruz breakfast burrito: two fried eggs, chile, cheese, and avocado wrapped in a tortilla. My favorite lunch is the Gertrude Stein sandwich, with Swiss cheese, tomato, red onion, sprouts, and mayonnaise. It comes with a generous portion of potato salad. Carlos's has outdoor tables set on a sunny patio, but many diners prefer to sit indoors, reading newspapers or chatting around the large common table. During the lunch hour it can be a busy, noisy place. Gospel and soul music play continually; paintings of churches and performers cover the walls.

125 Lincoln Ave. ⓒ **505/983-1841.** Menu items $3–$8. No credit cards. Mon–Sat 8–10:30am and 11am–3pm.

Guadalupe Cafe ★★ NEW MEXICAN   When I want New Mexican food, I go to this restaurant, and like many Santa Feans, I go there often. This casually elegant cafe is in a white stucco building that's warm and friendly and has a nice-size patio for dining in warmer months. Service is generally friendly and conscientious. For breakfast, try the spinach-mushroom burritos or huevos rancheros, and for lunch, the chalupas or stuffed *sopaipillas*. Any other time, I'd start with fresh roasted ancho chiles (filled with a combination of Montrachet and Monterey Jack cheeses and piñon nuts, and topped with your choice of chile) and move on to the sour-cream chicken enchilada or any of the other Southwestern dishes. Order both red and green chile ("Christmas") so that you can sample some of the best sauces in town. Beware, though: The chile here can be hot, and the chef won't put it on the side. Diners can order from a choice of delicious salads, such as a Caesar with chicken. There are also traditional favorites, such as chicken-fried steak and turkey piñon meatloaf. Daily specials are available, and don't miss the famous chocolate-amaretto adobe pie for dessert. Beer, wine, and margaritas are served.

422 Old Santa Fe Trail. ℂ **505/982-9762**. Breakfast $4.50–$8.75; lunch $6–$12; dinner $7–$15. DISC, MC, V. Tues–Fri 7am–2pm; Sat–Sun 8am–2pm; Tues–Sat 5:30–9pm.

La Choza ★★ NEW MEXICAN   This sister restaurant of The Shed (p. 95) offers some of the best New Mexican food in town at a convenient location near the intersection of Cerrillos Road and St. Francis Drive. When other restaurants are packed, you'll only wait a little while here. It's a warm, casual eatery with vividly painted walls; it's especially popular on cold days, when diners gather around the wood-burning stove and fireplace. Service is friendly and efficient. The menu offers enchiladas, tacos, and burritos on blue-corn tortillas, as well as green-chile stew, chile con carne, and carne adovada. The portions are medium-size, so if you're hungry, start with guacamole or nachos. For years, I've ordered the cheese or chicken enchilada, two dishes I will always recommend. My new favorite, though, is the blue-corn burritos (tortillas stuffed with beans and cheese) served with *posole;* the dish can be made vegetarian if you'd like. For dessert, you can't leave without trying the mocha cake (chocolate cake with a mocha pudding filling, served with whipped cream). Vegetarians and children have their own menus. Beer and wine are available.

905 Alarid St. ℂ **505/982-0909**. Lunch or dinner $7–$8.75. AE, DC, DISC, MC, V. Summer Mon–Sat 11am–9pm; winter Mon–Thurs 11am–8pm, Fri–Sat 11am–9pm.

Longevity Café ★ PACIFIC RIM   If peace and happiness could actually come in the form of tea, curry, and ambience, this is where you'd find it. Longevity Café defines New Age imagination. Set in a small downtown shopping center, it has boldly painted walls, well-spaced tables, and a counter where you order to have your food delivered to you. The fare is highly imaginative: elixirs, served hot or iced, top the menu, with specials running daily. I had an Andean Delight that was as tasty as a milkshake and had goodies such as macaroot (cures anything that ails you), soy milk, cinnamon, nutmeg, and honey. You may want to try the Virtual Buddha or the Blues Buster, made with herbs and spices. A long list of varied teas as well as chai and organic coffee are also available. The food is clean and light, with a small menu of dishes such as a teriyaki chicken bowl, with organic ingredients such as broccoli, edamame, carrots, and peas. The pad Thai is lighter than most but has excellent flavors. The dessert names are as enchant-ing as the flavors: Feast on ginger-gingko apple pie or ginseng-chai pumpkin pie. If that doesn't fill you, a local psychic or tarot card reader is often in residence, to give your mind plenty more to chew on.

122 W. San Francisco St. #214. ℂ **505/986-0403**. Lunch or dinner main courses $4–$9. AE, MC, V. Mon–Sat 11am–11pm; Sun noon–7pm.

Plaza Cafe ☆ AMERICAN/DELI/NEW MEXICAN/GREEK Santa Fe's best example of diner-style eating, this cafe has excellent food in a bright and friendly atmosphere right on the plaza. I like to meet friends here, sit in a booth, eat, and laugh about life. A restaurant since the turn of the 20th century, it's been owned by the Razatos family since 1947. The decor has changed only enough to stay comfortable and clean, with red upholstered banquettes, Art Deco tile, and a soda-fountain–style service counter. Service is always quick and conscientious, and only during the heavy tourist seasons will you have to wait long for a table. Breakfasts are excellent and large, and the hamburgers and sandwiches are good. I also like the soups and New Mexican dishes, such as the bowl of green-chile stew, or, if you're more adventurous, the pumpkin *posole*. Check out the Greek dishes, such as vegetable moussaka or beef and lamb gyros. Wash it down with an Italian soda, in flavors from vanilla to Amaretto. Alternatively, you can have a shake, a piece of coconut cream pie, or Plaza Cafe's signature dessert, *cajeta* (apple and pecan pie with Mexican caramel). Beer and wine are available.

54 Lincoln Ave. (on the plaza). © 505/982-1664. No reservations. Main courses $8–$15. AE, DISC, MC, V. Daily 7am–9pm.

Sage Bakehouse ☆ GOURMET CAFE Restaurants all over Santa Fe use elegantly sharp sourdough bread from this bakery on Cerrillos Road across from the Hotel Santa Fe. And whenever I'm going visiting, I'll stop and pick up a peasant loaf or some rich olive bread. If you're a bread lover, you might want to stop in for breakfast or lunch. The atmosphere is quiet and hip, with lots of marble and metal, a rounded counter, and a few small tables, as well as sidewalk seating during the warm months. Breakfasts include good espressos and mochas, and a bread basket that allows you to sample some of the splendid treats. There are also large blueberry muffins. Lunches are simple, with only a few sandwiches from which to choose, but you can bet they're good. Try the Black Forest ham and gruyere on rye or the roasted red bell pepper and goat cheese on olive. People all over town are talking about the chocolate chip cookies—rumor has it there's more chocolate than cookie in them.

535-C Cerrillos Rd. © 505/820-SAGE. All menu items under $8. MC, V. Mon–Sat 7am–5pm.

The Shed ☆☆ NEW MEXICAN This long-time locals' favorite is so popular that during lunch, lines often form outside. Half a block east of the plaza, a luncheon institution since 1953, it occupies several rooms and the patio of a rambling hacienda that was built in 1692. Festive folk art adorns the doorways and walls. The food is delicious, some of the best in the state, and a compliment to traditional Hispanic and Pueblo cooking. The cheese enchilada is renowned in Santa Fe. Tacos and burritos are good, too, all served on blue-corn tortillas, with pinto beans on the side. The green-chile soup is a local favorite. The Shed's Joshua Carswell has added vegetarian and low-fat Mexican foods to the menu, as well as a variety of soups and salads and grilled chicken and steak. Don't leave without trying the mocha cake, possibly the best dessert you'll ever eat. In addition to wine and a number of beers, there is full bar service.

113½ E. Palace Ave. © 505/982-9030. Reservations accepted at dinner. Lunch $5.75–$9.50; dinner $8–$17. AE, DC, DISC, MC, V. Mon–Sat 11am–2:30pm and 5:30–9pm.

Tía Sophia's ☆ *Finds* NEW MEXICAN If you want to see how real Santa Fe locals look and eat, go to this friendly downtown restaurant, now in its 31st year. You'll sit at big wooden booths and sip diner coffee. Daily breakfast specials include eggs with blue-corn enchiladas (Tues) and burritos with chorizo, potatoes, chile, and cheese (Sat). My favorites are the breakfast burrito and huevos rancheros (eggs over corn tortillas, smothered with chile). Beware of what you order because, as the menu states, Tía Sophia's is "not responsible for too hot chile." Because this is a popular place, be prepared to wait for a table.

210 W. San Francisco St. ℂ **505/983-9880.** Breakfast $2–$9.50; lunch $4–$9.50. MC, V. Mon–Sat 7am–1:55pm.

Tomasita's Cafe ★ NEW MEXICAN   When I was in high school, I used to eat at Tomasita's, a little dive on a back street. I always ordered a burrito, and I think people used to bring liquor in bags. It's now in a modern building near the train station, and its food has become renowned. The atmosphere is simple— hanging plants and wood accents—with lots of families sitting at booths or tables and a festive spillover from the bar, where many come to drink margaritas. Service is quick, even a little rushed, which is my biggest gripe about Tomasita's. Sure, the food is still tasty, but unless you go at some totally odd hour, you'll wait for a table, and once you're seated, you may eat and be out again in less than an hour. The burritos are still excellent, though you may want to try the chile rellenos, a house specialty. Vegetarian dishes, burgers, steaks, and daily specials are also offered. There's full bar service.

500 S. Guadalupe St. ℂ **505/983-5721.** No reservations; large parties call ahead. Lunch $5.25–$12; dinner $5.75–$13. DISC, MC, V. Mon–Sat 11am–10pm.

Upper Crust Pizza ★ (Kids) PIZZA/ITALIAN   Upper Crust serves Santa Fe's best pizzas, in an adobe house near the old San Miguel Mission. Meals-in-a-dish include the Grecian gourmet pizza (feta and olives) and the whole-wheat vegetarian pizza (topped with sesame seeds). You can either eat here or request free delivery (it takes about 30 min.) to your downtown hotel. Beer and wine are available, as are salads, calzones, sandwiches, and stromboli.

329 Old Santa Fe Trail. ℂ **505/982-0000.** Pizzas $7.25–$16. DISC, MC, V. Summer daily 11am–midnight; winter Sun–Thurs 11am–10pm, Fri–Sat 11am–11pm.

Zia Diner INTERNATIONAL/AMERICAN   Santa Fe's alternative weekly, *The Reporter,* awarded this local favorite the prize for the "Best Comfort Food" in town, and that phrase describes the place well. In a renovated 1880 coal warehouse, it's an Art Deco diner with a turquoise-and-mauve color scheme. It boasts a stainless-steel soda fountain and a shaded patio. Extended hours make it a convenient stopover after a movie or late outing; however, during key meals on weekends, it can get crowded and the wait can be long. The varied menu features homemade soups, salads, fish and chips, scrumptious piñon meatloaf, and, of course, enchiladas. Specials range from turkey potpie to Yankee pot roast to three-cheese calzone. I like the corn, green-chile, and asiago pie, as well as the soup specials. There are fine wines, a full bar, great desserts (for example, tapioca pudding, apple pie, and strawberry-rhubarb pie), and an espresso bar. You can get malts, floats, and shakes anytime.

326 S. Guadalupe St. ℂ **505/988-7008.** Reservations accepted only for parties of 6 or more. Lunch $5.75–$10; dinner $5.75–$17. AE, MC, V. Daily 11am–10pm.

3 The North Side

EXPENSIVE

El Nido ★ STEAK/SEAFOOD   This is my favorite place to eat when I'm with my friend Carla. Her family is old Santa Fe, as is this restaurant. In the warm atmosphere, decorated with birdcages and smooth adobe partitions and *bancos,* we always encounter interesting characters, and since Carla eats here weekly, she knows what to order. In fact, during our last visit, she pointed to a corner of the front room (where two fires blaze in winter) and jokingly said she was born there. In the 1950s and 1960s, her parents used to party and dance at El Nido into the wee hours of the morning. Indeed, El Nido (the Nest) has been a landmark for many years. Built as a residence in the 1920s, it was a dance hall and Ma Nelson's brothel before it became a restaurant in 1939.

The food here is fresh and well prepared, with just a touch of fusion (European and Cajun influences) added to the specials. I'd suggest coming here if you're a bit overloaded by the seasonings at restaurants such as Santacafé, Coyote Café, and the Anasazi. The place is roomy, and the service is friendly and informal. Carla insists on oysters Rockefeller for an appetizer, though you can also start with a lighter ceviche. For entrees, she always has the salmon, which is broiled, with a light dill sauce on the side. I enjoy the broiled lamb chops, served with a light and tasty spinach mint sauce. All meals come with salad and baked potato, rice, or french fries. For dessert, try the crème brûlée, or, if you're a chocolate lover, try the chocolate piñon torte. There's a full bar, including a good selection of wines and local microbrewed beers.

Bishop's Lodge Rd., at the center of Tesuque Village. ⓒ 505/988-4340. Reservations recommended. Main courses $15–$26. AE, DC, MC, V. Tues–Sun 5:30–9:30pm.

MODERATE

Tesuque Village Market AMERICAN/SOUTHWESTERN   You'll see sparkly Range Rovers parked alongside beat-up ranch trucks in front of this charming market and restaurant, an indication that the food here has broad appeal. Located under a canopy of cottonwoods at the center of this quaint village, the restaurant doesn't have the greatest food but makes for a nice adventure 15 minutes north of town. During warmer months, you can sit on the porch; in other seasons, the interior is comfortable, with plain wooden tables next to a deli counter and upscale market. For me, this is a breakfast place, where blue-corn pancakes rule. Friends of mine like the breakfast burritos and huevos rancheros. Lunch and dinner are also popular, and there's always a crowd (though, if you have to wait for a table, the wait is usually brief). For lunch, I recommend the burgers, and for dinner, one of the hearty specials, such as lasagna. For dessert, there's a variety of housemade pastries and cakes at the deli counter, as well as fancy granola bars and oversize cookies in the market. A kids' menu is available.

At the junction of Bishop's Lodge Rd. and NM 591, in Tesuque Village. ⓒ 505/988-8848. Reservations recommended for holidays. Main courses $5–$8 breakfast, $6–$12 lunch, $8–$20 dinner. MC, V. Summer daily 7am–10pm; winter daily 7am–9pm.

4 The South Side

Santa Fe's motel strip and other streets south of Paseo de Peralta have their share of good, reasonably priced restaurants.

MODERATE

Chow's ⓐ CREATIVE CHINESE   This upscale but casual restaurant, near the intersection of St. Francis and St. Michael's, is Chinese with a touch of health-conscious Santa Fe. The tasteful decor has lots of wood and earth tones, while the food is unconventional as well, and cooked without MSG. You can get standard pot stickers and fried rice, but you may want to investigate imaginatively named dishes such as Firecracker Dumplings (carrots, onions, ground turkey, and chile in a Chinese pesto-spinach sauce); Nuts and Birds (chicken, water chestnuts, and zucchini in a Szechuan sauce); or my favorite, Pearl River Splash (whole steamed boneless trout in a ginger-onion sauce). For dessert, try the chocolate-dipped fortune cookies. Wine by the bottle or glass as well as beer are available. Chow's has Chow's Chinese Bistro in Albuquerque, also with tasty food.

720 St. Michaels Dr. ⓒ 505/471-7120. Main courses $8–$17. MC, V. Mon–Sat 11:30am–2pm and 5–9pm.

mu du noodles ⭐⭐ PACIFIC RIM   If you're ready for a light, healthy meal with lots of flavor, head to this small restaurant about an 8-minute drive from downtown. There are two rooms, with plain pine tables and chairs and sparse Asian prints on the walls. The carpeted back room is cozier, and a woodsy-feeling patio is definitely worth requesting during the warmer months. The waitstaff is friendly and unimposing. I almost always order the Malaysian *laksa,* thick rice noodles in a blend of coconut milk, hazelnuts, onions, and red curry, stir-fried with chicken or tofu and julienned vegetables and sprouts. If you're eating with others, you may each want to order a different dish and share. The pad Thai is lighter and spicier than most, served with a chile/vinegar sauce. A list of beers, wines, and sakes is available, tailored to the menu. I'm especially fond of the ginseng ginger ale. Menu items change seasonally.

1494 Cerrillos Rd. ⓒ 505/983-1411. Reservations for parties of 3 or larger only. Main courses $9–$18. AE, DC, DISC, MC, V. Mon–Sat 5:30–9pm (sometimes 10pm in summer).

Steaksmith at El Gancho ⭐ STEAK/SEAFOOD   Surrounded by piñon and juniper about 15 minutes southeast of town on Old Pecos Trail, with a decor accented by raw wood, this steakhouse is a favorite for many Santa Fe locals. In fact, my mother and her best friend eat here regularly. They like the food and the festive atmosphere (there's often a crowd). I find the service quite uneven, especially for large parties. A creative appetizer menu of tapas ranges from ceviche to deep-fried avocado. My mother orders the grilled shrimp, and her friend orders the baby back ribs. Steak and Alaskan King crab are other friends' favorites. There is also a choice of salads, homemade desserts, and bread, plus a full bar and lounge (serving a tapas menu from 4pm) that even caters to cappuccino lovers.

At the intersection of Old Las Vegas Hwy. and El Gancho Way. ⓒ 505/988-3333. Reservations recommended. Main courses $9–$27. AE, DC, DISC, MC, V. Daily 4–9:30pm.

INEXPENSIVE

Felipe's Tacos MEXICAN   Locals buzz around this small rapid-food restaurant like *moscas en miel* (flies on honey), and it's no wonder—the food is *muy sabrosa* (very flavorful) and prepared with lean meats and fresh ingredients—no lard is used. You order at a counter, and the food generally comes quickly, ready for you to apply your own choice of a variety of salsas. As far as I'm concerned, there's only one thing to order here—it's so good, why bother with anything else? That's the original chicken burrito, charbroiled chicken with cheese, beans, avocado, and salsa. You can also get it with steak. I see plenty of quesadillas served as well, and during the morning hours, *la Mexicana burrito* (eggs, pico de gallo, potatoes, and beans) is popular. Avoid the tacos, which are bland. Nonalcoholic drinks are served.

1711 A Llano St., in St. Michael's Village. ⓒ 505/473-9397. All menu items under $7. No credit cards. Mon–Sat 9am–4:30pm.

Marisco's La Playa MEXICAN/SEAFOOD   What this Mexican seafood restaurant lacks in ambience, it makes up for in *comida sabrosa* (tasty food). Set

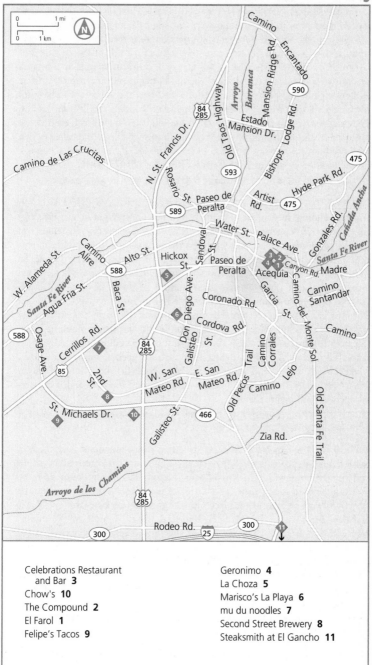

Celebrations Restaurant
  and Bar **3**
Chow's **10**
The Compound **2**
El Farol **1**
Felipe's Tacos **9**

Geronimo **4**
La Choza **5**
Marisco's La Playa **6**
mu du noodles **7**
Second Street Brewery **8**
Steaksmith at El Gancho **11**

in a small shopping mall not far from St. Francis Drive, it has a beach scene mural on one wall and stark luminescent lighting from above. It was opened by two cousins who wanted to bring good Mexican *playa* (beach) food to the dry-lands, and judging from the crowds here (you may have to wait 15–20 min., but it's worth it), they've succeeded. It features such dishes as shrimp or fish tacos and *pescado a la plancha* (trout seasoned with butter, garlic, and paprika). Some locals complain that the place is too pricey, but I say for good fish, it's a bargain. My Chinese doctor friend, Michael, says my favorite dish is excellent for my chi: The *caldo vuelve a la vida* (come-back-to-life soup) is a huge bowl, even if you order the small, of shrimp, octopus, scallops, clams, crab legs, and calamari in a tasty broth. Wash it down with a domestic or imported beer. There is a now a second location as well, at 2875 Cerrillos Rd. (② **505/473-4594**).

537 Cordova Rd. ② **505/982-2790**. Main courses $7–$13. AE, DISC, MC, V. Fri–Wed 11am–9pm.

Second Street Brewery MICROBREWERY/AMERICAN PUB FARE   In a metal building, tucked back off 2nd Street, this brewery has managed to cre-ate a lively pub scene and fairly warm atmosphere, and inside it's smoke-free. The walls, painted in gold hues, enclose a room containing interesting contem-porary art and wooden tables. It's a party type of place, especially during the warm months, when diners and beer savorers sit out on the patio. The beers are quite tasty—I had a hearty cream stout, and my friend enjoyed the amber ale. You can even get a 4-ounce sampler size for 75¢ and try a few different brews. The food isn't extremely memorable, but in winter, it can warm a hearty appetite with such home-style dishes as chicken potpie and shepherd's pie (a little too tomatoey for my taste). The jerk chicken breast is tasty, though it could use more sauce. The menu also offers lighter fare, such as quiches, soups, and salads. There's a kids' menu, and wines are available. Look for their "Hoppy" Hour, when beer prices are reduced. There are also darts all the time and live enter-tainment several nights a week.

1814 2nd St. (at the railroad tracks). ② **505/982-3030**. Main courses $4–$10. AE, DISC, MC, V. Sun–Thurs noon–10pm; Fri–Sat 11am–11pm (bar open later; call).

Tortilla Flats ✦ *Kids* NEW MEXICAN   This casual restaurant takes pride in its all-natural ingredients and vegetarian menu offerings (its vegetarian burrito is famous around town). The atmosphere is a bit like Denny's, but don't be fooled—the food is authentic. The blueberry pancakes are delicious, as are the fajitas and eggs with a side of black beans. I also like the blue-corn enchiladas and the chimichangas. The Santa Fe Trail steak (8 oz. of prime rib-eye smoth-ered with red or green chile and topped with grilled onions) will satisfy a big appetite. Above all, try the fresh tortillas and *sopaipillas,* made on the spot (you can even peek through a window into the kitchen and watch them being made). There's a full bar, with the legendary Ultimate Margarita, made with Grand Marnier and Cuervo Gold 1800 Tequila. A children's menu and a takeout serv-ice are available.

3139 Cerrillos Rd. ② **505/471-8685**. Breakfast $2–$8; lunch $5–$10; dinner $6–$11. DISC, MC, V. Sun–Thurs 7am–9pm (10pm in summer); Fri–Sat 7am–10pm.

What to See & Do in Santa Fe

One of the oldest cities in the United States, Santa Fe has long been a center for the creative and performing arts, so it's not surprising that most of the city's major sights are related to local history and the arts. The city's Museum of New Mexico, art galleries and studios, historic churches, and cultural sights associated with local Native American and Hispanic communities all merit a visit. It would be easy to spend a full week sightseeing in the city, without ever heading out to any nearby attractions. Of special note is the **Georgia O'Keeffe Museum.**

SUGGESTED ITINERARIES

If You Have 2 Days

Day 1 For an overview, start your first day at the Palace of the Governors; as you leave you might want to peruse the crafts and jewelry sold by Native Americans beneath the portal facing the plaza. After lunch, take a self-guided walking tour of old Santa Fe, starting at the plaza (see "Santa Fe Strolls," later in this chapter).

Day 2 Spend the morning at the Museum of Fine Arts and the afternoon browsing in the galleries on Canyon Road.

If You Have 3 Days

Day 3 Visit the cluster of museums on Camino Lejo—in particular, the Museum of International Folk Art, the Museum of Indian Arts & Culture, and the Wheelwright Museum of the American Indian. Then wander through the historic Barrio de Analco and spend the rest of the afternoon shopping.

If You Have 4 Days or More

Day 4 Devote your fourth day to exploring the pueblos, including San Juan Pueblo, headquarters of the Eight Northern Indian Pueblos Council, and San Ildefonso Pueblo, with its broad plaza.

Day 5 Go out along the High Road to Taos, with a stop at El Santuario de Chimayo, and return down the Rio Grande Valley. If you have more time, take a trip to Los Alamos, birthplace of the atomic bomb and home of the Bradbury Science Museum and Bandelier National Monument.

1 The Top Attractions

● **Museum of Fine Arts** ✪ Located opposite the Palace of the Governors, this was one of the first Pueblo Revival–style buildings constructed in Santa Fe (in 1917).

The museum's permanent collection of more than 20,000 works emphasizes regional art and includes landscapes and portraits by all the Taos masters, *los Cincos Pintores* (a 1920s organization of Santa Fe artists), and contemporary artists. The museum also has a collection of photographic works by such masters as Ansel Adams, Edward Weston, and Elliot Porter. Modern artists are featured in temporary exhibits throughout the year. Two sculpture gardens present a range of three-dimensional art, from the traditional to the abstract.

Graceful **St. Francis Auditorium,** patterned after the interiors of traditional Hispanic mission churches, adjoins the art museum (see "The Performing Arts," in chapter 9). A museum shop sells gifts, art books, prints, and postcards of the collection.

107 W. Palace (at Lincoln Ave.). © 505/476-5072. www.museumofnewmexico.org. Admission $7 adults, free for seniors Wed, free for children 16 and under, free for all Fri 5–8pm. 4-day passes (good at all 4 branches of the Museum of New Mexico and the Museum of Spanish Colonial Art) $15 for adults. Tues–Sun 10am–5pm (Fri until 8pm). Closed New Year's Day, Easter, Thanksgiving, Christmas.

Palace of the Governors ★★   In order to fully appreciate this structure, it's important to know that this is where the only successful Native American uprising took place in 1680. Prior to the uprising, this was the local seat of power, and after de Vargas reconquered the natives, it resumed that position. Built in 1610 as the original capitol of New Mexico, the palace has been in continuous public use longer than any other structure in the United States. A watchful eye can find remnants of the conflicts this building has seen through the years. Begin out front, where Native Americans sell jewelry, pottery, and some weavings under the protection of the portal. This is a good place to buy, and it's a fun place to shop, especially if you take the time to visit with the artisans about their work. When you buy a piece, you may learn its history, a treasure as valuable as the piece itself.

Inside, a map illustrates 400 years of New Mexico history, from the 16th-century Spanish explorations through the frontier era and modern times. A rickety stagecoach contains tools, such as farm implements and kitchen utensils, used by early Hispanic residents. There's a replica of a mid-19th-century chapel, with a simple, bright-colored altarpiece made in 1830 for a Taos church by folk artist José Rafael Aragón. What I find most interesting are the period photos scattered throughout. The building's exterior seems elaborate now, but it was once a simple flat-topped adobe with thin posts. You can see a fireplace and chimney chiseled into the adobe wall, and, in the west section of the museum, a cutaway of the adobe floor. Farther in that direction, unearthed in a recent excavation, are storage pits where the Pueblo Indians kept corn, wheat, barley, and other goods.

The museum focuses little on regional Native American culture. (Most Native American artifacts previously housed here have been moved to the Museum of Indian Arts & Culture.) However, a world-class collection of pre-Columbian art objects has been added. You'll see South and Central American ceramics, gold, and stonework dating from 1500 B.C. to A.D. 1500. There's also an impressive 18th-century Segesser Hide painting collection and an exhibit called "Jewish Pioneers of America."

Governors' offices from the Mexican and 19th-century U.S. eras have been restored and preserved. My favorite display is a set of spurs ranging from the 16th to the late 19th centuries, including a spur with 5-inch rowels. There are two shops of particular interest. One is the bookstore, which has one of the finest selections of art, history, and anthropology books in the Southwest. The other is the print shop and bindery, where limited-edition works are produced on hand-operated presses.

The palace is the flagship of the Museum of New Mexico system; the main office is at 113 Lincoln Ave. (© **505/476-5060**). The system comprises five state monuments and four Santa Fe museums: the Palace of the Governors, the

Downtown Santa Fe Attractions

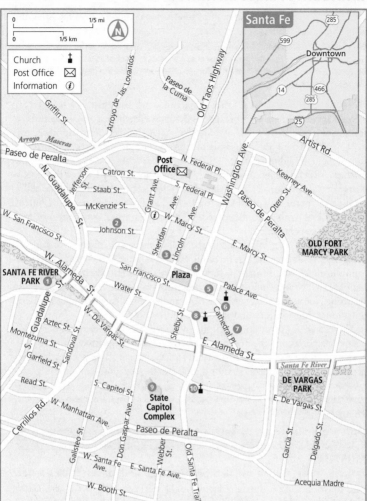

Catholic Museum & Lamy Garden **17**
Georgia O'Keeffe Museum **2**
Institute of American
   Indian Arts Museum **5**
Loretto Chapel Museum **8**
Mission of San Miguel **10**
Museum of Fine Arts **3**

New Mexico State Capitol
   (Roundhouse) **9**
Palace of the Governors **4**
Santuario de Nuestra Señora
   de Guadalupe **1**
St. Francis Cathedral **6**

Museum of Fine Arts, the Museum of International Folk Art, and the Museum of Indian Arts & Culture.

North plaza. ⓒ 505/476-5100. www.palaceofthegovernors.org. Admission $7 adults, free for children 16 and under, free for all Fri. 4-day passes (good at all 4 branches of the Museum of New Mexico and the Museum of Spanish Colonial Art) $15 for adults. Tues–Sun 10am–5pm. Closed New Year's Day, Thanksgiving, Christmas.

St. Francis Cathedral ⚹   Santa Fe's grandest religious structure is an architectural anomaly in Santa Fe because its design is French. Just a block east of the plaza, it was built between 1869 and 1886 by Archbishop Jean-Baptiste Lamy in the style of the great cathedrals of Europe. French architects designed the Romanesque building—named after Santa Fe's patron saint—and Italian masons assisted with its construction. The small adobe Our Lady of the Rosary chapel on the northeast side of the cathedral has a Spanish look. Built in 1807, it's the only portion that remains from Our Lady of the Assumption Church, founded along with Santa Fe in 1610. The new cathedral was built over and around the old church.

A wooden icon set in a niche in the wall of the north chapel, Our Lady of Peace, is the oldest representation of the Madonna in the United States. Rescued from the old church during the 1680 Pueblo Rebellion, it was brought back by Don Diego de Vargas on his (mostly peaceful) reconquest 12 years later—thus, the name. Today, Our Lady of Peace plays an important part in the annual Feast of Corpus Christi in June and July.

The cathedral's front doors feature 16 carved panels of historic note and a plaque memorializing the 38 Franciscan friars who were martyred during New Mexico's early years. There's also a large bronze statue of Bishop Lamy himself; his grave is under the main altar of the cathedral.

Cathedral Place at San Francisco St. ⓒ 505/982-5619. Donations appreciated. Open daily. Visitors may attend Mass Mon–Sat 7am and 5:15pm; Sun 8am, 10am, noon, and 5:15pm. Free parking in city lot next to the cathedral to attend church services.

2 More Attractions

MUSEUMS

Catholic Museum and the Archbishop Lamy Commemorative Garden
This museum will be especially interesting if you've read Willa Cather's *Death Comes for the Archbishop,* a fictional account of Archbishop Lamy's experience in northern New Mexico. If you haven't read it, as you visit the St. Francis Cathedral, The Bishop's Lodge, and other areas around Santa Fe, take special note of tales of the Archbishop because he is central to the area's history. The exhibition changes every few years, but you are likely to see a portrait of the determined, thin-lipped Frenchman—who resolutely battled what he felt was apostasy on the part of the Spanish clergy in New Mexico—and some of Lamy's personal items. All of the museum's changing exhibits feature objects and information about the 400-year-old history of the Catholic Church in New Mexico. The adjacent Lamy garden isn't much to see, but the gift shop has a nice collection of locally made religious articles.

223 Cathedral Place. ⓒ 505/983-3811. Donations appreciated. Mon–Fri 9am–4pm.

Georgia O'Keeffe Museum ⚹   For years, anxious visitors to Santa Fe asked, "Where are the O'Keeffes?" Locals flushed and were forced to answer: "The Metropolitan Museum of Art in New York and the National Gallery of Art in

Washington, D.C." Although this artist is known the world over for her haunting depictions of the shapes and colors of northern New Mexico, until rather recently, little of her work hung in the state.

The Georgia O'Keeffe museum, inaugurated in July 1997, contains the largest collection of O'Keeffes in the world: currently 117 oil paintings, drawings, watercolors, and pastels, and more than 50 works by other artists of note. It is the only museum in the United States dedicated solely to one woman's work. You can see such killer O'Keeffes as *Jimson Weed,* painted in 1932, and *Evening Star No. VII,* from 1917. The rich and varied collection adorns the walls of a cathedral-like, 13,000-square-foot space—a former Baptist church with adobe walls. O'Keeffe's images are tied inextricably to local desert landscapes. She first visited New Mexico in 1917 and returned for extended periods from the '20s through the '40s.

217 Johnson St. ℂ **505/946-1000.** www.okeeffemuseum.org. Admission $8, free for students, free for all Fri 5–8pm. July–Oct daily 10am–5pm (Fri until 8pm); Nov–June Thurs–Tues 10am–5pm (Fri until 8pm).

Indian Arts Research Center ⭐ Having grown up in New Mexico, surrounded by Native American arts, I had a hodgepodge knowledge of whose work looked like what. The center put my knowledge into an understandable framework. The School of American Research, of which the Indian Arts Research Center is a division, was established in 1907 as a center for advanced studies in anthropology and related fields. It sponsors scholarship, academic research, and educational programs, all in the name of keeping traditional arts alive.

The school has collected more than 10,000 objects, in the process compiling one of the world's finest collections of Southwest Indian pottery, jewelry, weavings, kachinas, paintings, baskets, and other arts that span from the prehistoric era (around 300–500 A.D.) to the present. You'll be led through temperature- and humidity-controlled rooms filled with work separated by tribe. Admission, however, is by tour only; see below for details.

School of American Research, 660 Garcia St. (off Canyon Rd.). ℂ **505/954-7205.** www.sarweb.org/ iarc/iarc.htm. Free admission for Native Americans and SAR members; $15 fee for others. Public tours given most Fri 2pm (call for reservations). Group tours can also be arranged. Limited parking.

Institute of American Indian Arts Museum ⭐ A visit to this museum (the most comprehensive collection of contemporary Native American art in the world) offers a profound look into the lives of a people negotiating two worlds: traditional and contemporary. Here, you'll see cutting-edge art that pushes the limits of many media, from creative writing to textile manufacturing to painting. One young artist says in a video, "I feel if I see one more warrior riding off into the sunset, I'm going to throw up." Much of the work originates from artists from The Institute of American Indian Arts (IAIA), the nation's only congressionally chartered institute of higher education devoted solely to the study and practice of the artistic and cultural traditions of all American Indian and Alaskan native peoples.

Exhibits change periodically, while a more permanent collection of Allan Houser's monumental sculpture is on display in the museum's Art Park. The museum store has a broad collection of contemporary jewelry, pottery, and other crafts, as well as books and music.

108 Cathedral Place. ℂ **505/983-8900.** www.iaiancad.org. Admission $4 adults, $2 seniors and students, free for children 16 and under. Oct–May Mon–Sat 10am–5pm, Sun noon–5pm; June–Sept daily 9am–5pm.

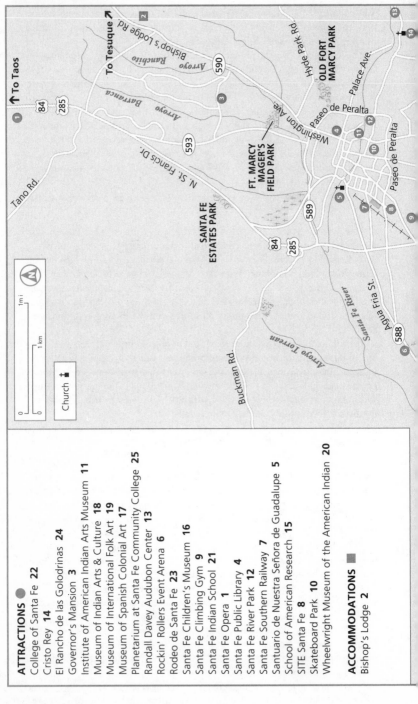

ATTRACTIONS ●

College of Santa Fe **22**
Cristo Rey **14**
El Rancho de las Golodrinas **24**
Governor's Mansion **3**
Institute of American Indian Arts Museum **11**
Museum of Indian Arts & Culture **18**
Museum of International Folk Art **19**
Museum of Spanish Colonial Art **17**
Planetarium at Santa Fe Community College **25**
Randall Davey Audubon Center **13**
Rockin' Rollers Event Arena **6**
Rodeo de Santa Fe **23**
Santa Fe Children's Museum **16**
Santa Fe Climbing Gym **9**
Santa Fe Indian School **21**
Santa Fe Opera **1**
Santa Fe Public Library **4**
Santa Fe River Park **12**
Santa Fe Southern Railway **7**
Santuario de Nuestra Señora de Guadalupe **5**
School of American Research **15**
SITE Santa Fe **8**
Skateboard Park **10**
Wheelwright Museum of the American Indian **20**

ACCOMMODATIONS ■

Bishop's Lodge **2**

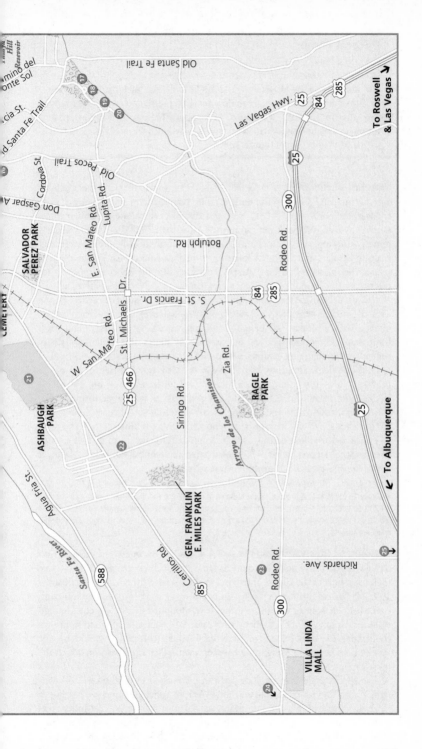

Cultural Chow

If you get hungry while visiting the Museum of Indian Arts & Culture, the Museum of International Folk Art, the Wheelwright Museum of the American Indian, and the Museum of Spanish Colonial Art (all located together, southeast of the plaza), you can now feast on more than your fingernails. The **Museum Hill Café** (© **505/820-1776**) opens Tuesday through Saturday for beverages and snacks at 10am, and a tasty lunch from 11am to 3pm; it serves Sunday brunch 11am to 3pm.

Museum of Indian Arts & Culture ★★   An interactive permanent exhibit here has made this one of the most exciting Native American museum experiences in the Southwest. "Here, Now and Always" takes visitors through thousands of years of Native American history. More than 70,000 pieces of basketry, pottery, clothing, carpets, and jewelry—much of it quite old—are on continual rotating display. You begin by entering through a tunnel that symbolizes the *sipapu,* the ancestral Puebloan (Anasazi) entrance into the upper worlds; you are greeted by the sounds of trickling water, drums, and Native American music. Videos show Native Americans telling creation stories. Visitors can reflect on the lives of modern-day Native Americans by juxtaposing a traditional Pueblo kitchen with a modern kitchen. You can step into a Navajo hogan and stroll through a trading post. The rest of the museum houses a lovely pottery collection as well as changing exhibits. There's always a contemporary show.

Look for demonstrations of traditional skills by tribal artisans and regular programs in a 70-seat multimedia theater. Call for information on year-round lectures and classes on native traditions and arts, as well as performances of Native American music and dancing by tribal groups. In February, look for an annual fiber show, and in June, a presentation on oral traditions.

The laboratory, founded in 1931 by John D. Rockefeller, Jr., is itself a point of interest. Designed by the well-known Santa Fe architect John Gaw Meem, it is an exquisite example of pueblo revival architecture.

710 Camino Lejo. © **505/476-1250.** www.miaclab.org. Admission $7 adults, free for kids 16 and under. 4-day passes (good at all 4 branches of the Museum of New Mexico and the Museum of Spanish Colonial Art) $15 for adults. Tues–Sun 10am–5pm. Drive southeast on Old Santa Fe Trail (beware: Old Santa Fe Trail takes a left turn; if you find yourself on Old Pecos Trail, you missed the turn). Look for signs pointing right onto Camino Lejo.

Museum of International Folk Art ★★ *Kids*   This branch of the Museum of New Mexico may not seem quite as typically Southwestern as other Santa Fe museums, but it's the largest of its kind in the world. With a collection of some 130,000 objects from more than 100 countries, it's my favorite city museum, well worth an hour or two of perusing. It was founded in 1953 by the Chicago collector Florence Dibell Bartlett, who said, "If peoples of different countries could have the opportunity to study each other's cultures, it would be one avenue for a closer understanding between men." That's the basis on which the museum operates today.

The special collections include Spanish colonial silver, traditional and contemporary New Mexican religious art, Mexican tribal costumes and majolica ceramics, Brazilian folk art, European glass, African sculptures, East Indian textiles, and the marvelous Morris Miniature Circus. Particularly delightful are numerous dioramas of people around the world at work and play in typical town, village, and home settings. Recent acquisitions include American weather vanes and quilts, Palestinian costume jewelry and amulets, and Bhutanese and Indonesian textiles.

Children love to look at the hundreds of toys on display throughout the museum, many of which are from a collection donated in 1982 by Alexander Girard, a notable architect and interior designer, and his wife, Susan. The couple spent their lives traveling the world collecting dolls, animals, fabrics, masks, and dioramas. They had a home in Santa Fe, where they spent many years before they died. Their donation included more than 100,000 pieces, 10,000 of which are exhibited at the museum.

The Hispanic Heritage Wing houses the country's finest collection of Spanish colonial and Hispanic folk art. Folk-art demonstrations, performances, and workshops are often presented here. The 80,000-square-foot museum also has a lecture room, a research library, and a gift shop, where a variety of folk art is available for purchase.

706 Camino Lejo. ℂ **505/476-1200.** www.moifa.org. Admission $7 adults, free for kids 16 and under. 4-day passes (good at all 4 branches of the Museum of New Mexico and the Museum of Spanish Colonial Art) $15 for adults. Tues–Sun 10am–5pm. The museum is located about 2 miles southeast of the plaza. Drive southeast on Old Santa Fe Trail (beware: Old Santa Fe Trail takes a left turn; if you find yourself on Old Pecos Trail, you missed the turn). Look for signs pointing right onto Camino Lejo.

Museum of Spanish Colonial Art ⭐   Beauty often follows in the tragic wake of imperialism. A good example of this point is Spanish colonial art, which has flourished from Europe across the Americas and even in the Philippines. This newer museum, located in the same compound as the Museum of International Folk Art, the Museum of Indian Arts & Culture, and the Wheelwright Museum of the American Indian, celebrates this art with a collection of 3,000 devotional and decorative works and utilitarian artifacts. Housed in a home built by noted architect John Gaw Meem, the museum displays *retablos* (religious paintings on wood), *bultos* (free-standing religious sculptures), furniture, metalwork, and textiles and, outside, an 18th-century wooden colonial house from Mexico.

750 Camino Lejo. ℂ **505/982-2226.** www.spanishcolonial.org. Admission $6 adults, free for kids 16 and under. 4-day passes (good at all 4 branches of the Museum of New Mexico and the Museum of Spanish Colonial Art) $15 for adults. Tues–Sun 10am–5pm. The museum is located about 2 miles southeast of the plaza. Drive southeast on Old Santa Fe Trail (beware: Old Santa Fe Trail takes a left turn; if you find yourself on Old Pecos Trail, you missed the turn). Look for signs pointing right onto Camino Lejo.

SITE Santa Fe ⭐   This not-for-profit, 18,000-square-foot contemporary art space without a permanent collection has made a place for itself in the City Different, as well as in the international art scene. It's no wonder, with shows by some of the world's most noted contemporary artists—in 2005, Jim Campbell will present his interactive multimedia works here, for example. As well as bringing cutting-edge visual art to Santa Fe, SITE sponsors an art and culture series of lectures, multidisciplinary programs, and artist dialogues. SITE sponsors other events, including a biennial exhibition that's well worth attending.

1606 Paseo de Peralta. ℂ **505/989-1199.** www.sitesantafe.org. $5 adults, $2.50 students and seniors, free for SITE Santa Fe members, free for all Fri. Wed–Sun 10am–5pm (Fri until 7pm). Closed Thanksgiving, Christmas Eve, Christmas, New Year's Eve, and New Year's Day. Call for information about docent tours and tours in Spanish.

Wheelwright Museum of the American Indian ⭐ *Kids*   Next door to the folk art museum, this museum resembles a Navajo hogan, with its doorway facing east (toward the rising sun) and its ceiling formed in the interlocking "whirling

---

Fun Fact Fetishes: Gifts of Power

According to Zuni lore, in the early years of human existence, the Sun sent down his two children to assist humans, who were under siege from earthly predators. The Sun's sons shot lightning bolts from their shields and destroyed the predators. For generations, Zunis, traveling across their lands in western New Mexico, have found stones shaped like particular animals. The Zunis believe the stones to be the remains of those long-lost predators, still containing their souls or last breaths.

Today, in many shops in Santa Fe you, too, can pick up a carved animal figure, called a *fetish*. According to belief, the owner of the fetish is able to absorb the power of that creature. Many fetishes were long ago used for protection and might in the hunt. Today, a person might carry a bear for health and strength or an eagle for keen perspective. A mole might be placed in a home's foundation for protection from elements underground, a frog buried with crops for fertility and rain, a ram carried in the purse for prosperity. For love, some locals recommend pairs of fetishes—often foxes or coyotes carved from a single piece of stone.

Many fetishes, arranged with bundles on top and attached with sinew, serve as an offering to the animal spirit that resides within the stone. Fetishes are still carved by many of the pueblos. A good fetish is not necessarily one that is meticulously carved. Some fetishes are barely carved at all, since the original shape of the stone already contains the form of the animal. When you have a sense of the quality and elegance available, decide which animal (and power) suits you best. Native Americans caution, however, that the fetish cannot be expected to impart an attribute you don't already possess. Instead, it will help elicit the power that already resides within you. Good sources for fetishes are **Dewey Galleries Limited,** 53 Old Santa Fe Trail, second floor (on the plaza; (C) **505/982-8632**) and **Keshi,** 227 Don Gaspar ((C) **505/989-8728**). Expect to pay $25 to $50 for a good one.

---

log" style. It was founded in 1937 by Boston scholar Mary Cabot Wheelwright, in collaboration with a Navajo medicine man, Hastiin Klah, to preserve and document Navajo ritual beliefs and practices. Klah took the designs of sand paintings used in healing ceremonies and adapted them into the woven pictographs that are a major part of the museum's treasure. In 1976, the museum's focus was altered to include the living arts of all Native American cultures. The museum offers three or four exhibits per year. You may see a basketry exhibit, mixed-media Navajo toys, or amazing contemporary Navajo rugs. An added treat here is the Case Trading Post, an arts-and-crafts shop built to resemble the typical turn-of-the-20th-century trading post found on the Navajo reservation. Docent tours of the exhibition are Monday to Wednesday and Friday at 2pm and Saturday at 11am. Year-round each Saturday and Tuesday morning at 10:15am and Sunday at 2pm, the Trading Post presents a lively and informative introduction to Southwestern Indian art. The museum has excellent access for travelers with disabilities.

704 Camino Lejo. ⓒ **800/607-4636** or 505/982-4636. Fax 505/989-7386. www.wheelwright.org. Donations appreciated. Mon–Sat 10am–5pm; Sun 1–5pm. Closed New Year's Day, Thanksgiving, and Christmas. Drive southeast on Old Santa Fe Trail (beware: Old Santa Fe Trail takes a left turn; if you find yourself on Old Pecos Trail, you missed the turn). Look for signs pointing right onto Camino Lejo.

CHURCHES

Cristo Rey   This Catholic church ("Christ the King," in Spanish), a huge adobe structure, was built in 1940 to commemorate the 400th anniversary of Coronado's exploration of the Southwest. Parishioners did most of the construction work, even making adobe bricks from the earth where the church stands. The local architect John Gaw Meem designed the building, in Mission style, as a place to keep some magnificent stone *reredos* (altar screens) created by the Spanish during the colonial era and recovered and restored in the 20th century.
Upper Canyon Rd. ⓒ **505/983-8528.** Free admission. Mon–Fri 8am–5pm.

● **Loretto Chapel Museum** ✦   Though no longer consecrated for worship, the Loretto Chapel is an important site in Santa Fe. Patterned after the famous Sainte-Chapelle church in Paris, it was constructed in 1873—by the same French architects and Italian masons who were building Archbishop Lamy's cathedral—as a chapel for the Sisters of Loretto, who had established a school for young women in Santa Fe in 1852.

The chapel is especially notable for its remarkable spiral staircase: It makes two complete 360-degree turns, with no central or other visible support. The structure is steeped in legend: The building was nearly finished in 1878, when workers realized the stairs to the choir loft wouldn't fit. Hoping for a solution more attractive than a ladder, the sisters made a novena to St. Joseph—and were rewarded when a mysterious carpenter appeared astride a donkey and offered to build a staircase. Armed with only a saw, a hammer, and a T-square, the master constructed this work of genius by soaking slats of wood in tubs of water to curve them and holding them together with wooden pegs. Then he disappeared without bothering to collect his fee.
207 Old Santa Fe Trail (between Alameda and Water sts.). ⓒ **505/982-0092.** www.lorettochapel.com. Admission $2.50 adults, $2 children 7–12 and seniors over 65, free for children 6 and under. Mon–Sat 9am–5pm; Sun 10:30am–5pm.

Mission of San Miguel   If you really want to get the feel of colonial Catholicism, visit this church. Better yet, attend Mass here. You won't be disappointed. Built in 1610, the church has massive adobe walls, high windows, an elegant altar screen (erected in 1798), and a 780-pound San José bell (now found inside), which was cast in Spain in 1356. If that doesn't impress you, perhaps the buffalo hide and deerskin Bible paintings used in 1630 by Franciscan missionaries to teach the Native Americans will. Anthropologists have excavated near the altar, down to the original floor that some claim to be part of a 12th-century pueblo. A small store just off the sanctuary sells religious articles.
401 Old Santa Fe Trail (at E. de Vargas St.). ⓒ **505/983-3974.** Admission $1 adults, free for children under 6. Mon–Sat 9am–5pm; Sun 10am–4pm. Summer hours start earlier. Mass Sun 5pm.

Santuario de Nuestra Señora de Guadalupe ✦   This church, built between 1776 and 1796 at the end of El Camino Real by Franciscan missionaries, is believed to be the oldest shrine in the United States honoring the Virgin of Guadalupe, the patron saint of Mexico. Better known as Santuario de Guadalupe, the shrine's adobe walls are almost 3 feet thick, and the deep-red plaster wall behind the altar was dyed with oxblood in traditional fashion when the church was restored early in the 20th century.

It is well worth a visit to see photographs of the transformation of the building over time; its styles have ranged from flat-topped pueblo to New England town meeting and today's northern New Mexico style. On one wall is a famous oil painting, *Our Lady of Guadalupe,* created in 1783 by the renowned Mexican artist José de Alzibar. Painted expressly for this church, it was brought from Mexico City by mule caravan.

100 S. Guadalupe St. ⓒ 505/988-2027. Donations appreciated. Mon–Sat 9am–4pm. Closed weekends Nov–Apr.

PARKS & REFUGES

Arroyo de los Chamisos Trail   This trail, which meanders through the southwestern part of town, is of special interest to those staying in hotels along Cerrillos Road. The 2.5-mile paved path follows a chamisa-lined arroyo (stream) and has mountain views. It's great for walking or bicycling; dogs must leashed.

Begin at Santa Fe High School on Yucca St. or on Rodeo Rd. near Sam's Club. ⓒ 505/955-2103.

Old Fort Marcy Park   Marking the 1846 site of the first U.S. military reservation in the Southwest, this park overlooks the northeast corner of downtown. Only a few mounds remain from the fort, but the Cross of the Martyrs, at the top of a winding brick walkway from Paseo de Peralta near Otero Street, is a popular spot for bird's-eye photographs. The cross was erected in 1920 by the Knights of Columbus and the Historical Society of New Mexico to commemorate the Franciscans killed during the Pueblo Rebellion of 1680. It has since played a role in numerous religious processions. Open daily 24 hours.

617 Paseo de Peralta (or travel 3 blocks up Artist Rd. and turn right).

Randall Davey Audubon Center ⭐   Named for the late Santa Fe artist who willed his home to the National Audubon Society, this wildlife refuge occupies 135 acres at the mouth of Santa Fe Canyon. Just a few minutes' drive from the plaza, it's an excellent escape. More than 100 species of birds and 120 types of plants live here, and varied mammals have been spotted—including black bears, mule deer, mountain lions, bobcats, raccoons, and coyotes. Trails winding through more than 100 acres of the nature sanctuary are open to day hikers, but not to dogs. There's also a natural history bookstore on site.

1800 Upper Canyon Rd. ⓒ 505/983-4609. Trail admission $1. Daily 9am–5pm. House tours conducted by appointment and sporadically during the summer $2 adults, $1 children under 12; call for hours. Gift shop daily 10am–4pm (call for winter hours). Free 1-hr. guided bird walk 1st Sat every month at 8:30am, 9am winter.

● **Santa Fe River Park**   This is a lovely spot for an early morning jog, a midday walk beneath the trees, or perhaps a sack lunch at a picnic table. The green strip, which does not close, follows the midtown stream for about 4 miles as it meanders along Alameda from St. Francis Drive upstream beyond Camino Cabra, near its source.

Alameda St. ⓒ 505/955-2103.

OTHER ATTRACTIONS

El Rancho de las Golondrinas ⭐ *Kids*   This 200-acre ranch, about 15 miles south of the plaza via I-25, was once the last stopping place on the 1,000-mile El Camino Real from Mexico City to Santa Fe. Today, it's a living 18th- and 19th-century Spanish village, comprising a hacienda, a village store, a schoolhouse, and several chapels and kitchens. There's also a working molasses mill, wheel-wright and blacksmith shops, shearing and weaving rooms, a threshing ground, a winery and vineyard, and four water mills, as well as dozens of farm animals. A walk around the entire property is 1¾ miles in length, with amazing scenery and plenty of room for the kids to romp.

The Spring Festival (the first full weekend of June) and the Harvest Festival (the first full weekend of Oct) are the year's highlights at Las Golondrinas (The Swallows). On these festival Sundays, the museum opens with a procession and Mass dedicated to San Ysidro, patron saint of farmers. Volunteers in authentic costumes demonstrate shearing, spinning, weaving, embroidery, wood carving, grain milling, blacksmithing, tinsmithing, soap making, and other activities. There's an exciting atmosphere of Spanish folk dancing, music, theater, and food.

334 Los Pinos Rd. 📞 **505/471-2261.** www.golondrinas.org. Admission $5 adults, $4 seniors and teens, $2 children 5–12, free for children under 5. Festival weekends $7 adults, $5 seniors and teens, $3 children 5–12. June–Sept Wed–Sun 10am–4pm; Apr–May and Oct open by advance arrangement. Closed Nov–Mar. From Santa Fe, drive south on I-25, taking exit 276; this will lead to NM 599 going north; turn left on W. Frontage Rd.; drive ½ mile; turn right on Los Pinos Rd.; travel 3 miles to the museum.

New Mexico State Capitol (Roundhouse)   Some are surprised to learn that this is the only round capitol building in the U.S. Built in 1966, it's designed in the shape of a Zia Pueblo emblem (or sun sign, which is also the state symbol). It symbolizes the Circle of Life: four winds, four seasons, four directions, and four sacred obligations. Surrounding the capitol is a lush 6½-acre garden boasting more than 100 varieties of plants, including roses, plums, almonds, nectarines, Russian olive trees, and sequoias. Inside you'll find standard functional offices, with New Mexican art hanging on the walls. Check out the Governor's Gallery and the Capitol Art Collection. Self-guided tours are available 8am to 5pm Monday through Friday year-round; Memorial Day to Labor Day guided tours are available Monday through Saturday at 10am and 2pm. All tours and self-guided brochures are free to the public.

Paseo de Peralta and Old Santa Fe Trail. 📞 **505/986-4589.** www.legis.state.nm.us. Free admission. Mon–Sat 8am–5pm. Free parking.

Santa Fe Climbing Gym   The walls of this two-story, cavernous gym are cov-ered with foot- and handholds, making it a perfect place to frolic, especially in winter. Rental gear is available.

825 Early St. 📞 **505/986-8944.** Daily passes $12 adults, $6 kids under 12. Weekdays 5–10pm; Sat 1–8pm.

Santa Fe Southern Railway ⋆   "Riding the old Santa Fe" always referred to riding the Atchison, Topeka & Santa Fe railroad. Ironically, the main route of the AT&SF bypassed Santa Fe, which probably forestalled some development for the capital city. A spur was run off the main line to Santa Fe in 1880, and today, an 18-mile ride along that spur offers views of some of New Mexico's most spectacular scenery.

The Santa Fe Depot is a well-preserved tribute to the Mission architecture that the railroad brought to the West in the early 1900s. Characterized by light-colored stuccoed walls, arched openings, and tile roofs, this style was part of an architectural revolution in Santa Fe at a time that builders snubbed the tradi-tional Pueblo style.

Inside the restored coach, passengers are surrounded by aged mahogany and faded velvet seats. The train snakes through Santa Fe and onto the New Mexico plains, broad landscapes spotted with piñon and chamisa, with views of the Sandia and Ortiz mountains. Arriving in the small track town of Lamy, you get another glimpse of a Mission-style station, this one surrounded by spacious lawns where passengers picnic. Check out the sunset rides on weekends and specialty trains throughout the year.

410 S. Guadalupe St. © **888/989-8600** or 505/989-8600. Fax 505/983-7620. www.sfsr.com. Tickets range from $15 (children) to $25 (adults), $30–$80 Fri–Sat evening rides (Apr–Oct). Depending on the season, trains depart the Santa Fe Depot (call to check winter schedule) 9:30am–1pm Mon–Sat. Rides also available Fri–Sat evening and Sun afternoon.

COOKING, ART & PHOTOGRAPHY CLASSES

If you're looking for something to do that's a little off the beaten tourist path, you might consider taking a class.

You can master the flavors of Santa Fe with an entertaining 3-hour demonstration cooking class at the **Santa Fe School of Cooking and Market** ★, on the upper level of the Plaza Mercado, 116 W. San Francisco St. (© **505/983-4511;** fax 505/983-7540; www.santafeschoolofcooking.com). The class teaches about the flavors and history of traditional New Mexican and contemporary Southwestern cuisines. "Cooking Light" classes are available as well. Prices range from $40 to $88 and include a meal; call for a class schedule. The adjoining market offers a variety of regional foods and cookbooks, with gift baskets available.

If Southwestern art has you hooked, you can take a drawing and painting class led by Santa Fe artist Jane Shoenfeld. Students sketch such outdoor subjects as the Santa Fe landscape and adobe architecture. In case of inclement weather, classes are held in the studio. Each class lasts for 3 hours, and art materials are included in the fee, which ranges from $85 to $90. Private lessons can also be arranged. All levels of experience are welcome. Children's classes can be arranged. You can create your own personal art adventure with one of Shoenfeld's 1-day classes at Ghost Ranch in Abiquiu, or a 5-day intensive class (also held at Ghost Ranch). Contact Jane at **Sketching Santa Fe,** P.O. Box 5912, Santa Fe, NM 87502 (© **505/986-1108;** fax 505/986-3845; www.skyfields.net).

Some of the world's most outstanding photographers convene in Santa Fe at various times during the year for the **Santa Fe Photography & Digital Workshops,** P.O. Box 9916, Santa Fe, NM 87504, at a delightful campus in the hills on the east side of town (© **505/983-1400;** www.santafeworkshops.com). Most courses are full-time, lasting a week. Food and lodging packages are available.

WINE TASTINGS

If you enjoy sampling regional wines, consider visiting the wineries within easy driving distance of Santa Fe: **Balagna Winery/Il Santo Cellars,** 223 Rio Bravo Dr., in Los Alamos (© **505/672-3678**), north on US 84/285 and then west on NM 502; **Santa Fe Vineyards,** with a retail outlet at 235 Don Gaspar Avenue, in Santa Fe (© **505/982-3474**), or the vineyard itself about 20 miles north of Santa Fe on US 84/285 (© **505/753-8100**); **Madison Vineyards & Winery,** in Ribera (© **505/421-8028**), about 45 miles east of Santa Fe on I-25 North; and the **Black Mesa Winery,** 1502 Hwy. 68, in Velarde (© **800/852-6372**), north on US 84/285 to NM 68. Be sure to call in advance to find out when the wineries are open for tastings and to get specific directions.

3 Especially for Kids

Don't miss taking the kids to the **Museum of International Folk Art,** where they'll love the international dioramas and the toys (discussed earlier in this chapter). Also visit the tepee at the **Wheelwright Museum of the American**

Indian (discussed earlier in this chapter), where storyteller Joe Hayes spins tra-ditional Spanish *cuentos,* Native American folk tales, and Wild West tall tales on weekend evenings. **The Bishop's Lodge** has extensive children's programs dur-ing the summer. These include horseback riding, swimming, arts-and-crafts pro-grams, and special activities, such as archery and tennis. Kids are sure to enjoy **El Rancho de las Golondrinas** (discussed above), a living 18th- and 19th-cen-tury Spanish village comprising a hacienda, a village store, a schoolhouse, and several chapels and kitchens.

The **Genoveva Chavez Community Center** is a full-service family recreation center on the south side of Santa Fe (3221 Rodeo Rd.). The complex includes a 50m pool, a leisure pool, a therapy pool, an ice-skating rink, three gyms, a work-out room, racquetball courts, and an indoor running track, as well as a spa and sauna. For hours and more information, call ℂ **505/955-4001.**

Planetarium at Santa Fe Community College
The planetarium offers imaginative programs, combining star shows with storytelling and other inter-active techniques. Among the planetarium's inventive programs: Rusty Rocket's Last Blast, in which kids launch a model rocket; and the Solar System Stakeout, in which kids build a solar system. There's also a 10-minute segment on the cur-rent night sky. Programs vary, from those designed for preschoolers to ones for high school kids.

6401 Richards Ave. (south of Rodeo Rd.). ℂ **505/428-1677,** or 505/428-1777, Option 6, for the information line. www.sfccnm.edu/planetarium. Admission $5 adults, $3 seniors and children 12 and under. Live lecture 1st Wed of month 7–8pm; Celestial Highlights (live program mapping the night sky for that particular month) 1st Thurs of month 7–8pm; pre-recorded shows 2nd and 4th Thurs of month.

Rockin' Rollers Event Arena
This roller rink offers public-skating sessions and lessons as well as rentals. There's a concession area where kids can get snacks. In-line skates are allowed.

2915 Agua Fria St. ℂ **505/473-7755.** Public skating sessions summers only Mon–Fri 1–3pm and 3–5pm.

Rodeo de Santa Fe 🌟
The rodeo is usually held sometime around June 21. It's a colorful and fun Southwestern event for kids, teens, and adults. (See "Northern New Mexico Calendar of Events," in chapter 2, for details.)

3237 Rodeo Rd. ℂ **505/471-4300.**

Santa Fe Children's Museum 🌟
This museum offers interactive exhibits and hands-on activities in the arts, humanities, and science. The most notable features include a 16-foot climbing wall that kids—outfitted with helmets and harnesses—can scale, and a 1-acre Southwestern horticulture garden, complete with animals, wetlands, and a greenhouse. This fascinating area serves as an out-door classroom for ongoing environmental educational programs. Special per-formances and hands-on sessions with artists and scientists are regularly scheduled. Recently, *Family Life* magazine named this as 1 of the 10 hottest chil-dren's museums in the nation.

1050 Old Pecos Trail. ℂ **505/989-8359.** www.santafechildrensmuseum.org. Admission $4; children under 12 must be accompanied by an adult. Wed–Sat 10am–5pm; Sun noon–5pm.

Santa Fe Public Library
Special programs, such as storytelling and magic shows, can be found here weekly throughout the summer. The library is located in the center of town, 1 block from the plaza.

145 Washington Ave. ℂ **505/955-6780.** www.santafelibrary.org. Mon–Thurs 10am–9pm; Fri–Sat 10am–6pm; Sun 1–5pm. Call for additional information.

Skateboard Park   Split-level ramps for daredevils, park benches for onlookers, and climbing structures for youngsters are located at this park near downtown.

At the intersection of de Vargas and Sandoval sts. (© 505/955-2100. Free admission. Open 24 hr.

4 Santa Fe Strolls

Santa Fe, with its intricate streets and resonant historical architecture, lends itself to walking. The city's downtown core extends only a few blocks in any direction from the plaza, and the ancient Barrio de Analco and the Canyon Road artists' colony are a mere stone's throw away.

WALKING TOUR 1   THE PLAZA AREA

Start:	The plaza.
Finish:	Loretto Chapel.
Time:	1 to 5 hours, depending on the length of visits to the museums and churches.
Best Times:	Any morning before the afternoon heat, but after the Native American traders have spread out their wares.

➊ The Plaza
This square has been the heart and soul of Santa Fe, as well as its literal center, since its concurrent establishment with the city in 1610. Originally designed as a meeting place, it has been the site of innumerable festivals and other historical, cultural, and social events. Long ago the plaza was a dusty hive of activity as the staging ground and terminus of the Santa Fe Trail. Today, those who congregate around the central monument enjoy the best people-watching in New Mexico. In 2004, they also enjoyed watching an excavation that revealed Native American treasures, with plans for continued work there. The dig came about as a result of construction on a new gazebo/bandstand. Santa Feans understandably feel nostalgic for the days when the plaza, now the hub of the tourist trade, still belonged to locals rather than outside commercial interests.

Facing the plaza on its north side is the:
➋ Palace of the Governors
Today the flagship of the New Mexico State Museum system (see "The Top Attractions," above), the Palace of the Governors has functioned continually

as a public building since it was erected in 1610 as the capitol of Nuevo Mexico. Every day, Native American artisans spread out their crafts for sale beneath its portal.

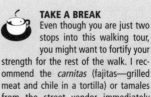

TAKE A BREAK
Even though you are just two stops into this walking tour, you might want to fortify your strength for the rest of the walk. I recommend the *carnitas* (fajitas—grilled meat and chile in a tortilla) or tamales from the street vendor immediately opposite the Palace, at Lincoln and Palace avenues.

If you stopped at Lincoln and Palace avenues for a *carnita*, you're now in front of the:
➌ Museum of Fine Arts
Located at 107 W. Palace Ave., the museum holds works by Georgia O'Keeffe and other famed 20th-century Taos and Santa Fe artists. The building is a fine example of Pueblo Revival–style architecture, and it is home to the renowned St. Francis Auditorium (see "The Top Attractions," above, and "The Performing Arts," in chapter 9).

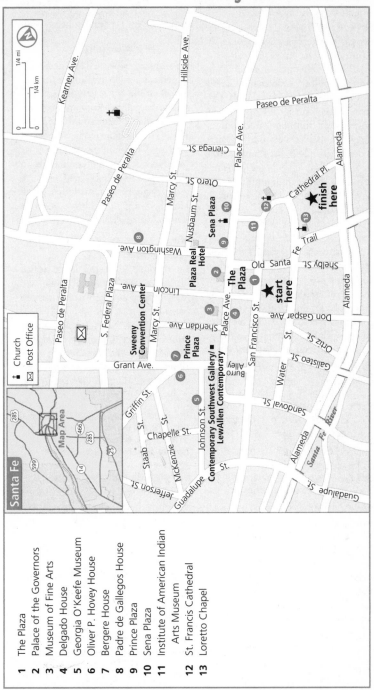

Santa Fe

Map Area

- 285
- 466
- 25
- 14
- 599

† Church
⊠ Post Office

1/4 mi
1/4 km
0
0

Kearney Ave.

Paseo de Peralta

Hillside Ave.

Paseo de Peralta

Cienega St.

Palace Ave.

Marcy St.

Otero St.

Nusbaum St.

Sena Plaza

Cathedral Pl.

Alameda

finish here ★

12

10

11

13

Washington Ave.

Plaza Real Hotel

8

2

Santa Fe Trail

9

Old Santa

Shelby St.

Paseo de Peralta

S. Federal Plaza

Lincoln

The Plaza

1

★ **start here**

Alameda

Marcy St.

Ave.

Palace Ave.

San Francisco St.

Don Gaspar Ave.

Sweeny Convention Center

3

Sheridan Ave.

4

Ortiz St.

Paseo de Peralta

Burro Alley

Water St.

Galisteo St.

Prince Plaza

7

Grant Ave.

6

Contemporary Southwest Gallery/ LewAllen Contemporary

Sandoval St.

Santa Fe River

Griffin St.

St.

Chapelle St.

Johnson St.

McKenzie

St.

Alameda

Guadalupe St.

Staab St.

Jefferson St.

Guadalupe

Virtually across the street is the:

④ Delgado House

This Victorian mansion (at 124 W. Palace Ave.) is an excellent example of local adobe construction, modified by late-19th-century architectural detail. It was built in 1890 by Felipe B. Delgado, a merchant most known for his business of running mule and ox freight trains over the Santa Fe Trail to Independence and the Camino Real to Chihuahua. The home remained in the Delgado family until 1970. It now belongs to the Historic Santa Fe Foundation.

If you continue west on Palace Avenue, you'll come to two galleries worth perusing. The first is the **Contemporary Southwest Gallery,** where you'll find lots of vivid landscapes, but little that extends the limits of the genre. Next door, however, you'll come to **LewAllen Contemporary,** where you'll find an array of paintings, sculptures, ceramics, and work in other media that may make you stop and ponder.

Nearby, you'll see a narrow lane—Burro Alley—jutting south toward San Francisco Street. You may want to head down the lane and peek into **Downtown Bed and Bath,** where you'll find a selection of bath and home accessories, including down pillows and comforters, aromatic candles, and furniture.

Head back to Palace Avenue, make your way north on Grant Avenue, and turn left on Johnson Street to the:

⑤ Georgia O'Keeffe Museum

Opened in 1997, this museum houses the largest collection of O'Keeffe works in the world. The 13,000-square-foot space is the largest museum in the United States dedicated solely to one woman's work. You might also want to stop at the museum's **O'Keeffe Café** (discussed in more detail in chapter 6) for one of its creative lunch or dinner entrees.

Head back to Grant Avenue, and continue north to number 136 Griffin St., where you'll find the:

⑥ Oliver P. Hovey House

Constructed between 1857 and 1859 in Territorial style, this adobe (located at 136 Griffin St.) is unique because it is actually painted brick. It's not surprising that a flamboyant man like Hovey would go to the trouble to dress up a home in such a fancy style (red brick was a rare commodity in this outpost town back then), but such stunts might be what made people call him the Great Lord Hovey, when he was no lord at all.

Across the street (no. 135 Griffin St.) is the:

⑦ Bergere House

Built around 1870, this house hosted U.S. President Ulysses S. Grant and his wife Julia during their 1880 visit to Santa Fe.

Proceed north on Grant, turning right on Marcy. On the north side of this corner is the **Sweeney Convention Center,** host of major exhibitions and home of the Santa Fe Convention and Visitors Bureau.

Three blocks farther east, through a residential, office, and restaurant district, turn left on Washington Avenue. Walk a short distance to 227–237 Washington Ave., where you'll see the:

⑧ Padre de Gallegos House

This house was built in 1857 in the Territorial style. Padre de Gallegos was a priest who, in the eyes of newly arrived Archbishop Jean-Baptiste Lamy, kept too high a social profile and was therefore defrocked in 1852. Gallegos later represented the territory in Congress and eventually became the federal superintendent of Native American affairs.

Reverse course and turn south again on Washington Avenue, passing en route the public library and some handsomely renovated accommodations such as the Territorial Inn.

TAKE A BREAK
This is a good time to stop for refreshments at a little cart in front of the Plaza Real; during summer, you'll find a variety of drinks served on the veranda, and in winter, the small bar inside can be quite cozy.

Leaving the hotel, you'll notice the entrance to the Palace of the Governors archives across the street. As you approach the plaza, turn left (east) on Palace Avenue. A short distance farther on your left, at 113 E. Palace Ave., is:

9 Prince Plaza
A former governor's home, this Territorial-style structure, which now houses **The Shed** restaurant, had huge wooden gates to keep out tribal attacks.

Next door is:

10 Sena Plaza
This city landmark offers a quiet respite from the busy streets, with its parklike patio. **La Casa Sena** restaurant (a great place to stop for lunch or dinner) is the primary occupant of what was once the 31-room Sena family adobe hacienda, built in 1831. The Territorial legislature met in the upper rooms of the hacienda in the 1890s.

Turn right (south) on Cathedral Place to no. 108, which is the:

11 Institute of American Indian Arts Museum
Here you'll find the most comprehensive collection of contemporary Native American art in the world (see "More Attractions," above).

Across the street, step through the doors of the:

12 St. Francis Cathedral
Built in Romanesque style between 1869 and 1886 by Archbishop Lamy, this is Santa Fe's grandest religious edifice. It has a famous 17th-century wooden Madonna known as *Our Lady of Peace* (see "The Top Attractions," above).

After leaving the cathedral, walk around the backside of the illustrious La Fonda Hotel—south on Cathedral Place and west on Water Street—to the intersection of the Old Santa Fe Trail. Here, in the northwest corner of the Hotel Loretto, you'll find the:

13 Loretto Chapel
This chapel is more formally known as the Chapel of Our Lady of Light. Lamy was also behind the construction of this chapel, built for the Sisters of Loretto. It is remarkable for its spiral staircase, which has no central or other visible support (see "More Attractions," above).

TAKE A BREAK
By now you may be tired and hungry. I recommend heading straight back to the plaza to a small store called **Five and Dime General Store**, where F. W. Woolworth's, the now-defunct, legendary five-and-dime store, once stood. Like Woolworth's, the store serves a cherished local delicacy called Frito pie: a bag of Fritos smothered in chile con carne, served in a plastic bag with a spoon and a napkin.

WALKING TOUR 2	BARRIO DE ANALCO & CANYON ROAD

Start:	Don Gaspar Avenue and East de Vargas Street.
Finish:	Any of the quaint restaurants on Canyon Road.
Time:	1 to 3 hours, depending on how long you spend in the art galleries.
Best Times:	Anytime.

The Barrio de Analco, now called East de Vargas Street, is one of the oldest continuously inhabited avenues in the United States. Spanish colonists, with their

Mexican and Native American servants, built homes here in the early 1600s, when Santa Fe was founded; some of the structures survive to this day.

Most of the houses you'll see as you walk east on de Vargas are private residences, not open for viewing. Even so, they are well worth looking at because of the feeling they evoke of a Santa Fe now relegated to bygone days. Most have interpretive historical plaques on their outer walls.

The first house you'll see is:

❶ Tudesqui House

Dating from the early 19th century, this house (129 E. de Vargas St.) is now recognizable for the wisteria growing over its adobe walls.

Across the street is the:

❷ Gregoria Crespin House

The records of this house (132 E. de Vargas St.) date back at least to 1747, when it was sold for 50 pesos. Originally of pueblo design, it later had Territorial embellishments added in the trim of bricks along its roofline.

Just down the road is the:

❸ Santa Fe Playhouse

Home to the oldest existing thespian group in New Mexico, this original adobe theater (at 142 E. de Vargas St.) still holds performances. (See "The Performing Arts," in chapter 9.)

In the next block, at 401 Old Santa Fe Trail, is the:

❹ Mission of San Miguel

Built around 1612, this ranks as one of the oldest churches in the United States (see "More Attractions," above). Today, it's maintained and operated by the Christian Brothers.

Across de Vargas Street from the Mission of San Miguel is the so-called:

❺ Oldest House in the United States

Whether or not this is true is anybody's guess, but this is among the last of the poured-mud adobe houses and may have been built by Pueblo people. The new owners, who run a crafts shop here, date the place between 1200 and 1646.

TAKE A BREAK
This might be a good time to stop in at **Jane's,** 237 E. de Vargas. Jane serves excellent coffee and tea and tasty sandwiches and soups under shady elm trees.

There are more homes at the east end of de Vargas, before its junction with Canyon Road. Among them is the:

❻ Boyle House

This house (located at 327 E. de Vargas St.) on the left side of the street was built in the mid–18th century as a hacienda.

Up the block and across the street is the:

❼ José Alarid House

Built in the 1830s, this house (at 338 E. de Vargas St.) is a one-story house with a pitched metal roof in the grand style of a hacienda.

East de Vargas crosses Paseo de Peralta, entering an alleyway. Immediately on the right is the:

❽ Adolph Bandelier House

This house (located at 352 E. de Vargas St.) was the home of the famous archaeologist who unearthed the prehistoric ruins at Bandelier National Monument. It has recently undergone a fine restoration.

Extending for a mile or so before you, Canyon Road was once a Native American trail used by the Pueblo tribes and traders. When the Pueblo tribes came to launch their

Travel Tip: He who finds the best hotel deal has more to spend on facials involving knobbly vegetables.

Hello, the Roaming Gnome here. I've been nabbed from the garden and taken round the world. The people who took me are so terribly clever. They find the best offerings on Travelocity. For very little cha-ching. And that means I get to be pampered and exfoliated till I'm pink as a bunny's doodah.

travelocity®

1-888-TRAVELOCITY / travelocity.com / America Online Keyword: Travel

Plan your vacation

- flights, hotels, car rentals
- cruises & vacation packages
- destination guides
- fare alerts
- go to yahoo.com, click travel

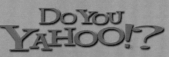

Walking Tour: Barrio de Analco & Canyon Road

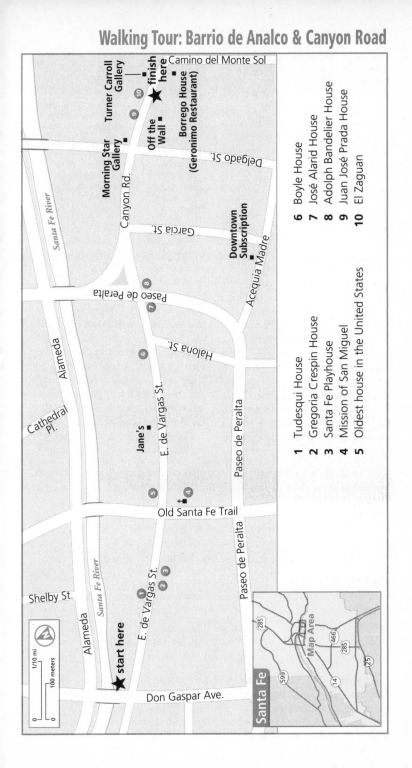

1 Tudesqui House
2 Gregoria Crespin House
3 Santa Fe Playhouse
4 Mission of San Miguel
5 Oldest house in the United States
6 Boyle House
7 José Alarid House
8 Adolph Bandelier House
9 Juan José Prada House
10 El Zaguan

1680 insurrection against the Spanish colonists, they used this route. Today it's lined with art galleries, shops, and restaurants. Its historic buildings include the:

⑨ Juan José Prada House

This house (at 519 Canyon Rd.) dates from about 1760. A few doors before you get to it, you'll come to **Morning Star Gallery,** a great place to glimpse and buy museum-quality Native American arts and artifacts.

Farther up the road is:

⑩ El Zaguan

This building (located at 545 Canyon Rd.) is a beautiful example of a Spanish hacienda. In warmer months, be sure to walk through the garden, subject of many Santa Fe paintings. El Zaguan is the headquarters of the **Historic Santa Fe Foundation** (© **505/983-2567;** www.historic santafe.com). A publication of the foundation, *Old Santa Fe Today* ($10 for non-members), gives detailed descriptions, with a map and photos, of approximately 80 sites within walking distance of the plaza. The office is generally open weekdays 9am to 5pm; closed Sunday.

> **TAKE A BREAK**
> If you're ready for a break, look for **Off the Wall,** a gallery and coffee shop on your right. It serves drinks and pastries in a cozy, colorful atmosphere. Farther up Canyon Road you may want to stop at the old Borrego House, which is now **Geronimo Restaurant,** for lunch or dinner. Across the street is **Turner Carroll Gallery,** where you'll find very eclectic art.

If you have the stamina to continue, I suggest that you turn right on Camino del Monte Sol, then right again on Camino del Poniente, and bear right onto Acequia Madre (Mother Ditch). This narrow lane winds through one of Santa Fe's oldest and most notable residential districts. It follows the mother ditch, used for centuries to irrigate gardens in the area. A 20- to 30-minute walk will bring you to **Downtown Subscription,** where you can have some excellent coffee and baked goods. From there, you can take Garcia Street north, back to the base of Canyon Road.

5 Organized Tours

BUS, CAR & TRAM TOURS

LorettoLine For an open-air tour of the city, contact LorettoLine. Tours last 1½ hours and are offered daily from April to October. Tour times are every hour on the hour during the day from 10am to 3pm.

At the Hotel Loretto, 211 Old Santa Fe Trail. © **505/983-3701.** Tours $12 adults, $6 children.

WALKING TOURS

As with the independent strolls described above, the following are the best way to get an appreciable feel for Santa Fe's history and culture.

A Foot in Santa Fe ⊛ Personalized 2-hour tours are offered year-round at 9:30am from the Hotel Loretto. Reservations are not required.

At the Hotel Loretto, 211 Old Santa Fe Trail. © **505/983-3701.** Tours $10.

Storytellers and the Southwest: A Literary Walking Tour ⊛ Barbara Harrelson, a former Smithsonian museum docent and local writer, takes you on a 2-hour literary walking tour of downtown, exploring the history, legends, characters, and authors of the region through its landmarks and historic sites. It's a great way to absorb the unique character of Santa Fe. Tours take place by appointment.

924 Old Taos Hwy. ✆ **505/989-4561**. www.sfaol.com/books/littour.html. Apr–Oct. Tours $15 per person, 2-person minimum.

Walking Tour of Santa Fe ✎   One of Santa Fe's best walking tours begins under the T-shirt tree at Tees & Skis, 107 Washington Ave., near the northeast corner of the plaza (at 9:30am and 1:30pm). It lasts about 2½ hours.

54½ E. San Francisco St. (tour meets at 107 Washington Ave.). ✆ **800/338-6877** or 505/983-6565. Tours $10 adults, free for children under 12.

MISCELLANEOUS TOURS

Pathways Customized Tours ✎   Don Dietz offers several planned tours, including a downtown Santa Fe walking tour, a full city tour, a trip to the cliff dwellings and native pueblos, a "Taos adventure," and a trip to Georgia O'Keeffe country (with a focus on the landscape that inspired the art now viewable in the O'Keeffe Museum). He will try to accommodate any special requests you might have. These tours last anywhere from 2 to 9 hours, depending on the one you choose. Don has extensive knowledge of the area's culture, history, geology, and flora and fauna, and will help you make the most of your precious vacation time.

161-F Calle Ojo Feliz. ✆ **505/982-5382**. www.santafepathways.com. Tours $60–$200+ per day per couple. Credit cards not accepted.

Rain Parrish ✎   A Navajo (or *Diné*) anthropologist, artist, and curator, Rain Parrish offers custom guide services focusing on cultural anthropology, Native American arts, and the history of the Native Americans of the Southwest. Some of these are true adventures to insider locations. Ms. Parrish includes visits to local Pueblo villages.

704 Kathryn St. ✆ **505/984-8236**. Tours $130 per couple for 4½ hr., $230 per couple for 7 hr.

Recursos de Santa Fe/Royal Road Tours   This organization is a full-service destination management company, emphasizing custom-designed itineraries to meet the interests of any group. They specialize in the archaeology, art, literature, spirituality, architecture, environment, food, and history of the Southwest. Call or visit the websites for a calendar and information about their annual writers' conferences and the international bead expo that they sponsor in Santa Fe on even years in March.

826 Camino de Monte Rey. ✆ **505/982-9301**. www.recursos.org.

Rojo Tours & Services   Customized and private tours are arranged to pueblos, cliff dwellings, ruins, hot air ballooning, backpacking, or whitewater rafting. Rojo also provides planning services for groups.

P.O. Box 15744. ✆ **505/474-8333**. Fax 505/474-2992. www.rojotours.com.

Santa Fe Detours ✎   Santa Fe's most extensive tour-booking agency accommodates almost all travelers' tastes, from bus and rail tours to river rafting, backpacking, and cross-country skiing. The agency can also facilitate hotel reservations, from budget to high end.

54½ San Francisco (summer tour desk, 107 Washington Ave.). ✆ **800/338-6877** or 505/983-6565. www. sfdetours.com.

Southwest Safaris ✎✎   This tour is one of the most interesting Southwestern experiences I've had. We flew in a small plane 1,000 feet off the ground from Santa Fe to the Grand Canyon while pilot Bruce Adams explained 300 million years of geologic history. We passed by the ancient ruins of Chaco Canyon and over the vivid colors of the Painted Desert, as well as over many land formations on Navajo Nation land so remote they remain nameless. Then, of course, there was the spectacular Grand Canyon, with ground transport to the South Rim and lunch on a canyon-side bench. Trips to many Southwestern destinations are available, including Monument Valley, Mesa Verde, Canyon de Chelly, Arches/ Canyonlands, as well as a trip to Capulin Volcano and the ruins at Aztec, New Mexico. Local 1- and 2-hour scenic flights are available as well, to places such as the Rio Grande Gorge, the back route in to Acoma Pueblo, and Abiquiu Valley—Georgia O'Keeffe country. Tours depart from the Santa Fe Airport. P.O. Box 945. ✆ **800/842-4246** or 505/988-4246. Tours $129–$699 per person.

6 Outdoor Activities

Set between the granite peaks of the Sangre de Cristo Mountains and the subtler volcanic Jemez Mountains, and with the Rio Grande flowing through, the Santa Fe area offers outdoor enthusiasts many opportunities to play. This is the land of high desert, where temperatures vary with the elevation, allowing for a full range of activities throughout the year.

BALLOONING
New Mexico is renowned for its spectacular Balloon Fiesta, which takes place annually in Albuquerque (p. 16). If you want to take a ride, you'll probably have to go to Albuquerque or Taos, but you can book your trip in Santa Fe through **Santa Fe Detours,** 54½ E. San Francisco St. (tour desk for summer, 107 Washington Ave.; ✆ **800/338-6877** or 505/983-6565). Flights take place early in the day. Rates begin at around $135 a flight. If you have your heart set on a balloon flight, I suggest that you reserve a time early in your trip because flights are sometimes canceled due to bad weather. That way, if you have to reschedule, you'll have enough time to do so.

BIKING
You can cycle along main roadways and paved country roads year-round in Santa Fe, but be aware that traffic is particularly heavy around the plaza—and all over town, motorists are not particularly attentive to bicyclists, so you need to be especially alert. Mountain-biking interest has exploded here and is especially popular in the spring, summer, and fall; the high-desert terrain is rugged and challenging, but mountain bikers of all levels can find exhilarating rides. The Santa Fe Convention and Visitors Bureau can supply you with bike maps.

I recommend the following trails: West of Santa Fe, the **Caja del Rio** area has nice dirt roads and some light-to-moderate technical biking; the **railroad tracks south of Santa Fe** provide wide-open biking on beginner-to-intermediate technical trails; and the **Borrego Trail** up toward the Santa Fe Ski Area is a challenging technical ride that links in with the **Windsor Trail,** a nationally renowned technical romp with plenty of verticality.

In Santa Fe bookstores, look for *Frommer's Great Outdoor Guide to Arizona and New Mexico* by Lesley King, *Mountain Biking in Northern New Mexico: Historical and Natural History Rides* by Craig Martin, and *The Mountain Biker's Guide to New Mexico* by Sarah Bennett. All of them are excellent guides to trails in Santa Fe, Taos, and Albuquerque, and outline tours for beginner, intermediate, and advanced riders. **Santa Fe Mountain Sports,** 606 Cerrillos Rd. (✆ **505/ 988-3337**), rents hard-tail mountain bikes for $20/half day and $25/full day, or full-suspension bikes for $35/full day. **Sun Mountain Bike Company,** 102 E.

Water St. (© **505/982-8986**), rents quality front-suspension mountain bikes for $30 a day. Add $7, and they'll deliver to and pick up from your hotel (in the Santa Fe area). Multiday rentals can be arranged, for $22 a day. Both shops supply accessories such as helmets, locks, water, maps, and trail information. **Sun Mountain Bike Company** also runs bike tours from April through October to some of the most spectacular spots in northern New Mexico. Trips range from an easy Glorieta Mesa tour to my favorite, the West Rim Trail, which snakes along the Taos Gorge, to the technical Glorieta Baldy, with prices from $60 to $109. All tours include bikes, transportation, and a snack.

FISHING

In the lakes and waterways around Santa Fe, anglers typically catch trout (there are five varieties in the area). Other local fish include bass, perch, and kokanee salmon. The most popular fishing holes are Cochiti and Abiquiu lakes as well as the Rio Chama, Pecos River, and the Rio Grande. A world-renowned fly-fishing destination, the **San Juan River,** near Farmington, is worth a visit and can make for an exciting 2-day trip in combination with a tour around **Chaco Culture National Historic Park** (see chapter 10). Check with the **New Mexico Game and Fish Department** (© **800/862-9310** or 505/476-8000) for information (including maps of area waters), licenses, and fishing proclamations. **High Desert Angler,** 435 S. Guadalupe St. (© **505/988-7688**), specializes in fly-fishing gear and guide services.

GOLF

There are three courses in the Santa Fe area: the 18-hole **Santa Fe Country Club,** on Airport Road (© **505/471-2626**); the often-praised 18-hole **Cochiti Lake Golf Course,** 5200 Cochiti Hwy., Cochiti Lake, about 35 miles southwest of Santa Fe via I-25 and NM 16 and 22 (© **505/465-2239**); and Santa Fe's newest 18-hole course, **Marty Sanchez Links de Santa Fe,** 205 Caja del Rio (© **505/955-4400**). Both the Santa Fe Country Club and the Marty Sanchez offer driving ranges as well.

HIKING

It's hard to decide which of the 1,000 miles of nearby national forest trails to tackle. Four wilderness areas are nearby, most notably **Pecos Wilderness,** with 223,000 acres east of Santa Fe. Also visit the 58,000-acre **Jemez Mountain National Recreation Area.** Information on these and other wilderness areas is available from the **Santa Fe National Forest,** P.O. Box 1689 (1474 Rodeo Rd.), Santa Fe, NM 87504 (© **505/438-7840**). If you're looking for company on your trek, contact the Santa Fe branch of the **Sierra Club,** 621 Old Santa Fe Trail, Suite 10 (© **505/983-2703**). You can pick up a hiking schedule in the local newsletter outside the office. Some people enjoy taking a chairlift ride to the summit of the **Santa Fe Ski Area** (© **505/982-4429;** www.skisantafe.com) and hiking around up there during the summer. You might also consider purchasing *The Hiker's Guide to New Mexico* (Falcon Press Publishing Co., Inc.) by Laurence Parent; it outlines 70 hikes throughout the state. *Frommer's Great Outdoor Guide to Arizona and New Mexico* (Wiley Publishing, Inc.), written by yours truly, details many of my favorite hikes. A popular guide with Santa Feans is *Day Hikes in the Santa Fe Area,* put out by the local branch of the Sierra Club. The most popular hiking trails are the **Borrego Trail,** a moderate 4-mile jaunt through aspens and ponderosa pines, ending at a creek; and **Aspen Vista,** an easy 1- to 5-mile hike through aspen forest with views to the east. Both are easy to find; simply head up Hyde Park Road toward Ski Santa Fe. The Borrego Trail is 8.25 miles up, while Aspen Vista is 10 miles. In recent years an energetic crew has cut the **Dale Ball Trails** (✆ **505/955-2103**), miles of hiking/biking trails throughout the Santa Fe foothills. The easiest access is off Hyde Park Road toward Ski Santa Fe. Drive 2 miles from Bishop's Lodge Road and watch for the trail head on the left.

HORSEBACK RIDING

Trips ranging in length from a few hours to overnight can be arranged by **Santa Fe Detours,** 54½ E. San Francisco St. (summer tour desk, 107 Washington Ave.; ✆ **800/338-6877** or 505/983-6565). You'll ride with "experienced wranglers" and can even arrange a trip that includes a cookout or brunch. Rides are also major activities at **The Bishop's Lodge** (see "The North Side," in chapter 5). The **Broken Saddle Riding Company** (✆ **505/424-7774**) offers rides through the stunning Galisteo Basin south of Santa Fe.

HUNTING

Elk and mule deer are taken by hunters in the Pecos Wilderness and Jemez Mountains, as are occasional black bears and bighorn sheep. Wild turkeys and grouse are frequently bagged in the uplands, geese and ducks at lower elevations. Check with the **New Mexico Game and Fish Department** (✆ **800/862-9310** or 505/476-8000) for information and licenses.

RIVER RAFTING & KAYAKING

Although Taos is the real rafting center of New Mexico, several companies serve Santa Fe during the April-to-October whitewater season. They include **Southwest Wilderness Adventures,** P.O. Box 9380, Santa Fe, NM 87504 (✆ **505/983-7262**); **New Wave Rafting,** 70 County Rd. 84B, Santa Fe, NM 87506 (✆ **800/984-1444** or 505/984-1444); **Santa Fe Rafting Co.,** 1000 Cerrillos Rd., Santa Fe, NM 87505 (✆ **800/467-RAFT** or 505/988-4914; www. santaferafting.com); and **Wolf Whitewater,** 4626 Palo Alto SE, Albuquerque, NM 87108 (✆ **505/262-1099;** www.wolfwhitewater.com). You can expect the cost of a full-day trip to range from about $85 to $105 before tax and the 3% federal land use fee. The day of the week (weekdays are less expensive) and group size may also affect the price.

RUNNING

Despite its elevation, Santa Fe is popular with runners and hosts numerous competitions, including the annual **Old Santa Fe Trail Run** on Labor Day. Each Wednesday, Santa Fe runners gather at 6pm at the plaza and set out on foot for runs in the surrounding area. This is a great opportunity for travelers to find their way and to meet some locals. **Santa Fe Striders** (www.santafestriders.org) sponsors various runs during the year.

SKIING

There's something available for every ability level at **Ski Santa Fe,** about 16 miles northeast of Santa Fe via Hyde Park (Ski Basin) Road. Lots of locals ski here, particularly on weekends; if you can, go on weekdays. It's a good family area and fairly small, so it's easy to split off from and later reconnect with your party. Built on the upper reaches of 12,000-foot Tesuque Peak, the area has an average annual snowfall of 225 inches and a vertical drop of 1,650 feet. Seven lifts, including a 5,000-foot triple chair and a new quad chair, serve 39 runs and

Getting Pampered: The Spa Scene

If traveling, skiing, or other activities have left you weary, a great place to treat your body and mind is **Ten Thousand Waves** ★★, a Japanese-style health spa about 3 miles northeast of Santa Fe on Hyde Park Road (© **505/982-9304**; www.tenthousandwaves.com). This serene retreat, nestled in a grove of piñon, offers hot tubs, saunas, and cold plunges, plus a variety of massage and other bodywork techniques. Bathing suits are optional in both the 10-foot communal hot tub (during the day) and the women's communal tub, where you can stay as long as you want for $14. Nine private hot tubs cost $20 to $27 an hour, with discounts for seniors and children. You can also arrange therapeutic massage, hot-oil massage, in-water *watsu* massage, herbal wraps, salt glows, facials, dry brush aromatherapy treatments, Ayurvedic treatments, and the much-praised Japanese Hot Stone Massage. If you call far enough in advance, you may be able to find lodging at **Ten Thousand Waves** as well (see chapter 5). The spa is open Sunday, Monday, Wednesday, and Thursday from 10am to 10pm; Tuesday from 4:30 to 10pm; and Friday and Saturday from 10am to 11pm (winter hours are shorter, so be sure to call). Reservations are recommended, especially on weekends.

Decorated in Southwestern-cum-Asian style, with clean lines and lots of elegant stone, Santa Fe's chicest option is **Avanu** ★★ at the La Posada de Santa Fe Resort and Spa (© **505/986-0000**). A full-service spa offering a range of treatments from massage to salt glows, this spot may initially seem expensive (about $95 for 50 min.), but treatments come with full use of the steam room, hot tub, and grass-surrounded pool.

Another option is **Vista Clara Ranch Spa Resort,** though you'll have to wait until 2006, when it reopens after a major remodel. Located 25 minutes south of Santa Fe, just outside Galisteo (© **888/663-9772** or 505/466-4772; www.vistaclara.com), this resort/spa has a stunning setting and some fine amenities and programs, including a cooking school in the summer.

Another south-of-town option, **Sunrise Springs Inn and Retreat,** 242 Los Pinos Rd. (© **505/471-3600**), offers spa stays in a lovely pond-side setting. Some accommodations here retain a group-meeting feel—the inn's bread and butter; to avoid these request their newest additions, which are lovely. Even if you don't stay here, plan a meal at the inn's **Blue Heron Restaurant** ★★, where you'll feast on delectable new American cuisine with a healthy flair.

590 acres of terrain, with a total capacity of 7,800 riders an hour. Base facilities, at 10,350 feet, center around **La Casa Mall,** with a cafeteria, lounge, ski shop, and boutique. Another restaurant, **Totemoff's,** has a mid-mountain patio.

The ski area is open daily from 9am to 4pm; the season often runs from Thanksgiving to early April, depending on snow conditions. Rates for all lifts are $47 for adults, $39 for teens (13–20 years), $35 for children and seniors, free for kids less than 46 inches tall (in their ski boots), and free for seniors 72 and older. For more information, contact **Ski Santa Fe,** 2209 Brothers Rd., Suite 220 (✆ **505/982-4429;** www.skisantafe.com). For 24-hour reports on snow conditions, call ✆ **505/983-9155. Ski New Mexico** (✆ **505/982-5300**) gives statewide reports. Ski packages are available through **Santa Fe Central Reservations** (✆ **800/745-9910**).

Cross-country skiers find seemingly endless miles of snow to track in the **Santa Fe National Forest** (✆ **505/438-7840**). A favorite place to start is at the Black Canyon campground, about 9 miles from downtown en route to the Santa Fe Ski Area. In the same area are the **Borrego Trail** (high intermediate), **Aspen Vista Trail,** and the **Norski Trail,** all en route to Santa Fe Ski Area as well. Other popular activities at the ski area in winter include snowshoeing, snowboarding, sledding, and inner tubing. Snowshoe and snowboard rentals are available at a number of downtown shops and the ski area.

SWIMMING

There's a public pool at the **Fort Marcy Complex** (✆ **505/955-2500**) on Camino Santiago, off Bishop's Lodge Road. Admission is $1.85 for adults, $1.50 for ages 13 to 18, 75¢ for ages 8 to 12, 30¢ for children 7 and under, and 75¢ for seniors.

TENNIS

Santa Fe has 44 public tennis courts and 4 major private facilities. The **City Recreation Department** (✆ **505/955-2100**) can help you locate indoor, outdoor, and lighted public courts.

Santa Fe Shopping

Each time I head out to shop in northern New Mexico, I'm amazed by the number of handcrafts, pieces of art, and artifacts I find. There's a broad range of work, from very traditional Native American crafts and Hispanic folk art to extremely innovative contemporary work.

Some call Santa Fe one of the top art markets in the world. Galleries speckle the downtown area, and as an artists' thoroughfare, Canyon Road is preeminent. Still, the greatest concentration of Native American crafts is displayed beneath the portal of the Palace of the Governors.

Any serious arts aficionado should try to attend one or more of the city's great arts festivals—the Spring Festival of the Arts in May, the Spanish Market in July, The Indian Market in August, and the Fall Festival of the Arts in October.

1 The Shopping Scene

Few visitors to Santa Fe leave the city without acquiring at least one item from the Native American artisans at the Palace of the Governors. When you are thinking of making such a purchase, keep the following pointers in mind.

Silver jewelry should have a harmony of design, clean lines, and neatly executed soldering. Navajo jewelry typically features large stones, with designs shaped around the stone. Zuni jewelry usually has patterns of small or inlaid stones. Hopi jewelry rarely uses stones; it's usually a silver-on-silver overlay, darkly oxidized so the image stands out.

Turquoise of a deeper color is usually higher quality, so long as it hasn't been color treated (undesirable because the process adds false color to the stone). Often, turquoise is "stabilized," which means it has resin baked into the stone. This makes the stone less fragile but also prevents it from changing color with age and contact with body oils. Many people find the aging effect desirable. Beware of "reconstituted turquoise." In this process the stone is disassembled and reassembled; it usually has a uniformly blue color that looks very unnatural.

Pottery is traditionally hand-coiled and of natural clay, not thrown on a potter's wheel using commercial clay. It is hand-polished with a stone, hand-painted, and fired in an outdoor oven (usually an open firepit) rather than an electric kiln. Look for an even shape; clean, accurate painting; a high polish (if it is a polished piece); and an artist's signature.

Navajo rugs are appraised according to tightness and evenness of weave, symmetry of design, and whether natural (preferred) or commercial dyes have been used.

The value of **kachina dolls** depends on the detail of their carving: fingers, toes, muscles, rib cages, feathers, and so on. Elaborate costumes are also desirable. Oil staining is preferred to the use of bright acrylic paints.

Sand paintings should display clean, narrow lines, even colors, balance, an intricacy of design, and smooth craftsmanship.

Local museums, particularly the Wheelwright Museum and the Institute of American Indian Arts Museum, can give you a good orientation to contemporary craftsmanship.

Contemporary artists are mainly painters, sculptors, ceramists, and fiber artists, including weavers. Peruse one of the outstanding **gallery catalogs** for an introduction to local dealers. They're available for free in many galleries and hotels. They include *The Collector's Guide to Art in Santa Fe and Taos* by Wingspread Incorporated (www.collectorsguide.com); *The Essential Guide* by Essential Guides, LLC (www.essentialguide.com); or *Performance de Santa Fe* by Cynthia Stearns (P.O. Box 8932, Santa Fe, NM 87504-8932). For a current listing of gallery openings, with recommendations on which ones to attend, purchase a copy of the monthly magazine the *Santa Fean* by Santa Fean, LLC (444 Galisteo, Santa Fe, NM 87501; www.santafean.com). Also check in the "Pasatiempo" section of the local newspaper, the *New Mexican* (www.santafenew mexican.com), every Friday.

Business hours vary quite a bit among establishments, but most are open at least Monday through Friday from 10am to 5pm, with mall stores open until 8 or 9pm. Most shops are open similar hours on Saturday, and many also open on Sunday afternoon during the summer. Winter hours tend to be more limited.

After the high-rolling 1980s, during which art markets around the country prospered, came the penny-pinching 1990s and the fearful 2000s. Many galleries in Santa Fe have been forced to shut their doors. Those that remain tend to specialize in particular types of art, a refinement process that has improved the gallery scene here. Still, some worry that the lack of serious art buyers in the area leads to fewer good galleries and more T-shirt and trinket stores. The plaza has its share of those but still has a good number of serious galleries, appealing to those buyers whose interests run to accessible art—Southwestern landscapes and the like. On Canyon Road, the art is often more experimental and more diverse.

2 The Top Galleries

CONTEMPORARY ART

Adieb Khadoure Fine Art   This is a working artists' studio, featuring contemporary artists Steven Boone, Hal Larsen, Robert Anderson, and Barry Lee Darling. Their works are shown in the gallery daily from 10am to 6pm. Adieb Khadoure also sells elegant rugs, furniture, and pottery from around the world. 610 Canyon Rd. ✆ 505/820-2666.

Canyon Road Contemporary Art   This gallery represents some of the finest emerging U.S. contemporary artists as well as internationally known artists. You'll find figurative, landscape, and abstract paintings, as well as raku pottery. 403 Canyon Rd. ✆ 505/983-0433.

Hahn Ross Gallery   Owners Tom Ross and Elizabeth Hahn, a children's book illustrator and surrealist painter, respectively, specialize in representing artists who create colorful, fantasy-oriented works. I'm especially fond of the wild party scenes by Susan Contreras. Check out the new sculpture garden here. 409 Canyon Rd. ✆ 505/984-8434.

La Mesa of Santa Fe ⭐ *Finds*   Step into this gallery and let your senses dance. Dramatically colored ceramic plates, bowls, and other kitchen items fill one room. Contemporary kachinas by Gregory Lomayesva—a real buy—line the walls, accented by steel lamps and rag rugs. An adventure. 225 Canyon Rd. © 505/984-1688.

Leslie Muth Gallery   Here, you'll find "Outsider Art," wild works made by untrained artists in a bizarre variety of media, from sculptures fashioned from pop-bottle lids to portraits painted on flattened beer cans; this is also the place to find Navajo folk art. Much of the work here is extraordinary and affordable. By appointment only. 221 E. de Vargas St. © 505/989-4620.

LewAllen Contemporary ⭐ *Finds*   This is one of my favorite galleries. You'll find bizarre and beautiful contemporary works in a range of media, from granite to clay to twigs. There are always exciting works on canvas. 129 W. Palace Ave. © 505/988-8997.

Linda Durham Contemporary Art ⭐   The opening of this broad and bright art space in summer 2004 marks the return of one of Santa Fe's best galleries. Longtime gallery owner Linda Durham had moved her gallery 25 miles south of town, but has now returned, with a strong roster of talent including Greg Erf and Judy Tuwaletstiwa. 1101 Paseo de Peralta. © 505/466-6600.

Peyton Wright Gallery ⭐   Housed within the Historic Spiegelberg House (a refurbished Victorian adobe), this excellent gallery offers contemporary, Spanish Colonial, African, Russian, Native American, and pre-Columbian art and antiquities. In addition to representing such artists as Kellogg Johnson, Larry Fodor, and Darren Vigil Gray, the gallery features monthly exhibitions—including contemporary paintings, sculptures, and works on paper. 237 E. Palace Ave. © 800/879-8898 or 505/989-9888.

Shidoni Foundry, Gallery, and Sculpture Gardens ⭐⭐ *Finds*   Shidoni Foundry is one of the area's most exciting spots for sculptors and sculpture enthusiasts. At the foundry, visitors may take a tour through the facilities to view casting processes. In addition, Shidoni Foundry includes a 5,000-square-foot contemporary gallery, a bronze gallery, and a wonderful sculpture garden. Bishop's Lodge Rd., Tesuque. © 505/988-8001.

Waxlander Gallery   Primarily featuring the whimsical acrylics and occasional watercolors of Phyllis Kapp, this is the place to browse if you like bold color. 622 Canyon Rd. © 800/342-2202 or 505/984-2202.

NATIVE AMERICAN & OTHER INDIGENOUS ART

Andrea Fisher Fine Pottery ⭐   This expansive gallery is a wonderland of authentic Southwestern Indian pottery. You'll find real showpieces here, including the work of renowned San Ildefonso Pueblo potter Maria Martinez. 100 W. San Francisco St. © 505/986-1234.

Frank Howell Gallery   If you've never seen the wonderful illustrative hand of the late Frank Howell, you'll want to visit this gallery. You'll find a variety of works by contemporary American Indian artists, such as Pablo Antonio Milan, as well as the Southwestern impressionism of Paula Shaw. The gallery also features sculpture, jewelry, and graphics. 103 Washington Ave. © 505/984-1074.

Morning Star Gallery ⭐⭐ *Finds*   This is one of my favorite places to browse. Throughout the rambling gallery are American Indian art masterpieces, all elegantly displayed. You'll see a broad range of works, from late-19th-century Navajo blankets to 1920s Zuni needlepoint jewelry. 513 Canyon Rd. ℭ **505/982-8187.**

Ortega's on the Plaza A hearty shopper could spend hours here, perusing inventive turquoise and silver jewelry and especially fine strung beadwork, as well as rugs and pottery. An adjacent room showcases a wide array of clothing, all with a hip Southwestern flair. 101 W. San Francisco St. ℭ **505/988-1866.**

PHOTOGRAPHY

Andrew Smith Gallery ⭐ I'm always amazed when I enter this gallery and see works I've seen reprinted in major magazines for years. There they are, photographic prints, large and beautiful, hanging on the wall. Here, you'll see famous works by Edward Curtis, Henri Cartier-Bresson, Ansel Adams, Annie Leibovitz, and others. 203 W. San Francisco St. ℭ **505/984-1234.**

Photo-Eye Gallery You're bound to be surprised each time you step into this gallery a few blocks off Canyon Road. Dealing in contemporary photography, the gallery represents both internationally renowned and emerging artists. 370 Garcia St. ℭ **505/988-5152.**

SPANISH & HISPANIC ART

Montez Gallery This shop is rich with New Mexican (and Mexican) art, decorations, and furnishings such as *santos* (saints), *retablos* (paintings), *bultos* (sculptures), and *trasteros* (armoires). Sena Plaza Courtyard, 125 E. Palace Ave., Suite 33. ℭ **505/982-1828.**

TRADITIONAL ART

Altermann Galleries This is a well of interesting traditional art, mostly 19th-, 20th-, and 21st-century American paintings and sculpture. The gallery represents Remington and Russell, in addition to Taos founders, Santa Fe artists, and members of the Cowboy Artists of America and the National Academy of Western Art. Stroll through the sculpture garden among whimsical bronzes of children and dogs. 225 Canyon Rd. ℭ **505/983-1590.**

Gerald Peters Gallery ⭐⭐ Displayed throughout a two-story Pueblo-style building, the works here are so fine you'll feel as though you're in a museum. You'll find 19th-, 20th-, and 21st-century American painting and sculpture, featuring the art of Georgia O'Keeffe, William Wegman, and the founders of the Santa Fe and Taos artist colonies, as well as more contemporary works. 1011 Paseo de Peralta. ℭ **505/954-5700.**

The Mayans Gallery Ltd. Established in 1977, this is one of the oldest galleries in Santa Fe. You'll find 20th-century American and Latin American paintings, photography, prints, and sculpture. 601 Canyon Rd. ℭ **505/983-8068.**

Nedra Matteucci Galleries ⭐ As you approach this gallery, note the elaborately crafted stone and adobe wall that surrounds it, merely a taste of what's to come. The gallery specializes in 19th-, 20th-, and 21st-century American art. Inside, you'll find a lot of high-ticket works such as those of early Taos and Santa Fe painters, as well as classic American Impressionism, historical Western modernism, and contemporary Southwestern landscapes and sculpture. 1075 Paseo de Peralta. ℭ **505/982-4631.**

Owings-Dewey Fine Art ⭐ These are treasure-filled rooms. You'll find 19th-, 20th-, and 21st-century American painting and sculpture, including works by Georgia O'Keeffe, Robert Henri, Maynard Dixon, Fremont Ellis, and

Andrew Dasburg, as well as antique works such as Spanish colonial *retablos, bultos,* and tin works. Don't miss the Day of the Dead exhibition around Halloween. 76 E. San Francisco St., upstairs. ✆ **505/982-6244.**

Zaplin Lampert Gallery ★★   Art aficionados as well as those who just like a nice landscape will enjoy this gallery, one of Santa Fe's classics. Hanging on old adobe walls are works by some of the region's early masters, including Bert Phillips, Gene Kloss, and Gustauve Baumann. 651 Canyon Rd. ✆ **505/982-6100.**

3 More Shopping A to Z

ANTIQUES

El Paso Import Company ★   Whenever I'm in the vicinity of this shop, I always stop in. It's packed—and I mean packed—with colorful, weathered colonial and ranchero furniture. The home furnishings and folk art here are imported from Mexico. 418 Sandoval St. ✆ **505/982-5698.**

Jackalope ★ *Kids* *Value*   Spread over 7 acres of land, this is a wild place to spend a morning or an afternoon browsing through exotic furnishings from India and Mexico, as well as imported textiles, pottery, jewelry, and clothing. It's a great place to find gifts. Kids will love the new petting zoo and prairie-dog village. 2820 Cerrillos Rd. ✆ **505/471-8539.**

BELTS

Desert Son of Santa Fe ★ *Moments*   From belts to mules, everything in this narrow little shop is hand-tooled, hand-carved, and/or hand-stamped. As well as leather items, look for cowboy hats and exotic turquoise jewelry. It's a slip of a shop with lots of character, presided over by the artist herself, Mindy Adler. 725 Canyon Rd. ✆ **505/982-9499.**

BOOKS

Borders   With close to 200 stores nationwide, this chain provides a broad range of books, music, and videos, and it hosts in-store appearances by authors, musicians, and artists. 500 Montezuma Ave. ✆ **505/954-4707.**

Nouveau Shopping on the Plaza

Opened in 2004, the **Santa Fe Arcade,** 60 E. San Francisco St. (✆ **505/995-0219**), on the south side of the plaza, offers three stories of shops in a sleek, glassy European-style space. It's a far cry from the Woolworth's that once lived there. Showy Western wear, fine Indian jewelry, and hip clothing fill the display windows of some 60 spaces in the mall, with two restaurants planned. Local favorite **Back at the Ranch** ★ (suite 127; ✆ **800/962-6687** or 505/989-8110; www.backattheranch.com) has a satellite shop in the arcade, where they display a portion of what they call the "largest selection of handmade cowboy boots in the country." Prima Fine Jewelry's **Oro Fino** (suite 218; ✆ **505/983-9699**) has also opened up, selling contemporary and Southwestern inlaid jewelry in silver, gold, and platinum.

Collected Works Bookstore   This is a good downtown book source, with carefully recommended books up front, in case you're not sure what you want, and shelves of Southwest, travel, nature, and other books. 208–B W. San Francisco St. ℂ 505/988-4226.

Horizons—The Discovery Store *Kids*   Here, you'll find adult and children's books, science-oriented games and toys, telescopes, binoculars, and a variety of unusual educational items. I always find interesting gifts for my little nieces in this store. 328 S. Guadalupe St. ℂ 505/983-1554.

Nicholas Potter, Bookseller   This bookstore handles rare and used hard-cover books, as well as tickets to many local events. 211 E. Palace Ave. ℂ 505/983-5434.

CRAFTS

Davis Mather Folk Art Gallery   This small shop is a wild animal adventure. You'll find New Mexican animal woodcarvings in shapes of lions, tigers, and bears—even chickens—as well as other folk and Hispanic arts. 141 Lincoln Ave. ℂ 505/983-1660.

Nambe Outlets ★ *Finds*   Here, you'll find cooking, serving, and decorating pieces, fashioned from an exquisite sand-cast and handcrafted alloy. These items are also available at the Nambe Outlet stores at 104 W. San Francisco St. (ℂ **505/988-3574**) and in Taos in Yucca Plaza, 113A Paseo del Pueblo Norte (ℂ **505/758-8221**). 924 Paseo De Peralta. ℂ **505/988-5528.**

FASHIONS

Judy's Unique Apparel   Judy's has eclectic separates made locally and imported from around the globe. You'll find a wide variety of items here, many at surprisingly reasonable prices. 714 Canyon Rd. ℂ 505/988-5746.

Origins ★ *Moments*   A little like a Guatemalan or Turkish marketplace, this store is packed with wearable art, folk art, and the work of local designers. Look for good buys on ethnic jewelry. Throughout the summer there are trunk shows, which offer opportunities to meet the artists. 135 W. San Francisco St. ℂ **505/988-2323.**

Overland Sheepskin Company   The rich smell of leather will draw you in the door, and possibly hold onto you until you purchase a coat, blazer, hat, or other finely made leather item. 74 E. San Francisco St. ℂ 505/983-4727.

Finds **Gypsy Time**

Even if you don't shop, you'll want to wander down Gypsy Alley, one of Canyon Road's older artist enclaves. Though the once-crooked shops and studios have been replaced by sleek galleries, it still retains a row of whimsically painted mail boxes—a great photo op. **Gypsy Baby,** 708 Canyon Rd. nos. 3 and 4. (ℂ **505/820-1898**), sells bright clothes, beaded slippers, and mustang rocking horses, all mindful of the slogan "Born to be spoiled." **Chiaroscuro Gallery,** 708 Canyon Rd. (ℂ **505/986-9197**), presents contemporary fine art and photography. Especially look for Willy Heeks's lovely textured paintings.

FOOD

The Chile Shop   This store has too many cheap trinketlike items for me, but many find novelty items to take back home. You'll find everything from salsas to cornmeal and tortilla chips. The shop also stocks cookbooks and pottery items. 109 E. Water St. 🕿 **505/983-6080**.

Cookworks   For the chef or merely the wannabe, this is a fun place for browsing. You'll find inventive food products and cooking items spread across three shops. Cookworks also offers gourmet food and cooking classes. 316 S. Guadalupe St. 🕿 **505/988-7676**.

Señor Murphy Candy Maker   This candy store is unlike any you'll find in other parts of the country—everything here is made with local ingredients. The chile piñon-nut brittle is a taste sensation! Señor Murphy has another shop in the Villa Linda Mall (🕿 **505/471-8899**). 100 E. San Francisco St. (La Fonda Hotel). 🕿 **505/982-0461**.

FURNITURE

Asian Adobe   One of the Santa Fe Railyard district's new treats, this shop marries the warmth of Southwestern decor with the austere grace of Asian. You'll find weathered wood tables and trasteros, colorful wall hangings and moody rugs. 530 S. Guadalupe (in the Gross Kelly Warehouse). 🕿 **505/992-6846**.

Casa Nova   In the Santa Fe Railyard district, this colorful shop offers everything from dishware to furniture, all in bold and inventive colors. Those with whimsical natures will get happily lost here. 530 S. Guadalupe St. (in the Gross Kelly Warehouse). 🕿 **505/983-8558**.

Southwest Spanish Craftsmen   The Spanish colonial and Spanish provincial furniture, doors, and home accessories in this store are a bit too elaborate for my tastes, but if you find yourself dreaming of carved wood, this is your place. 328 S. Guadalupe St. 🕿 **505/982-1767**.

Taos Furniture   Here you'll find classic Southwestern furnishings handcrafted in solid ponderosa pine—both contemporary and traditional. Prices are a little better here than in downtown shops. 219 Galisteo St. 🕿 **800/443-3448** or **505/988-1229**.

GIFTS & SOUVENIRS

El Nicho *Value*   If you want to take a little piece of Santa Fe home with you, you'll likely find it at this shop. You'll find handcrafted Navajo folk art as well as jewelry and other items by local artisans, including woodcarvings (watch for the *santos!*) by the renowned Ortega family. 227 Don Gaspar Ave. 🕿 **505/984-2830**.

HATS

Montecristi Custom Hat Works ✦   This fun shop hand-makes fine Panama and felt hats in a range of styles, from Australian outback to Mexican bolero. 322 McKenzie St. 🕿 **505/983-9598**. www.montecristihats.com.

JEWELRY

Packards ✦   Opened by a notable trader, Al Packard, and later sold to new owners, this store on the plaza is worth checking out to see some of the best jewelry available. You'll also find exquisite rugs and pottery. 61 Old Santa Fe Trail. 🕿 **505/983-9241**.

Tresa Vorenberg Goldsmiths   You'll find some wildly imaginative designs in this jewelry store, where more than 40 artisans are represented. All items are handcrafted, and custom commissions are welcomed. 656 Canyon Rd. ✆ **505/988-7215.**

MALLS & SHOPPING CENTERS

de Vargas Center   There are approximately 50 merchants and restaurants in this mall just northwest of downtown. This is Santa Fe's small, struggling mall. Though there are fewer shops than at Villa Linda, this is where I shop because I don't tend to get the mall phobia I get in the more massive places. Open Monday to Friday 10am to 7pm, Saturday 10am to 6pm, and Sunday noon to 5pm. N. Guadalupe St. and Paseo de Peralta. ✆ **505/982-2655.**

Sanbusco Market Center ✯   Unique shops and restaurants occupy this remodeled warehouse near the old Santa Fe Railyard. Many of the shops are overpriced, but it's a fun place to window-shop. Open Monday to Saturday 10am to 6pm, Sunday noon to 5pm. 500 Montezuma St. ✆ **505/989-9390.**

Santa Fe Premium Outlets   Outlet shopping fans will enjoy this open-air mall on the south end of town. Anchors include Brooks Brothers, Jones New York, Nautica, and Coach. 8380 Cerrillos Rd. ✆ **505/474-4000.**

Villa Linda Mall   Santa Fe's largest mall is near the southwestern city limits, not far from the I-25 on-ramp. If you're from a major city, you'll probably find shopping here very provincial. Anchors include JCPenney, Sears, Dillard's, and Mervyn's. Open Monday to Saturday 10am to 9pm, Sunday noon to 6pm. 4250 Cerrillos Rd. (at Rodeo Rd.). ✆ **505/473-4253.**

MARKETS

Farmers' Market ✯ *(Finds*   The farmers' market has everything from fruits, vegetables, and flowers to cheeses, cider, and salsas. Great local treats! If you're an early riser, stroll through and enjoy good coffee and excellent pastries. Open April to mid-November, Saturday and Tuesday 7am to noon. In the Santa Fe Railyard, off S. Guadalupe behind Tomasita's. ✆ **505/983-4098.**

Tesuque Flea Market ✯ *(Moments*   If you're a flea-market hound, you'll be happy to find this one. More than 500 vendors here sell everything from used cowboy boots (you might find some real beauties) to clothing, jewelry, books, and furniture, all against a big northern New Mexico view. Open March to late November, Friday to Sunday. Vendors start selling at about 7:30am and stay open until about 6:30pm, weather permitting. US 84/285 (about 8 miles north of Santa Fe). No phone.

NATURAL ART

Mineral & Fossil Gallery of Santa Fe   You'll find ancient artwork here, from fossils to geodes in all sizes and shapes. There are also natural mineral jewelry and decorative items for the home, including lamps, wall clocks, furniture, art glass, and carvings. Mineral & Fossil also has galleries in Taos, and in Scottsdale and Sedona, Arizona. 127 W. San Francisco St. ✆ **800/762-9777** or 505/984-1682.

Stone Forest *(Finds*   Proprietor Michael Zimber travels to China and other Asian countries every year to collaborate with the stone carvers who create the fountains, sculptures, and bath fixtures that fill this inventive shop and garden not far from the plaza. 833 Dunlap. ✆ **505/986-8883.**

POTTERY & TILES

Artesanos Imports Company ⭐ *Moments*   This is like a trip south of the border, with all the scents and colors you'd expect on such a journey. You'll find a wide selection of Talavera tile and pottery, as well as light fixtures and many other accessories for the home. There's even an outdoor market where you can buy fountains, sculpture items, and outdoor furniture. A second store is located at 1414 Maclovia St. (℗ **505/471-8020**). 222 Galisteo St. ℗ **505/983-1743**.

Santa Fe Pottery   The work of more than 120 master potters from New Mexico and the Southwest is on display here; you'll find everything from mugs to lamps. From June to December, the shop hosts a series of six one-man and -woman and group/theme shows, with openings for each. 323 S. Guadalupe St. ℗ **505/989-3363**.

RUGS

Seret & Sons Rugs, Furnishings, and Architectural Pieces ⭐   If you're like me and find Middle Eastern decor irresistible, you need to wander through this shop. You'll find kilims and Persian and Turkish rugs, as well as some of the Moorish-style ancient doors and furnishings that you see around Santa Fe. 224 Galisteo St. ℗ **505/988-9151** or 505/983-5008.

9

Santa Fe After Dark

Santa Fe is a city committed to the arts, so it's no surprise that the Santa Fe night scene is dominated by high-brow cultural events, beginning with the world-famous Santa Fe Opera. The club and popular music scene runs a distant second.

Information on all major cultural events can be obtained from the **Santa Fe Convention and Visitors Bureau** (© 800/777-CITY or 505/955-6200) or from the **City of Santa Fe Arts Commission** (© 505/955-6707). Current listings are published each Friday in the "Pasatiempo" section of *The New Mexican* (www.santafenewmexican.com), the city's daily newspaper, and in the *Santa Fe Reporter* (www.sfreporter.com), published every Wednesday.

Nicholas Potter, Bookseller, 211 E. Palace Ave. (© 505/983-5434),

sells tickets to select events. **Candyman,** 851 St. Michaels Dr. (© 505/983-5906), and **CD Café,** 301 N. Guadalupe (© 505/986-0735), sell tickets for Paramount Lounge events. You can also order by phone from **Ticketmaster** (© 505/883-7800). Discount tickets may be available on the night of a performance; for example, the opera offers standing-room tickets on the day of the performance. Sales start at 10am.

A variety of free concerts, lectures, and other events are presented in the summer, co-sponsored by the City of Santa Fe and the Chamber of Commerce. Many of these musical and cultural events take place on the plaza; check in the "Pasatiempo" section for current listings and information.

1 The Performing Arts

No fewer than 24 performing-arts groups flourish in this city of 65,000. Many of them perform year-round, but others are seasonal. The acclaimed Santa Fe Opera, for instance, has just a 2-month summer season: July and August.

Note: Many companies noted here perform at locations other than their listed addresses, so check the site of the performance you plan to attend.

MAJOR PERFORMING ARTS COMPANIES
CHORAL GROUPS

Desert Chorale This 28-member vocal ensemble recruits members from all over the U.S. It's nationally recognized for its eclectic blend of Renaissance melodies and modern avant-garde compositions. During summer months, the chorale performs classical concerts at various locations, including the Loretto Chapel, as well as smaller cameo concerts at more intimate settings throughout Santa Fe and Albuquerque. The chorale also performs a popular series of Christmas concerts during December. Most concerts begin at 8pm. 811 St. Michael's Dr., Suite 208. © 800/244-4011 or 505/988-2282. www.desertchorale.org. Tickets $10–$40 adults, half price for students.

Sangre de Cristo Chorale   This 34-member ensemble has a repertoire ranging from classical, baroque, and Renaissance works to more recent folk music and spirituals, much of it presented a cappella. The group gives concerts in Santa Fe, Los Alamos, and Albuquerque. The Christmas dinner concert is extremely popular. P.O. Box 4462. ℂ **505/662-5445**. www.sdc-chorale.org. Tickets $15–$60, depending on the season.

Santa Fe Women's Ensemble   This choral group of 13 semiprofessional singers offers classical works sung a cappella as well as with varied instrumental accompaniment during February, March, and December. The "Spring Offering" concert (in Feb and Mar) is held at the Santuario de Guadalupe (100 S. Guadalupe St.), and the "Christmas Offering" concert (in mid-Dec) is held in the Loretto Chapel (Old Santa Fe Trail at Water St.). Call for tickets. 424 Kathryn Place. ℂ **505/954-4922**. www.sfwe.org. Tickets $20, $15 students.

OPERA & CLASSICAL MUSIC

Santa Fe Opera ★★★   Many rank the Santa Fe Opera second only to the Metropolitan Opera of New York in the United States. Established in 1957, it consistently attracts famed conductors, directors, and singers. At the height of the season, the company is 500 strong. It's noted for its performances of the classics, little-known works by classical European composers, and American premieres of 21st-century works. The theater, completed for the 1998 season, sits on a wooded hilltop 7 miles north of the city, off US 84/285. It's partially open-air, with open sides. A controversial structure, this new theater replaced the original, built in 1968, but preserved the sweeping curves attuned to the contour of the surrounding terrain. At night, the lights of Los Alamos can still be seen in the distance under clear skies.

The 8-week, 40-performance opera season runs from late June through late August. Highlights for 2005 include the opera's first Spanish work in almost 30 years, Osvaldo Golijov's *Ainadamar,* based on the life of poet and playwright Federico García Lorca. Also slated are Puccini's arresting *Turandot,* Rossini's comic *The Barber of Seville,* Mozart's grand *Lucio Silla,* and Britten's tragic *Peter Grimes.* All performances begin at 9pm, until the last 2 weeks of the season when performances begin at 8:30pm. A small screen in front of each seat shows the libretto during the performance. A gift shop has been added, as has additional parking. The entire theater is wheelchair accessible. P.O. Box 2408. ℂ **800/280-4654** or 505/986-5900. www.santafeopera.org. Tickets $20–$130; standing room $10; Opening Night Gala $1,000–$2,500. Backstage tours July–Aug Mon–Sat at noon; $5 adults, free for children ages 5–17.

A Home for the Arts

The Santa Fe arts scene has gained an exciting addition: The **Lensic Performing Arts Center,** 211 W. San Francisco St. (ℂ **505/988-7050**), now hosts many of the city's major performances, including the Santa Fe Chamber Music Festival and the Santa Fe Symphony Orchestra and Chorus, among others. The setting is wonderfully atmospheric; a multi-million-dollar face-lift brought out the 1931 movie palace's Arabian Nights charm.

ORCHESTRAL & CHAMBER MUSIC

Santa Fe Pro Musica Chamber Orchestra & Ensemble This chamber ensemble performs everything from Bach to Vivaldi to contemporary masters. During Holy Week, the Santa Fe Pro Musica presents its annual Mozart and Hayden Concert at the St. Francis Cathedral. Christmas brings candlelight chamber ensemble concerts. Pro Musica's season runs September to May. 430 Manhattan, Suite 10. ✆ **505/988-4640**. www.santafepromusica.com. Tickets $15–$50.

Santa Fe Symphony Orchestra and Chorus This 60-piece professional symphony orchestra has grown rapidly in stature since its founding in 1984. Matinee and evening performances of classical and popular works are presented in a subscription series at the Lensic Performing Arts Center from October to May. There's a pre-concert lecture before each performance. During the spring, the orchestra presents music festivals (call for details). P.O. Box 9692. ✆ **800/480-1319** or 505/983-1414. www.sf-symphony.org. Tickets $15–$48 (5 seating categories).

Serenata of Santa Fe This professional chamber-music group specializes in bringing lesser-known works of the masters to the concert stage. Concerts are presented September to May. Call for location, dates, and details. P.O. Box 8410. ✆ **505/989-7988**. Tickets $12 general admission, $15–$20 reserved seats.

MUSIC FESTIVALS & CONCERT SERIES

Santa Fe Chamber Music Festival ★★ An extraordinary group of international artists comes to Santa Fe every summer for this festival. Its 6-week season runs mid-July to mid-August and is held in the St. Francis Auditorium and the Lensic Performing Arts Center. Each festival features chamber-music masterpieces, new music by a composer in residence, jazz, free youth concerts, pre-concert lectures, and open rehearsals. Performances are Monday, Tuesday, Thursday, and Friday at 8pm; Saturday at various evening times; and Sunday at 6pm. Open rehearsals, youth concerts, and pre-concert lectures are free to the public. 239 Johnson St., Suite B (P.O. Box 2227). ✆ **505/983-2075** or 505/982-1890 for box office (after June 22). www.sfcmf.org. Tickets $15–$40.

Santa Fe Concert Association Founded in 1937, this oldest musical organization in northern New Mexico has a September-to-May season that includes approximately 17 annual events. Among them are a "Great Performances" series and an "Adventures" series, both featuring renowned instrumental and vocal soloists and chamber ensembles. The association also hosts special holiday concerts around Christmas. Performances are held at the Lensic Performing Arts Center and the St. Francis Auditorium; tickets are available at the Lensic box office (✆ **505/988-1234**) and at ✆ **800/905-3315** (www.tickets.com) or 505/984-8759. 210 E. Marcy St. (P.O. Box 4626, 87502). Tickets $16–$75.

THEATER COMPANIES

Greer Garson Theater Center In this graceful, intimate theater, the College of Santa Fe's Performing Arts Department produces four plays annually, with six presentations of each, given between October and May. Usually, the season consists of a comedy, a drama, a musical, and a classic. The college also sponsors studio productions and various contemporary music concerts. College of Santa Fe, 1600 St. Michael's Dr. ✆ **505/473-6511**. www.csf.edu. Tickets $8–$17 adults, $5 students.

Santa Fe Playhouse Founded in the 1920s, this is the oldest extant theater group in New Mexico. Still performing in a historic adobe theater in the Barrio de Analco, it attracts thousands for its dramas, avant-garde theater, and musical comedy. Its popular one-act melodramas call on the public to boo the sneering villain and swoon for the damsel in distress. 142 E. de Vargas St.. $\textcircled{C}$ 505/988-4262. www.santafeplayhouse.org. Tickets "Pay What You Wish"–$20, depending on the show.

Santa Fe Stages ★★ Most locals couldn't imagine international theater and dance troupes coming to Santa Fe, but it began happening in 1994, with the founding of this theater. Year-round performances are presented at the Firestone Plaza and the Lensic Performing Arts Center. In recent years, the company has hosted such distinguished performances as the Tony Award–wining play *Copenhagen* and the Paul Taylor Dance Company. 422 N. W. San Francisco St. $\textcircled{C}$ 505/982-6683. www.santafestages.org. Tickets $15–$52.

Theater Grottesco ★ *Finds* This troupe combines the best of comedy, drama, and dance in its original productions performed each spring and summer in a renovated space at the Center for Contemporary Arts. Expect to be romanced, shocked, intellectually stimulated, and, above all, struck silly with laughter. Look for upcoming winter shows as well. 551 W. Cordova Rd. #8400. $\textcircled{C}$ 505/474-8400. www.theatergrottesco.org. Tickets $7–$20.

Theaterwork Studio ★ A critic for the *Santa Fe New Mexican* called Theaterwork's performance of Chekhov's *Uncle Vanya* "the most rewarding experience I have yet had at a Santa Fe theater." That high praise is well deserved by this community theater that goes out of its way to present refreshing, at times risky, plays. In an intimate theater on the south end of town, Theaterwork offers seven main-stage productions a year, a broad variety including new plays and classics by regional and national playwrights. Expect to see works by such names as Brecht, Shakespeare, and Victor Hugo. 1336 Rufina Circle (mail: P.O. Box 842). $\textcircled{C}$ 505/471-1799. www.theaterwork.org. Tickets $10–$15. Call for performance times.

DANCE COMPANIES
María Benitez Teatro Flamenco ★★ *Finds* You won't want to miss this cultural treat. True flamenco is one of the most thrilling of dance forms, displaying the inner spirit and verve of the gypsies of Spanish Andalusia, and María Benitez, trained in Spain, is a fabulous performer. The Benitez Company's "Estampa Flamenca" summer series is performed nightly except Tuesday from late June to early September. The María Benitez Theater at the Radisson Hotel is modern and showy, and yet it's intimate enough so you're immersed in the art. Institute for Spanish Arts, P.O. Box 8418. For tickets call $\textcircled{C}$ 888/435-2636, or the box office (June 16–Sept 3, $\textcircled{C}$ 505/982-1237). www.mariabenitez.com. Tickets $18–$42.

MAJOR CONCERT HALLS & ALL-PURPOSE AUDITORIUMS
Center for Contemporary Arts and Cinematheque CCA presents the work of internationally, nationally, and regionally known contemporary artists in art exhibitions, dance, new music concerts, poetry readings, performance-art events, theater, and video screenings. The Cinematheque screens films from around the world nightly, with special series presented regularly. CCA's galleries are open daily noon to 7pm. 1050 Old Pecos Trail. $\textcircled{C}$ 505/982-1338. www.ccasantafe.org. Film tickets $7.50. Art exhibitions are free; performances range broadly in price.

St. Francis Auditorium This atmospheric music hall, patterned after the interiors of traditional Hispanic mission churches, is noted for its excellent acoustics. The hall hosts a wide variety of musical events, including the Santa Fe Chamber Music Festival in July and August. Museum of Fine Arts, Lincoln and Palace aves. $\textcircled{C}$ 505/476-5072. Ticket prices vary; see above for specific performing-arts companies.

Sweeney Convention Center Santa Fe's largest indoor arena hosts a wide variety of trade expositions and other events during the year. The Berkshire Choral visits every year in May. 201 W. Marcy St. ✆ **800/777-2489** or 505/955-6200. Tickets $10–$30, depending on seating and performances. Tickets are never sold at Sweeney Convention Center; event sponsors handle ticket sales.

2 The Club & Music Scene

In addition to the clubs and bars listed below, there are a number of hotels whose bars and lounges feature some type of entertainment (see chapter 5.)

COUNTRY, JAZZ & LATIN

Cowgirl Hall of Fame It's difficult to categorize what goes on in this bar and restaurant, but there's live entertainment nightly. Some nights there's blues guitar, others folk music; you might also find "progressive rock," comedy, or cowboy poetry. In the summer, this is a great place to sit under the stars and listen to music. 319 S. Guadalupe St. ✆ **505/982-2565.** No cover for music Sun, Mon, and Wed. Tue and Thurs–Sat $3 cover. Special performances $10.

Eldorado Hotel In a grand lobby-lounge full of fine art, classical guitarists and pianists perform nightly. 309 W. San Francisco St. ✆ **505/988-4455.**

El Farol This original neighborhood bar of the Canyon Road artists' quarter (its name means "the lantern") is the place to head for local ambience. Its low ceilings and dark brown walls are home to Santa Fe's largest and most unusual selection of tapas (bar snacks and appetizers). Jazz, swing, folk, and ethnic musicians— some of national note—perform most nights. 808 Canyon Rd. ✆ **505/983-9912.** Cover $7.

La Fiesta Lounge ⭐ Set in the notable La Fonda hotel on the plaza, this nightclub offers excellent country bands on weekends, with old- and new-timers two-stepping across the floor. This lively lobby bar offers cocktails, an appetizer menu, and live entertainment nightly. It's a great authentic Santa Fe spot. La Fonda Hotel, 110 E. San Francisco St. ✆ **505/982-5511.**

Rodeo Nites A real locals' spot, this club offers dancing to a variety of types of music, including New Mexican, Mexican, and, on weekends, country. Open Wednesday through Sunday. 2911 Cerrillos Rd. ✆ **505/473-4138.** Cover varies, averaging $6.

ROCK & DISCO

Catamount Bar and Grille The post-college crowd hangs out at this bar, where there's live rock and blues music on weekends. Food is served until midnight, and there is also a billiards room. 125 E. Water St. ✆ **505/988-7222.**

Paramount Lounge and Night Club This hip nightspot presents an ambitious array of entertainment—from live music to comedy to weekly DJ dance nights. "Trash Disco" on Wednesday nights (a blend of disco hits from the '70s and more contemporary "house" music) is especially popular and always draws an eclectic crowd. On other nights, the dance floor transforms into a listening room for live music; recent performances included J. J. Cale and Buckwheat Zydeco.

In the back of the building you'll find Bar B, a much smaller room with more of an intimate, martini-lounge atmosphere. Along with a happy hour Monday to Friday, weekly live jazz, and changing art shows, Bar B hosts many musical acts—often "unplugged" singer-songwriters.

The **Candyman** (𝒞 505/983-5906) and the **CD Café** (𝒞 505/986-0735) sell tickets for Paramount Lounge events. 331 Sandoval St. 𝒞 505/982-8999. Cover $5 for dance nights; call for music performances.

3 The Bar Scene

The Dragon Room ★ A number of years ago, *International Newsweek* named the Dragon Room at The Pink Adobe (see chapter 6) one of the top 20 bars in the world. The reason is its spirited but comfortable ambience, which draws students, artists, politicians, and even an occasional celebrity. The decor theme is dragons, which you'll find carved on the front doors as well as hanging from the ceiling, all within low-lit, aged elegance akin to the Pink Adobe's interior. Live trees also grow through the roof. In addition to the tempting lunch and bar menu, there's always a complimentary bowl of popcorn close at hand. 406 Old Santa Fe Trail. 𝒞 505/983-7712.

El Paseo Bar and Grill You can almost always catch live music at this casual, unpretentious place (yet it's not a "sports bar"). The crowd here is somewhat younger than at most other downtown establishments, and on certain nights, the bar is completely packed. In addition to the open mic night on Tuesdays, a variety of local bands play here regularly—cranking out many types of music, from blues to rock to jazz to bluegrass. 208 Galisteo St. 𝒞 505/992-2848. Cover $3–$5 weekends.

Evangelo's A popular downtown hangout, this bar can get raucous at times. It's an interesting place, with tropical decor and a mahogany bar. More than 60 varieties of imported beer are available, and pool tables are an added attraction. On Friday and Saturday nights starting at 9pm and Wednesdays at 7:30pm, live bands play (jazz, rock, or reggae). Evangelo's is extremely popular with the local crowd. You'll find your share of business people, artists, and even bikers here. Open Monday to Saturday noon to 1:30am and Sundays until midnight. 200 W. San Francisco St. 𝒞 505/982-9014. Cover for special performances only.

Swig ★ *Finds* Santa Fe's most happening club stirs a splash of '60s retro in with a good shot of contemporary chic. The result? A smooth sip of fun. Catering to a broad variety of clientele, this martini bar serves classic and cutting-edge drinks along with delectable small plates of Asian food. The lounge serves until 11pm on weekdays and midnight on weekends, making it one of the few Santa Fe spots for late-night food. Open Tuesday through Saturday from 5pm to 2am. 135 W. Palace Ave., level 3. 𝒞 505/955-0400.

Vanessie of Santa Fe ★ This is unquestionably Santa Fe's most popular piano bar. The talented Doug Montgomery and Charles Tichenor have a loyal local following. Their repertoire ranges from Bach to Billy Joel, Gershwin to Barry Manilow. They play nightly from 8pm until closing, which could be anywhere from midnight to 2am. There's an extra microphone, so if you're daring (or drunk), you can stand up and accompany the piano and vocals (though this is *not* a karaoke scene). National celebrities have even joined in—including Harry Connick, Jr. (and he wasn't even drunk). Vanessie's offers a great bar menu. 434 W. San Francisco St. 𝒞 505/982-9966.

10

Excursions from Santa Fe

Native American pueblos and ruins, a national monument and national park, Los Alamos (the A-bomb capital of the United States), and the scenic and fascinating High Road to Taos are all easy day trips from Santa Fe. A longer drive will take you to Chaco Culture National Historic Park (well worth the time).

1 Exploring the Northern Pueblos

Of the eight northern pueblos, Tesuque, Pojoaque, Nambe, San Ildefonso, San Juan, and Santa Clara are within about 30 miles of Santa Fe. Picuris (San Lorenzo) is on the High Road to Taos (see section 3, below), and Taos Pueblo is just outside the town of Taos (p. 206).

The six pueblos described in this section can easily be visited in a single day's round-trip from Santa Fe, though I suggest visiting just the two that really give a feel of the ancient lifestyle: San Ildefonso, with its broad plaza, and San Juan, including its arts cooperative. In an easy day-trip from Santa Fe you can take in both, with some delicious New Mexican food in Española en route. If you're in the area at a time when you can catch certain rituals, that's when to see some of the other pueblos.

TESUQUE PUEBLO

Tesuque (te-*soo*-keh) Pueblo is located about 9 miles north of Santa Fe on US 84/285. You will know that you are approaching the pueblo when you see a large store near the highway. If you're driving north and you get to the unusual Camel Rock and a large roadside casino, you've missed the pueblo entrance.

The 400 pueblo dwellers at Tesuque are faithful to their traditional religion, rituals, and ceremonies. Excavations confirm that a pueblo has existed here at least since the year A.D. 1200; accordingly, this pueblo is now on the National Register of Historic Places. When you come to the welcome sign at the pueblo, turn right, go a block, and park on the right. You'll see the plaza off to the left. There's not a lot to see; in recent years renovation has brought a new look to some of the homes around it. There's a big open area where dances are held, and the **San Diego Church,** completed in 2004 on the site of an 1888 structure that burned down recently. It's the fifth church on the pueblo's plaza since 1641. Visitors are asked to remain in this area.

Some Tesuque women are skilled potters; Ignacia Duran's black-and-white and red micaceous pottery and Teresa Tapia's miniatures and pots with animal figures are especially noteworthy. You'll find many crafts at a gallery on the plaza's southeast corner. The **San Diego Feast Day,** which may feature harvest, buffalo, deer, flag, or Comanche dances, is November 12.

The Tesuque Pueblo address is Route 5, Box 360-T, Santa Fe, NM 87501 (© **505/983-2667**). Admission to the pueblo is free; however, there is a $20 charge for use of still cameras; special permission is required for movie cameras,

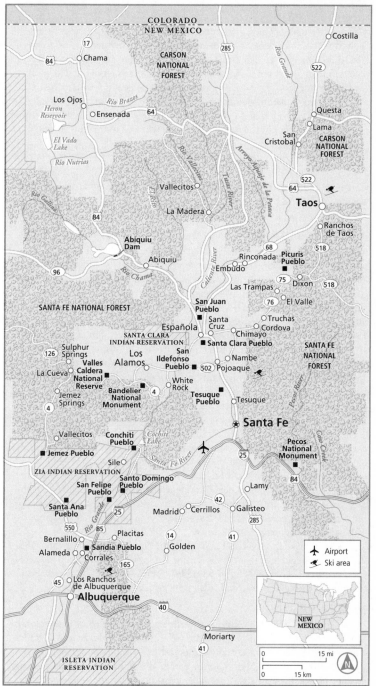

Pueblo Etiquette

When you visit pueblos, it is important to observe certain rules of etiquette. These are personal dwellings and/or important historic sites and must be respected as such. Don't climb on the buildings or peek into doors or windows. Don't enter sacred grounds, such as cemeteries and kivas. If you attend a dance or ceremony, remain silent while it is taking place and refrain from applause when it's over. Many pueblos prohibit photography or sketches; others require you to pay a fee for a permit. If you don't respect the privacy of the Native Americans who live at the pueblo, you'll be asked to leave.

---

sketching, and painting. The pueblo is open daily 9am to 5pm. **Camel Rock Casino** (© 505/984-8414) is open Sunday to Wednesday 8am to 4am, Thursday to Saturday 24 hours; it has a snack bar on the premises.

POJOAQUE PUEBLO

About 6 miles farther north of Tesuque Pueblo on US 84/285, at the junction of NM 502, Pojoaque (Po-*hwa*-keh) Pueblo provides a roadside peek into Pueblo arts. Though small (pop. 200) and without a definable village (more modern dwellings exist now), Pojoaque is important as a center for traveler services; in fact, Pojoaque, in its Tewa form, means "water-drinking place." The historical accounts of the Pojoaque people are sketchy, but we do know that in 1890, smallpox took its toll on the Pojoaque population, forcing most of the pueblo residents to abandon their village. Since the 1930s, the population has gradually increased, and in 1990, a war chief and two war captains were appointed. Today, visitors won't find much to look at, but the **Poeh Cultural Center and Museum,** on US 84/285, operated by the pueblo, features a museum, a cultural center, and artists' studios. It's situated within a complex of adobe buildings, including the three-story Sun Tower. There are frequent artist demonstrations, exhibitions, and, in the warmer months, traditional ceremonial dances. Indigenous pottery, embroidery, silverwork, and beadwork are available for sale at the Pojoaque Pueblo Visitor Center nearby.

If you leave US 84/285 and travel on the frontage road back to where the pueblo actually was, you'll encounter lovely orchards and alfalfa fields backed by desert and mountains. A modern community center is located near the site of the old pueblo and church. On December 12, the annual feast day of **Our Lady of Guadalupe** features a buffalo dance.

The pueblo's address is Rt. 11, Box 71, Santa Fe, NM 87506 (© 505/455-2278). The pueblo is open every day during daylight hours. The Poeh Center is at 78 Cities of Gold Rd. (© 505/455-3334). Admission is free. Open daily 8am to 5pm. Sketching, cameras, and video cameras are prohibited.

NAMBE PUEBLO

If you're still on US 84/285, continue north from Pojoaque about 3 miles until you come to NM 503; turn right, and travel until you see the Bureau of Reclamation sign for Nambe Falls; turn right on NP 101. Approximately 2 miles farther is Nambe ("mound of earth in the corner"), a 700-year-old Tewa-speaking pueblo (pop. 450), with a solar-powered tribal headquarters, at the foot of the Sangre de Cristo range. Only a few original pueblo buildings remain, including a large round kiva, used today in ceremonies. Pueblo artisans make woven belts,

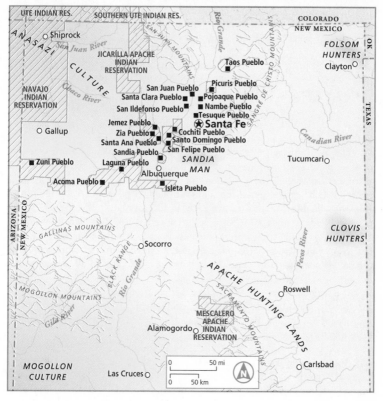

beadwork, and brown micaceous pottery. One of my favorite reasons for visiting this pueblo is to see the small herd of bison that roam on 179 acres set aside for them.

Nambe Falls make a stunning three-tier drop through a cleft in a rock face about 4 miles beyond the pueblo. You can reach the falls via a 15-minute hike on a rocky, clearly marked path that leaves from the picnic area. A recreational site at the reservoir offers fishing, boating (non-motor boats only), hiking, camping, and picnicking. The **Waterfall Dances** on July 4 and the **Saint Francis of Assisi Feast Day** on October 4, which has buffalo and deer dances, are observed at the pueblo. Recent dry weather has caused cancellations; before setting out, call the pueblo.

The address is Route 1, Box 117-BB, Santa Fe, NM 87501 (✆ **505/455-2036,** or 505/455-2304 for the Ranger Station). Admission to the pueblo is free, but there is a $10 charge for still cameras, $20 for movie cameras, and $25 for sketching. The pueblo is open daily 8am to 5pm. The recreational site is open in March 7am to 6pm, in April and May 7am to 8pm, in June to August 6am to 8pm, and in September and October 7am to 7pm.

SAN ILDEFONSO PUEBLO ★★

Pox Oge, as San Ildefonsos Pueblo is called in its own Tewa language, means "place where the water cuts down through," possibly because of the way the Rio Grande cuts through the mountains nearby. Turn left on NM 502 at Pojoaque, and drive about 6 miles to the turnoff. This pueblo has a broad, dusty plaza, with a kiva on one side, ancient dwellings on the other, and a church at the far end. It's nationally famous for its matte-finish, black-on-black pottery, developed by tribeswoman María Martinez in the 1920s. One of the most visited pueblos in northern New Mexico, San Ildefonso attracts more than 20,000 visitors a year.

The San Ildefonsos could best be described as rebellious because this was one of the last pueblos to succumb to the reconquest spearheaded by Don Diego de Vargas in 1692. Within view of the pueblo is the volcanic Black Mesa, a symbol of the San Ildefonsos people's strength. Through the years, each time San Ildefonso felt itself threatened by enemy forces, the residents, along with members of other pueblos, would hide out up on the butte, returning to the valley only when starvation set in. Today, a visit to the pueblo is valuable mainly in order to see or buy rich black pottery. A few shops surround the plaza, and there's the **San Ildefonso Pueblo Museum** tucked away in the governor's office beyond the plaza. I especially recommend visiting during ceremonial days. **San Ildefonso Feast Day,** on January 23, features the buffalo and Comanche dances in alternate years. **Corn dances,** held in late August or early September, commemorate a basic element in pueblo life, the importance of fertility in all creatures—humans as well as animals—and plants.

The pueblo has a 4½-acre fishing lake that is surrounded by *bosque* (Spanish for "forest"), open April to October. Picnicking is encouraged, though you may want to look at the sites before you decide to stay; some are nicer than others. Camping is not allowed.

The pueblo's address is Route 5, Box 315A, Santa Fe, NM 87506 (© **505/ 455-3549**). The admission charge is $3 per car. The charge for using a still camera is $10; you'll pay $20 to use a video camera and $25 for sketching. If you plan to fish, the charge is $10 for adults and $8 for seniors and children under 12 years, but you'll want to call to be sure the lake is open. The pueblo is open in the summer, daily 8am to 5pm; call for weekend hours. In the winter, it is open Monday to Friday 8am to 4:30pm. It's closed for major holidays and tribal events.

SAN JUAN PUEBLO ⊛

If you continue north on US 84/285, you will reach San Juan Pueblo via NM 74, a mile off NM 68, about 4 miles north of Española.

The largest (pop. 1,950) and northernmost of the Tewa-speaking pueblos and headquarters of the Eight Northern Indian Pueblos Council, San Juan is located on the east side of the Rio Grande—opposite the 1598 site of San Gabriel, the first Spanish settlement west of the Mississippi River and the first capital of New Spain. In 1598, the Spanish, impressed with the openness and helpfulness of the people of San Juan, decided to establish a capital there (it was moved to Santa Fe 10 years later), making San Juan Pueblo the first to be subjected to Spanish colonization. The Indians were generous, providing food, clothing, shelter, and fuel—they even helped sustain the settlement when its leader Conquistador Juan de Oñate became preoccupied with his search for gold and neglected the needs of his people. Unfortunately, the Spanish subjugation of the Indians left them virtual slaves, forced to provide the Spanish with corn, venison, cloth, and labor. They were compelled to participate in Spanish religious ceremonies and to abandon their own religious practices. Under no circumstances were Indian ceremonies allowed; those caught participating in them were punished. In 1676, several Indians were accused of sorcery and jailed in Santa Fe. Later they were led to the plaza, where they were flogged or hanged. This despicable incident became a turning point in Indian–Spanish relations, generating an overwhelming feeling of rage in the Indian community. One of the accused, a San Juan Pueblo Indian named Po'Pay, became a leader in the Great Pueblo Revolt, which led to freedom from Spanish rule for 12 years.

The past and present cohabit here. Though many of the tribe members are Catholics, most of the San Juan tribe still practice traditional religious rituals. Thus, two rectangular kivas flank the church in the main plaza, and *caciques* (pueblo priests) share power with civil authorities. The annual **San Juan Fiesta** is held June 23 and 24; it features buffalo and Comanche dances. Another annual ceremony is the **turtle dance** on December 26. The **Matachine dance,** performed here Christmas day, vividly depicts the subjugation of the Native Americans by the Catholic Spaniards (p. 290).

The address of the pueblo is P.O. Box 1099, San Juan Pueblo, NM 87566 (**©** **505/852-4400** or 505/852-4210). Admission is free. Photography or sketching may be allowed with prior permission from the governor's office. For information, call the number above. The charge for fishing is $8 for adults and $5 for children and seniors. The pueblo is open every day during daylight hours.

The **Eight Northern Indian Pueblos Council** (**©** **505/852-4265**) is a sort of chamber of commerce and social-service agency.

A crafts shop, **Oke Oweenge Arts and Crafts Cooperative** (**©** **505/852-2372**), specializes in local wares. This is a fine place to seek out San Juan's distinctive red pottery, a lustrous ceramic incised with traditional geometric symbols. Also displayed for sale are seed, turquoise, and silver jewelry; wood and stone carvings; indigenous clothing and weavings; embroidery; and paintings. Artisans often work on the premises, allowing visitors to watch. The co-op is open Monday through Saturday 9am to 4:30pm in winter, until 5pm in summer (but is closed San Juan Feast Day, June 24). **Sunrise Crafts,** another crafts shop, is located to the right of the co-op. There, you'll find one-of-a-kind hand-crafted pipes, beadwork, and burned and painted gourds.

Fishing and picnicking are encouraged at the **San Juan Tribal Lakes,** open year-round. **Ohkay Casino** (**©** **505/747-1668**) offers table games and slot machines, as well as live music nightly Tuesday through Saturday. It's open every day, 24 hours.

SANTA CLARA PUEBLO

Close to Española (on NM 5), Santa Clara, with a population of about 1,800, is one of the largest pueblos, and it's the one most special to me. I've spent a good bit of time here, writing about the Santa Clara people. You'll see the village sprawling across the river basin near the beautiful Black Mesa, rows of tract homes surrounding an adobe central area. Although it's in an incredible setting, the pueblo itself is not much to see; however, a trip through it will give a real feel for the contemporary lives of these people. Though stories vary, the Santa Clarans teach their children that their ancestors once lived in cliffside dwellings named Puye and migrated down to the river bottom in the 13th century. This pueblo is noted for its language program. Artisan elders work with children to teach them their native Tewa language, on the brink of extinction because so many now speak English. This pueblo is also the home of noted potter Nancy Youngblood, who comes from a long line of famous potters and now does alluring contemporary work.

Follow the main route to the old village, where you come to the visitor center, also known as the neighborhood center. There you can get directions to small shops that sell distinctive black incised Santa Clara pottery, red burnished pottery, baskets, and other crafts. One stunning sight here is the cemetery. Stop on the west side of the church and look over the 4-foot wall. It's a primitive site, with plain wooden crosses and some graves adorned with plastic flowers.

There are corn and harvest dances on **Santa Clara Feast Day** (Aug 12); information on other special days (including the corn or harvest dances, as well as children's dances) can be obtained from the pueblo office.

The famed **Puye Cliff Dwellings** (see below) are on the Santa Clara reservation.

The pueblo's address is P.O. Box 580, Española, NM 87532 (© **505/753-7326**). Admission is free. The charge for still cameras is $5; video cameras and sketching are not allowed. The pueblo is open every day 9am to 4pm; the visitor center is open Monday to Friday 8am to 4:30pm.

PUYE CLIFF DWELLINGS 😊⋆

Well worth visiting, the Puye Cliff Dwellings offer a view of centuries of culture so well preserved you can almost hear ancient life clamoring around you. Unfortunately, recent fires devastated the area, so Santa Clara has closed the ruins and recreation area indefinitely. Call before setting out.

If you do get to see them, you'll first encounter dwellings believed to have been built around 1450. Above, on a 200-foot cliff face, are dwellings dating from 1200. By 1540, this dwelling's population was at its height, and Puye was the center for a number of villages of the Pajarito Plateau. Today, this settlement, which typifies Pajaritan culture in the placement of its houses and its symbolic decorations, is a series of rooms and caves reached by sturdy ladders and steps that visitors can climb up and down, clambering in and out of the homes.

If you would like to visit the cliff dwellings, call © **505/753-7326** for opening times and admissions information (before the area was closed, admission was $6 for adults, $5 for children and seniors). To reach Puye: At the intersection of NM 502 and NM 30, head north for 4 miles to Indian Road 601. Travel this paved road for 7 miles.

2 Los Alamos & the Ancient Cliff Dwellings of Bandelier National Monument

Pueblo tribes lived in the rugged Los Alamos area for well over 1,000 years, and an exclusive boys' school operated atop the 7,300-foot plateau from 1918 to 1943. Then, the **Los Alamos National Laboratory** was established here in secrecy, code-named Site Y of the Manhattan Project, the hush-hush wartime program that developed the world's first atomic bombs.

Project director J. Robert Oppenheimer, later succeeded by Norris E. Bradbury, worked along with thousands of scientists, engineers, and technicians in research, development, and production of those early weapons. Today, more than 10,000 people work at the Los Alamos National Laboratory, making it the largest employer in northern New Mexico. Operated from the beginning by the University of California, currently under a contract through the U.S. Department of Energy, its 2,200 individual facilities and 47 separate technical areas occupy 43 square miles of mesa-top land.

The laboratory is known today as one of the world's foremost scientific institutions. While primarily focused on nuclear weapons research—the Trident and

Minuteman strategic warheads were designed here, for example—it has many other interdisciplinary research programs, including international nuclear safeguards and nonproliferation, space, and atmospheric studies; supercomputing; theoretical physics; biomedical and materials science; and environmental restoration.

Current plans call on Los Alamos National Laboratory, in 2007, to begin building a limited number of replacement plutonium pits for use in the enduring U.S. nuclear weapons stockpile. The lab has the only plutonium-processing facility in the United States that is capable of producing those components.

ORIENTATION/USEFUL INFORMATION

Los Alamos is located about 35 miles west of Santa Fe and about 65 miles southwest of Taos. From Santa Fe, take US 84/285 north approximately 16 miles to the Pojoaque junction, then turn west on NM 502. Driving time is only about 50 minutes.

Los Alamos is a town of 18,000, spread over the colorful, fingerlike mesas of the Pajarito Plateau, between the Jemez Mountains and the Rio Grande Valley. As NM 502 enters Los Alamos from Santa Fe, it follows Trinity Drive, where accommodations, restaurants, and other services are located. Central Avenue parallels Trinity Drive and has restaurants, galleries, and shops, as well as the **Los Alamos Historical Museum** (1921 Juniper St.; © 505/662-4493; free) and the **Bradbury Science Museum** (15th St. and Central Ave.; © 505/667-4444; free). In the spring of 2000, the town was evacuated due to a forest fire that destroyed 400 families' homes. Though no lives were lost, the appearance of Los Alamos and particularly the forest surrounding it—47,000 acres of which burned—were forever changed.

The **Los Alamos Chamber of Commerce,** P.O. Box 460, Los Alamos, NM 87544 (© 505/662-8105; fax 505/662-8399), runs a visitor center that is open Monday to Friday 9am to 5pm, Saturday 9am to 4pm, and Sunday 10am to 3pm. It's located at 109 Central Park Square (across from the Bradbury Science Museum).

EVENTS

The Los Alamos events schedule includes a **Sports Skiesta** in mid-March; **arts-and-crafts fairs** in May, August, and November; a **county fair, rodeo, and arts festival** in August; and a **triathlon** in August/September.

WHAT TO SEE & DO

Aside from the sights described below, Los Alamos offers the **Pajarito Mountain ski area,** Camp May Road (P.O. Box 155), Los Alamos, NM 87544 (© 505/662-5725), with five chairlifts—it's only open on Friday through Sunday and federal holidays. It's an outstanding ski area that rarely gets crowded; many trails are steep and have moguls. Los Alamos also offers the **Los Alamos Golf Course,** 4250 Diamond Dr. (© 505/662-8139), at the edge of town, where greens fees are around $20; and the **Larry R. Walkup Aquatic Center,** 2760 Canyon Rd. (© 505/662-8170), the highest-altitude indoor Olympic-size swimming pool in the United States. Not far from downtown is an outdoor ice-skating rink, with a snack bar and skate rentals, open Thanksgiving to late February (© 505/662-4500). It's located at 4475 West Rd. (take Trinity Dr. to Diamond St., turn left and watch for the sign on your right). There are no outstanding restaurants in Los Alamos, but if you get hungry, you can stop at the **Blue Window,** 800 Trinity Dr. (© 505/662-6305), a country-style restaurant serving pasta, sandwiches, and salads, with a view of the Sangre de Cristo Mountains. The Chamber of Commerce has maps for self-guided historical walking tours, and you can find self-guided driving-tour tapes at stores and hotels around town.

The Art Center at Fuller Lodge This is a public showcase for work by visual artists from northern New Mexico and the surrounding region. Two annual arts-and-crafts fairs are also held here—in August and October. The gallery shop sells local crafts at good prices.

In the same building is the **Los Alamos Arts Council** (© 505/663-0477), a multidisciplinary organization that sponsors two art fairs (May and Nov), as well as evening and noontime cultural programs.

2132 Central Ave., Los Alamos. © 505/662-9331. www.artfulnm.org. Free admission. Mon–Sat 10am–4pm.

Black Hole *Finds* This store/museum is an engineer's dream world, a creative photographer's heaven, and a Felix Unger nightmare. Owned and run by Edward Grothus, it's an old grocery store packed to the ceiling with the remains of the nuclear age, from Geiger counters to giant Waring blenders. If you go, be sure to visit with Grothus. He'll point out an A-frame building next door that he's christened the "First Church of High Technology," where he says a "critical mass" each Sunday. In this business for over 50 years, Grothus has been written about in *Wired* magazine and has supplied props for the movies *Silkwood, Earth II,* and *The Manhattan Project.*

4015 Arkansas, Los Alamos. © 505/662-5053. Free admission. Mon–Sat 10am–5pm.

Bradbury Science Museum ★ This is a great place to get acquainted with what goes on at a weapons production facility after nuclear proliferation. Though the museum is run by Los Alamos National Laboratory, which definitely puts a positive spin on the business of producing weapons, it's a fascinating place to explore and includes more than 35 hands-on exhibits. Begin in the History Gallery, where you'll learn about the evolution of the site from the Los Alamos Ranch School days through the Manhattan Project to the present, including a 1939 letter from Albert Einstein to President Franklin D. Roosevelt, suggesting research into uranium as a new and important source of energy. Next, move into the Research and Technology Gallery, where you can see work that's been done on the Human Genome Project, including a computer map of human DNA. You can try out a laser and learn about the workings of a particle accelerator. Meanwhile, listen for announcement of the film *The Town That Never Was,* an 18-minute presentation on this community that grew up shrouded in secrecy (shown in the auditorium). Further exploration will take you to the Defense Gallery, where you can test the heaviness of plutonium against that of other substances, see an actual 5-ton Little Boy nuclear bomb (like the one dropped on Hiroshima), and see firsthand how Los Alamos conducts worldwide surveillance of nuclear explosions. The museum has added a new exhibit on national defense. It presents issues related to nuclear weapons: why we have them, how they work, how scientists ensure that aging weapons will still work, what treaties govern them, and what environmental problem sites resulted from their production. It includes a 16-minute film, computer-based activities for visitors, and displays of bombs, a cruise missile, and warhead casings.

15th St. and Central Ave., Los Alamos. © 505/667-4444. Free admission. Tues–Fri 9am–5pm; Sat–Mon 1–5pm. Closed Thanksgiving, Christmas, and New Year's Day.

Los Alamos Historical Museum ⭐   Fuller Lodge, a massive vertical-log building built by John Gaw Meem in 1928, is well worth the visit. The log work is intricate and artistic, and the feel of the old place is warm and majestic. It once housed the dining and recreation hall for the Los Alamos Ranch School for boys and is now a National Historic Landmark. It is accessible to people with disabilities. Its current occupants include the museum office and research archives and The Art Center at Fuller Lodge (see above). The museum, located in the small log-and-stone building to the north of Fuller Lodge, depicts area history from prehistoric cliff dwellers to the present. Exhibits range from Native American artifacts to school memorabilia and an excellent Manhattan Project exhibit that offers a more realistic view of the devastation resulting from use of atomic bombs than is offered at the Bradbury Science Museum.

1921 Juniper St., Los Alamos. ✆ **505/662-4493.** Free admission. Summer Mon–Sat 9:30am–4:30pm, Sun 11am–5pm; winter Mon–Sat 10am–4pm, Sun 1–4pm. Closed Thanksgiving, Dec 25, and Easter.

NEARBY

Bandelier National Monument ⭐⭐⭐   Less than 15 miles south of Los Alamos along NM 4, this National Park Service area contains stunningly preserved ruins of the ancient cliff-dwelling ancestral Puebloan (Anasazi) culture within 46 square miles of canyon-and-mesa wilderness. The national monument is named after the Swiss-American archaeologist Adolph Bandelier, who explored here in the 1880s. During busy summer months, head out early; there can be a waiting line for cars to park.

After an orientation stop at the visitor center and museum to learn about the culture that flourished here between 1100 and 1550, most visitors follow a trail along Frijoles Creek to the principal ruins. The pueblo site, including an underground kiva, has been stabilized. The biggest thrill for most folks is climbing hardy ponderosa pine ladders to visit an alcove—140 feet above the canyon floor—that was once home to prehistoric people. Tours are self-guided or led by a National Park Service ranger. Be aware that dogs are not allowed on trails.

On summer nights, rangers offer campfire talks about the history, culture, and geology of the area. The guided night walks offered some summer evenings reveal a different, spooky aspect of the ruins and cave houses, outlined in the two-dimensional chiaroscuro of the thin light from the starry sky. During the day, nature programs are sometimes offered for adults and children. The small museum at the visitor center displays artifacts found in the area.

Elsewhere in the monument area, 70 miles of maintained trails lead to more tribal ruins, waterfalls, and wildlife habitats. However, a recent fire has decimated parts of this area, so periodic closings will take place in order to allow the land to reforest.

The separate **Tsankawi** section, reached by an ancient 2-mile trail close to **White Rock,** has a large unexcavated ruin on a high mesa overlooking the Rio Grande Valley. The town of White Rock, about 10 miles southeast of Los Alamos on NM 4, offers spectacular panoramas of the river valley in the direction of Santa Fe; the **White Rock Overlook** is a great picnic spot. Within Bandelier, areas have been set aside for picnicking and camping.

While you're in the area, check out the **Valles Caldera National Preserve,** past Bandelier National Monument on NM 4, beginning about 15 miles from Los Alamos. The reserve is all that remains of a volcanic caldera created by a collapse after eruptions nearly a million years ago. When the mountain spewed ashes and dust as far away as Kansas and Nebraska, its underground magma chambers collapsed, forming this great valley—one of the largest volcanic calderas in the world. Lava domes that pushed up after the collapse obstruct a full view across the expanse, but the beauty of the place is still within grasp. Visitors have many guided options for exploring the preserve, from sleigh rides in winter to fly-fishing in summer. For more information check out www.vallescaldera.gov.

NM 4 (HCR 1, Box 1, Suite 15, Los Alamos). *©* **505/672-3861**, ext 517. www.nps.gov/band. Admission $10 per vehicle. Open daily during daylight hours. No pets allowed on trails. Closed Christmas and New Year's Day.

3 Along the High Road to Taos ★★

Unless you're in a hurry to get from Santa Fe to Taos, the High Road—also called the Mountain Road or the King's Road—is by far the most fascinating route between the two cities. It begins in lowlands of mystically formed pink and yellow stone, passing by apple and peach orchards and chile farms in the weaving village of **Chimayo.** Then it climbs toward the highlands to the village of **Cordova,** known for its woodcarvers, and higher still to **Truchas,** a renegade arts town where Hispanic traditions and ways of life continue much as they did a century ago. Though I've described this tour from south to north, the most scenic way to see it is from north to south, on your return from Taos.

CHIMAYO

About 28 miles north of Santa Fe on NM 76/285 is the historic weaving center of Chimayo. It's approximately 16 miles past the Pojoaque junction, at the junction of NM 520 and NM 76 via NM 503. In this small village, families still maintain the tradition of crafting hand-woven textiles initiated by their ancestors seven generations ago, in the early 1800s. One such family is the Ortegas, and both **Ortega's Weaving Shop** (*©* **505/351-4215**) and **Galeria Ortega** (*©* **505/351-2288**), both at the corner of NM 520 and NM 76, are fine places to take a close look at this ancient craft. A more humble spot is **Trujillo Weavings** (*©* **505/351-4457**) on NM 76. If you're lucky enough to find the proprietors in, you might get a weaving history lesson. You can see an 80-year-old loom and a 100-year-old shuttle carved from apricot wood. The weavings you'll find are some of the best of the Rio Grande style, with rich patterns, many made from naturally dyed wool. Also on display are some fine Cordova woodcarvings.

One of the best places to shop in Chimayo, **Chimayo Trading and Mercantile** (*©* **505/351-4566**), on Highway 76, is a richly cluttered store carrying local arts and crafts as well as select imports. It has a good selection of kachinas and Hopi corn maidens, as well as specialty items such as elaborately beaded cow skulls. Look for George Zarolinski's "smoked porcelain."

Many people come to Chimayo to visit **El Santuario de Nuestro Señor de Esquipulas (the Shrine of Our Lord of Esquipulas)** ★★, better known simply as "El Santuario de Chimayo." Ascribed with miraculous powers of healing, this church has attracted thousands of pilgrims since its construction in 1814 to 1816. Up to 30,000 people participate in the annual Good Friday pilgrimage, many of them walking from as far away as Albuquerque.

Although only the earth in the anteroom beside the altar is presumed to have the gift of healing powers, the entire shrine radiates true serenity. A National Historic Landmark, the church has five beautiful *reredos* (panels of sacred paintings)—one behind the main altar and two on each side of the nave. Each year during the fourth weekend in July, the military exploits of the

9th-century Spanish saint Santiago are celebrated in a weekend fiesta, including the historic play *Los Moros y Los Cristianos (The Moors and the Christians).*

A good place to stop for a quick bite, **Leona's Restaurante de Chimayo** (© 505/351-4569) is right next door to the Santuario de Chimayo. Leona herself presides over this little taco and burrito stand with plastic tables inside and, during warm months, out. Leona has gained national fame for her flavored tortilla—such delicacies as raspberry and chocolate really are tasty. Burritos and soft tacos made with chicken, beef, or veggie-style with beans will definitely tide you over en route to Taos or Santa Fe. Open 11am to 5pm, closed Tuesday and Wednesday.

Nearby **Santa Cruz Lake** provides water for Chimayo Valley farms and also offers a recreation site for trout fishing and camping at the edge of the Pecos Wilderness. During busy summer months, trash might litter its shores. To reach the lake from Chimayo, drive 2 miles south on NM 520, then turn east on NM 503 and travel 4 miles.

WHERE TO STAY

Casa Escondida ⓐ On the outskirts of Chimayo, this inn offers a lovely retreat and a good home base for exploring the Sangre de Cristo Mountains and their many soulful farming villages. This hacienda-feeling place has a cozy living room with a large kiva fireplace. Decor is simple and classic, with Mission-style furniture lending a colonial feel. The breakfast room is a sunny atrium with French doors that open out in summer to a grassy yard spotted with apricot trees. The rooms are varied; all of my favorites are within the main house. The Sun Room catches all that passionate northern New Mexico sun upon its red brick floors and on its private flagstone patio as well. It has an elegant feel and connects with a smaller room, so it's a good choice for families. The Vista is on the second story. Its dormer windows give it an oddly shaped roofline. It has a wrought-iron queen-size bed as well a twin, and it opens out onto a large deck offering spectacular sunset views. The casita adjacent to the main house has a kiva fireplace, a stove, and a minirefrigerator, as well as nice meadow views.

P.O. Box 142, Chimayo, NM 87522. © 800/643-7201 or 505/351-4805. Fax 505/351-2575. www.casaescondida.com. 8 units. $85–$145 double. Rates include full breakfast. MC, V. Pets welcome for a small fee; pre-arrangement required. **Amenities:** Jacuzzi; in-room massage; laundry service.

WHERE TO DINE

Restaurante Rancho de Chimayo ⓐ NEW MEXICAN For as long as I can remember, my family and many of my friends' families have scheduled trips into northern New Mexico to coincide with lunch- or dinnertime at this fun restaurant. Located in an adobe home built by Hermenegildo Jaramillo in the 1880s, it is now run as a restaurant by his descendants. Unfortunately, over the years the restaurant has become so famous that tour buses now stop here. However, the food has suffered only a little. In the warmer months, request to dine on the terraced patio. During winter, you'll be seated in one of a number of cozy rooms with thick viga ceilings. The food is native New Mexican, prepared from generations-old Jaramillo family recipes. You can't go wrong with the enchiladas, served layered, northern New Mexico style, rather than rolled. For variety you might want to try the *combinación picante* (carne adovada, tamale, enchilada, beans, and posole). Each plate comes with two *sopaipillas*. With a little honey, who needs dessert? The full bar serves delicious margaritas.

P.O. Box 11, Chimayo, (CTR 98). © 505/351-4444. Reservations recommended. Lunch $7.50–$13; dinner $10–$15. AE, DC, DISC, MC, V. Daily 11:30am–9pm; Sat–Sun breakfast 8:30–10:30am. Closed Mon Nov 1–Apr 30.

CORDOVA

Just as Chimayo is famous for its weaving, the village of Cordova, about 7 miles east on NM 76, is noted for its wood carvers. It's easy to whiz by this village, nestled below the High Road, but don't. Just a short way through this truly traditional northern New Mexico town is a gem: **The Castillo Gallery** ✮ (✆ **505/351-4067**), a mile into the village of Cordova, carries moody and colorful acrylic paintings by Paula Castillo, as well as her found-art welded sculptures. It also carries the work of Terry Enseñat Mulert, whose contemporary woodcarvings are treasures of the high country. En route to the Castillo, you may want to stop in at two other local carvers' galleries. The first you'll come to is that of **Sabinita Lopez Ortiz;** the second belongs to her cousin, **Gloria Ortiz.** Both are descendants of the well-noted José Dolores Lopez. Carved from cedar wood and aspen, the works range from simple statues of saints *(santos)* to elaborate scenes of birds.

TRUCHAS

Robert Redford's 1988 movie *The Milagro Beanfield War* featured the town of Truchas (which means "trout"). A former Spanish colonial outpost built on top of an 8,000-foot mesa, 4 miles east of Cordova, it was chosen as the site for the film in part because traditional Hispanic culture is still very much in evidence. Subsistence farming is prevalent here. The scenery is spectacular: 13,101-foot Truchas Peak dominates one side of the mesa, and the broad Rio Grande Valley dominates the other.

Be sure to find your way into **The Cordovas' Handweaving Workshop** (✆ **505/689-2437**). Located in the center of town, this tiny shop is run by Harry Cordova, a fourth-generation weaver with a unique style. His works tend to be simpler than many Rio Grande weavings, utilizing mainly stripes in the designs.

Just down the road from Cordovas' is **Hand Artes Gallery** (✆ **800/ 689-2441** or 505/689-2443), a definite surprise in this remote region. Here you'll find an array of contemporary as well as representational art from noted regional artists. Look for Sheila Keeffe's worldly painted panels, Susan Christie's monoprints and subtly textured paintings, and Norbert Voelkel's colorful paintings.

About 6 miles east of Truchas on NM 76 is the small town of **Las Trampas,** noted for its **San José Church,** which, with its thick walls and elegant lines, might possibly be the most beautiful of all New Mexico churches built during the Spanish colonial period.

PICURIS (SAN LORENZO) PUEBLO

Near the regional education center of Peñasco, about 24 miles from Chimayo, near the intersection of NM 75 and NM 76, is the Picuris (San Lorenzo) Pueblo (✆ **505/587-2519**). The 375 citizens of this 15,000-acre mountain pueblo, native Tewa speakers, consider themselves a sovereign nation: Their forebears never made a treaty with any foreign country, including the United States. Thus, they observe a traditional form of tribal council government. A few of the original mud-and-stone houses still stand, as does a lovely church. A striking aboveground ceremonial kiva called "the Roundhouse," built at least 700 years ago, and some historic excavated kivas and storerooms are located on a hill above the pueblo and are open to visitors. The **annual feast days** at San Lorenzo Church are August 9 and 10.

The people here are modern enough to have fully computerized their public showcase operations as Picuris Tribal Enterprises. Besides running the Hotel Santa Fe in the state capital, they own the **Picuris Pueblo Museum and Visitor's Center,** where weaving, beadwork, and distinctive reddish-brown clay cooking pottery are exhibited daily 9am to 6pm. Self-guided tours through the old village ruins begin at the museum and cost $5; the camera fee is $6; sketching and video camera fees are $25. There's also an information center, crafts shop, and restaurant. Fishing permits ($11 for adults, $8 for seniors, and $7 for children) are available, as are permits to camp ($8) at Tu-Tah Lake, which is regularly stocked with trout.

About a mile east of Peñasco on NM 75 is **Vadito,** the former center for a conservative Catholic brotherhood, the Penitentes, early in the 20th century. You'll see a small adobe chapel on the left. Also watch for Penitente crosses scattered about the area, often on hilltops.

DIXON & EMBUDO

Taos is about 24 miles north of Peñasco via NM 518, but day-trippers from Santa Fe can loop back to the capital by taking NM 75 west from Picuris Pueblo. Dixon, approximately 12 miles west of Picuris, and its twin village Embudo, a mile farther on NM 68 at the Rio Grande, are home to many artists and craftspeople who exhibit their works during the annual **autumn show** sponsored by the Dixon Arts Association. If you get to Embudo at mealtime, stop in at **Embudo Station** (© 800/852-4707 or 505/852-4707), a restaurant right on the banks of the Rio Grande. From mid-April to October—the only time it's open—you can sit on the patio under giant cottonwoods and sip the restaurant's own microbrewed beer (try the green-chile ale, its most celebrated) and signature wines while watching the peaceful Rio flow by. The specialty here is Southwestern food, but you'll find other tantalizing tastes as well. Try the rainbow trout roasted on a cedar plank. The restaurant is generally open Tuesday to Sunday noon to 9pm, but call before making plans. It is especially known for its Jazz on Sunday, an affair that PBS once featured. For more taste of the local grape, you can follow signs to **La Chiripada Winery** (© 505/579-4437), whose product is surprisingly good, especially to those who don't know that New Mexico has a long winemaking history. Local pottery is also sold in the tasting room. The winery is open Monday to Saturday 10am to 5pm, Sunday noon to 5pm.

Two more small villages lie in the Rio Grande Valley at 6-mile intervals south of Embudo on NM 68. **Velarde** is a fruit-growing center; in season, the road here is lined with stands selling fresh fruit or crimson chile ristras and wreaths of native plants. **Alcalde** is the site of Los Luceros, an early-17th-century home that is to be refurbished as an arts and history center. The unique **Dance of the Matachines,** a Moorish-style ritual brought from Spain, is performed here on holidays and feast days (p. 290).

ESPAÑOLA

The commercial center of Española (pop. 7,000) no longer has the railroad that led to its establishment in the 1880s, but it may have New Mexico's greatest concentration of **low riders.** These are late-model customized cars, so called because their suspension leaves them sitting quite close to the ground. For details, see the box below.

Sights of interest in Española include the **Bond House Museum** (© 505/747-8535), a Victorian-era adobe home that exhibits local history and art; and

---

Fun Fact   **Lowriders: Car Art**

While cruising Española's main drag, don't drop your jaw if you see the front of a car raise up off the ground and then sink down again, or if you witness another that appears to be scraping its underbelly on the pavement. These novelties are part of a car culture that thrives in northern New Mexico. Traditionally, the owners use late-model cars, which they soup up with such novelties as elaborate chrome, metal chain steering wheels, even portraits of Our Lady of Guadalupe painted on the hood. If you're interested in seeing the "Custom Car and Truck Show" put on by local car clubs (and often co-sponsored by local casinos), call the Española Valley Chamber of Commerce for information (© **505/753-2831**).

---

the **Santa Cruz Church,** built in 1733 and renovated in 1979, which houses many fine examples of Spanish colonial religious art. The **Convento,** built to resemble a colonial cathedral, on the Española Plaza (at the junction of NM 30 and US 84), houses a variety of shops, including a trading post and an antiques gallery, as well as a display room for the Historical Society. Major events include the July **Fiesta de Oñate,** commemorating the valley's founding in 1596; the October **Tri-Cultural Art Festival** on the Northern New Mexico Community College campus; the weeklong **Summer Solstice** celebration staged in June by the nearby Ram Dass Puri ashram of the Sikhs (© **888/346-2420** or 505/367-1310); and **Peace Prayer Day,** an outdoor festival in mid-June—featuring art, music, food, guest speakers, and more—in the Jemez mountains (© **877/707-3223**).

Complete information on Española and the vicinity can be obtained from the **Española Valley Chamber of Commerce,** 710 Paseo de Onate, Española, NM 87532 (© **505/753-2831**).

If you admire the work of Georgia O'Keeffe, try to plan a short trip to **Abiquiu,** a tiny town at a bend of the Rio Chama, 14 miles south of Ghost Ranch and 22 miles north of Española on US 84. When you see the surrounding terrain, it will be clear that this was the inspiration for many of her startling landscapes. **O'Keeffe's adobe home** ✿ (where she lived and painted) is open for public tours. However, a reservation must be made in advance; the minimum requested donation is $22 for a 1-hour tour. A number of tours are given each week—on Tuesday, Thursday, and Friday (Mar–Nov only)—and a limited number of people are accepted per tour. Visitors are not permitted to take pictures. Fortunately, O'Keeffe's home remains as it was when she lived there (until 1986). Call several months in advance for reservations (© **505/685-4539**).

WHERE TO STAY & DINE

El Paragua ✿ NORTHERN NEW MEXICAN   This Española restaurant is a great place to stop en route to Taos, though some Santa Feans make a special trip here. Every time I enter El Paragua (which means "the umbrella"), with its red-tile floors and colorful Saltillo-tile trimmings, I feel as though I've stepped into Mexico. The restaurant opened in 1958 as a small taco stand owned by two brothers, and through the years it has flourished. It has received praise from many sources, including *Gourmet Magazine* and N. Scott Momaday, writing for the *New York Times*. You can't go wrong ordering the enchilada suprema, a chicken and cheese enchilada with onion and sour cream. Also on the menu are fajitas and a variety of seafood dishes and steaks, including the *churrasco Argentino*. Served at your table in a hot brazier, it's cooked in a green herb *salsa chimichurri*. There's a full bar from which you may want to try Don Luis's Italian coffee, made with a coffee-flavored liquor called Tuaca. For equally excellent

Georgia O'Keeffe & New Mexico: A Desert Romance

In June 1917, during a short visit to the Southwest, the painter Georgia O'Keeffe (born 1887) visited New Mexico for the first time. She was immediately enchanted by the stark scenery; even after her return to the energy and chaos of New York City, her mind wandered frequently to New Mexico's arid land and undulating mesas. However, not until coaxed by the arts patron and "collector of people" Mabel Dodge Luhan 12 years later did O'Keeffe return to the multihued desert of her daydreams.

O'Keeffe was reportedly ill, both physically and emotionally, when she arrived in Santa Fe in April 1929. New Mexico seemed to soothe her spirit and heal her physical ailments almost magically. Two days after her arrival, Mabel Dodge Luhan persuaded O'Keeffe to move into her home in Taos. There, she would be free to paint and socialize as she liked.

In Taos, O'Keeffe began painting what would become some of her best-known canvases—close-ups of desert flowers and objects such as cow and horse skulls. "The color up there is different . . . the blue-green of the sage and the mountains, the wildflowers in bloom," O'Keeffe once said of Taos. "It's a different kind of color from any I've ever seen—there's nothing like that in north Texas or even in Colorado." Taos transformed not only her art, but her personality as well. She bought a car and learned to drive. Sometimes, on warm days, she ran naked through the sage fields. That August, a new, rejuvenated O'Keeffe rejoined her husband, photographer Alfred Stieglitz, in New York.

The artist returned to New Mexico year after year, spending time with Mabel Dodge Luhan as well as staying at the isolated Ghost Ranch. She drove through the countryside in her snappy Ford, stopping to paint in her favorite spots along the way. Until 1949, O'Keeffe always returned to New York in the fall. Three years after Stieglitz's death, though, she relocated permanently to New Mexico, spending each winter and spring in Abiquiu and each summer and fall at Ghost Ranch. Georgia O'Keeffe died in Santa Fe in 1986.

A great way to see Ghost Ranch is on a hike that climbs above the mystical area. Take US 84 north from Española about 36 miles to Ghost Ranch and follow the road to the Ghost Ranch office. The ranch is managed by the Presbyterian Church, and the staff will supply you with a primitive map for the **Kitchen Mesa** and **Chimney Rock** hikes.

but faster food, skip next door to the kin restaurant **El Paragua** and order a chicken taco—the best ever.

603 Santa Cruz Rd., Española (off the main drag; turn east at Long John Silver's). $\textcircled{C}$ **505/753-3211.** Reservations recommended. Main courses $9–$20. AE, DISC, MC, V. Daily 11am–9pm.

Rancho de San Juan ★★ Located between Española and Ojo Caliente, this inn provides an authentic northern New Mexico desert experience with the comfort of a luxury hotel. It's the passion of architect and chef John Johnson, responsible for the design and cuisine, and interior designer David Heath, responsible for the elegant interiors. The original part of the inn comprises four rooms around a central courtyard. Thirteen additional casitas have been added in the outlying hills. The original rooms are a bit small but very elegant, with European antiques and spectacular views of desert landscapes and distant, snow-capped peaks. The Kiva suite is the most innovative, with a round bedroom and a skylight just above the bed, perfect for stargazing.

Tuesday through Saturday evenings, a four-course prix-fixe dinner is served. The meal ranges in price from $45 per person on up, depending on the wine.

A few minutes' hike from the inn is the **Grand Chamber,** an impressive shrine that the innkeepers commissioned to be carved into a sandstone outcropping, where weddings and other festivities are held.

US 285 (en route to Ojo Caliente), P.O. Box 4140, Fairview Station, Española, NM 87533. $\textcircled{C}$ **505/753-6818.** www.ranchodesanjuan.com. 17 units. $175–$400 double; $25 added for single-night lodging. AE, DISC, MC, V. **Amenities:** Restaurant; concierge; in-room massage and other spa treatments; laundry service. *In room:* Stocked fridge, coffeemaker, hair dryer.

OJO CALIENTE & CHAMA

Many locals from the area like to rejuvenate at **Ojo Caliente Mineral Springs,** Ojo Caliente, NM 87549 ($\textcircled{C}$ **800/222-9162** or 505/583-2233); it's on US 285, 50 miles (a 1-hr. drive) northwest of Santa Fe and 50 miles southwest of Taos. This National Historic Site was considered sacred by prehistoric tribes. When Spanish explorer Cabeza de Vaca discovered and named the springs in the 16th century, he called them "the greatest treasure that I found these strange people to possess." No other hot spring in the world has Ojo Caliente's combination of iron, soda, lithium, sodium, and arsenic. If the weather is warm enough, the outdoor mud bath is a real treat. The dressing rooms are fairly new and in good shape; however, the whole place has an earthy feel. If you're a fastidious type, you won't be comfortable here. The resort offers herbal wraps and massages, lodging, and meals. It's open daily 8am to 8pm (9pm Fri–Sat).

If you find yourself enamored with this part of New Mexico, you may want to explore farther north to the **Chama** area, where, between late May and mid-October, you can ride the **Cumbres & Toltec Scenic Railroad** ($\textcircled{C}$ **505/756-2151**). Built in 1880, America's longest and highest narrow-gauge steam railroad operates on a 64-mile track between Chama and Antonito, Colorado.

4 Pecos National Monument

About 15 miles east of Santa Fe, I-25 meanders through **Glorieta Pass,** site of an important Civil War skirmish. In March 1862, volunteers from Colorado and New Mexico, along with Fort Union regulars, defeated a Confederate force marching on Santa Fe, thereby turning the tide of Southern encroachment in the West.

Follow NM 50 east to **Pecos** for about 7 miles. This quaint town, well off the beaten track since the interstate was constructed, is the site of a noted **Benedictine monastery.** About 26 miles north of here on NM 63 is the village of **Cowles,** gateway to the natural wonderland of the **Pecos Wilderness.** There are many camping, picnicking, and fishing locales en route.

Pecos National Historical Park ★★ (© **505/757-6414;** www.nps.gov/peco), about 2 miles south of the town of Pecos off NM 63, contains the ruins of a 15th-century pueblo and 17th- and 18th-century missions that jut up spectacularly from a high meadow. Coronado mentioned Pecos Pueblo in 1540: "It is feared through the land," he wrote. The approximately 2,000 Native Americans here farmed in irrigated fields and hunted wild game. Their pueblo had 660 rooms and many kivas. By 1620, Franciscan monks had established a church and convent. Military and natural disasters took their toll on the pueblo, and in 1838, the 20 surviving Pecos went to live with relatives at the Jemez Pueblo.

The **E. E. Fogelson Visitor Center** tells the history of the Pecos people in a well-done, chronologically organized exhibit, complete with dioramas. A 1.5-mile loop trail begins at the center and continues through Pecos Pueblo and the **Misión de Nuestra Señora de Los Angeles de Porciuncula** (as the church was formerly called). This excavated structure—170 feet long and 90 feet wide at the transept—was once the most magnificent church north of Mexico City.

Pecos National Historical Park is open Memorial Day to Labor Day, daily 8am to 6pm; the rest of the year, daily 8am to 5pm. It's closed January 1 and December 25. Admission is $3 per person over age 16.

5 Chaco Culture National Historic Park ★★★

A combination of a stunning setting and well-preserved ruins makes the long drive to **Chaco Culture National Historic Park,** often referred to as Chaco Canyon, worth the trip. Whether you come from the north or south, you drive in on a dusty (and sometimes muddy) road that seems to add to the authenticity and adventure of this remote New Mexico experience.

When you finally arrive, you walk through stark desert country that seems perhaps ill suited as a center of culture. However, the ancient Anasazi people successfully farmed the lowlands and built great masonry towns, which connected with other towns over a wide-ranging network of roads crossing this desolate place.

What's most interesting here is how changes in architecture—beginning in the mid-800s, when the Anasazi started building on a larger scale than they had previously—chart the area's cultural progress. The Anasazi used the same masonry techniques that tribes had used in smaller villages in the region (walls one stone thick, with generous use of mud mortar), but they built stone villages of multiple stories with rooms several times larger than in the previous stage of their culture. Within a century, six large pueblos were under way. This pattern of a single large pueblo with oversize rooms, surrounded by conventional villages, caught on throughout the region. New communities built along these lines sprang up. Old villages built similarly large pueblos. Eventually there were more than 75 such towns, most of them closely tied to Chaco by an extensive system of roads. Aerial photos show hundreds of miles of roads connecting these towns with the Chaco pueblos, one of the longest running 42 miles straight north to Salmon Ruins and the Aztec Ruins. It is this road network that leads some scholars to believe that Chaco was the center of a unified Anasazi society.

This progress led to Chaco becoming the economic center of the San Juan Basin by A.D. 1000. As many as 5,000 people may have lived in some 400 settlements in and around Chaco. As masonry techniques advanced through the years, walls rose more than four stories in height. Some of these are still visible today.

Chaco's decline after 1½ centuries of success coincided with a drought in the San Juan Basin between A.D. 1130 and 1180. Scientists still argue vehemently over why the site was abandoned and where the Chacoans went. Many believe that an influx of outsiders may have brought new rituals to the region, causing a schism among tribal members. Most agree, however, that the people drifted away to more hospitable places in the region and that their descendants live among the Pueblo people today.

This is an isolated area, and there are **no services** available within or close to the park—no food, gas, auto repairs, firewood, lodging (besides the campground), or drinking water (other than at the visitor center) are available. Overnight camping is permitted year-round. If you're headed towards Santa Fe after a day at the park and looking for a place to spend the night, one nice option is the **Casa del Rio–Riverside Inn,** 16445 Scenic Hwy. 4, Jemez Springs, NM 87025 (℅ **505/829-4377;** www.canondelrio.com).

ESSENTIALS

GETTING THERE   To get to Chaco from Santa Fe, take I-25 south to Bernalillo, then US 550 northwest. Turn off US 550 at CR 7900 (3 miles southeast of Nageezi and about 50 miles west of Cuba at mile 112.5). Follow the signs from US 550 to the park boundary (21 miles). This route includes 5 miles of paved road (CR 7900) and 16 miles of rough dirt road (CR 7950). This is the recommended route. NM 57 from Blanco Trading Post is closed. The trip takes about 3½ to 4 hours. Farmington is the nearest population center, a 1½-hour drive away. The park can also be reached from Grants via I-40 west to NM 371, then north on NM 57 (with the final 19 miles ungraded dirt). This route is rough to impassable and is not recommended for RVs.

Whichever way you come, call ahead to inquire about **road conditions** (℅ **505/786-7014**) before leaving the paved highways. The dirt roads can get extremely muddy and dangerous after rain or snow, and afternoon thunderstorms are common in late summer. Roads often flood when it rains.

VISITOR INFORMATION   Ranger-guided walks and campfire talks are available in the summer at the visitor center where you can get self-guiding trail brochures and permits for the overnight campground (see "Camping," below). If you want information before you leave home, write to the Superintendent, Chaco Culture National Historical Park, 1808 County Rd. 7950, Nageezi, NM 87037 (℅ **505/786-7014;** www.nps.gov/chcu).

ADMISSION FEES & HOURS   Admission is $8 per car; a campsite is $10 extra. The visitor center is open daily from 8am to 5pm. Trails are open from sunrise to sunset.

SEEING THE HIGHLIGHTS

Exploring the ruins and hiking are the most popular activities here. A series of pueblo ruins stand within 5 or 6 miles of each other on the broad, flat, treeless canyon floor. Plan to spend at least 3 to 4 hours here driving to and exploring the different pueblos. A one-way road from the visitor center loops up one side of the canyon and down the other. Parking lots are scattered along the road near the various pueblos; from most, it's only a short walk to the ruins.

You may want to focus your energy on seeing **Pueblo Bonito,** the largest prehistoric Southwest Native American dwelling ever excavated. It contains giant kivas and 800 rooms covering more than 3 acres. Also, the **Pueblo Alto Trail** is a nice hike that takes you up on the canyon rim so that you can see the ruins from above—in the afternoon, with thunderheads building, the views are spectacular. If you're a cyclist, stop at the visitor center to pick up a map outlining ridable trails.

CAMPING

Gallo Campground, located within the park, is quite popular with hikers. It's located about 1 mile east of the visitor center; fees are $10 per night. The campground has 47 sites (group sites are also available), with fire grates (bring your own wood or charcoal), central toilets, and nonpotable water. Drinking water is available only at the visitor center. The campground cannot accommodate trailers over 30 feet.

As I said above, there's no place to stock up on supplies once you start the arduous drive to the canyon, so if you're camping, make sure to be well supplied, especially with water, before you leave home base.

6 Chama: Home of the Cumbres & Toltec Scenic Railroad

Some of my best outdoor adventuring has taken place in the area surrounding this pioneer village of 1,250 people at the base of the 10,000-foot Cumbres Pass. With backpack on, I cross-country skied high into the mountains and stayed the night in a *yurt* (Mongolian hut), the next day waking to hundreds of acres of snowy fields to explore. Another time, we headed down **Rio Chama,** an official wild and scenic river, on rafts and in kayaks following the course that Navajos, Utes, and Comanches once traveled to raid the Pueblo Indians down river. The campsites along the way were pristine, with mule deer threading through the trees beyond our tents. In my most recent visit to the village, it was summertime, and I'd just come from Durango, which was packed with tourists, to hike, raft, and ride the train. Chama was still quiet, and I realized Chama is New Mexico's undiscovered Durango, without the masses. And now, with some new additions, the town is really looking up. A park, clock-tower, and, drum-roll please . . . sidewalks! give it a more friendly tone.

Bordered by three wilderness areas, the Carson, Rio Grande, and Santa Fe national forests, the area is indeed prime for hunting, fishing, cross-country skiing, snowmobiling, snowshoeing, and hiking.

Another highlight here is America's longest and highest narrow-gauge coal-fired steam line, the **Cumbres & Toltec Scenic Railroad,** which winds through valleys and mountain meadows 64 miles between Chama and Antonito, Colorado. The village of Chama boomed when the railroad arrived in 1881. A rough-and-ready frontier town, the place still maintains that flavor, with lumber and ranching making up a big part of the economy.

Landmarks to watch for are the **Brazos Cliffs** and waterfall and **Heron and El Vado lakes.** Tierra Amarilla, the Rio Arriba County seat, is 14 miles south, and is at the center—along with Los Ojos and Los Brazos—of a wool-raising and weaving tradition where local craftspeople still weave masterpieces. Dulce, governmental seat of the Jicarilla Apache Indian Reservation, is 27 miles west.

ESSENTIALS

GETTING THERE   From Santa Fe, take US 84 north (2 hr.). From Taos, take US 64 west (2½ hr.). From Farmington, take US 64 east (2¼ hr.).

VISITOR INFORMATION   The **New Mexico Visitor Information Center,** P.O. Box 697, Chama, NM 87520 (© **505/756-2235**), is at 2372 NM 17. It's open daily from 8am to 6pm in the summer, from 8am to 5pm in the winter. At the same address is the **Chama Valley Chamber of Commerce** (ⓒ **800/477-0149** or 505/756-2306).

ALL ABOARD THE HISTORIC C&T RAILROAD

Cumbres & Toltec Scenic Railroad   If you have a passion for the past and for incredible scenery, climb aboard America's longest and highest narrow-gauge steam railroad, the historic C&T. It operates on a 64-mile track between Chama and Antonito, Colorado. Built in 1880 as an extension of the Denver and Rio Grande line to serve the mining camps of the San Juan Mountains, it is perhaps the finest surviving example of what once was a vast network of remote Rocky Mountain railways.

The C&T passes through forests of pine and aspen, past striking rock formations, and over the magnificent Toltec Gorge of the Rio de los Pinos. It crests at the 10,015-foot Cumbres Pass, the highest in the United States used by scheduled passenger trains.

Halfway through the route, at Osier, Colorado, the *New Mexico Express* from Chama meets the *Colorado Limited* from Antonito. They stop to exchange greetings, engines, and through passengers. Round-trip day passengers return to their starting point after enjoying a picnic or catered lunch beside the old water tank and stock pens in Osier. Through passengers continue on to Antonito and return by van. Be aware that both trips are nearly full-day events. Those who find it uncomfortable to sit for long periods may instead want to opt for hiking or skiing in the area. Ask about their Parlor Car, a more luxurious alternative to coach seating.

A walking-tour brochure, describing 23 points of interest in the Chama railroad yards, can be picked up at the 1899 depot in Chama. A registered National Historic Site, the C&T is owned by the states of Colorado and New Mexico. Special cars with lifts for people with disabilities are available with a 7-day advance reservation.

After all the sitting while you're on the train, you may want to stroll a while, hitting a few of the shops in Chama. One of note is the **Local Color Gallery** (ⓒ **888/756-2604** or 505/756-2604) in the center of town. Here you'll find all kinds of locally made arts and crafts, from flashy broomstick skirts to moody candles painted with petroglyph symbols to picturesque watercolors of the Chama area.

P.O. Box 789, Chama. ⓒ **888/CUMBRES** or 505/756-2151. Fax 505/756-2694. www.cumbresandtoltec.com. Lunch is included with all fares. Round-trip to Osier: adults $70, children age 11 and under $37. Through trip to Antonito, return by van (or to Antonito by van, return by train): adults $65, children $35. Reservations highly recommended. Memorial Day to mid-Oct trains leave Chama daily at 10am; vans depart for Antonito at 8am.

WHERE TO STAY IN CHAMA

Most accommodations in this area are found on NM 17 or south of the US 64/84 junction, known as the "Y."

HOTELS/LODGES

Chama Trails Inn   This stucco building adorned with chile *ristras* (decorative strung chiles) houses nice motel-style rooms at a reasonable price. The place is impeccably kept, all rooms with queen-size beds, custom-made pine furnishings, and minirefrigerators, some with suite-like configurations. Be aware that the ceilings are fairly low and rooms are a bit dark. A few rooms have ceiling fans, gas fireplaces, and/or Mexican-tile bathroom floors. Some have newer mattresses than others, so ask for a new one.

2362 Hwy. 17 (P.O. Box 975), Chama, NM 87520. © **800/289-1421** or 505/756-2156. Fax 505/756-2855. www.chamatrailsinn.com. 15 units. $50–$85 double, depending on the season. AE, DC, DISC, MC, V. Pets accepted with $10 fee. **Amenities:** Exercise room; Jacuzzi; sauna. *In room:* TV, dataport, fridge, coffeemaker, iron.

River Bend Lodge   Set on a bend of the Chama River, this lodging offers the best cabins in town and clean motel rooms. If you can reserve cabin no. 40, 50, or 60 at the back of the property, you'll have a sweet riverside stay. Some of these cabins are split level, with a queen-size sleeping loft and a bedroom—not great for privacy, but good for a family that doesn't mind sharing space. Others are similar, but without the loft. Every cabin has a fold-out futon in the living room, an efficient little kitchen, and a small bathroom. The motel rooms are medium-size, with basic furnishing and a long portal to relax on in the afternoons.

2625 US 64/285, Chama, NM 87520. © **800/288-1371** or 505/756-2264. Fax 505/756-2664. www. chamariverbendlodge.com. 20 units. Motel rooms $65–$78 double; cabins $89–$129 double. Additional person $10. Children under 13 stay free in parent's room. AE, DC, DISC, MC, V. Pets accepted with $10 fee. **Amenities:** Jacuzzi; river for fishing and wading. *In-room:* A/C, TV, fridge, coffeemaker (upon request), microwave (upon request).

The Timbers at Chama ⭑   This luxury lodge, set on 400 acres of meadow, with only streams, birds, and elk to disturb your sleep, is one of the region's real gems. Designed as a hunting and fishing lodge, the place has an elegant great room on the first floor, with vaulted ceilings, a giant stone fireplace, and a big-screen TV. One wall is devoted to a vast display of game heads, a detail that non-hunters may find disturbing. Outside is a broad deck with a hot tub and outdoor fireplace overlooking a little pond. The rooms, all decorated in an elegant Montana ranch style, are medium-size (the suite is large) with heavy pine furniture, views, and medium-size bathrooms. The beds are comfortably firm and have fine linens. All rooms have VCRs, jet tubs, and robes, and are decorated with original art. An adjacent guest house has a kitchen—a great place for families. Hunting and fishing guides are available, as are horses for guests to ride, all for an additional charge.

Off NM 512 to the Brazos (HC 75, Box 136), Chama, NM 87520. © **505/588-7950.** Fax 505/588-7051. www.thetimbersatchama.com. 5 units. $100–$175 double. Guest house $200 double. Rates include full breakfast, except for guest house. DISC, MC, V. **Amenities:** Jacuzzi. *In room:* TV/VCR, coffeemaker, hair dryer, safe.

BED & BREAKFASTS

Gandy Dancer Bed & Breakfast Inn ⭑   Located in a 1912 two-story Victorian from the early railroad era, this B&B offers an old-world feel with up-to-date amenities. New owners have added color and a cozy atmosphere to the place. Rooms range in size, all with medium-size bathrooms and comfortable beds. Attractive antiques make each room—all named with railroad lingo—unique. The upstairs Caboose, with a king-size bed, sky blue walls, and lots of light from all directions, is one pick of the place, but my favorite is the downstairs Main Line, a large room with a king-size bed and a purple iris theme. The full breakfast is well worth waking up for. The spinach quiche served with Canadian bacon and an almond French pancake from my last stay is still memorable. Ask about their winter packages, including home-cooked German dinners.

299 Maple Ave. (P.O. Box 810), Chama, NM 87520. © **800/424-6702** or 505/756-2191. Fax 505/756-2649. www.gandydancerbb.com. 7 units. Summer $95–$125 double; winter $85 double. Additional person $15. Rates include full breakfast. AE, DISC, MC, V. **Amenities:** Jacuzzi. *In room:* A/C, TV, VCR.

CAMPING

At **Rio Chama RV Campground** (© **505/756-2303**), you're within easy walking distance of the Cumbres & Toltec Scenic Railroad depot. This shady campground with 94 sites along the Rio Chama is ideal for RVers and tenters who plan to take train rides. The campground also offers great photo opportunities of the old steam trains leaving the depot. Hot showers, a dump station, and complete hookups are available. It's open from mid-May to mid-October only. The campground is located 2¼ miles north of the US 84/64 junction on NM 17.

Twin Rivers Trailer Park (© **505/756-2218;** www.twinriversonline.net) has 50 sites and 40 full hookups; phone hookups are offered. Tenting is available, as are laundry facilities and ice and picnic tables. River swimming and fishing are popular activities; other sports facilities include basketball, volleyball, badminton, and horseshoes. Twin Rivers is open from April 15 to November 15 and is located 100 yards west of the junction of NM 17 and US 84/64.

WHERE TO DINE IN CHAMA

High Country Restaurant and Saloon ★ STEAKS/SEAFOOD/NEW MEXICAN   This is definitely a country place, with functional furniture, orange vinyl chairs, brown carpet, and a big stone fireplace. But it's *the* place innkeepers recommend, and one traveling couple I spoke to had eaten lunch and dinner here every day of their weeklong stay. The steaks are a big draw here. More sophisticated appetites may like the *trucha con piñon,* trout dusted in flour and cooked with pine nuts, garlic, and shallots. Meals are served with a salad and choice of potato. The New Mexican food is also good. The attached saloon has a full bar and bustles with people eating peanuts and throwing the shells on the floor. Breakfast on Sunday is country-style, with offerings such as steak and eggs and biscuits and gravy topping the menu, as well as pancakes and huevos rancheros (eggs atop tortillas smothered in chile sauce).

Main St. (¹⁄₁₀ mile north of the "Y"), Chama. © **505/756-2384.** Main courses $4–$10 breakfast, $6–$12 lunch, $6–$17 dinner. AE, DISC, MC, V. Mon–Sat 11am–10pm; Sun 8am–10pm. Closed Easter, Thanksgiving, and Christmas.

Village Bean ★ BAKERY/SANDWICHES   Sunny colored walls and lots of space encourage coffee lovers to linger in this new cafe in the center of town. The owner roasts his own coffee beans, so you can count on your espresso, cappuccino, or just plain Joe being tasty. The food follows in the same thoughtful vein. For breakfast, select from a variety of home-baked goods. At lunch, creations such as the Hot and Spicy Pastrami (with cream cheese, provolone, green chiles, and red onions) and the Blue Spruce (with three cheeses, cucumbers, avocado, and sprouts) come on home-baked bread. A variety of soups and salads round out the menu. You can even get boxed lunches to take on Chama outings. Call to see if a Monday night open-mic is happening (until 8pm).

425 Terrace Ave., Chama. © **505/756-1663.** All menu items under $7. No credit cards. Daily 7am–4pm.

Viva Vera's Mexican Kitchen NEW MEXICAN/AMERICAN   A locals' favorite, Vera's serves tasty sauces over the rich enchiladas and burritos, followed by fluffy *sopaipillas* soaked with honey. Some complain that the chile is too hot, but I say bring it on. The setting is pastoral, with fields of gazing horses stretching to the river. The porch is *the* place to sit on warmer days. Inside, the restaurant has a vaulted ceiling and typical Mexican memorabilia hangs on the walls—even sequined sombreros. The tables are well spaced, and a TV rests in the corner. Beer and wine are served, but the favorite seems to be wine margaritas, frothy and frozen, served in big glasses. For breakfast try the huevos rancheros (eggs atop corn tortillas smothered in chile sauce).

2202 Hwy. 17, Chama. ℭ 505/756-2557. Main courses $4–$7 breakfast, $4–$12 lunch and dinner. AE, MC, V. Daily 8am–8pm.

CHAMA AFTER DARK

Summer evenings in Chama now include entertainment beyond watching the river flow in its banks or the beer flow in the local tavern. The Elkhorn Lodge, 2663 S. US 84 (ℭ **800/532-8874** or 505/756-2105; www.elkhornlodge.net), sponsors a **Chuckwagon Cowboy Dinner** Saturday and Sunday evenings. Guests chow down on beef brisket, beans, and corn bread while watching a historical western narrative told through guitar music and singing. Kids like the food and the fun story. Reservations required; contact Elkhorn Lodge. Performances start at 6:30pm, and prices run $16 for adults and $9 for children under 14; under 2 eat free.

ON THE ROAD: WHAT TO SEE & DO ON US 84 SOUTH

Distinctive yellow earth provided a name for the town of **Tierra Amarilla,** 14 miles south of Chama at the junction of US 84 and US 64. Throughout New Mexico, this name is synonymous with a continuing controversy over the land-grant rights of the descendants of the original Hispanic settlers. But the economy of this community of 1,000 is dyed in the wool—literally.

The organization *Ganados del Valle* (Livestock Growers of the Valley) is at work to save the longhaired Spanish churro sheep from extinction, to introduce other unusual wool breeds to the valley, and to perpetuate a 200-year-old tradition of shepherding, spinning, weaving, and dyeing. Many of the craftspeople work in conjunction with **Tierra Wools** ⋆, P.O. Box 229, Los Ojos, NM 87551 (ℭ **505/588-7231;** www.handweavers.com), which has a showroom and workshop in a century-old mercantile building just north of Tierra Amarilla. One-of-a-kind blankets and men's and women's apparel are among the products displayed and sold.

Just down the street, across from the Los Ojos General Store, is an interesting little art studio worth checking out. **Yellow Earth Studio** (ℭ **505/588-7807**), the passion of Paul Trachtman, the resident artist, is a great place to see and purchase enchanting scenes of the Los Ojos area in the form of paintings and monotype, woodcut, and metal engraving prints. His work is part of the permanent collection of the New Mexico State Capitol. Paul will likely be working away in his studio in back, and if you're fortunate, he'll guide you through some of his techniques.

Two state parks are a short drive west from Tierra Amarilla. **El Vado Lake State Park,** 14 miles southwest on NM 112 (ℭ **505/588-7247**), offers boating and water-skiing, fishing, and camping in summer; cross-country skiing and ice fishing in winter. **Heron Lake State Park,** 11 miles west on US 64 and NM 95 (ℭ **505/588-7470**), has a no-wake speed limit for motor vessels, adding to its appeal for fishing, sailing, windsurfing, canoeing, and swimming. The park has an interpretive center, plus camping, picnic sites, hiking trails, and cross-country skiing in the winter. The 5.5-mile Rio Chama trail connects the two lakes.

East of Tierra Amarilla, the Rio Brazos cuts a canyon through the Tusas Mountains and around 11,403-foot Brazos Peak. Just north of Los Ojos, NM 512 heads east 7½ miles up the **Brazos Box Canyon.** High cliffs that rise straight from the valley floor give it a Yosemite-like appearance—which is even more apparent from an overlook on US 64, 18 miles east of Tierra Amarilla en route to Taos. **El Chorro,** an impressive waterfall at the mouth of the canyon, usually flows only from early May to mid-June. Several resort lodges are in the area.

About 37 miles south of Tierra Amarilla on US 84, and 3 miles north of Ghost Ranch, is **Echo Canyon Amphitheater** (℃ 505/684-2486), a U.S. Forest Service campground and picnic area. The natural "theater," hollowed out of sandstone by thousands of years of erosion, is a natural work of art with layers of stone ranging from pearl-color to blood red. The walls send back eerie echoes and even clips of conversations. It's just a 10-minute walk from the parking area. The fee is $3. Some 13 miles west of here, via the dirt Forest Service road 151 into the Chama River Canyon Wilderness, is the isolated **Monastery of Christ in the Desert** (www.christdesert.org), built in 1964 by Benedictine monks. The chapel is a graceful structure set against bold cliffs, worth visiting if you like a taste of solemnity. The brothers produce crafts, sold at a small gift shop, and operate a guest house.

Along the same road (FS 151) is access to the Chama River, a good place to hike, mountain bike, kayak, and camp. The **Rim Vista Trail** will take you to the top of the rim, with vast views out across Abiquiu Lake and Ghost Ranch. Primitive campsites can be found all along the river.

A 3-mile drive from there is **Ghost Ranch,** a collection of adobe buildings that make up an adult study center maintained by the United Presbyterian Church. A number of hauntingly memorable hikes originate from this place, which gets its name from the *brujas,* or witches, said to inhabit the canyons. Most notable among the hikes is **Kitchen Mesa,** directions for which can be obtained at the visitor center. World-renowned painter Georgia O'Keeffe spent time at Ghost Ranch painting these canyons and other land formations. Eventually she bought a portion of the ranch and lived in a humble adobe house there. The ranch now offers seminars on a variety of topics, ranging from art to literature to religion, that are open to all. For information, contact **Ghost Ranch,** 401 Old Taos Hwy., Santa Fe (℃ **505/982-8539;** www.ghostranch. org).

The **Florence Hawley Ellis Museum of Anthropology** has interpretative exhibits of a Spanish ranch house and Native American anthropology, and the **Ruth Hall Paleontology Museum** (both museums ℃ **505/685-4333;** www. ghostranch.org) displays fossils of the early dinosaur named coelophysis found on the ranch. A lightly built creature, it was very fast when chasing prey. It roamed the area 250 million years ago, making it the oldest dinosaur found in New Mexico.

Many dinosaur skeletons have been found in rocks along the base of cliffs near **Abiquiu Reservoir** (℃ **505/685-4371**), a popular boating and fishing spot formed by the Abiquiu Dam.

A good place to stay in the area is the **Abiquiu Inn,** a small country inn, restaurant, art gallery, and gift shop, ½ mile north of the village of Abiquiu (℃ **505/685-4378**). The casitas are especially nice. Rates are $109 to $189.

Heading south from Abiquiu, watch for **Dar al Islam** (℃ **505/685-4515**), a spiritual center with a circular Middle Eastern–style mosque made of adobe; the small community of **Mendanales,** where you'll find the shop of renowned weaver Cordelia Coronado; and **Hernandez,** the village immortalized in Ansel Adams's famous 1941 photograph *Moonrise, Hernandez, New Mexico.*

Rancho de San Juan is a great nearby place to stay and dine. See "Española," earlier in this chapter.

11

Getting to Know Taos

New Mexico's favorite arts town sits in a masterpiece setting. It's wedged between the towering peaks of the Rocky Mountains and the plunging chasm of the Rio Grande Gorge.

Located about 70 miles north of Santa Fe, this town of 5,000 residents combines 1960s hippiedom (thanks to communes set up in the hills back then) with the ancient culture of Taos Pueblo (some people still live without electricity and running water, as their ancestors did 1,000 years ago). It can be an odd place, where some completely eschew materialism and live "off the grid" in half-underground houses called earthships. But there are plenty of more mainstream attractions as well—Taos boasts some of the best restaurants in the state, a hot and funky arts scene, and incredible outdoors action, including world-class skiing.

Its history is rich. Throughout the Taos valley, ruins and artifacts attest to a Native American presence dating back 5,000 years. The Spanish first visited this area in 1540, colonizing it in 1598. In the last 2 decades of the 17th century, they put down three rebellions at Taos Pueblo. During the 18th and 19th centuries, Taos was an important trade center: New Mexico's annual caravan to Chihuahua, Mexico, couldn't leave until after the annual midsummer **Taos Fair.** French trappers began attending the fair in 1739. Even though the Plains tribes often attacked the pueblos at other times, they would attend the market festival under a temporary annual truce. By the early 1800s, Taos had become a meeting place for American mountain men, the most famous of whom, Kit Carson, made his home in Taos from 1826 to 1868.

Taos remained loyal to Mexico during the U.S.–Mexican War of 1846. The town rebelled against its new U.S. landlord in 1847, even killing newly appointed Governor Charles Bent in his Taos home. Nevertheless, the town was eventually incorporated into the Territory of New Mexico in 1850. During the Civil War, Taos fell into Confederate hands for 6 weeks; afterward, Carson and two other men raised the Union flag over Taos Plaza and guarded it day and night. Since that time, Taos has had the honor of flying the flag 24 hours a day.

Taos's population declined when the railroad bypassed it in favor of Santa Fe. In 1898, two East Coast artists—Ernest Blumenschein and Bert Phillips—discovered the dramatic, varied effects of sunlight on the natural environment of the Taos valley and depicted them on canvas. By 1912, thanks to the growing influence of the **Taos Society of Artists,** the town had gained a worldwide reputation as a cultural center. Today, it is estimated that more than 15% of the population are painters, sculptors, writers, or musicians, or in some other way earn their income from artistic pursuits.

The town of Taos is merely the focal point of the rugged 2,200-square-mile Taos County. Two features dominate this sparsely populated region: the high desert mesa, split in two by the 650-foot-deep chasm of the **Rio Grande;** and the **Sangre de Cristo** range, which tops out at 13,161-foot Wheeler Peak, New Mexico's highest mountain. From the forested uplands to the sage-carpeted mesa, the county is home to a large variety of wildlife. The human element includes Native Americans who are still living in ancient pueblos and Hispanic farmers who continue to irrigate their farmlands using centuries-old methods.

Taos is also inhabited by many people who have chosen to retreat from, or altogether drop out of, mainstream society. There's a laid-back attitude here, even more pronounced than the general *mañana* attitude for which New Mexico is known. Most Taoseños live here to play here—and that means outdoors. Many work at the ski area all winter (skiing whenever they can) and work for raft companies in the summer (to get on the river as much as they can). Others are into rock climbing, mountain biking, and backpacking. That's not to say that Taos is just a resort town. With the Hispanic and Native American populations' histories in the area, there's a richness and depth here that most resort towns lack.

Taos's biggest task these days is to try to stem the tide of overdevelopment that is flooding northern New Mexico. In the "Life Today—From Flamenco to Craps" section of the appendix, I address the city's success in battling back airport expansion and some housing developments. A grassroots community program has been implemented that gives neighborhoods a say in how their area is developed.

1 Orientation

ARRIVING

BY PLANE   The **Taos Municipal Airport** (© 505/758-4995) is about 8 miles northwest of town on US 64. **Rio Grande Air** (© 877/435-9742 or 505/737-9790; www.riograndeair.com) runs daily flights between Albuquerque and Taos. Most people opt to fly into Albuquerque International Sunport, rent a car, and drive up to Taos from there. The drive takes approximately 2½ hours. If you'd rather be picked up at Albuquerque International Sunport, call **Faust's Transportation, Inc.** (© 505/758-3410), which offers daily service, as well as taxi service between Taos and Taos Ski Valley.

BY BUS   The **Taos Bus Center** is located 5 miles south of the plaza at 1386 Paseo del Pueblo Sur (© 505/758-1144). **TNM&O** (© 505/242-4998) arrives and departs from this depot several times a day. For more information on this and other bus services to and from Albuquerque and Santa Fe, see "Getting There," in chapter 2.

BY CAR   Most visitors arrive in Taos via either NM 68 or US 64. Northbound travelers should exit I-25 at Santa Fe, follow US 285 as far as San Juan Pueblo, and then continue on the divided highway when it becomes NM 68. Taos is about 79 miles from the I-25 junction. Southbound travelers from Denver on I-25 should exit about 6 miles south of Raton at US 64 and then follow it about 95 miles to Taos. Another major route is US 64 from the west (214 miles from Farmington).

VISITOR INFORMATION

The **Taos County Chamber of Commerce,** at the junction of NM 68 and NM 585 (P.O. Drawer I), Taos, NM 87571 (© **800/732-TAOS** or 505/758-3873; www.taoschamber.com), is open in summer, daily 9am to 5pm. It's closed on

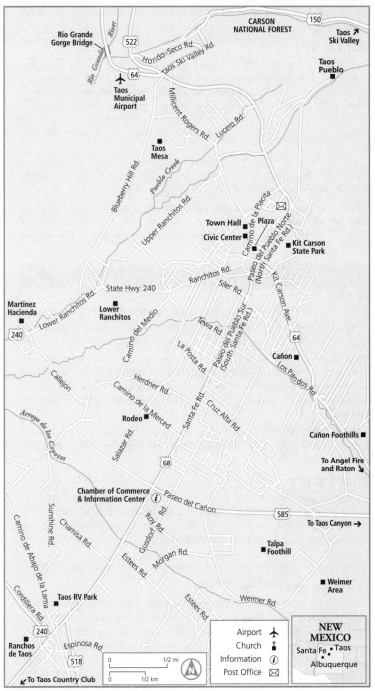

major holidays. **Carson National Forest** also has an information center in the same building.

CITY LAYOUT

The **plaza** is a short block west of Taos's major intersection—where US 64 (Kit Carson Rd.) from the east joins NM 68, **Paseo del Pueblo Sur.** US 64 proceeds north from the intersection as **Paseo del Pueblo Norte. Camino de la Placita (Placitas Rd.)** circles the west side of downtown, passing within a block of the other side of the plaza. Many of the streets that join these thoroughfares are winding lanes lined by traditional adobe homes, many of them over 100 years old.

Most of the art galleries are located on or near the plaza, which was paved over with bricks several years ago, and along neighboring streets. Others are located in the **Ranchos de Taos** area a few miles south of the plaza.

MAPS   To find your way around town, pick up a free Taos map from the **Chamber of Commerce at Taos Visitor Center,** 1139 Paseo del Pueblo Sur (© **505/758-3873**). Good, detailed city maps can be found at area bookstores as well (see "Shopping," in chapter 14).

2 Getting Around

BY CAR

With offices at the Taos airport, **Enterprise** (© **800/369-4226** or 505/751-7490) is reliable and efficient. Other car-rental agencies are available out of Albuquerque. See "Getting Around," in chapter 15, for details.

PARKING   Parking can be difficult during the summer rush, when the stream of tourists' cars moving north and south through town never ceases. If you can't find parking on the street or in the plaza, check out some of the nearby roads (Kit Carson Rd., for instance); there are plenty of metered and unmetered lots in Taos.

ROAD CONDITIONS   Information on highway conditions throughout the state can be obtained from the **State Highway Department** (© **800/432-4269**).

BY BUS & TAXI

If you're in Taos without a car, you're in luck because there is now a local bus service, provided by **Chile Line Town of Taos Transit** (© **505/751-4459**). It operates on the half-hour Monday to Saturday 7am to 7pm in summer, 7am to 6pm in winter, and on the hour Sunday 8am to 5pm. Two simultaneous routes

---

(Warning **Warning for Drivers**

En route to many recreation sites, reliable paved roads often give way to poorer forest roads. When you get off the main roads, you don't find gas stations or cafes. Four-wheel-drive vehicles are recommended on snow and much of the unpaved terrain of the region. If you're doing some off-road adventuring, it's wise to go with a full gas tank, extra food and water, and warm clothing—just in case. At the higher-than-10,000-foot elevations of northern New Mexico, sudden summer snowstorms are not unheard of.

---

run southbound from Taos Pueblo and northbound from the Ranchos de Taos Post Office. Each route makes stops at the casino and various hotels in town, as well as at Taos RV Park. Bus fares are 50¢ one-way, $1 round-trip, $5 for a 7-day pass, and $20 for 31-day pass.

In addition, **Faust's Transportation** (© **505/758-3410**) has a taxi service linking town hotels and Taos Ski Valley. Faust's Transportation also offers shuttle service and on-call taxi service daily from 7am to 9pm, with fares of about $8 anywhere within the city limits for up to two people ($2 per additional person).

BY BICYCLE

Bicycle rentals are available from **Gearing Up Bicycle Shop,** 129 Paseo del Pueblo Sur (© **505/751-0365**); daily rentals run $35 for a full day and $25 for a half day for a mountain bike with front suspension. From April to October, **Native Sons Adventures,** 1033-A Paseo del Pueblo Sur (© **800/753-7559** or 505/758-9342), rents no-suspension bikes for $15/half day and $20/full day, front-suspension bikes for $25/half day and $35/full day, and full-suspension bikes for $35/half day and $45/full day. It also rents car racks for $5. Each shop supplies helmets and water bottles with rentals.

FAST FACTS: Taos

Airport See "Orientation," above.

Area Code The telephone area code for all of New Mexico is 505; however, at press time, plans were in the works to add new codes.

ATMs You can find ATMs (also known as *cash pueblos*) all over town, at supermarkets, banks, and drive-throughs.

Business Hours Most **businesses** are open at least Monday to Friday 10am to 5pm, though some may open an hour earlier and close an hour later. Many **tourist-oriented shops** are also open on Saturday morning, and some **art galleries** are open all day Saturday and Sunday, especially during peak tourist seasons. **Banks** are generally open Monday to Thursday 9am to 5pm and often for longer hours on Friday. Some may be open Saturday morning. Most branches have cash machines available 24 hours. Call establishments for specific hours.

Car Rentals See "Getting Around Northern New Mexico," in chapter 2, or "Getting Around," above.

Climate Taos's climate is similar to that of Santa Fe. Summer days are dry and sunny, except for frequent afternoon thunderstorms. Winter days are often bracing, with snowfalls common but rarely lasting too long. Average **summer temperatures** range from 50°F to 87°F (10°C–31°C). **Winter temperatures** vary between 9°F and 40°F (-13°C–4°C). **Annual rainfall** is 12 inches; annual snowfall is 35 inches in town and 300 inches at Taos Ski Valley, where the elevation is 9,207 feet. (A foot of snow is equal to an inch of rain.)

Currency Exchange Foreign currency can be exchanged at the **Centinel Bank of Taos,** 512 Paseo del Pueblo Sur (© **505/758-6700**).

Dentists If you need dental work, try **Dr. Walter Jakiela,** 1392 Weimer Rd. (© **505/758-8654**); **Dr. Michael Rivera,** 107 Plaza Garcia, Suite E (© **505/ 758-0531**); or **Dr. Tom Simms,** 1392 Weimer Rd. (© **505/758-8303**).

Doctors Members of the **Taos Medical Group,** on Weimer Road (© 505/758-2224), are highly respected. Also recommended are **Family Practice Associates of Taos,** 630 Paseo del Pueblo Sur, Suite 150 (© 505/758-3005).

Embassies & Consulates See "Fast Facts: For the International Traveler," in chapter 3.

Emergencies Dial © **911** for police, fire, and ambulance.

Hospital **Holy Cross Hospital,** 1397 Weimer Rd., off Paseo del Canyon (© 505/758-8883), has 24-hour emergency service. Serious cases are transferred to Santa Fe or Albuquerque.

Hot Lines The **crisis hot line** (© 505/758-9888) is available for emergency counseling.

Information See "Visitor Information," under "Orientation," above.

Internet Access You can retrieve your e-mail at **Magic Circle Bagels,** 710 Paseo del Pueblo Sur (© 505/758-0045).

Library The **Taos Public Library,** 402 Camino de la Placita (© 505/758-3063 or 505/737-2590), has a general collection for Taos residents, a children's library, and special collections on the Southwest and Taos art.

Liquor Laws The legal drinking age is 21 in New Mexico, as it is throughout the United States. Bars may remain open until 2am Monday to Saturday and until midnight on Sunday. Wine, beer, and spirits are sold at licensed supermarkets and liquor stores, but there are no package sales on election days until after 7pm. It is illegal to transport liquor through most Native American reservations.

Lost Property Check with the **Taos police** at © 505/758-2216.

Newspapers & Magazines **The Taos News** (© 505/758-2241; www.taosnews.com) and the **Sangre de Cristo Chronicle** (© 505/377-2358; www.sangrechronicle.com) are published every Thursday. **Taos Magazine** is also a good source of local information. The **Albuquerque Journal** (www.abqjournal.com) and the **New Mexican** (from Santa Fe; www.santafenewmexican.com) are easily obtained at book and convenience stores.

Pharmacies There are several full-service pharmacies in Taos. **Raley's Pharmacy** (© 505/758-1203), **Smith's Pharmacy** (© 505/758-4824), and **Wal-Mart Pharmacy** (© 505/758-2743) are all located on Pueblo Sur and are easily seen from the road.

Police In case of emergency, dial © **911.** All other inquiries should be directed to the **Taos police,** Civic Plaza Drive (© 505/758-2216). The **Taos County Sheriff,** with jurisdiction outside the city limits, is located in the county courthouse on Paseo del Pueblo Sur (© 505/758-3361).

Post Offices The main **Taos post office** is at 318 Paseo del Pueblo Norte (© 505/758-2081), a few blocks north of the plaza traffic light. There are smaller offices in **Ranchos de Taos** (© 505/758-3944) and at **El Prado** (© 505/758-4810). The zip code for Taos is 87571.

Radio A local station is **KTAO-FM** (101.7), which broadcasts an entertainment calendar daily (© 505/758-1017); National Public Radio can be found on **KUNM-FM** (98.5) from Albuquerque.

Taxes Gross receipts tax for the city of Taos is 7%, and for Taos County it's 6.31%. There is an additional local bed tax of 4.5% in the city of Taos and 5% on hotel rooms in Taos County.

Taxis See "Getting Around," above.

Television **Channel 2,** the local access station, is available in most hotels. For a few hours a day it shows local programming. Cable networks carry Santa Fe and Albuquerque stations.

Time As is true throughout New Mexico, Taos is on **Mountain Standard Time.** It's 2 hours earlier than New York, 1 hour earlier than Chicago, and 1 hour later than Los Angeles. Daylight saving time is in effect from early April to late October.

Useful Telephone Numbers For **emergency road service** in the Taos area, call the state police at ✆ **505/758-8878;** for **road conditions** dial ✆ **800/ 432-4269** (within New Mexico) for the state highway department. **Taos County offices** are at ✆ **505/737-6300.**

Weather For weather forecasts, Taos has no number to call, but if you're hooked up, log on to www.taoschamber.com.

12

Where to Stay in Taos

A tiny town with a big tourist market, Taos has thousands of rooms in hotels, motels, condominiums, and bed-and-breakfasts. Many new properties have recently opened, turning this into a buyer's market. In the slower seasons, in January through early February and April through early May, when competition for travelers is steep, you may even want to try bargaining your room rate down. Most of the hotels and motels are located on Paseo del Pueblo Sur and Norte, with a few scattered just east of the town center, along Kit Carson Road. The condos and bed-and-breakfasts are generally scattered throughout Taos's back streets.

During peak seasons, visitors without reservations may have difficulty finding vacant rooms. **Taos Central Reservations,** P.O. Box 1713, Taos, NM 87571 (© **800/821-2437**), might be able to help.

Fifteen hundred or so of Taos County's beds are in condominiums and lodges at or near Taos Ski Valley. The **Taos Valley Resort Association,** P.O. Box 85, Taos Ski Valley, NM 87525 (© **800/776-1111** or 505/776-2233; fax 505/776-8842; www.visitnewmexico.com), can book these,

as well as rooms in Taos and all the rest of northern New Mexico, and it can book private home rentals.

Reservations of Taos, 1033-A Paseo del Pueblo Sur, Taos, NM 87571 (© **505/751-1292**), will help you find accommodations from bed-and-breakfasts to home rentals, hotels, RV parks, and cabins throughout Taos and the rest of northern New Mexico. It'll also help you arrange package prices for outdoor activities such as whitewater rafting, horseback riding, hot-air ballooning, snowmobiling, fishing, and skiing.

There are two high seasons in Taos: winter (the Christmas-to-Easter ski season, except for Jan, which is notoriously slow) and summer. Spring and fall are shoulder seasons, often with lower rates. The period between Easter and Memorial Day is also slow in the tourist industry here, and many proprietors of restaurants and other businesses take their annual vacations at this time. Book well ahead for ski holiday periods (especially Christmas) and for the annual arts festivals (late May to mid-June and late Sept to early Oct).

1 The Taos Area

HOTELS/MOTELS
EXPENSIVE

El Monte Sagrado ★★★ (Moments) For those like me who are blessed, or cursed, with sensitive senses, El Monte Sagrado (the Sacred Mountain), Taos' new resort near the center of town, is pure heaven. Often while traveling I find I'm accosted by sounds, scents, even sights, but at this resort my senses rejoice. Water running over falls, clear air, and delicious food and drink lull guests into

Taos Area Accommodations

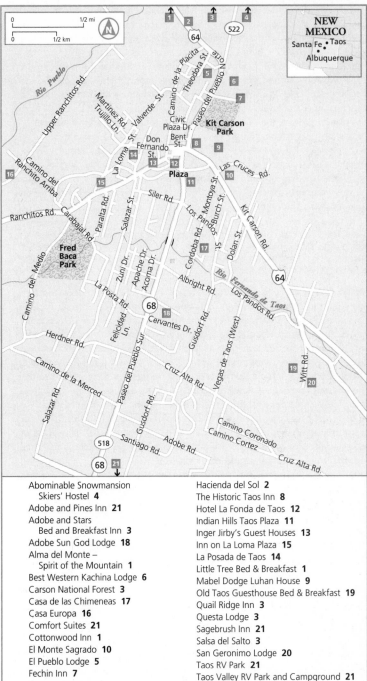

Abominable Snowmansion
  Skiers' Hostel **4**
Adobe and Pines Inn **21**
Adobe and Stars
  Bed and Breakfast Inn **3**
Adobe Sun God Lodge **18**
Alma del Monte –
  Spirit of the Mountain **1**
Best Western Kachina Lodge **6**
Carson National Forest **3**
Casa de las Chimeneas **17**
Casa Europa **16**
Comfort Suites **21**
Cottonwood Inn **1**
El Monte Sagrado **10**
El Pueblo Lodge **5**
Fechin Inn **7**

Hacienda del Sol **2**
The Historic Taos Inn **8**
Hotel La Fonda de Taos **12**
Indian Hills Taos Plaza **11**
Inger Jirby's Guest Houses **13**
Inn on La Loma Plaza **15**
La Posada de Taos **14**
Little Tree Bed & Breakfast **1**
Mabel Dodge Luhan House **9**
Old Taos Guesthouse Bed & Breakfast **19**
Quail Ridge Inn **3**
Questa Lodge **3**
Sagebrush Inn **21**
Salsa del Salto **3**
San Geronimo Lodge **20**
Taos RV Park **21**
Taos Valley RV Park and Campground **21**

a sweet *samadhi,* or state of relaxation, while the eyes luxuriate in the beauty of rooms impeccably decorated. These range in theme from the Caribbean Casita, a medium-size room with a medium-size bathroom, which evokes the feel of an African jungle; to the China Casita, a large two-bedroom suite with two large bathrooms, all bathed in gold, with its own patio and outdoor hot tub; to the Kamasutra Suite, with suggestive carvings throughout, a room resort owner Tom Worrell describes as "the first honeymoon suite to come with instructions." All rooms are quiet and lovely, with patios or balconies and views. In line with Worrell's plan to preserve the earth's environment through responsible development and sustainable technologies, the resort recycles its water and makes much of its own electricity. All rooms rim a grassy, cottonwood-shaded "Sacred Circle," which also has trout and koi ponds. The intimate spa offers a full range of treatments in softly shaped rooms. The **Anaconda Bar** (see chapter 14) and **De La Tierra restaurant** (see chapter 13) combine a contemporary feel with elegant Asian touches.

317 Kit Carson Rd., Taos, NM 87571. © **800/828-TAOS** or 505/758-3502. www.elmontesagrado.com. 36 units. $245–$375 historic 1-bedroom casita; $295–$395 1-bedroom junior suite; $395–$795 1-bedroom exclusive casita; $1,095–$1,495 2-bedroom global suite. AE, DC, DISC, MC, V. Free parking. **Amenities:** Restaurant; bar; indoor pool; well-equipped health club and spa; Jacuzzi; concierge; babysitting; laundry service. *In room:* A/C, TV, dataport, hair dryer, safe.

Fechin Inn 𝄫𝄫 This masterfully created luxury hotel provides comfort, quiet, and lots of amenities. Built next door to Russian artist Nicolai Fechin's 1927 home (see the discussion of the Taos Art Museum in chapter 14), the hotel features elegantly carved wood furniture and artwork by Jeremy Morelli of Santa Fe. The hotel is located right next to Kit Carson Park, a short walk from the plaza. The two-story lobby is airy, with a bank of windows and French doors looking south to a portal where diners can eat breakfast in the warmer months. The spacious rooms have Southwestern decor with nice touches such as guest robes, hickory furniture, and flagstone-topped tables; some have balconies or patios. Suites have kiva fireplaces. The bathrooms are delightful, with Italian tile and warm, adjustable lighting. There's a library where you can play chess or backgammon. For an additional cost, you can eat an elaborate continental breakfast. In the evenings, drinks are available.

227 Paseo del Pueblo Norte, Taos, NM 87571. © **800/811-2933** or 505/751-1000. Fax 505/751-7338. www.fechininn.com. 84 units. $114–$177 double; $282–$512 suite. Rates vary according to season. Additional person $15. AE, DC, DISC, MC, V. Free parking. Pets accepted with some restrictions and extra fee. **Amenities:** Medium-size health club; Jacuzzi; car-rental desk; room service; massage; coin-op laundry; same-day dry-cleaning and laundry service. *In room:* A/C, TV, dataport, fridge, coffeemaker, hair dryer.

The Historic Taos Inn 𝄫 It's rare to see a hotel that has withstood the years with grace. The Historic Taos Inn has. Here, you'll be surrounded by 20th-century luxury without ever forgetting that you're within the thick walls of a number of 19th-century Southwestern homes. Dr. Thomas Paul Martin, the town's first physician, purchased the complex in 1895. In 1936, a year after the doctor's death, his widow, Helen, enclosed the plaza—now the inn's darling two-story lobby—and turned it into a hotel. In 1981–82, the inn was restored; it's now listed on both the State and National Registers of Historic Places.

The lobby doubles as the **Adobe Bar,** a popular local gathering place, with adobe *bancos* (benches) and a sunken fireplace, all surrounding a wishing well that was once the old town well. A number of rooms open onto a balcony that overlooks this area. If you like community and don't mind the sound of jazz and flamenco drifting up toward your room, these rooms are for you. However, if you appreciate solitude and silence, request one of the courtyard rooms downstairs. All the rooms are unique and comfortable, decorated with Spanish colonial art, Taos-style furniture, and interesting touches, such as hand-woven Oaxacan bedspreads and little niches decorated with Mexican pottery; many rooms have fireplaces.

I should note that in recent years I've had complaints from guests about the temperamental nature of these old buildings. You may encounter problems such as windows not staying open and some not having screens. I've also had complaints about the service here.

Doc Martin's, with good nouveau Southwestern cuisine and a hint of Asia, is a good bet for dinner (see chapter 13).

125 Paseo del Pueblo Norte, Taos, NM 87571. $\textcircled{C}$ **800/TAOS-INN** or 505/758-2233. Fax 505/758-5776. www.taosinn.com. 36 units. $65–$225, depending on the type of room and season. AE, DISC, MC, V. **Amenities:** Restaurant; bar; seasonal outdoor pool; Jacuzzi; room service; coffee or refreshments in lobby. *In room:* A/C, TV, VCR on request, hair dryer, iron.

Hotel La Fonda de Taos ★   Finally, Taos has a recommendable hotel on the plaza. A $3-million renovation to this historic property built in 1880 has turned it into a comfortable, fun spot with a stellar location. The charismatic Taos figure Saki Kavaras put this hotel on the society map in the 1930s, when, most notably, British author D. H. Lawrence frequented it. His legacy is preserved in a unique D. H. Lawrence Forbidden Art Museum, where some of his risqué paintings hang—a must-see even if you don't stay here (free for guests; $3 for non-guests). Rooms are set off broad hallways, each styled in earth tones, Southwestern furnishings, and tile bathrooms. Standards are small, each with a queen-size bed. Your better bet is to reserve a plaza or deluxe plaza room, or a suite. These are larger, with king beds. My favorite rooms are nos. 201 and 301, which overlook the plaza. Groups can rent the whole top floor, which includes a full kitchen suite.

108 South Plaza, Taos, NM 87571. $\textcircled{C}$ **800/833-2211** or 505/758-2211. Fax 505/758-8508. www.hotel lafonda.com. 24 units. $99–$169 standard double; $129–$219 plaza and deluxe double; $169–$229 suite. AE, DC, DISC, MC, V. Free parking. **Amenities:** Restaurant; coffee shop; bar. *In room:* A/C, TV, hair dryer, iron.

Inger Jirby's Guest Houses ★★   You can't have a better address in Taos than this artist has, 2 blocks from the plaza, between the R.C. Gorman Gallery and the Ernest L. Blumenschein Museum. Inger Jirby has chosen this for her gallery space as well as a home for travelers. From the remains of a 400-year-old adobe, she's carved and added these lively dwellings and adorned them with her unique style. Full of rich Mexican and Balinese art, and then accented by her own vivid landscapes of the Southwest and beyond, the casitas are artsy as well as comfortable. Each has a full kitchen, with range, dishwasher, microwave, and washer/dryer. The larger two have flagstone floors, large windows, and sleeping lofts. (Very big people might have trouble maneuvering the spiral staircases in these.) These also have foldout couches, so they're a great option for families. The third casita has a large kitchen, a smaller bedroom, and an atrium. All are equipped with stereos and robes. More than anywhere in town, these casitas provide a real home away from home.

207 Ledoux St., Taos, NM 87571. $\textcircled{C}$ **505/758-7333.** www.jirby.com. 3 units. $125–$175 double; $175–$250 double during holidays. Rates include self-prepared breakfast. Additional person $25. *In room:* TV/VCR, kitchen, hair dryer.

MODERATE

Best Western Kachina Lodge & Meeting Center ★ *Kids*   Built in the early 1960s, this lodge on the north end of town, in walking distance of the plaza, has a lot of charm despite the fact that it's really a motor hotel. Though it has traditionally been a good spot for families and travelers, in recent years management has begun catering so much to convention traffic that the service has suffered for others. Remodeling is ongoing in the solidly built Southwestern-style rooms—some have couches and most have Taos-style *trasteros* (armoires) that hold the TVs. Rooms are placed around a grassy courtyard studded with huge blue spruce trees, allowing kids room to run. In the center is a stage where a family from Taos Pueblo builds a bonfire and dances nightly in the summer and explains the significance of the dances—a real treat for anyone baffled by the Pueblo rituals.

413 Paseo del Pueblo Norte (P.O. Box NM), Taos, NM 87571. (C) **800/522-4462** or 505/758-2275. Fax 505/758-9207. www.kachinalodge.com. 118 units. $59–$129 double. Additional person $10. Children under 12 stay free in parent's room. AE, DC, DISC, MC, V. **Amenities:** 2 restaurants; lounge; outdoor pool; salon; coin-op laundry. *In room:* A/C, TV, coffeemaker, hair dryer, iron.

Comfort Suites   New, clean, predictable: That's what you'll get in this recent addition to the Taos accommodations scene. Each room has a small living/dining area, with a sleeper sofa, microwave, minirefrigerator, and coffeemaker, and a bedroom with hand-crafted wood furniture and a comfortable king-size or queen-size bed. If you have kids, you might want a ground-floor poolside room. Though the pool isn't landscaped, it's warm, roomy, and accompanied by a hot tub.

1500 Paseo del Pueblo Sur (P.O. Box 1268), Taos, NM 87571. (C) **888/751-1555** or 505/751-1555. Fax 505/751-1991. www.comfortsuites.com. 62 units. $69–$149 double. Rates include continental breakfast. AE, DC, DISC, MC, V. **Amenities:** Outdoor pool; Jacuzzi; sauna; car-rental desk; in-room massage; same-day dry cleaning. *In room:* A/C, TV, dataport, fridge, microwave, coffeemaker, hair dryer.

(Kids Family-Friendly Hotels

The Bavarian Lodge (p. 188)   Just feet from the slopes and with sleeping lofts in the rooms, this is a fun spot for kids.

Best Western Kachina Lodge & Meeting Center (above)   An outdoor swimming pool and Pueblo Indian presentations keep kids well entertained.

El Pueblo Lodge (p. 182)   A slide, year-round swimming pool, and hot tub set on 3½ acres of land will please the kids; a barbecue, some minikitchens with microwave ovens, laundry facilities, and the rates will please their parents.

Indian Hills Inn Taos Plaza (p. 182)   With a pool, picnic tables, barbecue grills, and acres of grass, this inn offers plenty of room for families to spread out.

Kandahar Condominiums (p. 190)   These two-story condos offer privacy and a convenient location close to the children's center at Taos Ski Valley.

Quail Ridge Inn (p. 181)   The year-round swimming pool and tennis courts will keep active kids busy during the day when it's time for mom and dad's siesta.

Quail Ridge Inn *Kids*   Pueblo-style adobe condominiums surround tennis courts at this sports resort, a place for those who spend more time out of their rooms than in them. Located 4 miles north of Taos en route to Taos Ski Valley, it was built between 1977 and 1982. In 1999, the resort completed an interior and exterior renovation. Families and ski pals tend to stay here. Rooms range in size from standard hotel rooms, to one- and two-bedroom condominiums, to large two-bedroom casitas, all decorated in some form of Southwestern style. All condo and casita units have fully stocked kitchens with refrigerators, microwaves, stoves/ovens, coffeemakers, toasters, and dishwashers. Every room features a fireplace and full shower/tub bathrooms. With its nice-size outdoor pool (heated year-round) and hot tub, and its surroundings among the sage, this is a nice stopping place, but don't expect luxury accommodations.

Ski Valley Rd. (P.O. Box 707), Taos, NM 87571. ℭ **800/624-4448** or 505/776-2211. Fax 505/776-2949. www. quailridgeinn.com. 110 units. $89–$130 double; $160–$395 suite. Additional person $10. Children under 18 stay free in parent's room. AE, DC, MC, V. **Amenities:** Year-round outdoor heated pool; 10 tennis courts; Jacuzzi; sauna; coin-op laundry; bocce court; putting green; summer volleyball pit. *In room:* TV.

Sagebrush Inn *★*   Three miles south of Taos, surrounded by acres of sage, this inn is housed in an adobe building that has been added on to decade after decade, creating an interesting mix of accommodations. The original structure was built in 1929. It had three floors and 12 rooms, hand-sculpted from adobe; the roof was held in place with hand-hewn vigas. That part still remains, and the rooms are small and cozy and have the feel of old Taos—in fact, Georgia O'Keeffe lived and worked here for 10 months in the late 1930s. But for those more accustomed to refined style, it might feel dated.

The treasure of this place is the large grass courtyard dotted with elm trees, where visitors sit and read in the warm months. Beware that some of the rooms added in the '50s through '70s have a tackiness not overcome by the vigas and tile work. More recent additions (to the west) are more skillful; these suites away from the hotel proper are spacious and full of amenities, but they have noisy plumbing.

The lobby-cum-cantina has an Old West feel that livens at night when it becomes a venue for country/western dancing and one of Taos's most active nightspots for live music (see "Taos After Dark," in chapter 14). Traditionally, this has been a family hotel, but with a new convention center and the addition of a Comfort Suites hotel on the property, management is working to appeal to convention guests as well.

1508 Paseo del Pueblo Sur (P.O. Box 557), Taos, NM 87571. ℭ **800/428-3626** or 505/758-2254. Fax 505/ 758-5077. www.sagebrushinn.com. 100 units. $70–$95 double; $90–$155 deluxe or small suite; $105–$185 executive suite. Additional person $10. Children under 18 stay free in parent's room. Rates include breakfast. AE, DC, DISC, MC, V. Pets welcome. **Amenities:** 2 restaurants; bar; 2 outdoor pools; tennis courts; Jacuzzi; courtesy shuttle; business center; in-room massage; same-day dry cleaning; executive-level rooms. *In room:* A/C, TV, dataport, fridge, coffeemaker, hair dryer, iron.

INEXPENSIVE

Abominable Snowmansion Skiers' Hostel   Since I was a kid, I've traveled past this hostel and marveled at the name; it was a treat for me to finally experience the inside. Set in the quaint village of Arroyo Seco, about 8 miles north of Taos and 10 miles from Taos Ski Valley, it offers clean beds (in dorm rooms or private ones) for reasonable prices, and a nice community experience. The common room has a pool table, piano, and circular fireplace. Best of all are the tepees that sit out around a grassy yard. They each sleep two to four people; an outdoor kitchen, showers, and toilets are nearby.

476 Taos Ski Valley Rd. (Hwy. 150), Arroyo Seco (P.O. Box GG), Taos, NM 87571. (C) **505/776-8298.** Fax 505/
776-2107. http://taoswebb.com/hotel/snowmansion. 60 beds. $15–$22 bed; $40–$54 double, depending on
size of accommodation and season; $34 cabins and teepees; $12 camping. Rates include continental breakfast in winter. MC, V.

Adobe Sun God Lodge   For a comfortable, economical stay with a northern
New Mexico ambience, this is a good choice. This hotel, a 5-minute drive from
the plaza, has three distinct parts spread across 1½ acres of landscaped grounds.
The oldest was solidly built in 1958 and has some court-motel charm, with a
low ceiling and large windows. To update the rooms, the owners added tile
sinks, Taos-style furniture, and new carpeting. To the south is a section built in
1988. The rooms are small but have little touches that make them feel cozy, such
as little *nichos* (niches) and hand-carved furnishings. In back to the east are the
newest buildings, built in 1994. These are two-story structures with portal-style
porches and balconies. Some rooms have kitchenettes, which include
microwaves, refrigerators, and stoves; others have kiva fireplaces. The two suites
on the northeast corner of the property are the quietest and have the best views.

919 Paseo del Pueblo Sur, Taos, NM 87571. (C) **800/821-2437** or 505/758-3162. Fax 505/758-1716.
www.sungodlodge.com. 53 units. $49–$99 double; $69–$139 suite. AE, DISC, MC, V. Pets allowed for $10 per
day. **Amenities:** Jacuzzi. *In room:* A/C, TV, dataport, coffeemaker.

El Pueblo Lodge *Value* *Kids*   Considering its location and setting, this hotel is
a bargain, especially for families, although you'll want to reserve carefully. It's set
on 3½ grassy, cottonwood-shaded acres, on the north end of town, a reasonable
walk from the plaza. Three buildings form a U-shape, each with its own high
and low points. The oldest part, to the south, was once a 1950s court motel, and
it maintains that cozy charm, with heavy vigas and most with tiny kitchenettes.
This section could use some updating, but despite that, it's worth the price. To
the north is a two-story building, constructed in 1972, that lacks charm but provides lots of space. The newest section (to the west) is one of Taos's best bargains,
with nicely constructed suites and double rooms decorated in blonde pine with
kiva fireplaces and doors that open onto the center yard or balconies. Almost all
rooms have air-conditioning, but in summer, ask to be sure yours does.

412 Paseo del Pueblo Norte, Taos, NM 87571. (C) **800/433-9612** or 505/758-8700. Fax 505/758-7321.
www.elpueblolodge.com. 56 units. $69–$89 double; $125–$255 suite. Call for Christmas rates. Additional
person $10. Rates include continental breakfast. AE, DISC, MC, V. Pets permitted for $10. **Amenities:** Outdoor
pool open and heated year-round; 2 Jacuzzis; tour desk; in-room massage; babysitting; coin-op laundry; laundry service. *In room:* TV, dataport, fridge, hair dryer upon request, iron upon request.

Indian Hills Inn Taos Plaza *Kids*   With its close location to the plaza
(3 blocks), this is a good choice if you're looking for a decent, functional night's
stay. There are two sections to the hotel: one built in the 1950s, the other completed in 1996. The older section has received a major face-lift. However, for a
few more dollars you can stay in the newer section, where the rooms are larger,
with gas-log fireplaces, and the bathrooms are fresher, though noise can travel
from nearby guest rooms. Both sections sit on a broad lawn studded with towering blue spruce trees. Picnic tables and barbecue grills add to the place's charm
and functionality and provide families a bit of respite from the restaurant scene.
The hotel offers golf, ski, and rafting packages at reduced rates, as well as Cumbres and Toltec Scenic Railroad tickets.

233 Paseo del Pueblo Sur (P.O. Box 1229), Taos, NM 87571. (C) **800/444-2346** or 505/758-4293. www.taos
net.com/indianhillsinn. 55 units. $49–$99 double. Group and package rates available. Rates include continental breakfast. AE, DC, DISC, MC, V. Small pets welcome with prior arrangements. **Amenities:** Outdoor
pool; tour desk; free laundry. *In room:* A/C, TV.

BED & BREAKFASTS
EXPENSIVE

Adobe & Pines Inn ⭐⭐   This inn seeks to create a magical escape. It succeeds. Much of it is located in a 150-year-old adobe directly off NM 68, less than half a mile south of St. Francis Plaza (about a 10-min. drive from Taos Plaza). The inn is set around a courtyard marked by an 80-foot-long grand portal and surrounded by pine and fruit trees. Each room has a private entrance and fireplace (three even have fireplaces in their bathrooms), and each is uniquely decorated. The theme here is the use of colors, which are richly displayed on the walls and in the furnishings. There's Puerta Azul, a cozy blue room with thick adobe walls, and Puerta Turquese, a separate whimsically painted guest cottage with a full kitchen. The two newest rooms, completed in 1996, have bold maroon and copper-yellow themes. The walls have handprints and petroglyph motifs, and each room is furnished with rich and comfortable couches. Most of the inn's rooms also have Jacuzzi tubs. Since this inn is near the highway, at times cars can be heard, but the rooms themselves are quiet. Morning brings a delicious full gourmet breakfast in the glassed-in breakfast room.

NM 68, Ranchos de Taos, NM 87557. ℂ **800/723-8267** or 505/751-0947. Fax 505/758-8423. www.adobe pines.com. 7 units, 3 casitas. $95–$195 double. Rates include full gourmet breakfast. MC, V. Pets accepted with prior arrangement. **Amenities:** In-room massage; complimentary laundry facility available evenings. *In room:* TV, no phone.

Adobe and Stars Bed and Breakfast Inn ⭐   On first appearance, this modern inn looks stark, sitting on the mesa between Taos town and Taos Ski Valley. However, once you're inside, you can see that innkeeper Judy Salathiel has an eye for detail. The breakfast area and common room are sunny, with large windows facing the mountains. A few rooms are upstairs, such as La Luna, my favorite, with views in every direction and a heart-shaped Jacuzzi tub for two. All rooms have kiva fireplaces and private decks or patios. Most of the downstairs rooms open onto a portal. All are decorated with hand-crafted Southwestern-style furniture, and many have Jacuzzi tubs. The full breakfast may vary from New Mexican dishes (such as breakfast burritos served with green-chile stew) to baked goods (apple and strawberry turnovers). In the afternoons, New Mexico wines are served with the inn's special salsa and blue-corn chips, as are sweets such as chocolate cake and piñon lemon bars.

At the corner of State Hwy. 150 and Valdez Rim Rd. (P.O. Box 2285), Taos, NM 87571. ℂ **800/211-7076** or 505/776-2776. Fax 505/776-2872. www.taosadobe.com. 8 units. $95–$185 double. Rates include full breakfast and hors d'oeuvres. AE, MC, V. Pets accepted with $20 per-pet fee and $50 damage deposit. **Amenities:** Jacuzzi; in-room massage. *In room:* Dataport, hair dryer.

Alma del Monte (Spirit of the Mountain) ⭐   If you like views and the quiet of the country, you'll enjoy this bed-and-breakfast. Situated halfway between the ski area and the plaza, this house is a hacienda-shaped, pueblo-style adobe. Each room opens onto the courtyard, which is outfitted with a fountain and, in warm weather, hammocks. Proprietors Jan and Phyllis Waye have decorated the place with a bit of a hodgepodge of lovely antiques and modern furnishings that works better in some cases than in others. Each room has a Jacuzzi tub and kiva-style fireplace. Many have picture-window views and skylights, and some have private gardens. Above all, the rooms are quiet because no roads border the property. The three-course breakfast includes a smoothie and a specialty such as baked French toast. In the library, guests enjoy high-speed Internet access, television, and a good CD library.

372 Hondo Seco Rd., Taos, NM 87571. ℂ 800/273-7203 or 505/776-2721. Fax 505/776-8888. www. almaspirit.com. 5 units. $160–$200 double; prices vary with seasons and holidays. Rates include full breakfast and afternoon refreshments. AE, MC, V. Pets welcome to stay in the strawbail dog house. *In room:* Hair dryer, iron, CD player.

Casa de las Chimeneas ★★★ This 82-year-old adobe home has, since its opening in 1988, been a model of Southwestern elegance. Now, with new additions, it has become a full-service luxury inn as well. The addition includes a spa with a small fitness room and sauna, as well as complete massage and facial treatments for an additional charge. I highly recommend the Rio Grande and Territorial rooms, which are air-conditioned. Both of these rooms have heated Saltillo-tile floors, gas kiva fireplaces, and Jacuzzi tubs. If you prefer a more antique-feeling room, try the delightful older section, especially the Library Suite. Each room in the inn is decorated with original works of art and has elegant bedding, a private entrance, robes, and a minirefrigerator stocked with complimentary soft drinks, juices, and mineral water. All rooms have kiva fireplaces, and most look out on flower and herb gardens. Breakfasts are delicious. Specialties include an artichoke-heart and mushroom omelet or ricotta cream-cheese blintz, plus innkeeper Susan Vernon's special fruit frappé. In the evenings she serves a light supper. During one evening I had canapés with avocado, cheese, and tomato; a spicy broccoli soup; and moonshine cake. End the day at the large hot tub in the courtyard. Smoking is not permitted. Ask about the spa specials.

405 Cordoba Rd., at Los Pandos Rd. (5303 NDCBU), Taos, NM 87571. ℂ 877/758-4777 or 505/758-4777. Fax 505/758-3976. www.visittaos.com. 8 units. $165–$290 double; $325 suite for 2. Rates include breakfast and evening supper. AE, DC, DISC, MC, V. **Amenities:** Small exercise room; spa; Jacuzzi; sauna; concierge; car-rental desk; in-room massage; coin-op laundry; laundry service; all units nonsmoking. *In room:* TV/VCR, dataport, free stocked minibar, coffeemaker, hair dryer, iron, free movies.

Casa Europa ★ This cream-colored Territorial-style adobe (just 1¾ miles west of the plaza) under giant cottonwoods is surrounded by open pastures dotted with grazing horses, with lovely views of the mountains in the distance. Some rooms here date from the 1700s; however, a 1983 renovation made this a contemporary two-story luxury inn. Elegant rooms, all with fireplaces, each with a sitting area and full bathroom (two rooms have two-person Jacuzzis) with robes, are furnished with interesting antiques. The regional artwork in the rooms can be purchased. There's a sitting area with a TV upstairs and a common sitting room for reading and/or conversation downstairs, where coffee and pastries are offered each day at 3pm; during ski season hors d'oeuvres are served. A full gourmet breakfast (specialties include cheese blintzes with warm strawberry sauce and vegetarian eggs Benedict) is served each morning in the formal dining room. Smoking is not permitted.

840 Upper Ranchitos Rd. (HC 68, Box 3F), Taos, NM 87571. ℂ 888/758-9798 or 505/758-9798. www. casaeuropanm.com. 7 units. $95–$165 double. Additional person $20. Rates include full breakfast and afternoon pastries. AE, DISC, MC, V. **Amenities:** Jacuzzi; sauna; concierge; all units nonsmoking. *In room:* TV, hair dryer.

Cottonwood Inn ★ This inn provides cozy comfort in a rural setting. Built in 1947 by a flamboyant artist, it has high ceilings with vigas, and almost every room has a kiva fireplace. Innkeepers Kit and Bill Owen have made the place luxurious, using thick carpeting in many of the rooms and Saltillo tile in the bathrooms, as well as adding Jacuzzi tubs and steam baths to some rooms. The rooms have down pillows and comforters on the beds and are decorated in a subtle

Southwestern style. The inn's location, halfway between Taos and the ski area, lends a pastoral quality to your stay, with a herd of sheep wandering in a meadow to the west. My favorite rooms are the ones that open into the main part of the house, but if you prefer a private entrance, you have that option, too. Smoking is not allowed here.

2 State Rd. 230 (HCR 74, Box 24609), Taos, NM 87529. ℂ **800/324-7120** or 505/776-5826. Fax 505/776-1141. www.taos-cottonwood.com. 8 units. $95–$195 double. Rates include full breakfast and afternoon snack. AE, DISC, MC, V. **Amenities:** Jacuzzi; concierge; in-room massage; all units nonsmoking. *In room:* Hair dryer.

Hacienda del Sol ★★   What's unique about this bed-and-breakfast is its completely unobstructed view of Taos Mountain. Because the 1¼-acre property borders Taos Pueblo, the land is pristine. The inn also has a rich history. It was once owned by arts patron Mabel Dodge Luhan, and it was here that author Frank Waters wrote *The People of the Valley.* You'll find bold splashes of color from the gardens—where in summer tulips, pansies, and flax bloom—to the rooms themselves—where woven bedspreads and original art lend a Mexican feel. The main house is 190 years old, so it has the wonderful curves of adobe as well as thick vigas. Some guest rooms are in this section. Others range from 3 to 10 years in age. These newer rooms are finely constructed, and I almost recommend them over the others because they're a little more private and the bathrooms are more refined. All rooms have robes and CD players, most have fireplaces, three have private Jacuzzis, and three have private steam rooms. Some have minirefrigerators. A full and delicious breakfast as well as evening hors d'oeuvres are served in the Spanish-hacienda-style dining area. The outdoor hot tub has a mountain view and is available for private guest use in half-hour segments.

109 Mabel Dodge Lane (P.O. Box 177), Taos, NM 87571. ℂ **505/758-0287.** Fax 505/758-5895. www.taos haciendadelsol.com. 11 units. $85–$245 double. Rates include full breakfast and evening hors d'oeuvres. AE, DISC, MC, V. **Amenities:** Jacuzzi; sauna; concierge; in-room massage. *In room:* TV, dataport, fridge, hair dryer, CD player.

Inn on La Loma Plaza ★★   Named by *American Historic Inns* as 1 of the 10 most romantic inns in America, the Inn on La Loma Plaza provides the comfortable intimacy of a B&B with the service and amenities of an inn. It's located on a historic neighborhood plaza, complete with dirt streets and a tiny central park, which was once a 1796 neighborhood stronghold—adobe homes built around a square, with thick outer walls to fend off marauders. The building, a 10-minute walk from Taos Plaza, is a 200-year-old home, complete with aged vigas and maple floors, decorated tastefully with comfortable furniture and Middle Eastern rugs. Each room is unique, most with sponge-painted walls and Talavera tile in the bathrooms to provide an eclectic ambience. All have robes, slippers, lighted makeup mirrors, bottled water, and fireplaces, and most have balconies or terraces and views. Some have special touches, such as the Happy Trails Room, with knotty pine paneling, a brass bed, old chaps, and decorative hanging spurs. Some rooms have kitchenettes. Guests dine on such delights as breakfast burritos or green-chile strata (a casserole) in a plant-filled sunroom or on the patio.

315 Ranchitos Rd., Taos, NM 87571. ℂ **800/530-3040** or 505/758-1717. Fax 505/751-0155. www.vacation taos.com. 7 units. $125–$225 double; $250–$325 artist's studios; $475–$550 suite. Additional person $20. Children 12 and under stay free in parent's room. Discounts available. Rates include full breakfast. AE, DISC, MC, V. **Amenities:** Pool and spa privileges at nearby Taos Spa; Jacuzzi. *In room:* TV/VCR, hair dryer, iron.

La Posada de Taos ☆ This cozy inn just a few blocks from the plaza rests within thick and cozy adobe walls and is decorated with a combination of Mexican tile and country antiques. The three rooms off the common area are the coziest. All the rooms except one have fireplaces and private patios. El Solecito and the Beutler Room have Jacuzzi tubs. The place lights with special touches such as old Mexican doors opening onto a patio in the Lino, a view of Taos Mountain from the Taos room, and a skylight over the bed in La Casa de la Luna Miel, the honeymoon suite, which is set in a cottage separate from the rest of the inn. Expect such breakfast treats as baked apple French toast or spinach frittata. Special ski packages include a free pass to Taos Spa.

309 Juanita Lane (P.O. Box 1118), Taos, NM 87571. ℂ 800/645-4803 or 505/758-8164. www.laposadade taos.com. 5 units, 1 cottage. $100–$215 double. Winter discounts available, except during holidays. Additional person $15. Rates include full breakfast and homemade afternoon snack. AE, DISC, MC, V. **Amenities:** In-room massage. *In room:* Hair dryer.

Little Tree Bed & Breakfast ☆☆ *Finds* Little Tree is one of my favorite Taos bed-and-breakfasts, partly because it's located in a beautiful, secluded setting, and partly because it's constructed with real adobe that's been left in its raw state, lending the place an authentic hacienda feel. Located 2 miles down a country road, about midway between Taos and the ski area, it's surrounded by sage and piñon. The charming and cozy rooms have radiant heat under the floors, queen-size beds (one with a king-size), nice medium-size baths (one with a Jacuzzi tub), and access to the portal and courtyard garden, at the center of which is the little tree for which the inn is named. The Piñon (my favorite) and Juniper rooms are equipped with fireplaces and private entrances. The Piñon and Aspen rooms offer sunset views. The Spruce Room, Victorian in ambience, is decorated with quilts. In the main building, the living room has a traditional viga-and-*latilla* ceiling and *tierra blanca* adobe (adobe that's naturally white; if you look closely at it, you can see little pieces of mica and straw). Visiting hummingbirds enchant guests as they enjoy a scrumptious breakfast on the portal during warmer months. On arrival, guests are treated to refreshments.

County Road B-143 (P.O. Box 509), Taos, NM 87513. ℂ 800/334-8467 or 505/776-8467. www.littletree bandb.com. 4 units. $105–$175 double. Rates include breakfast and afternoon snack. MC, V. *In room:* TV/VCR.

Mabel Dodge Luhan House This National Historic Landmark is also called "Las Palomas de Taos" because of the throngs of doves *(palomas)* that live in enchanting weathered birdhouses on the property. Like so many other free spirits, they were attracted by the flamboyant Mabel Dodge (1879–1962), who came to Taos in 1916. A familiar figure in these parts, she and her fourth husband, a full-blooded Pueblo named Tony Luhan, enlarged this 200-year-old home to its present size of 22 rooms in the 1920s. If you like history and don't mind the curves and undulations it brings to a building, this is a good choice, but it doesn't quite compete with the other B&Bs in town. The place has a mansion feel, evoking images of the glitterati of the 1920s—writers, artists, adventurers— sitting on the terrace under the cottonwoods, drinking margaritas. The entrance is marked by a Spanish colonial–style portal.

All main rooms have thick vigas, arched pueblo-style doorways, hand-carved doors, kiva fireplaces, and dark hardwood floors. Guest rooms in the main building feature antique furnishings and six have fireplaces. Most rooms have private bathrooms; others must share. Eight newer guest rooms are equipped with fireplaces. Many educational workshops are held here throughout the year, the rooms often reserved for participants.

240 Morada Lane, Taos, NM 87571. ℂ **800/846-2235** or 505/751-9686. www.mabeldodgeluhan.com. 18 units, 16 with bathroom. $95–$220 double. Additional person $20. During holiday season add $10. Rates include full breakfast. AE, MC, V.

Salsa del Salto ⍟   Situated between Taos town and Taos Ski Valley, Salsa del Salto is a good choice for those seeking a secluded retreat equipped like a country club. The main house was built in 1971 and has the modernity of that era's architecture. The rooms here are tastefully decorated with a Southwestern motif but don't have the ambience of inns such as the Little Tree or Adobe & Pines. Each room offers views of the mountains or mesas of Taos, and the bathrooms are modern and spacious. Three newer rooms (my favorites) are well designed, decorated in a whimsical Southwestern style, and each includes two queen-size beds, a minirefrigerator, fireplace, TV, VCR, and Jacuzzi tub. The focus here is on relaxation and outdoor activities. Salsa del Salto is the only bed-and-breakfast in Taos with a pool, Jacuzzi, and private tennis courts. The innkeepers, both with years of hospitality experience, serve guests' needs well and share information about favorite activities in the area.

543 State Hwy. 150 (Taos Ski Valley Rd.), Arroyo Seco, NM 87529. ℂ **800/530-3097** or 505/776-2422. Fax 505/776-5734. www.bandbtaos.com. 10 units. $85–$165 double. Rates include full breakfast. Additional person $20. AE, DISC, MC, V. **Amenities:** Outdoor heated pool, open seasonally; tennis court; Jacuzzi; concierge; massage by arrangement. *In room:* Fridge, coffeemaker, hair dryer.

MODERATE

Old Taos Guesthouse Bed & Breakfast ⍟   Less than 2 miles from the plaza, this 180-year-old adobe hacienda sits on 7½ acres and provides a cozy northern New Mexico rural experience. Once a farmer's home and later an artist's estate, it's been restored by owners and incorrigible ski bums Tim and Leslie Reeves, who, for more than 15 years, have carefully maintained the country charm: Mexican tile in the bathrooms, vigas on the ceilings, and kiva-style fireplaces in most of the rooms. Each room has an entrance from the outside, some off the broad portal that shades the front of the hacienda, some from a grassy lawn in the back, with a view toward the mountains. Some rooms are more utilitarian, some quainter, so make a request depending on your needs. One of my favorites is the Taos Suite, with a king-size bed, a big picture window, and a full kitchen that includes an oven, a stove, a minirefrigerator, and a microwave. A nature path and healthy breakfast complete the rural experience.

1028 Witt Rd., Taos, NM 87571. ℂ **800/758-5448** or 505/758-5448. www.oldtaos.com. 9 units. $85–$160 double. Rates include an expanded continental breakfast. DISC, MC, V. Pets accepted in some rooms with $25 fee. **Amenities:** Jacuzzi; concierge; tour desk; in-room massage; babysitting. *In room:* Hair dryer, iron.

San Geronimo Lodge ⍟   Built in 1925 in the style of a grand old lodge, this inn has high ceilings and rambling verandas, all situated on 2½ acres of grounds with views of Taos Mountain, yet it's a 5-minute drive from the plaza. The lodge received a major renovation in 1994. Common areas are filled with artwork for sale, from landscapes to portraits. The guest rooms are cozy and comfortable, eight with kiva fireplaces, all with furniture hand-built by local craftspeople and Mexican tile in the bathrooms. Guests feast on a full breakfast and afternoon snacks in the grand dining room, which looks out on elaborate gardens. There's an outdoor swimming pool, unusual for a B&B.

1101 Witt Rd., Taos, NM 87571. ℂ **800/894-4119** or 505/751-3776. Fax 505/751-1493. www.sangeronimo lodge.com. 18 units. $95–$150 double. Rates include full breakfast and afternoon snack. AE, DISC, MC, V. Pets accepted with prior arrangements. **Amenities:** Outdoor pool (summer only); Jacuzzi; concierge; massage. *In room:* TV, hair dryer.

2 Taos Ski Valley

For information on the skiing and the facilities offered at Taos Ski Valley, see "Skiing," in chapter 14.

LODGES
EXPENSIVE

The Bavarian Lodge ⭐ *Kids*   This mountain getaway offers the quintessence of Bavaria at the base of Taos Ski Valley's back bowls. At an elevation of 10,200 feet, the lodge has interesting accommodations and excellent food. The first-floor restaurant/reception area is a study in Bavaria—lots of aged pine paneling accented by an antler chandelier. Upstairs, the rooms combine antique and modern elements—not always successfully, but with good intent. All are fairly spacious, with large bathrooms, most with lofts to accommodate kids. The rooms aren't cozy, and some have odd configurations, but they all utilize faux painting to evoke old Europe; some have kitchenettes and balconies. The sun deck is the place to be on sunny ski days, and The Bavarian Restaurant (see chapter 13) is worth visiting even if you aren't a guest. The lodge offers nature hikes in summer.

100 Kachina Rd. (P.O. Box 653), Taos Ski Valley, NM 87525. ℂ 888/205-8020 or 505/776-8020. Fax 888/304-5301. www.thebavarian.com. 4 units. Dec 15–Jan 8 and Feb 10–Apr 6 $335–$395; late Nov–Dec 15 and Jan 9–Feb 9 $285–$350; summer $155–$195. AE, MC, V. Free parking. **Amenities:** Restaurant; bar; courtesy shuttle to and from the ski area. *In room:* TV, coffeemaker, microwave, no phone.

Chalet Montesano ⭐⭐   This chalet, constructed from a turn-of-the-20th-century miner's cabin, is a nice romantic ski vacation retreat. A 5-minute walk from restaurants and the lift, it's a woodsy and secluded place, just what innkeepers Victor and Karin Frohlich, who have been in Taos Ski Valley since the 1960s, set out to create. All rooms have a Bavarian feel, with nice touches such as CD players, VCRs, coffeemakers, and minirefrigerators; some have fireplaces. In the studio apartments, you'll find Murphy beds that fold into handcrafted chests to leave plenty of room for daytime living. These and the one-bedroom apartment have kitchenettes or full kitchens, with stoves, ovens, microwaves, and dishwashers. On the west side of the building are a picturesque lap pool, health club, and Jacuzzi, banked by windows, with views of the runs and forest. Smoking is not allowed here.

Pattison Loop #3 (P.O. Box 77), Taos Ski Valley, NM 87525. ℂ 800/723-9104 or 505/776-8226. Fax 505/776-8760. www.chaletmontesano.com. 7 units. Ski season $170–$220 double, $135–$330 apt (for 2 people); summer $85–$120 double; $120–$140 apt (for 2 people). Weekly rates $1,190–$2,560 during ski season, depending on type of room and number of people. AE, DISC, MC, V. Children under 14 not accepted. **Amenities:** Indoor pool; exercise room; Jacuzzi; sauna; in-room massage; coin-op laundry; all units nonsmoking. *In room:* TV/VCR, dataport, fridge, coffeemaker, hair dryer, iron, safe, CD player.

Edelweiss Lodge & Spa   Set to open in 2005, this lodge at the very base of the mountain is a remake of a 1960s classic. Now, it's a brand new condo-hotel, with the only full spa facility in Taos Ski Valley. At press time, it had yet to open, so I can't rate its quality. However, the owners have been excellent hosts since they purchased the property in 1997, so I'm confident it will be well planned and run. The condominiums are upscale, each with a fireplace and full kitchen with stainless steel appliances, and many with balconies; the hotel rooms are planned to be more standard. Check their website for a glimpse of rooms and other facilities.

106 Sutton Place, Taos Ski Valley, NM 87525. ℂ 800/I-LUV-SKI or 505/776-2301. Fax 505/776-2533. www.edelweisslodgeandspa.com. 46 units. Ski week includes gourmet meals, lift tickets, and lessons: $1,145–$1,590 per person double; shorter stays winter $145–$270, summer $100–$150 per day. AE, DISC,

MC, V. **Amenities:** Restaurant; bar; health club and full spa; 2 Jacuzzis; sauna; concierge; massage. *In room:* TV, fridge, coffeemaker, hair dryer.

Inn at Snakedance ✦✦   With all the luxuries of a full-service hotel, the Snakedance can please most family members. Skiers will appreciate the inn's location, just steps from the lift, as well as amenities like ski storage and boot dryers. The original structure that stood on this site (part of which has been restored for use today) was known as the Hondo Lodge. Before there was a Taos Ski Valley, Hondo Lodge served as a refuge for fishermen, hunters, and artists. Constructed from enormous pine timbers that had been cut for a copper-mining operation in the 1890s, it was literally nothing more than a place for the men to bed down for the night. The Inn at Snakedance today offers comfortable guest rooms; many feature wood-burning fireplaces, and all have humidifiers. All the furnishings are modern, the decor stylish, and the windows (many of which offer views) open to let in the mountain air. Some rooms adjoin, connecting a standard hotel room with a fireplace room—perfect for families. Smoking is prohibited in the guest rooms and most public areas. The Hondo Restaurant and Bar offers dining and entertainment daily during the ski season (schedules vary off-season) and also sponsors wine tastings and wine dinners. Grilled items, salads, and snacks are available on an outdoor deck. The hotel also offers shuttle service to and from nearby shops and restaurants.

110 Sutton Place (P.O. Box 89), Taos Ski Valley, NM 87525. © **800/322-9815** or 505/776-2277. Fax 505/776-1410. www.innsnakedance.com. 60 units. Christmas holiday $270 double; rest of ski season $225 double; value season $165 double; summer $75 double. AE, DC, DISC, MC, V. Children 6 and under not accepted. Free parking at Taos Ski Valley parking lot. Closed mid-Apr to mid-June and mid-Oct to mid-Nov. **Amenities:** Restaurant; bar; exercise room; spa; Jacuzzi; sauna; massage; convenience store (with food, sundries, video rental, and alcoholic beverages); all units nonsmoking. *In room:* Satellite TV, fridge, coffeemaker, hair dryer, humidifier.

Powderhorn Suites and Condominiums ✦✦ *(Finds)*   A cozy, homelike feel and Euro-Southwestern ambience make this inn one of the best buys in Taos Ski Valley, just a 2-minute walk from the lift. You'll find consistency and quality here, with impeccably clean medium-size rooms, mountain views, vaulted ceilings, spotless bathrooms, and comfortable beds. The larger suites have stoves, balconies, and fireplaces. Adjoining rooms are perfect for families. You can expect conscientious and expert service as well. There's no elevator, so if stairs are a problem for you, make sure to ask for a room on the ground floor.

5 Ernie Blake Rd. (P.O. Box 69), Taos Ski Valley, NM 87525. © **800/776-2346** or 505/776-2341. Fax 505/776-2341, ext. 103. www.taoswebb.com/powderhorn. 17 units. Ski season $99–$165 double, $130–$200 suite, $195–$400 condo; summer $69–$129 2- to 6-person occupancy. MC, V. Valet parking. **Amenities:** 2 Jacuzzis; massage. *In room:* TV, dataport, kitchenette.

MODERATE

Alpine Village Suites ✦   Alpine Village is a small village within Taos Ski Valley, a few steps from the lift. Owned by John and Barbara Cottam, the complex also houses a ski shop and bar/restaurant. The Cottams began with seven rooms, still nice rentals, above their ski shop. Each has a sleeping loft for the agile who care to climb a ladder, as well as sunny windows. The newer section has nicely decorated rooms, with attractive touches such as Mexican furniture and inventive tile work done by locals. Like most other accommodations at Taos Ski Valley, the rooms are not especially soundproof. Fortunately, most skiers go to bed early. All rooms have VCRs and small kitchenettes equipped with stoves, microwaves, and minirefrigerators. In the newer building, rooms have fireplaces and private balconies. Request a south-facing room for a view of the slopes. The Jacuzzi has a fireplace and a view of the slopes.

100 Thunderbird Rd. (P.O. Box 98), Taos Ski Valley, NM 87525. © **800/576-2666** or 505/776-8540. Fax 505/776-8542. www.alpine-suites.com. 29 units. Ski season $70–$145 suite for 2, $265–$335 suite for up to 6; summer $80–$120 suite for 2 (includes continental breakfast). AE, DISC, MC, V. Covered valet parking $10 per night. **Amenities:** Jacuzzi; sauna; massage. *In room:* TV/VCR, kitchenette.

Austing Haus Hotel   About 1½ miles from the ski resort, the Austing Haus is a beautiful example of a timber-frame building. It was hand-built by owner Paul Austing, who will gladly give you details of the process. Though an interesting structure, at times it feels a bit fragile. The guest rooms have a cute mountain-inn feel. There are boot lockers available for skiers.

1282 State Hwy. 150. (P.O. Box 8), Taos Ski Valley, NM 87525. © **800/748-2932** or 505/776-2649. Fax 505/776-8751. http://taoswebb.com/hotel/austinghaus. 23 units. $49–$170 double. Rates include lavish continental breakfast. AE, MC, V. Free parking. Pets stay free. **Amenities:** Jacuzzi. *In room:* TV.

Thunderbird Lodge ★   Owners Elisabeth and Tom Brownell's goal at this Bavarian-style lodge is to bring people together, and they accomplish it—sometimes a little too well. The lodge sits on the sunny side of the ski area. The lobby has a stone fireplace, raw pine pillars, and tables accented with copper lamps. There's a sun-lit room ideal for breakfast and lunch, with a bank of windows looking out toward the notorious Al's Run and the rest of the ski village. Adjoining is a large bar/lounge with booths, a grand piano, and a fireplace, where live entertainment plays during the evenings through the winter. The rooms are small, some tiny, and noise travels up and down the halls, giving these three stories a dormitory atmosphere. I suggest when making reservations that you request their widest room; otherwise, you may feel as though you're in a train car.

Across the road, the Thunderbird also has a chalet with larger rooms and a brilliant sun porch. Food is the big draw at the Thunderbird. Gourmet breakfast and dinner are included in your stay—you'll be dining on some of the best food available in the region. For breakfast, we had blueberry pancakes and bacon, with our choice from a table of continental breakfast accompaniments; and for dinner, we had four courses highlighted by rack of lamb Provençal. You can eat at your own table or join the larger communal one and get to know the guests, some of whom have been returning for as many as 30 years.

3 Thunderbird Rd. (P.O. Box 87), Taos Ski Valley, NM 87525. © **800/776-2279** or 505/776-2280. Fax 505/776-2238. www.thunderbird-taos.com. 32 units. $126–$147 per person. 7-day ski week package $1,190–$1,260 per person double occupancy (7 days room, 14 meals, 6 lift tickets, and ski lessons), depending on season and type of accommodations. Rates include 2 full meals per day. AE, MC, V. Free valet parking. **Amenities:** Jacuzzi; his-and-hers saunas; game room; business center; massage; babysitting by prior arrangement; laundry service.

CONDOMINIUMS
EXPENSIVE

Kandahar Condominiums *Kids*   These condos have almost the highest location on the slopes—and with it, ski-in/ski-out access; you actually ski down to the lift from here. Built in the 1960s, the condos have been maintained well and are sturdy and functional. Two stories and private bedrooms allow for more privacy than most condos offer. Each unit is privately owned, so decor varies, although a committee makes suggestions to owners for upgrading. Situated just above the children's center, it offers good access for families with young children.

35 Firehouse Rd. (P.O. Box 72), Taos Ski Valley, NM 87525. (C) 800/756-2226 or 505/776-2226. Fax 505/776-2481. www.kandahar-taos.com. 27 units. Ski season $275–$425; May–Oct $100–$150. Rates based on 4–6 people per unit. AE, MC, V. Pets accepted with prior arrangements, depending on season and size of pet. Valet parking. **Amenities:** Spa; Jacuzzi; steam room; game room; massage; coin-op laundry; laundry service. *In room:* TV/VCR, dataport, kitchen, hair dryer, safe.

Sierra del Sol Condominiums ⭐ I have wonderful memories of these condominiums, which are just a 2-minute walk from the lift; family friends used to invite me to stay with them when I was about 10. I was happy to see that the units, built in the 1960s, with additions through the years, have been well maintained. Though they're privately owned, and therefore decorated at the whim of the owners, management does inspect them every year and make suggestions. They're smartly built and come in a few sizes: studio, one-bedroom, and two-bedroom. The one- and two-bedroom units have big living rooms with fireplaces and porches that look out on the ski runs. The bedrooms are spacious, and some have sleeping lofts. Each has a full kitchen, with a dishwasher, stove, oven, and refrigerator. Most units also have microwaves and humidifiers. Two-bedroom units sleep up to six. Grills and picnic tables on the grounds sit near a mountain river.

13 Thunderbird Rd. (P.O. Box 84), Taos Ski Valley, NM 87525. (C) 800/523-3954 or 505/776-2981. Fax 505/776-2347. www.sierrataos.com. 32 units. Prices range from $70 for studio in summer to $395 for 2-bedroom condo in high season. AE, DISC, MC, V. Free parking. **Amenities:** 2 Jacuzzis; 2 saunas; massage; babysitting; coin-op laundry. *In room:* TV/VCR, kitchen, hair dryer upon request, iron upon request, safe.

MODERATE

Taos Mountain Lodge *Value*   About a mile west of Taos Ski Valley on the road from Taos, these loft suites (which can each accommodate up to six) provide airy, comfortable lodging for a good price. Built in 1990, the place has undergone some renovation over the years. Don't expect a lot of privacy in these condominiums, but they're good for a romping ski vacation. Each unit has a small bedroom downstairs and a loft bedroom upstairs, as well as a foldout or futon couch in the living room. Regular rooms have kitchenettes, with minirefrigerators and stoves, and deluxe rooms have more full kitchens, with full refrigerators, stoves, and ovens.

Taos Ski Valley Road (P.O. Box 202), Taos Ski Valley, NM 87525. (C) 866/320-8267 or 505/776-2229. Fax 505/776-3982. www.taosmountainlodge.com. 10 units. Ski season $119–$280 suite; May–Oct $80–$100 suite. Ski packages available. AE, DISC, MC, V. *In room:* Kitchen or kitchenette.

3 RV Parks & Campgrounds

Carson National Forest   There are nine national-forest camping areas within 20 miles of Taos; these developed areas are open from Memorial Day to Labor Day. They range from woodsy, streamside sites on the road to Taos Ski Valley to open lowlands with lots of sage. Call the Forest Service to discuss the best location for your needs.

208 Cruz Alta Rd., Taos, NM 87571. (C) 505/758-6200. www.fs.fed.us/r3/carson. Fees range from $7–$15 per night. No credit cards.

Questa Lodge   On the banks of the Red River, this RV camp is just outside the small village of Questa. It's a nice pastoral setting. The cabins aren't in the best condition, but the RV and camping accommodations are pleasant—all with amazing mountain views.

Lower Embargo Road #8 (P.O. Box 155), Questa, NM 87556. ⓒ **505/586-0300**. 24 sites. Full RV hookup $20 per day, $200 per month. 4 cabins for rent in summer. AE, DISC, MC, V. Closed Nov–Apr.

Taos RV Park   This RV park, located on the edge of town, offers a convenient location but a city atmosphere. It has very clean and nice bathrooms and showers. Two tepees rent for around $25 each, but beware: They're right on the main drag and may be noisy. The park is located on a local bus line. Senior discounts are available.

1802 NM 68, Taos, NM 87557. ⓒ **800/323-6009** or 505/758-1667. Fax 505/758-1989. www.taosbudget host.com. 33 spaces. $17 without RV hookup; $25 with RV hookup. DISC, MC, V.

Taos Valley RV Park and Campground   Just 2½ miles south of the plaza, this campground is surrounded by sage and offers views of the surrounding mountains. Each site has a picnic table and grill. The place has a small store, a laundry room, a playground, and tent shelters, as well as a dump station and very clean restrooms. Pets are welcome.

120 Este Rd., off NM 68 (7204 NDCBU), Taos, NM 87571. ⓒ **800/999-7571** or 505/758-4469. Fax 505/758-4469. www.camptaos.com/rv. 92 spaces. $18 without RV hookup; $24–$27 with RV hookup. MC, V.

13

Where to Dine in Taos

Taos is one of my favorite places to eat. Informality reigns; at a number of restaurants you can dine on world-class food while wearing jeans or even ski pants. Nowhere is a jacket and tie mandatory. This informality doesn't extend to reservations, however;

especially during the peak season, it is important to make reservations well in advance and keep them or else cancel. Also, be aware that Taos is not a late-night place; most restaurants finish serving at about 9pm.

1 Restaurants by Cuisine

AMERICAN
The Apple Tree ✷ ($$, p. 197)
Bravo ✷ ($$, p. 198)
De La Tierra ✷✷✷ ($$$, p. 194)
Gypsy 360° ✷ ($, p. 202)
Michael's Kitchen ($, p. 201)
Old Blinking Light ✷ ($$, p. 198)

ASIAN
Gypsy 360° ✷ ($, p. 202)

BAVARIAN
The Bavarian Restaurant ✷
   ($, p. 201)

CONTEMPORARY AMERICAN
Lambert's of Taos ✷✷ ($$$, p 196)

CONTINENTAL
Stakeout Grill & Bar ✷ ($$$, p. 196)

DELI/CAFE
Bent Street Cafe & Deli ✷ ($$, p. 198)
Bravo ✷ ($$, p. 198)
Caffe Tazza ($, p. 200)

INTERNATIONAL
Bent Street Cafe & Deli ✷
   ($$, p. 198)
Ogelvie's Bar & Grill ($$, p. 198)
Trading Post Café ✷✷ ($$, p. 199)

ITALIAN
Taos Pizza Out Back ✷ ($$, p. 199)
Trading Post Café ✷✷ ($$, p. 199)
Villa Fontana ✷ ($$$, p. 197)

MEDITERRANEAN
Joseph's Table ✷✷ ($$$, p 194)

MEXICAN
Guadalajara Grill ✷ ($, p. 200)

NEW AMERICAN
Doc Martin's ✷ ($$$, p. 194)
Joseph's Table ✷✷ ($$$, p. 194)
Momentitos de la Vida ✷✷
   ($$$, p. 196)

NEW MEXICAN
Michael's Kitchen ($, p. 201)
Orlando's New Mexican Café ✷
   ($, p. 201)

PIZZA
Taos Pizza Out Back ✷ ($$, p. 199)

SOUTHWESTERN
The Apple Tree ✷ ($$, p. 197)
Eske's Brew Pub and Eatery ✷
   ($, p. 200)

STEAK/SEAFOOD
Stakeout Grill & Bar ✷
   ($$$, p. 196)

Key to Abbreviations: $$$$ = Very Expensive $$$ = Expensive $$ = Moderate $ = Inexpensive

2 Expensive

De La Tierra ★★★ REGIONAL AMERICAN   This hot spot not far from the plaza always leaves me with an exotic and buoyant sense that I must attribute to its setting and cuisine. Located at the new eco-resort El Monte Sagrado, this restaurant creates an elegance of old-world Orient, with an open high ceiling and comfortable black silk chairs, while serving imaginative American fare with an emphasis on wild game. Service is excellent, even down to the master sommelier overseeing the wine selections. The chef utilizes seasonal and local ingredients, including organic ones when he can. For starters, I recommend the Dungeness crab cake, or, for a more exotic treat, try the yak satay, the meat from the resort owner's high-mountain cattlelike animals. For a main course, I've enjoyed the venison medallions, served over garlic mashed potatoes and with roasted spring mushrooms. My mother likes the rosemary skewered shrimp, served with white-corn polenta and chard. Tasty food is served during the day at The Gardens, a more casual spot, with lots of exotic plants and a lovely patio (try the yak cheese frittata). Tapas are served at the Anaconda Bar.

In the El Monte Sagrado hotel, 317 Kit Carson Rd. ✆ **800/828-TAOS** or 505/758-3502. Reservations recommended. The Gardens breakfast $5–$11; lunch $8–$16; De La Tierra dinner $19–$34. AE, DC, DISC, MC, V. The Gardens daily 7–10am and 11am–2:30pm; De La Tierra daily 5:30–10pm.

Doc Martin's ★ NEW AMERICAN   Doc Martin's serves innovative food in a historic setting. The restaurant comprises Dr. Thomas Paul Martin's former home, office, and delivery room. In 1912, painters Bert Philips (Doc's brother-in-law) and Ernest Blumenschein hatched the concept of the Taos Society of Artists in the dining room. Art still predominates here, in both the paintings that adorn the walls and the cuisine offered. The food is often good here, but it can be inconsistent.

The wine list has received numerous "Awards of Excellence" from *Wine Spectator* magazine. In a rich atmosphere, with bins of yellow squash, eggplants, and red peppers set near the kiva fireplace, diners feast on Southwestern breakfast fare such as huevos rancheros (fried eggs on a blue-corn tortilla smothered with chile and Jack cheese). Lunch might include the house specialty, the Doc Chile relleno or chipolte shrimp on corn cake. For dinner, a good bet is the piñon-encrusted salmon or the Southwest lacquered duck served with *posole* and mango relish. If you still have room, there's always a nice selection of desserts—try the chocolate mousse cake or the *capirotada* (New Mexican bread pudding). The Adobe bar has live jazz with no cover charge. Brunch is served on Sundays from 7:30am to 2:30pm.

In the Historic Taos Inn, 125 Paseo del Pueblo Norte. ✆ **505/758-1977.** www.taosinn.com. Reservations recommended. Breakfast $5–$8; lunch $5.50–$11; dinner $14–$28; fixed-price menu $23. AE, DISC, MC, V. Daily 7:30–11am, 11:30am–2:30pm, and 5:30–9pm.

Joseph's Table ★★ (Finds) NEW AMERICAN/MEDITERRANEAN   Taos funk meets European flair at this intimate restaurant on the plaza. Recently moved to the renovated Hotel La Fonda de Taos, this notable eatery now occupies a larger space, but it can still fill up. Chef/owner Joseph Wrede (once selected as 1 of the 10 "Best New Chefs" in America by *Food and Wine Magazine*) creates such delicacies as a six-way duck and a lovely steak au poivre, inventively prepared and served. The duck is literally cooked six different ways, ranging from roasted to sliced thinly, prosciutto style, and paired with a delicate corn crème brûlée. Meanwhile, the steak sits atop a layer of smooth mashed

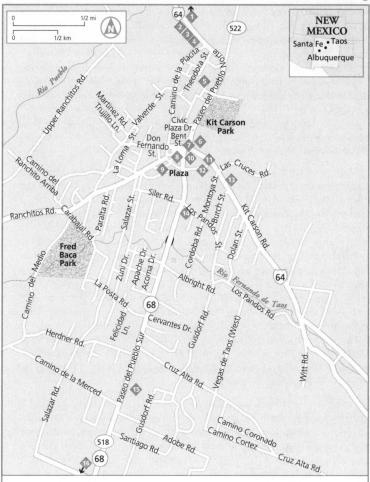

The Apple Tree **7**

The Bavarian Restaurant **1**

Bent Street Cafe & Deli **8**

Bravo **15**

Caffe Tazza **11**

De La Tierra **13**

Doc Martin's **6**

Eske's Brew Pub and Eatery **12**

Guadalajara Grill **3, 16**

Gypsy 360° **1**

Joseph's Table **9**

Lambert's of Taos **14**

Michael's Kitchen **5**

Momentitos de la Vida **1**

Ogelvie's Bar & Grill **10**

Old Blinking Light **1**

Orlando's New Mexican Café **2**

Taos Pizza Out Back **4**

Stakeout Grill & Bar **16**

Trading Post Café **16**

Villa Fontana **1**

potatoes and is crowned with an exotic mushroom salad. The offerings are not for the faint of palate, though. Wrede likes complex flavors, so those who prefer more conservative food might opt for Lambert's. The servers can help guide you through the complex menu, so be sure to ask. As for comfort, be aware that in winter parts of the restaurant can be cold. For dessert, try such delicacies as the mescal chocolate bar with lime sorbet or the black-pepper roasted pineapple-bread pudding. An eclectic selection of beers and wines by the bottle and glass is available.

In the Hotel La Fonda de Taos, 108-A South Taos Plaza. ✆ 505/751-4512. www.josephstable.com. Reservations recommended. Main courses $8–$18 lunch, $18–$35 dinner. AE, DISC, MC, V. May–Aug daily 11:30am–2:30pm and 5:30–10pm; ski season 4:30–10pm; rest of year 5:30–10pm.

Lambert's of Taos ★★ CONTEMPORARY AMERICAN   Zeke Lambert, once the head chef at Doc Martin's, opened this fine dining establishment in late 1989 in the historic Randall Home near Los Pandos Road. It's a sparsely decorated place with contemporary art on the walls—a nice spot for a romantic evening. The service is friendly and efficient, and the meal always begins with a complimentary aperitif. I found the house salad nicely prepared with butter lettuce and radicchio. Appetizers include a Mediterranean olive plate and chile-dusted rock shrimp. I ordered the restaurant's signature dish, the pepper-crusted lamb. If you like strong flavors, this is your dish—very peppery, served with a red-wine demi-glace and linguine. I also tasted the shepherd's pie, lamb stew served with mashed potatoes, and wasn't overly impressed with the sauce. Others I've spoken to have enjoyed the grilled salmon with tomato-sage sauce. For dessert, the white chocolate ice cream and Zeke's chocolate mousse with raspberry sauce are quite delicious. Espresso coffees, beers, and wine are served.

309 Paseo del Pueblo Sur. ✆ 505/758-1009. Reservations recommended. Main courses $17–$30. AE, DC, DISC, MC, V. Daily 5pm–closing, usually 9pm or so.

Momentitos de la Vida ★★ NEW AMERICAN   For years, this personable adobe building housed the Casa Cordova, where, in the '60s and '70s, the jet-set après ski crowd hung out, drinking martinis. Well, as long as martinis are back in style, why not revamp this spot on the outskirts of Arroyo Seco and once again make it the place to be? That was what owner/chefs Chris and Kelly Maher had in mind for this restaurant. The atmosphere is moody; the service is refined and attentive. Though locals call the place too pricey, the food is very thoughtfully prepared, with real attention to imaginative detail: The excellent sourdough bread comes with a squash butter spread, and the dishes' ingredients include such novelties as parsnips and purple potatoes. You might start with a smoked trout éclair or grilled habañero prawns. One of the most popular main courses is the blackened filet mignon, served with root mashed potatoes (a tasty mixture of rutabaga and parsnip), wilted greens, and asparagus. The vegan shepherd's pie is also a tasty option. There are fish dishes as well. Finish with a hot berry cobbler or tiramisu. In warm months, you can enjoy your meal on the patio, surrounded by a plum orchard. Jazz plays fireside Friday to Sunday.

5 miles north of the intersection of NM 150 and NM 522, Arroyo Seco. ✆ 505/776-3333. Reservations recommended on weekends. Bistro menu $8–$15; main dining room $19–$36. AE, MC, V. Tues–Sun 5:30–10pm; bar 4:30pm–closing.

Stakeout Grill & Bar ★ CONTINENTAL/STEAKS/SEAFOOD   Drive about a mile up a dirt road toward the base of the Sangre de Cristo Mountains to this restaurant, and dine looking down on the Taos gorge while the sun sets over the Jemez Range. The warm, rustic decor includes paneled walls, creaking hardwood floors, and a crackling fireplace in the winter. The fare, which focuses on steak and seafood, is fresh and thoughtfully prepared. Start with baked brie with sliced almonds and apples, or escargots baked with walnuts, herbs, white wine, and garlic. Move on to a filet mignon served with béarnaise sauce, or, for something more exotic, try the duck Cumberland (half a duck roasted with apples and prunes and served with orange-currant sauce). Try to time your reservation so you can see the sunset. A full bar, an extensive wine list, and cigars are available.

101 Stakeout Dr. (9 miles south of Taos, just off Hwy. 68). © 505/758-2042. www.stakeoutrestaurant.com. Reservations recommended. Main courses $15–$37. AE, DC, DISC, MC, V. Daily 5–9:30pm.

Villa Fontana ★ ITALIAN   Carlo and Siobhan Gislimberti have received wide acclaim for their restaurant on the north end of town. They like to talk about *peccato di gola* ("lust of the palate"), which they brought with them to Taos when they left their home in Italy. They have their own herb garden, and Carlo, a master chef, is a member of the New Mexico Mycological Society—wild mushrooms play an important role in his menu. The decor is country European. Romantic opera plays while tuxedoed waiters carefully serve each course. Meals are truly gourmet, but the word around town is that the food is not always consistent, and I have to agree. A must for a starter is the cream of wild mushroom soup, light and buttery. You also may want to try the cured salmon cocktail with lemon and capers. For a main course, the duck with brandy is very flavorful, as are the pork medallions sautéed with roasted peppers. For dessert, the profiterole is excellent. Outdoor dining in the summer offers pleasant mountain and valley views.

NM 522, 5 miles north of Taos. © 505/758-5800. Reservations recommended. Main courses $8–$16 lunch, $19–$25 dinner. AE, DC, DISC, MC, V. Mon–Sat 5:30–9pm. June–Sept lunch Mon–Fri 11:30am–2pm.

3 Moderate

The Apple Tree ★ SOUTHWESTERN/AMERICAN   Eclectic music pervades the four adobe rooms of this restaurant, a block north of the plaza. Original paintings by Taos masters watch over the candlelit service indoors. Outside, diners sit at wooden tables beneath a spreading apple tree.

This restaurant is popular among locals and travelers, but it isn't my favorite. Though the chefs use fresh and tasty ingredients, the recipes often try too hard. I suggest ordering what looks simplest, either from the menu or from the daily specials. The Apple Tree salad (greens sprinkled with dried cranberries, walnuts, and blue cheese served with a vinaigrette) is very good, as is the *calabasa* (squash) quesadilla. A very popular dish is mango chicken enchiladas (chicken simmered with onions and spices, layered between blue-corn tortillas with mango chutney, sour cream, and salsa fresca, and smothered with green chile), but beware: They're sweet. I prefer the salmon alfredo, made with sun-dried tomatoes and New Mexico goat cheese. The best thing here is the chile-jalapeño bread, served with the meal. The brunch offerings are worth sampling, even more so when eaten out on the lovely patio under the restaurant's namesake. Such standards as French toast and eggs Benedict are good, but the specials usually outshine them, especially the fresh fruit crepes, such as blueberry or peach, served with whipped cream. The Apple Tree has an award-winning wine list, and the desserts are prepared fresh daily.

123 Bent St. ⓒ **505/758-1900.** Reservations recommended. Main courses $5–$11 brunch, $6–$12 lunch, $12–$30 dinner. AE, DC, DISC, MC, V. Mon–Sat 11:30am–3pm; daily 5:30–9pm; brunch Sun 11am–3pm.

Bent Street Cafe & Deli ⓖ CAFE/INTERNATIONAL   This popular cafe, a short block north of the plaza, has inventive, reliable food in a country-home atmosphere. Outside, a flower box surrounds sidewalk seating that is heated in winter. Inside, baskets and bottles of homemade jam accent wooden tables. The menu features breakfast burritos and homemade granola in the morning; for lunch, you can choose from 18 deli sandwiches, plus a "create-your-own" column, as well as a nice selection of salads. At dinner, select a special such as beef tenderloin medallions served over fettuccine with chipotle-Fontina cream sauce, or, from the menu, *camarones di pesto* (tiger prawns with sun-dried tomatoes, artichoke hearts, and green-chile pesto). To grab a picnic to go, head for the deli, which offers carryout service.

120 Bent St. ⓒ **505/758-5787.** Reservations accepted. Breakfast $2–$8; lunch $2.50–$8; dinner $11–$20. MC, V. Mon–Sat 8am–9pm.

Bravo ⓖ AMERICAN/CAFE   This bustling cafe on the south end of town offers a refreshing big-city mix of atmosphere and flavors. As well as a restaurant, it is a specialty wine and beer shop, package liquor store, and gourmet deli—a great place to stock your lunch basket. There's a large communal table at the restaurant's heart. The menu is eclectic, offering good-size portions of very tasty food. With owner/chef Lionel Garnier's French background lending magic, the flavors are refined. Locals rave about the three-cheese pizza—my favorite is the Bravo, with roasted vegetables. The Caesar salad with chicken is also popular, as is the elaborate salad bar, complete with pasta and bean concoctions. A variety of sandwiches fills the menu as well, and in the evenings, you can order Continental dishes. During busy hours, service is slow but congenial. There's also a martini and beer bar here with specials, such as a beer sampler and enough types of martinis to make you really wonder how many things you should mix with gin or vodka.

1353-A Paseo del Pueblo Sur, Ranchos de Taos. ⓒ **505/758-8100.** Lunch $6–$12; dinner $8–$18. AE, DISC, MC, V. Mon–Sat 11am–9pm.

Ogelvie's Bar & Grille INTERNATIONAL   The only real reason to go to this restaurant is to have a cocktail right on the plaza. In the warm months, there's a nice balcony where diners can sit and drink margaritas and indulge in chips or other appetizers, such as potato skins, or even burgers. Otherwise, the food here is not flavorful, and the atmosphere inside is dated.

103E. Plaza Suite I. ⓒ **505/758-8866.** Lunch $6–$12; dinner $8.50–$25. AE, DC, DISC, MC, V. Daily 11am–9pm dining, 10pm bar.

Old Blinking Light ⓖ AMERICAN   This newer restaurant on the Ski Valley Road provides tasty American food in a casual atmosphere. Decorated with Spanish colonial furniture and an excellent art collection, this restaurant is a good place to stop after skiing. The service is friendly and efficient. To accompany the free chips and house-made salsa, order a margarita—preferably their standard, made with Sauza Gold Tequila—and sip it next to the patio bonfire, open evenings year-round. The menu is broad, ranging from salads and burgers to steaks, seafood, and Mexican food. I say head straight for the fajitas, especially the jumbo shrimp wrapped in bacon and stuffed with poblano peppers and jack cheese. Leave room for the Old Blinking Light mud pie, made with local Taos Cow Ice Cream. Live music plays Monday and Friday nights.

(Kids) Family-Friendly Restaurants

Michael's Kitchen (p. 201)   With a broad menu, comfy booths, and a very casual, diner-type atmosphere, Michael's Kitchen makes both kids and their parents feel at home here.

Orlando's New Mexican Café (p. 201)   The relaxed atmosphere and playfully colorful walls will please the kids almost as much as the tacos and quesadillas made especially for them.

Taos Pizza Out Back (p. 199)   The pizza will please both parents and kids, and so will all the odd decorations, such as the chain with foot-long links hanging over the front counter.

US 150, mile marker 1. © **505/776-8787.** Reservations recommended weekends and Mon nights. Main courses $9–$26. AE, MC, V. Wine shop daily 11:30am–10pm. Restaurant daily 5–10pm.

Taos Pizza Out Back ★ *Kids* PASTA AND GOURMET PIZZA   My kayaking buddies always go here after a day on the river. That will give you an idea of the level of informality (very), as well as the quality of the food and beer (great), and the size of the portions (large). It's a raucous old hippie-decorated adobe restaurant, with a friendly and eager waitstaff. What to order? I have one big word here: PIZZA. Sure the spicy Greek pasta is good, as is the Veggie Zone (a calzone filled with stir-fried veggies and two cheeses)—but, why? The pizzas are incredible. All come with a delicious thin crust (no sogginess here) that's folded over on the edges and sprinkled with sesame seeds. The sauce is unthinkably tasty, and the variations are broad. There's Thai chicken pizza (pineapple, peanuts, and a spicy sauce); The Killer, with sun-dried tomatoes, Gorgonzola, green chile, and black olives; and my favorite, pizza Florentine, (spinach, basil, sun-dried tomatoes, chicken breast, mushrooms, capers, and garlic, sautéed in white wine). Don't leave without trying either a Dalai Lama bar (coconut, chocolate, and caramel) or the Taos Yum (a "mongo" chocolate-chip cookie with ice cream, whipped cream, and chocolate sauce). Check out the small selection of wines and large selection of microbrews.

712 Paseo del Pueblo Norte (just north of Allsup's). © **505/758-3112.** Reservations recommended weekends and holidays. Pizzas $12–$26; pastas and calzones $7–$12. MC, V. Summer daily 11am–10pm; winter Sun–Thurs 11am–9pm, Fri–Sat 11am–10pm.

Trading Post Café ★★ *Finds* NORTHERN ITALIAN/INTERNATIONAL One of my tastiest writing assignments was when I did a profile of this restaurant for the *New York Times.* Chef/owner René Mettler spent 3 hours serving course after course of dishes prepared especially for us. If you think this gastronomical orgy might color my opinion, just ask anyone in town where they most like to eat. Even notables such as R. C. Gorman, Dennis Hopper, and Gene Hackman will likely name the Trading Post. What draws the crowds is a gallery atmosphere, where rough plastered walls washed with an orange hue are set off by sculptures, paintings, and photographs. The meals are also artistically served. "You eat with your eyes," says Mettler. If you show up without reservations, be prepared to wait for a table, and don't expect quiet romance here: The place bustles. A bar encloses an open-exhibition kitchen. If you're dining alone or just don't feel like waiting for a table, the bar is a fun place to sit. Although the focus is on the fine food, diners can feel comfortable here, even if trying three appetizers and skipping the main course. The outstanding Caesar salad has an interesting twist—garlic chips. If you like pasta, you'll find a nice variety on the menu. The fettuccine alla carbonara is tasty, as is the seafood pasta. Heartier appetites might like the New Zealand lamb chops with tomato-mint sauce. There's also a fresh fish of the day and usually some nice stews and soups at very reasonable prices. A good list of beers and wines round out the experience. For dessert, try the tarts.

4179 Paseo del Pueblo Sur, Ranchos de Taos. © 505/758-5089. Reservations accepted. Menu items $6–$28. AE, DC, DISC, MC, V. Tues–Sat 11:30am–9:30pm; Sun 5–9pm.

4 Inexpensive

Caffe Tazza CAFE   This cozy three-room cafe, with a summer patio, attracts local community groups, artists, performers, and poets. Plays, films, comedy, and musical performances are given here on weekends (and some weeknights in summer), including appearances by such notable authors as John Nichols *(The Milagro Beanfield War)* and Natalie Goldberg *(Writing Down the Bones)*. The walls are always hung with the works of local emerging artists who have not yet made it to the Taos gallery scene. You can read one of the assorted periodicals available (including the *New York Times*) while sipping a cappuccino or *cafe Mexicano* (espresso with steamed milk and Mexican chocolate), made from organic coffee beans. The food is quite good. Usually, there are two homemade soups from which to choose. I recommend the veggie red chile with tofu. Breakfast burritos are also tasty, as are the bagel sandwiches. Pastries, which are imported from many bakeries around the region, are almost as big a draw here as the Taos Cow ice cream. Choose from 15 flavors.

122 Kit Carson Rd. © 505/758-8706. Reservations not accepted. All menu items under $10. No credit cards. Winter 7am–5pm; May–Oct 6:30am–9pm.

Eske's Brew Pub and Eatery ✦ SOUTHWESTERN PUB FARE   I have a fondness for this place that one might have for an oasis in the desert. The first time I ate here, I'd been on assignment ice climbing and just spent 8 hours in the shadow of a canyon, hacking my way up an 80-foot frozen waterfall. I sat down at one of the high tables in the main room, dipped into a big bowl of Wanda's green-chile turkey stew, and felt the blood return to my extremities. My climbing buddies ordered The Fatty (a whole-wheat tortilla filled with beans, mashed potatoes, onions, and feta and cheddar cheeses, smothered in greenchile turkey stew). Eske's also serves bratwurst, burgers, and vegetarian dishes. With our meal, we enjoyed a tasty black and tan (a mixture of barley wine and stout, the heavier beer sinking to the bottom), and a Mesa pale ale. When I asked the owner, Steve "Eske" Eskeback, which was his favorite beer, he replied "the one in my hand," meaning he recommends all the beers, which are his own recipes. The service is friendly and informal. The crowd is local, a few people sitting at the bar, where they can visit and watch the beer-pouring and food preparation. At times it can be a rowdy place, but mostly it's just fun, with lots of ski patrollers and mountain guides showing up to swap stories. In summer, you can eat on picnic tables outside.

106 Des Georges Lane. © 505/758-1517. All menu items under $10. MC, V. Mar–Sept and peak times such as spring and winter breaks daily 11:30am–10pm; rest of winter Fri–Sun 11:30am–10pm.

Guadalajara Grill ✦ MEXICAN   My organic-lettuce-farmer friend Joe introduced me to this authentic Mexican restaurant; then he disappeared into Mexico, only communicating occasionally by e-mail. Did the incredible food lure him south? I wonder. The restaurant shares a building with a car wash, but don't let that put you off; the food here is excellent. It's Mexican rather than New Mexican, a refreshing treat. I recommend the tacos, particularly pork or chicken, served in soft homemade corn tortillas, the meat artfully seasoned and grilled. The burritos are large and smothered in chile. *Platos* are served with rice and beans, and half orders are available for smaller appetites. There are also some seafood dishes available—try the *mojo de ajo* (shrimp cooked with garlic), served with rice, beans, and guacamole. Beer and wine are served.

1384 Paseo del Pueblo Sur. ℂ **505/751-0063.** All items under $15. MC, V. Mon–Sat 10:30am–9pm; Sun 11am–9pm. A second location, at 1822 Paseo del Pueblo Norte (ℂ **505/737-0816**), is open Mon–Sat 10:30am–9pm; Sun 11am–8:30pm.

Michael's Kitchen *(Kids* NEW MEXICAN/AMERICAN A couple blocks north of the plaza, this eatery provides big portions of okay food in a relaxed atmosphere. Between its hardwood floor and viga ceiling are various knick-knacks: a deer head here, a Tiffany lamp there. Seating is at booths and tables. Breakfast dishes, including a large selection of pancakes and egg preparations (with names like the "Moofy," and "Omelette Extra-ordinaire") are served all day, as are lunch sandwiches (including Philly cheesesteak, tuna melt, and a veggie sandwich). Some people like the generically (and facetiously) titled "Health Food" meal, a double order of fries with red or green chile and cheese. Dinners range from veal cordon bleu to plantation-fried chicken. For breakfast, try one of the excellent donuts served from Michael's bakery.

304 C Paseo del Pueblo Norte. ℂ **505/758-4178.** No reservations. Breakfast $3–$8; lunch $4–$9.50; dinner $6–$14. AE, DISC, MC, V. Daily 7am–8:30pm (except major holidays).

Orlando's New Mexican Café ★ *(Kids* NEW MEXICAN Festivity reigns in this spicy little cafe on the north end of town. Serving some of northern New Mexico's best chile, this place has colorful tables set around a bustling open kitchen and airy patio dining during warmer months. Service is friendly but minimal. Try the Los Colores, their most popular dish, with three enchiladas (chicken, beef, and cheese) smothered in chile and served with beans and *posole*. The taco salad is another favorite. Portions are big here, and you can order a Mexican or microbrew beer, or a New Mexican or California wine.

114 Don Juan Valdez Lane. (1¾ miles north of the plaza, off Paseo del Pueblo Norte). ℂ **505/751-1450.** Reservations not accepted. Main courses under $10. No credit cards. Daily 10:30am–9pm.

NORTH OF TOWN
The Bavarian Restaurant ★ *(Finds* BAVARIAN Enter through 300-year-old castle doors into a high alpine world full of Bavaria. This restaurant, sitting high above Taos Ski Valley at an elevation of 10,200 feet, creates, with beamed ceilings, aged pine paneling, and an antler lamp all set around an authentic kachelofe, a Bavarian-style stove, a feel both rustic and elegant. Service is uneven but well intentioned. At lunch, the porch fills with sun-worshipers. Dishes include traditional foods such as goulash (a hearty beef and paprika stew) and spaetzle (Bavarian-style pasta) at lunch. Dinnertime brings classic dishes such as Wiener schnitzel (Viennese veal cutlet) and sauerbraten (beef roast). Most dishes come with a potato dish and fresh vegetable. For dessert try the apple strudel. Accompany your meal with a selection from the well-chosen European wine list or with a beer, served in an authentic stein. The road to The Bavarian is easily drivable in summer. In winter, most diners ski here or call to arrange for a shuttle to pick them up at the Taos Ski Valley parking lot. Proust!

In The Bavarian Lodge, Taos Ski Valley. © **888/205-8020** or 505/776-8020. Reservations recommended at dinner. Lunch $7.50–$15; dinner $17–$35. AE, MC, V. Daily ski season 11:30am–3pm and 6–9pm; summer Thurs–Sun 11:30am–3:30pm and 5:30pm–closing.

Gypsy 360° ★ *Finds* ASIAN/AMERICAN   This funky cafe on a side street is as cute as the village of Arroyo Seco where it resides. And the food is tasty and inventive. During the winter diners sit in a sunny atrium or a more enclosed space, all casual with lawn-style furnishings and bright colors. In warm months, a sunny patio opens up the place. Service is accommodating though at times overworked. The food ranges from sushi to Thai to sandwiches. My Berkley Bowl salad had lots of spring greens and crisp goodies such as carrots and jicama, and the chef accommodated my request for grilled salmon on top. The pesto dressing is now my all-time favorite. My mother's angus burger was thick and juicy, topped with crisp bacon and bleu cheese; her potato salad had fresh dill. Other times I've enjoyed the noodle bowls, such as a Sri Lankan red curry or pad Thai. If you're staying in Taos, this spot makes for a great destination, with plenty of fun shops to peruse when your tummy's full.

480 NM 150, Seco Plaza, Arroyo Seco. © **505/776-3166.** Main courses $7.50–$15. MC, V. Tues–Wed and Sat 8am–4pm; Thurs–Fri 8am–8pm; Sun 9am–3pm.

14

What to See & Do in Taos

With a history shaped by pre-Columbian civilization, Spanish colonialism, and the Wild West; outdoor activities that range from ballooning to world-class skiing; and a clustering of artists, writers, and musicians, Taos has something to offer almost everybody. Its pueblo is the most accessible in New Mexico, and its museums represent a world-class display of regional history and culture.

SUGGESTED ITINERARIES
If You Have Only 1 Day
Spend at least 2 hours at Taos Pueblo. You'll also have time to see the Millicent Rogers Museum and to browse in some of the town's fine art galleries. Try to make it to Ranchos de Taos to see the San Francisco de Asis Church and to shop on the plaza there.

If You Have 2 Days
On the second day, explore the Taos Historic Museums—the Martinez Hacienda, the Kit Carson Home, and the Ernest L. Blumenschein Home. Then head out of town to enjoy the view from the Rio Grande Gorge Bridge.

If You Have 3 Days or More
On your third day, drive the "Enchanted Circle" through Red River, Eagle Nest, and Angel Fire, or head to the Taos Art Museum. You may want to allow a full day for shopping or perhaps drive up to Taos Ski Valley for a chairlift ride or a short hike. Of course, if you're here in the winter with skis, the mountain is your first priority.

1 The Top Attractions

Millicent Rogers Museum of Northern New Mexico ✸ This museum will give you a glimpse of some of the finest Southwestern arts and crafts anywhere, but it's small enough to avoid being overwhelming. It was founded in 1953 by Millicent Rogers's family members after her death. Rogers was a wealthy Taos émigré who in 1947 began acquiring a magnificent collection of beautiful Native American arts and crafts. Included are Navajo and Pueblo jewelry, Navajo textiles, Pueblo pottery, Hopi and Zuni kachina dolls, paintings from the Rio Grande Pueblo people, and basketry from a wide variety of Southwestern tribes. The museum also presents exhibitions of Southwestern art, crafts, and design.

Since the 1970s, the scope of the museum's permanent collection has been expanded to include Anglo arts and crafts and Hispanic religious and secular arts and crafts, from Spanish and Mexican colonial to contemporary times. Included are *santos* (religious images), furniture, weavings, *colcha* embroideries, and decorative tinwork. Agricultural implements, domestic utensils, and craftspeople's tools dating from the 17th and 18th centuries are also displayed.

Tips **A Tip for Museumgoers**

If you would like to visit five museums that comprise the Museum Association of Taos—Blumenschein Home, Martinez Hacienda, Harwood Museum, Millicent Rogers Museum, and Taos Art Museum—you'll save money by purchasing a combination ticket for $20. The ticket allows one-time entry to each museum during a 1-year period and is fully transferable. You may purchase the pass at any of the five museums. For more information, call ℂ **505/758-0505.**

The museum gift shop has a fine collection of superior regional art. Classes and workshops, lectures, and field trips are held throughout the year.

Off NM 522, 4 miles north of Taos Plaza, on Millicent Rogers Rd. ℂ **505/758-2462.** www.millicentrogers. org. Admission $6 adults, $5 students and seniors, $15 family rate, $1 children 6–16. Daily 10am–5pm. Closed Mon Nov–Mar, Easter, Thanksgiving, Christmas, and New Year's Day. Self-parking.

Taos Historic Museums ★★ Two historical homes are operated as museums, affording visitors a glimpse of early Taos lifestyles. The Martinez Hacienda and Ernest Blumenschein home each has unique appeal.

The **Martinez Hacienda,** Lower Ranchitos Road, Highway 240 (ℂ **505/758-1000**), is the only Spanish colonial hacienda in the United States that's open to the public year-round. This was the home of the merchant, trader, and *alcalde* (mayor) Don Antonio Severino Martinez, who bought it in 1804 and lived here until his death in 1827. His eldest son was Padre Antonio José Martinez, northern New Mexico's controversial spiritual leader from 1826 to 1867. Located on the west bank of the Rio Pueblo de Taos, about 2 miles southwest of the plaza, the museum is remarkably beautiful, with thick, raw adobe walls. The hacienda has no exterior windows—this was to protect against raids by Plains tribes.

Twenty-one rooms were built around two *placitas,* or interior courtyards. They give you a glimpse of the austerity of frontier lives, with only a few pieces of modest period furniture in each. You'll see bedrooms, servants' quarters, stables, a kitchen, and a large fiesta room. Exhibits tell the story of the Martinez family and life in Spanish Taos between 1598 and 1821, when Mexico gained control.

Taos Historic Museums has developed the Martinez Hacienda into a living museum with weavers, blacksmiths, and wood carvers. Demonstrations are scheduled daily, and during the **Taos Trade Fair** (held in late Sept) they run virtually nonstop. The Trade Fair commemorates the era when Native Americans, Spanish settlers, and mountain men met here to trade with each other.

The **Ernest L. Blumenschein Home & Museum,** 222 Ledoux St. (ℂ **505/758-0505**), 1½ blocks southwest of the plaza, re-creates the lifestyle of one of the founders of the Taos Society of Artists (founded 1915). An adobe home with garden walls and a courtyard, parts of which date from the 1790s, it became the home and studio of Blumenschein (1874–1960) and his family in 1919. Period furnishings include European antiques and handmade Taos furniture in Spanish colonial style.

Blumenschein was born and raised in Pittsburgh. In 1898, after training in New York and Paris, he and fellow painter Bert Phillips were on assignment for

Taos Attractions

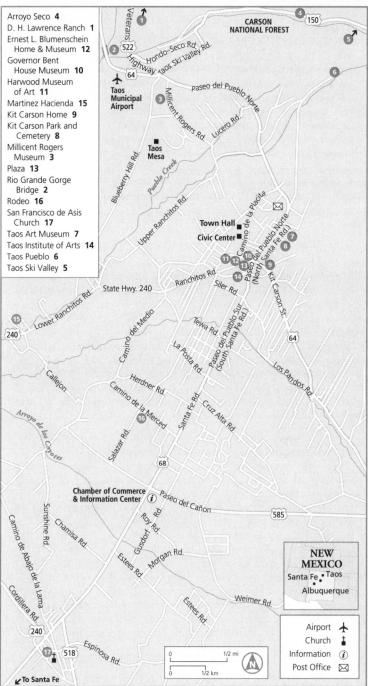

CARSON NATIONAL FOREST

Taos Municipal Airport

Taos Mesa

Town Hall
Civic Center

Chamber of Commerce & Information Center

NEW MEXICO
Santa Fe • Taos
• Albuquerque

To Santa Fe

Airport ✈
Church ✝
Information ⓘ
Post Office ✉

0   1/2 mi
0   1/2 km

The Kit Carson Home

Previously, the Kit Carson Home and Museum, East Kit Carson Road, located a short block east of the plaza intersection, was the town's general museum of Taos history. The 12-room adobe home was built in 1825 and purchased in 1843 by Carson, the famous mountain man, Indian agent, and scout, as a wedding gift for his young bride, Josefa Jaramillo. It remained their home for 25 years, until both died (exactly a month apart) in 1868. At press time, the owners of the home, the Masonic Lodge, had taken possession of it and closed it, with the intent of reopening it as a new museum. The Kit Carson collection, however, remains in the hands of the Taos Historic Museums, many pieces of which are now on display at the Martinez Hacienda.

Harper's and *McClure's* magazines of New York when a wheel of their wagon broke 30 miles north of Taos. Blumenschein drew the short straw and thus was obliged to bring the wheel by horseback to Taos for repair. He later recounted his initial reaction to the valley he entered: "No artist had ever recorded the New Mexico I was now seeing. No writer had ever written down the smell of this air or the feel of that morning sky. I was receiving . . . the first great unforgettable inspiration of my life. My destiny was being decided."

That spark later led to the foundation of Taos as an art colony. An extensive collection of works by early-20th-century Taos artists, including some by Blumenschein's daughter, Helen, is on display in several rooms of the home.

222 Ledoux St. ✆ **505/758-0505** (information for both museums can be obtained at this number). www. taoshistoricmuseums.com. Admission for each museum $5 adults, $3 children ages 6–16, free for children under 6; $10 families. Summer daily 9am–5pm; call for winter hours.

Taos Pueblo ★★★   It's amazing that in our frenetic world, more than 100 Taos Pueblo residents still live much as their ancestors did 1,000 years ago. When you enter the pueblo, you'll see two large buildings, both with rooms piled on top of each other, forming structures that echo the shape of Taos Mountain (which sits to the northeast). Here, a portion of Taos residents lives without electricity and running water. The remaining 2,000 residents of Taos Pueblo live in conventional homes on the pueblo's 95,000 acres.

The main buildings' distinctive flowing lines of shaped mud, with a straw-and-mud exterior plaster, are typical of Pueblo architecture throughout the Southwest. It's architecture that blends in with the surrounding land. Bright blue doors are the same shade as the sky that frames the brown buildings.

The northernmost of New Mexico's 19 pueblos, Taos Pueblo has been home to the Tiwa tribes for more than 900 years. Many residents here still practice ancestral rituals. The center of their world is still nature; women use hornos to bake bread, and most still drink water that flows down from the sacred Blue Lake. Meanwhile, arts and crafts and other tourism-related businesses support the economy, along with government services, ranching, and farming.

The village looks much the same today as it did when a regiment from Coronado's expedition first came upon it in 1540. Though the Tiwa were essentially a peaceful agrarian people, they are perhaps best remembered for spearheading the only successful revolt by Native Americans in history. Launched by Pope (poh-*pay*) in 1680, the uprising drove the Spanish from Santa Fe until 1692 and from Taos until 1698.

As you explore the pueblo, you can visit the residents' studios, sample home-made bread, look into the **San Geronimo Chapel,** and wander past the fascinating ruins of the old church and cemetery. You're expected to ask permission from individuals before taking their photos; some will ask for a small payment. Do not trespass into kivas (ceremonial rooms) and other areas marked as restricted.

The **Feast of San Geronimo** (the patron saint of Taos Pueblo), on September 29 and 30, marks the end of the harvest season. The feast day is reminiscent of an ancient trade fair for the Taos Indians, when tribes from as far south as South America and as far north as the Arctic would come and trade for wares, hides, clothing, and harvested crops. The day is filled with foot races, pole climbing done by traditional Indian clowns, and artists and craftspeople mimicking the early traders. Dances are performed the evening of September 29. Other annual events include a **turtle dance** on New Year's Day, **deer or buffalo dances** on Three Kings Day (Jan 6), and **corn dances** on Santa Cruz Day (May 3), San Antonio Day (June 13), San Juan Day (June 24), Santiago Day (July 25), and Santa Ana Day (July 26). The annual **Taos Pueblo Powwow,** a dance competition and parade that brings together tribes from throughout North America, is held the second weekend of July on tribal lands off NM 522 (see "Northern New Mexico Calendar of Events," in chapter 2). The pueblo Christmas celebration begins on Christmas Eve, with bonfires and a procession with children's dances. On Christmas day, the deer or **Matachine dances** take place (p. 290).

During your visit to the pueblo you will have the opportunity to purchase traditional fried and oven-baked bread as well as a variety of arts and crafts. If you would like to try traditional feast-day meals, the **Tiwa Kitchen,** near the entrance to the pueblo, is a good place to stop. Close to Tiwa Kitchen is the **Oo-oonah Children's Art Center,** where you can see the creative works of pueblo children.

As with many of the other pueblos in New Mexico, Taos Pueblo has opened a casino. **Taos Mountain Casino** (© **888/WIN-TAOS**) is located on the main road to Taos Pueblo and features slot machines, blackjack, and poker.

Veterans Hwy. (P.O. Box 1846), Taos Pueblo. © 505/758-1028. www.taospueblo.com. Admission cost, as well as camera, video, and sketching fees, subject to change on a yearly basis; be sure to ask about telephoto lenses and digital cameras; photography not permitted on feast days. Daily 8am–4:30pm, with a few exceptions. Guided tours available. Closed for 45 consecutive days every year late winter or early spring (call ahead). Also, because this is a living community, you can expect periodic closures. From Paseo del Pueblo Norte, travel north 2 miles on Veterans Hwy.

2 More Attractions

D. H. Lawrence Ranch   A trip to this ranch north of Taos leads you into odd realms of devotion for the controversial early-20th-century author who lived and wrote in the area in the early '20s. A short uphill walk from the ranch home (not open to visitors), is the D. H. Lawrence Memorial, a shedlike structure that's a bit of a forgotten place, where people have left a few mementos such as juniper berries and sticks of gum. The guest book is also interesting: One couple wrote of trying for 24 years to get here from England.

Lawrence lived in Taos on and off between 1922 and 1925. The ranch was a gift to his wife, Frieda, from the art patron Mabel Dodge Luhan. Lawrence repaid Luhan the favor by giving her the manuscript of *Sons and Lovers*. When

Lawrence died in southern France in 1930 of tuberculosis, his ashes were returned here for burial. The grave of Frieda, who died in 1956, is outside the memorial. The memorial is the only public building at the ranch, which is operated today by the University of New Mexico as an educational and recreational retreat.

NM 522, San Cristobal. ℰ **505/776-2245.** Free admission. Daily 8am–5pm. To reach the site, head north from Taos about 15 miles on NM 522, then another 6 miles east into the forested Sangre de Cristo Range via a well-marked dirt road.

Governor Bent House Museum (Kids)

Located a short block north of the plaza, this residence of Charles Bent, New Mexico Territory's first American governor, offers an interesting peek into the region's at-times brutal history. Bent, a former trader who established Fort Bent, Colorado, was murdered during the 1847 Native American and Hispanic rebellion, while his wife and children escaped by digging through an adobe wall into the house next door. The hole is still visible. Period art and artifacts are on display.

117 Bent St. ℰ **505/758-2376.** Admission $2 adults, $1 children 8–15, free for children under 8. MC, V. Summer daily 9:30am–5pm; winter daily 10am–5pm. Closed Easter, Thanksgiving, Christmas, and New Year's Day. Street parking.

Harwood Museum of Art of the University of New Mexico ★

With its high ceilings and broad wood floors, this recently restored museum is a lovely place to wander among New Mexico–inspired images. A cultural and community center since 1923, the museum displays paintings, drawings, prints, sculpture, and photographs by Taos-area artists from 1800 to the present. Featured are paintings from the early days of the art colony by members of the Taos Society of Artists, including Oscar Berninghaus, Ernest Blumenschein, Herbert Dunton, Victor Higgins, Bert Phillips, and Walter Ufer. Also included are works by Emil Bisttram, Andrew Dasburg, Agnes Martin, Larry Bell, and Thomas Benrimo.

Upstairs are 19th-century pounded-tin pieces and *retablos,* religious paintings of saints that have traditionally been used for decoration and inspiration in the homes and churches of New Mexico. The permanent collection includes sculptures by Patrociño Barela, one of the leading Hispanic artists of 20th-century New Mexico—well worth seeing, especially his 3-foot-tall "Death Cart," a rendition of Doña Sebastiána, the bringer of death.

The museum also schedules more than eight changing exhibitions a year, many of which feature works by celebrated artists currently living in Taos.

238 Ledoux St. ℰ **505/758-9826.** www.harwoodmuseum.org. Admission $5. Tues–Sat 10am–5pm; Sun noon–5pm.

Kit Carson Park and Cemetery

Major community events are held in the park in summer. The cemetery, established in 1847, contains the graves of Carson, his wife, Governor Charles Bent, the Don Antonio Martinez family, Mabel Dodge Luhan, and many other noted historical figures and artists. Their lives are described briefly on plaques.

Paseo del Pueblo Norte. ℰ **505/758-8234.** Free admission. Daily 24 hr.

Rio Grande Gorge Bridge ★ (Kids)

This impressive bridge, west of the Taos airport, spans the Southwest's greatest river. At 650 feet above the canyon floor, it's one of America's highest bridges. If you can withstand the vertigo, it's interesting to come more than once, at different times of day, to observe how the changing light plays tricks with the colors of the cliff walls. A curious aside is that the wedding scene in the movie *Natural Born Killers* was filmed here.

US 64, 10 miles west of Taos. Admission free. Daily 24 hr.

San Francisco de Asis church ★★ On NM 68, about 4 miles south of Taos, this famous church appears as a modern adobe sculpture with no doors or windows, an image that has often been photographed and painted. Visitors must walk through the garden on the east side to enter the two-story church and get a full perspective of its massive walls, authentic adobe plaster, and beauty.

A video presentation is given in the church office every hour on the half-hour. Also, displayed on the wall is an unusual painting, *The Shadow of the Cross,* by Henri Ault (1896). Under ordinary light it portrays a barefoot Christ at the Sea of Galilee; in darkness, however, the portrait becomes luminescent, and the perfect shadow of a cross forms over the left shoulder of Jesus' silhouette. The artist reportedly was as shocked as everyone else to see this. The reason for the illusion remains a mystery. A few crafts shops surround the square.

Ranchos de Taos Plaza. (© 505/758-2754. Admission $3 for video and mystery painting. Mon–Sat 9am–4pm. Visitors may attend Mass Mon–Fri 5:30pm, Sat 6pm (Mass rotates from this church to the 3 mission chapels), Sun 7 (Spanish), 9, and 11:30am. Closed to the public 1st 2 weeks in June, when repairs are done; however, services still take place.

Taos Art Museum ★ *Finds* Set in the home of Russian artist Nicolai Fechin (*Feh*-shin), this collection displays works of the Taos Society of Artists, which give a sense of what Taos was like in the late 19th and early 20th centuries. The works are rich and varied, including panoramas and images of the Native American and Hispanic villagers. The setting in what was Fechin's home from 1927 until 1933 is truly unique. The historic building commemorates his career. Born in Russia in 1881, Fechin came to the United States in 1923, already acclaimed as a master of painting, drawing, sculpture, architecture, and woodwork. In Taos, he renovated the home and embellished it with hand-carved doors, windows, gates, posts, fireplaces, and other features of a Russian country home. Fechin died in 1955.

227 Paseo del Pueblo Norte. (© 505/758-2690. www.taosmuseums.org. Admission $6 adults, $3 children 6–16, free for under 6. Summer Thurs–Sun 10am–5pm; call for winter hours.

ART CLASSES

If you'd like to pursue an artistic adventure of your own in Taos, check out the weeklong classes in such media as writing, sculpting, painting, jewelry making, photography, clay working, and textiles that are available at the **Taos Institute of Arts,** 108-B Civic Plaza Dr. (© **800/822-7183** or 505/758-2793; www. tiataos.com). Class sizes are limited, so if you're thinking about giving these workshops a try, call for information well in advance. The fees vary from class to class and usually don't include the cost of materials.

3 Organized Tours

An excellent opportunity to explore the historic downtown area of Taos is offered by **Taos Historic Walking Tours** (© **505/758-4020**). Tours cost $10 and take 1½ to 2 hours, leaving from the Mabel Dodge Luhan house at 10:30am Monday to Saturday (May–Sept). Closed Sundays and holidays. Call to make an appointment during the off season.

If you'd really like a taste of Taos history and drama, call **Enchantment Dreams Walking Tours** ★ (© **505/776-2562**). Roberta Courtney Meyers, a theater artist, dramatist, and composer, will tour you through Taos's history while performing a number of characters, such as Georgia O'Keeffe and Kit Carson. Walking tours cost $20 per person.

4 Skiing ★★★

DOWNHILL

Five alpine resorts are within an hour's drive of Taos; all offer complete facilities, including equipment rentals. Although exact opening and closing dates vary according to snow conditions, the season usually begins around Thanksgiving and continues into early April.

Ski clothing can be purchased, and ski equipment can be rented or bought, from several Taos outlets. Among them are **Cottam's Ski & Outdoor Shops,** with four locations (call ℂ **800/322-8267** or 505/758-2822 for the one nearest you); and **Taos Ski Valley Sportswear, Ski & Boot Co.,** in Taos Ski Valley (ℂ **505/776-2291**).

Taos Ski Valley ★★★, P.O. Box 90, Taos Ski Valley, NM 87525 (ℂ **505/776-2291;** www.skitaos.org), is the preeminent ski resort in the southern Rocky Mountains. It was founded in 1955 by a Swiss-German immigrant, Ernie Blake. According to local legend, Blake searched for 2 years in a small plane for the perfect location for a ski resort comparable to what he was accustomed to in the Alps. He found it at the abandoned mining site of Twining, high above Taos. Today, under the management of two generations of Blakes, the resort has become internationally renowned for its light, dry powder (as much as 320 in. annually), its superb ski school, and its personal, friendly service.

Taos Ski Valley can best be appreciated by the more experienced skier. It offers steep, high-alpine, high-adventure skiing. The mountain is more intricate than it might seem at first glance, and it holds many surprises and challenges—even for the expert. The *London Times* called the valley "without any argument the best ski resort in the world. Small, intimate, and endlessly challenging, Taos simply has no equal." And, if you're sick of dealing with yahoos on snowboards, you will be pleased to know that they're not permitted on the slopes of Taos Ski Valley, at least for now: You may see a number of "Free Taos" bumper stickers on your trip, part of a campaign by snowboarders to open up the slopes (go to www.free taos.com for more information). The quality of the snow here (light and dry) is believed to be due to the dry Southwestern air and abundant sunshine.

Between the 11,819-foot summit and the 9,207-foot base, there are 72 trails and bowls, more than half of them designated for expert and advanced skiers. Most of the remaining trails are suitable for advanced intermediates; there is little flat terrain for novices to gain experience and mileage. However, many beginning skiers find that after spending time in lessons they can enjoy the **Kachina Bowl,** which offers spectacular views as well as wide-open slopes.

The area has an uphill capacity of 15,000 skiers per hour on its five double chairs, one triple, four quads, and one surface tow. Full-day lift tickets, depending on the season, cost $33 to $51 for adults, $21 to $31 for children 7 to 12,

---

Kids Skiing with Kids

With its children's ski school, Taos Ski Valley has always been an excellent location for skiing families, but with the 1994 addition of an 18,000-square-foot children's center (Kinderkäfig Center), skiing with your children in Taos is even better. Kinderkäfig offers every service imaginable, from equipment rental for children to babysitting services. Call ahead for more information.

$19 to $40 for teens ages 13 to 17, $38 for seniors ages 65 to 69, and are free for seniors over 70 and for children 6 and under with an adult ticket purchase. Full rental packages are $20 for adults and $13 for children. Taos Ski Valley is open daily 9am to 4pm from Thanksgiving to around the second week of April. *Note:* Taos Ski Valley has one of the best ski schools in the country, specializing in teaching people how to negotiate steep and challenging runs.

Taos Ski Valley has many lodges and condominiums, with nearly 1,500 beds. (See "Taos Ski Valley," in chapter 12, for details on accommodations.) All offer ski-week packages; four of them have restaurants. There are three restaurants on the mountain in addition to the many facilities of Village Center at the base. For reservations, call the **Taos Valley Resort Association** (© **800/776-1111** or 505/776-2233; www.visitnewmexico.com).

Not far from Taos Ski Valley is **Red River Ski & Snowboard Area,** P.O. Box 900, Red River, NM 87558 (© **800/331-7669** for reservations; 505/754-2223 for information; www.redriverskiarea.com). One of the bonuses of this ski area is that lodgers at Red River can walk out their doors and be on the slopes. Two other factors make this 40-year-old, family-oriented area special: First, most of its 57 trails are geared toward the intermediate skier, though beginners and experts also have some trails; and second, good snow is guaranteed early and late in the year by snowmaking equipment that can work on 87% of the runs, more than any other in New Mexico. However, be aware that this human-made snow tends to be icy, and the mountain is full of inexperienced skiers, so you really have to watch your back. Locals in the area refer to this as "Little Texas" because it's so popular with Texans and other southerners. A very friendly atmosphere, with a touch of redneck attitude, prevails.

There's a 1,600-foot vertical drop here to a base elevation of 8,750 feet. Lifts include four double chairs, two triple chairs, and a surface tow, with a capacity of 7,920 skiers per hour. The cost of a lift ticket for all lifts is $47 for adults for a full day, $37 for half-day; $42 for teens 13 to 17 for a full day, $32 half-day; $33 for children ages 7 to 12 and seniors 65 and over, $24 for a half-day. All rental packages start at $17 for adults, $14 for children. Lifts run daily 9am to 4pm Thanksgiving to about March 28.

Also quite close to Taos is **Angel Fire Resort** ✿, P.O. Drawer B, Angel Fire, NM 87710 (© **800/633-7463** or 505/377-6401; www.angelfireresort.com). If you (or your kids) don't feel up to skiing steeper Taos Mountain, Angel Fire is a good choice. The 62 trails are heavily oriented to beginner and intermediate skiers and snowboarders, with a few runs for more advanced skiers and snowboarders. The mountain has received over $7 million in improvements in past years. This is not an old village like you'll find at Taos and Red River. Instead, it's a Vail-style resort, built in 1960, with a variety of activities other than skiing (see "Exploring Beyond Taos: A Driving Tour of the Enchanted Circle," later in this chapter). The snowmaking capabilities here are excellent, and the ski school is good, though I hear it's so crowded that it's difficult to get in during spring break. With the only two high-speed quad lifts in New Mexico, you can get to the top fast and have a long ski to the bottom. There are also three double lifts and one surface lift. There are a large snowboard park (with a banked slalom course, rails, jumps, and other obstacles) and some new hike-access advanced runs; note, however, that the hike is substantial. Cross-country skiing, snow-shoeing, and snowbiking are also available. All-day lift tickets cost $48 for adults, $31 for teens (ages 13–17), and $26 for children (ages 7–12). Kids 6 and under and seniors 65 and over ski free. Open from approximately Thanksgiving to March 29 (depending on the weather) daily 9am to 4pm.

The oldest ski area in the Taos region, founded in 1952, **Sipapu Ski and Summer Resort,** NM 518, Rte. Box 29, Vadito, NM 87579 (✆ **505/587-2240;** www.sipapunm.com), is 25 miles southeast of Taos, on NM 518 in Tres Ritos Canyon. It prides itself on being a small local ski area, especially popular with schoolchildren. It has two triple chairs and two surface lifts, with a vertical drop of 1,025 feet to the 8,200-foot base elevation. There are 31 trails, half classified as intermediate, and two terrain park trails have been added. It's a nice little area, tucked way back in the mountains, with excellent lodging rates. Be aware that because the elevation is fairly low, runs get very icy. Lift tickets are $35 for adults for a full day, $26 half-day; $26 for children under 12 for a full day, $22 half-day; $23 for seniors (ages 65–69) for a half or full day; and free for seniors age 70 and over, as well as children 5 and under. A package including lift tickets, equipment rental, and a lesson costs $49 for adults and $42 for children. Sipapu is open from about December 12 to April 1st, and lifts run daily from 9am to 4pm.

CROSS COUNTRY

Numerous popular Nordic trails exist in **Carson National Forest.** If you call or write ahead, the ranger will send you a booklet titled *Where to Go in the Snow,* which gives cross-country skiers details about the maintained trails. One of the more popular trails is **Amole Canyon,** off NM 518 near the Sipapu Ski Area, where the Taos Nordic Ski Club maintains set tracks and signs along a 3-mile loop. It's closed to snowmobiles, a comfort to lovers of serenity.

Just east of Red River, with 16 miles of groomed trails (in addition to 6 miles of trails strictly for snowshoers) in 400 acres of forestlands atop Bobcat Pass, is the **Enchanted Forest Cross Country Ski Area** (✆ 505/754-6112; www. enchantedforestxc.com). Full-day trail passes, good 9am to 4:30pm, are $10 for adults; $8 for teens 13 to 17 and seniors 62 to 69; $3 for children age 7 to 12; and free for seniors age 70 and over, as well as for children 6 and under. In addition to cross-country ski and snowshoe rentals, the ski area also rents pulk sleds—high-tech devices in which children are pulled by their skiing parents. The ski area offers a full snack bar. Equipment rentals and lessons can be arranged either at Enchanted Forest or at **Miller's Crossing** ski shop at 417 W. Main St. in Red River (✆ **505/754-2374**). Nordic skiers can get instruction in cross-country classic as well as freestyle skating.

Taos Mountain Outfitters, 114 S. Plaza (✆ **505/758-9292**), offers telemark and cross-country sales, rentals, and guide service, as does **Los Rios Whitewater Ski Shop** (✆ **800/544-1181** or 505/776-8854).

Southwest Nordic Center (✆ **505/758-4761;** www.southwestnordiccenter. com) offers rental of five *yurts* (Mongolian-style huts), four of which are in the Rio Grande National Forest near Chama. The fifth and newest addition is located outside the Taos Ski Valley (offering access to high Alpine terrain) and is twice as big as the others. These are insulated and fully equipped accommodations, each with a stove, pots, pans, dishes, silverware, mattresses, pillows, a table and benches, and wood-stove heating. Skiers trek into the huts, carrying their clothing and food in backpacks. Guide service is provided, or people can go in on their own, following directions on a map. The yurts are rented by the night and range from $65 to $125 per group. Call for reservations as much in advance as possible as they do book up. The season is mid-November through April, depending on snow conditions.

5 More Outdoor Activities

Taos County's 2,200 square miles embrace a great diversity of scenic beauty, from New Mexico's highest mountain, 13,161-foot **Wheeler Peak,** to the 650-foot-deep chasm of the **Rio Grande Gorge** ★★. Carson National Forest, which extends to the eastern city limits of Taos and cloaks a large part of the county, contains several major ski facilities as well as hundreds of miles of hiking trails through the Sangre de Cristo Range.

Recreation areas are mainly in the national forest, where pine and aspen provide refuge for abundant wildlife. Forty-eight areas are accessible by road, including 38 with campsites. There are also areas on the high desert mesa, carpeted by sagebrush, cactus, and, frequently, wildflowers. Two beautiful areas within a short drive of Taos are the **Valle Vidal Recreation Area,** north of Red River, and the **Wild Rivers Recreation Area,** near Questa. For complete information, contact **Carson National Forest,** 208 Cruz Alta Rd. (✆ **505/758-6200**), or the **Bureau of Land Management,** 226 Cruz Alta Rd. (✆ **505/758-8851**).

BALLOONING

As in many other towns throughout New Mexico, hot-air ballooning is a top attraction. Recreational trips over the Taos Valley and Rio Grande Gorge are offered by **Paradise Hot Air Balloon Adventure** (✆ **505/751-6098**). The company also offers ultra-light rides.

The **Taos Mountain Balloon Rally,** P.O. Box 3096 (✆ **800/732-8267**), is held each year in late October. (See "Northern New Mexico Calendar of Events," in chapter 2.)

BIKING

Even if you're not an avid cyclist, it won't take long for you to realize that getting around Taos by bike is preferable to driving. You won't have the usual parking problems, and you won't have to sit in the line of traffic as it snakes through the center of town. If you feel like exploring the surrounding area, Carson National Forest rangers recommend several biking trails in the greater Taos area. Head to the **Taos Box West Rim** for a scenic and easy ride. To reach the trail, travel NM 68 south for 17 miles to Pilar; turn west onto NM 570. Travel along the river for 6¼ miles, cross the bridge, and drive to the top of the ridge. Watch for the trail marker on your right. For a more technical and challenging ride, go to **Devisadero Loop:** From Taos drive out of town on US 64 to your first pull-out on the right, just as you enter the canyon at El Nogal Picnic Area. To ride the notorious **South Boundary Trail,** a 20-mile romp for advanced riders, contact Native Sons Adventures (below). Native Sons can arrange directions, a shuttle, and a guide, if necessary. The **U.S. Forest Service** office, 208 Cruz Alta Rd. (✆ **505/758-6200**), has excellent trail information. Also look for the *Taos Trails* map (created jointly by Carson National Forest, Native Sons Adventures, and Trails Illustrated) at area bookstores.

Bicycle rentals are available from the **Gearing Up Bicycle Shop,** 129 Paseo del Pueblo Sur (✆ **505/751-0365**); daily rentals run $35 for a mountain bike with front suspension. **Native Sons Adventures,** 1033-A Paseo del Pueblo Sur (✆ **800/753-7559** or 505/758-9342), rents bikes ranging from regular (unsuspended) to full-suspension bikes for $15 to $35/half-day and $20 to $45/full-day; it also rents some car racks. All these prices include use of helmets and water bottles.

Annual touring events include Red River's **Enchanted Circle Century Bike Tour** (© 505/754-2366) on the weekend following Labor Day.

FISHING

In many of New Mexico's waters, fishing is possible year-round, though, due to conditions, many high lakes and streams are fishable only during the warmer months. Overall, the best fishing is in the spring and fall. Naturally, the Rio Grande is a favorite fishing spot, but there is also excellent fishing in the streams around Taos. Taoseños favor the Rio Hondo, Rio Pueblo (near Tres Ritos), Rio Fernando (in Taos Canyon), Pot Creek, and Rio Chiquito. Rainbow, cutthroat, German brown trout, and kokanee (a freshwater salmon) are commonly stocked and caught. Pike and catfish have been caught in the Rio Grande as well. Jiggs, spinners, or woolly worms are recommended as lure, or worms, corn, or salmon eggs as bait; many experienced anglers prefer fly-fishing.

Licenses are required, of course, and are sold, along with tackle, at several Taos sporting-goods shops. For backcountry guides, try **Deep Creek Wilderness Outfitters and Guides,** P.O. Box 721, El Prado, NM 87529 (© **505/776-8423** or **505/776-5901**), or **Taylor Streit Flyfishing Service,** 405 Camino de la Placita (© **505/751-1312**; www.streitflyfishing.com).

FITNESS FACILITIES

The **Taos Spa and Tennis Club,** 111 Dona Ana Dr. (across from Sagebrush Inn; © **505/758-1980**; www.taosspa.com), is a fully equipped fitness center that rivals any you'd find in a big city. It has a variety of cardiovascular machines, bikes, and weight-training machines, as well as saunas, indoor and outdoor Jacuzzis, a steam room, and indoor and outdoor pools. Classes range from yoga to Pilates to water fitness. In addition, it has tennis and racquetball courts. Therapeutic massage, facials, and physical therapy are available daily by appointment. Children's programs include a tennis camp and swimming lessons, and babysitting programs are available in the morning and evening. The spa is open Monday to Friday 5am to 9pm; Saturday and Sunday 7am to 8pm. Monthly memberships are available for individuals and families, as are summer memberships and punchcards. For visitors, there's a daily rate of $12.

The **Northside Health and Fitness Center,** at 1307 Paseo del Pueblo Norte (© **505/751-1242**), is also a full-service facility, featuring top-of-the-line Cybex equipment, free weights, and cardiovascular equipment. Aerobics classes are scheduled daily (Jazzercise classes weekly), and there are indoor/outdoor pools and four tennis courts, as well as children's and seniors' programs. Open weekdays 6am to 9pm, weekends 8am to 8pm. The daily visitors' rate is $10.

GOLF

Since the summer of 1993, the 18-hole golf course at the **Taos Country Club,** 54 Golf Course Dr., Ranchos de Taos (© **800/758-7375** or 505/758-7300), has been open to the public. Located on Country Road 110, just 6 miles south of the plaza, it's a first-rate championship golf course designed for all levels of play. It has open fairways and no hidden greens. The club also features a driving range, practice putting and chipping green, and instruction by PGA professionals. Greens fees are seasonal and start at $48; cart and club rentals are available. The country club has also added a clubhouse, featuring a restaurant and full bar. It's always advisable to call ahead for tee times 1 week in advance, but it's not unusual for people to show up unannounced and still manage to find a time to tee off.

The par-72, 18-hole course at the **Angel Fire Resort Golf Course** (© **800/ 633-7463** or 505/377-3055) is PGA endorsed. Surrounded by stands of ponderosa pine, spruce, and aspen, at 8,500 feet, it's one of the highest regulation golf courses in the world. It also has a driving range and putting green. Carts and clubs can be rented at the course, and the club pro provides instruction. Greens fees range from $45 to $65.

HIKING

There are hundreds of miles of hiking trails in Taos County's mountain and high-mesa country. The trails are especially well traveled in the summer and fall, although nights turn chilly and mountain weather may be fickle by September.

Free materials and advice on all **Carson National Forest** trails and recreation areas can be obtained from the **Forest Service Building,** 208 Cruz Alta Rd. (© **505/758-6200**), open Monday to Friday 8am to 4:30pm. Detailed USGS topographical maps of backcountry areas can be purchased from **Taos Mountain Outfitters,** South Plaza (© **505/758-9292**).

The 19,663-acre **Wheeler Peak Wilderness** is a wonderland of alpine tundra, encompassing New Mexico's highest peak (13,161 ft.). A favorite (though rigorous) hike to Wheeler Peak's summit (15 miles round-trip with a 3,700-ft. elevation gain) makes for a long but fun day. The trail head is at Taos Ski Valley. For year-round hiking, head to the **Wild Rivers Recreation Area** (© **505/770-1600**), near Questa (see "Exploring Beyond Taos: A Driving Tour of the Enchanted Circle," later in this chapter).

HORSEBACK RIDING

The sage meadows and pine-covered mountains around Taos make it one of the West's most romantic places to ride. **Taos Indian Horse Ranch** ★★, on Pueblo land off Ski Valley Road, just before **Arroyo Seco** (© **505/758-3212**), offers a variety of guided rides. Open by appointment, the ranch provides horses for all types of riders (English, Western, Australian, and bareback) and ability levels. Call ahead to reserve and for prices, which will likely run about $85 for a 2-hour trail ride.

Horseback riding is also offered by **Rio Grande Stables,** P.O. Box 2122, El Prado (© **505/776-5913;** www.lajitasstables.com/taos.htm), with rides taking place during the summer months at Taos Ski Valley. Most riding outfitters offer lunch trips and overnight trips. Call for prices and further details.

HUNTING

Hunters in **Carson National Forest** bag deer, turkey, grouse, band-tailed pigeons, and elk by special permit. Hunting seasons vary year to year, so it's important to inquire ahead with the New Mexico **Game and Fish Department** in Santa Fe (© **505/476-8101**).

ICE-SKATING AND SKATEBOARDING

If a latent Michelle Kwan or Brian Boitano dwells in you, try your blades at **Taos Youth Family Center** (© **505/758-4160**), located at 406 Paseo del Cañon (2 miles south of the plaza and about ¾ mile off Paseo del Pueblo Sur). The rink is open daily from early November thorough mid-March. Call for hours. Skate rentals are available for adults and children. Admission is $4. Also at the center is a in-line skate and skateboarding park, open when there's no snow or ice. Admission is free.

JOGGING

The paved paths and grass of Kit Carson Park (see "More Attractions," earlier in this chapter) provide a quiet place to stretch your legs.

LLAMA TREKKING

For a taste of the unusual, you might want to try letting a llama carry your gear and food while you walk and explore, free of any heavy burdens. They're friendly, gentle animals that have keen senses of sight and smell. Often, other animals, such as elk, deer, and mountain sheep, are attracted to the scent of the llamas and will venture closer to hikers if the llamas are present. **El Paseo Llama Expeditions** ★★ (© 800/455-2627 or 505/758-3111; www.elpaseollama. com) utilizes U.S. Forest Service–maintained trails that wind through canyons and over mountain ridges. The llama expeditions are scheduled May to mid-October, and day hikes are scheduled year-round. Gourmet meals are provided. Half-day hikes cost $59, day hikes $79, and 2- to 8-day hikes run $249 to $989.

Wild Earth Llama Adventures ★★ (© 800/758-LAMA [5262] or 505/586-0174; www.llamaadventures.com) offers a "Take a Llama to Llunch" day hike—a full day of hiking into the Sangre de Cristo Mountains, complete with a gourmet lunch for $75. Wild Earth also offers a variety of custom multi-day wilderness adventures tailored to trekkers' needs and fitness levels for $125 per person per day. Children under 12 receive discounts. Camping gear and food are provided. On the trips, experienced guides provide information about native plants and local wildlife, as well as natural and regional history of the area. The head guide has doubled as a chef in the off season, so the meals on these treks are quite tasty.

RIVER RAFTING

Half- or full-day whitewater rafting trips down the Rio Grande and Rio Chama originate in Taos and can be booked through a variety of outfitters in the area. The wild **Taos Box** ★★★, a steep-sided canyon south of the Wild Rivers Recreation Area, offers a series of class IV rapids that rarely let up for some 17 miles. The water drops up to 90 feet per mile, providing one of the most exciting 1-day whitewater tours in the West. May and June, when the water is rising, is a good time to go. Experience is not required, but you will be required to wear a life jacket (provided), and you should be willing to get wet.

Most of the companies listed run the **Taos Box** ($99–$109 per person) and **Pilar Racecourse** ($40–$48 per person for a half-day) on a daily basis.

I highly recommend **Los Rios River Runners** ★ in Taos, P.O. Box 2734 (© 800/544-1181 or 505/776-8854; www.losriosriverrunners.com). Other safe bets are **Native Sons Adventures,** 1033-A Paseo del Pueblo Sur (© 800/753-7559 or 505/758-9342; www.nativesonsadventures.com); and **Far Flung Adventures,** P.O. Box 707, El Prado (© 800/359-2627 or 505/758-2628; www.farflung.com).

Safety warning: Taos is not the place to experiment if you are not an experienced rafter. Do yourself a favor and check with the **Bureau of Land Management** (© 505/758-8851) to make sure that you're fully equipped to go whitewater rafting without a guide. Have them check your gear to make sure that it's sturdy enough—this is serious rafting!

ROCK CLIMBING

Mountain Skills, P.O. Box 206, Arroyo Seco, NM 87514 (© **505/776-2222;** www.climbingschoolusa.com), offers rock-climbing instruction for all skill levels,

Getting Pampered: The Spa Scene

Taos doesn't have the spa scene that Tucson and Phoenix do, but you can get pampered at **Taos Spa and Tennis Club** (see "Fitness Facilities," above).

If you'd like to stay at a spa, **El Monte Sagrado,** 317 Kit Carson Rd. (© **800/828-TAOS** or 505/758-3502; www.elmontesagrado.com), and **Casa de las Chimineas,** 405 Cordoba Rd. (© **877/758-4777** or 505/758-4777; www.visittaos.com), offer a variety of treatments to their guests (see chapter 12).

from beginners to more advanced climbers who would like to fine-tune their skills or just find out about the best area climbs.

SNOWMOBILING AND ATV RIDING

Native Sons Adventures, 1033-A Paseo del Pueblo Sur (© **800/753-7559** or 505/758-9342), runs fully guided tours in the Sangre de Cristo Mountains. Rates run $64 to $150. Advanced reservations required.

SWIMMING

The **Don Fernando Pool** (© **505/737-2622**), on Civic Plaza Drive at Camino de la Placita, opposite the new Convention Center, admits swimmers over age 8 without adult supervision.

TENNIS

Quail Ridge Inn (© **800/624-4448** or 505/776-2211; www.quailridgeinn. com; p. 181) on Ski Valley Road has outdoor tennis courts available to those staying in Quail Ridge condos. **Taos Spa and Tennis Club** (see "Fitness Facilities," above) has four courts, and the **Northside Health and Fitness Center** (see "Fitness Facilities," above) has three tennis courts. In addition, there are four free public courts in Taos, two at **Kit Carson Park,** on Paseo del Pueblo Norte, and two at **Fred Baca Memorial Park,** on Camino del Medio, south of Ranchitos Road.

6 Shopping

Given the town's historical associations with the arts, it isn't surprising that many visitors come to Taos to buy fine art. Some 50-odd galleries are located within easy walking distance of the plaza, and a couple dozen more are just a short drive from downtown. Galleries and shops are generally open 7 days a week during summer and closed Sundays during winter. Hours vary but generally run from 10am to 5 or 6pm. Some artists show their work by appointment only.

The best-known artist in modern Taos is R. C. Gorman, a Navajo from Arizona who has made his home in Taos for more than 2 decades. He is internationally acclaimed for his bright, somewhat surrealistic depictions of Navajo women. His **Navajo Gallery,** at 210 Ledoux St. (© **505/758-3250**), is a showcase for his widely varied work: acrylics, lithographs, silk screens, bronzes, tapestries, hand-cast ceramic vases, etched glass, and more.

My favorite new spot to shop is the village of **Arroyo Seco** ✪ on NM 150, about 5 miles north of Taos en route to Taos Ski Valley. Not only is there a lovely

1834 church, La Santísima Trinidad, but there are a few cute little shops lining the winding lane through town. My favorites are the **Taos Sunflower** (*C* 505/776-5644), selling specialty yarns and fibers, just off the highway near the Gypsy 360° cafe and **Arroyo Seco Mercantile** (*C* 505/776-8806) at 488 NM 150, which is full of cowboy hats, antiques, and country home items.

ART

Act I Gallery This gallery has a broad range of works in a variety of media. You'll find watercolors, *retablos,* furniture, paintings, Hispanic folk art, pottery, jewelry, and sculpture. 218 Paseo del Pueblo Norte. *C* 800/666-2933 or 505/758-7831.

Fenix Gallery The Fenix Gallery focuses on Taos artists with national and/or international collections and reputations who live and work in Taos. The work is primarily nonobjective and very contemporary. Some "historic" artists are represented as well. Recent expansion has doubled the gallery space. 228B N. Pueblo Rd. *C* 505/758-9120.

Franzetti Metalworks This gallery's work appeals to some more than to others. The designs are surprisingly whimsical for metalwork. Much of the work is functional; you'll find laughing-horse switch plates and "froggie" earthquake detectors. 120-G Bent St. *C* 505/758-7872.

Gallery A The oldest gallery in town, Gallery A has contemporary and traditional paintings and sculpture, including Gene Kloss etchings, watercolors, and oils, as well as regional and national collections. 105–107 Kit Carson Rd. *C* 505/758-2343.

Inger Jirby Gallery ★ *Finds* The word *expressionist* could have been created to define the work of internationally known artist Inger Jirby. Full of bold color and passionate brush strokes, Jirby's oils record the lives and landscapes of villages from the southwestern U.S. to Guatemala to Bali. This gallery, which meanders back through a 400-year-old adobe house, is a feast for the eyes and soul. 207 Ledoux St. *C* 505/758-7333.

Lumina of New Mexico ★★ *Finds* Located in the historic Victor Higgins home, next to the Mabel Dodge Luhan estate, Lumina is one of the loveliest galleries in New Mexico. You'll find a large variety of fine art, including paintings, sculpture, and photography. This place is as much a tourist attraction as any of the museums and historic homes in town. Look for wonderful paintings and sculptures of Enrico Embrilo, and take a stroll through the new 2-acre Ridhwan sculpture garden with a pond and waterfall—where you'll find large outdoor pieces from all over the United States. About 8 minutes from town is **Lumina North** in Arroyo Seco, which features 3 acres of Buddhist sculpture and a tea house. 239 Morada Rd. (off Kit Carson Rd.). *C* 505/758-7282. Lumina North: 11 Des Moines Rd. *C* 505/776-3957.

Michael McCormick Gallery ★ *Finds* Nationally renowned artists dynamically play with Southwestern themes in the works hanging at this gallery, steps from the plaza. Especially notable are the bright portraits by Miguel Martinez and the moody architectural pieces by Margaret Nes. If the gallery's namesake is in, strike up a conversation about art or poetry. 106C Paseo del Pueblo Norte. *C* 800/279-0879 or 505/758-1372.

New Directions Gallery Here you'll find a variety of contemporary abstract works such as the beautiful blown glasswork of Tony Jojola. My favorites, though, are the Impressionistic works depicting northern New Mexico villages by Tom Noble. 107 North Plaza Suite B. *C* 800/658-6903 or 505/758-2771.

Nichols Taos Fine Art Gallery   Here you will find traditional works in all media, including Western and cowboy art. 403 Paseo del Pueblo Norte. ℭ 505/758-2475.

Parks Gallery ⭐   Some of the region's finest contemporary art decks the walls of this gallery just off the plaza. Some of the top artists here include Melissa Zink, Jim Wagner, Susan Contreres, and Erin Currier. 127 Bent St. ℭ **505/751-0343.**

Philip Bareiss Gallery   The works of some 30 leading Taos artists, including sculptor and painter Ron Davis, sculptor Gray Mercer, and watercolorist Patricia Sanford, are exhibited here. 15 Rt. 150. ℭ **505/776-2284.** bareiss@taosartappraisal.com.

R. B. Ravens   A trader for many years, including 21 on the Ranchos Plaza, R. B. Ravens is skilled at finding incredible period artwork. Here, you'll see (and have the chance to buy) Navajo rugs, and pottery, all in the setting of an old home with raw pine floors and hand-sculpted adobe walls. 4146 NM 68 (across from the St. Francis Church Plaza), Ranchos de Taos. ℭ **505/758-7322.**

Shriver Gallery   This gallery sells traditional paintings, drawings, etchings, and bronze sculptures. 401 Paseo del Pueblo Norte. ℭ **505/758-4994.**

BOOKS

Brodsky Bookshop   This shop has an exceptional inventory of fiction, non-fiction, Southwestern and Native American–studies books, children's books, used books, cards, tapes, and CDs. 226 Paseo del Pueblo Norte. ℭ **888/223-8730** or 505/758-9468.

Moby Dickens Bookshop ⭐   This is one of Taos's best bookstores. You'll find children's and adults' collections of Southwest, Native American, and out-of-print books. The shop has comfortable places to sit and read. 124A Bent St. ℭ **888/442-9980** or 505/758-3050.

CRAFTS

Clay & Fiber Gallery   Clay & Fiber represents more than 150 artists from around the country. Merchandise changes frequently, but you should expect to see a variety of ceramics, fiber arts, jewelry, and wearables. 201 Paseo del Pueblo Sur. ℭ **505/758-8093.**

Southwest Moccasin & Drum ⭐ *Kids*   Home of the All One Tribe Drum, this favorite local shop carries a large variety of drums in all sizes and styles, handmade by master Native American drum makers from Taos Pueblo. The shop also has the country's second-largest selection of moccasins, as well as an incredible inventory of indigenous world instruments and tapes, sculpture, weavings, rattles, fans, fetishes, bags, decor, and many handmade one-of-a-kind items. Kids enjoy the instruments as well as other colorful goods. A percentage of the store's profits goes to support Native American causes. 803 Paseo del Pueblo Norte. ℭ **800/447-3630** or 505/758-9332. www.swnativecrafts.com.

Taos Artisans Cooperative Gallery *Value*   This seven-member cooperative gallery, owned and operated by local artists, sells local handmade jewelry, wearables, clay work, glass, leather work, and garden sculpture. You'll always find an artist in the shop. 107C Bent St. ℭ **505/758-1558.**

Taos Blue   This gallery has fine Native American and contemporary handcrafts. 101A Bent St. ℭ **505/758-3561.**

Twining Weavers and Contemporary Crafts   Here, you'll find an interesting mix of hand-woven wool rugs and pillows by owner Sally Bachman, as well as creations by other gallery artists in fiber, basketry, and clay. 133 Kit Carson Rd. ℂ 505/758-9000.

Weaving Southwest   Contemporary tapestries by New Mexico artists, as well as one-of-a-kind rugs, blankets, and pillows, are the woven specialties found here. 216B Paseo del Pueblo Norte. ℂ 505/758-0433.

FASHIONS

Artemisia   Wearable art in bold colors defines this little shop a block from the plaza. Goods are pricey but unique, most hand-woven or hand-sewn, all for women. 115 Bent St. ℂ 505/737-9800.

Mariposa Boutique   What first caught my eye in this little shop were bright chile-pepper-print overalls for kids. Closer scrutiny brought me to plenty of finds for myself, such as suede and rayon broomstick skirts and Mexican-style dresses, perfect for showing off turquoise jewelry. 120-F Bent St. ℂ 505/758-9028.

Overland Sheepskin Company ★ (Finds   You can't miss the romantically weathered barn sitting on a meadow north of town. Inside, you'll find anything you can imagine in leather: coats, gloves, hats, slippers. The coats here are exquisite, from oversize ranch styles to tailored blazers in a variety of leathers from sheepskin to buffalo hide. NM 522 (a few miles north of town). ℂ 505/758-8820.

FOOD

Cid's Food Market   This store has the best selection of natural and gourmet foods in Taos. It's a great place to stock your picnic basket with such items as roasted chicken and barbequed brisket, or with lighter fare, such as sushi, Purple Onion–brand sandwiches, black-bean salad, and fresh hummus and tabbouleh. 623 Paseo del Pueblo Norte. ℂ 505/758-1148.

Xocoatl   Set in a cozy enclave connected to Michael McCormick Gallery, this fun chocolate and wine shop offers some of the tastiest truffles I've had. Tim Van Rixel makes such delicacies as mango truffles and pineapple coconut truffles. A bar serves Italian sodas, and plans are in the works for contemporary snacks such as cracker-crust pizzas and salads. 107-B Juan Largo Lane. ℂ 505/751-7549.

FURNITURE

Country Furnishings of Taos   Here, you'll find unique hand-painted folk-art furniture. The pieces are as individual as the styles of the local folk artists who make them. There are also home accessories, unusual gifts, clothing, and jewelry. 534 Paseo del Pueblo Norte. ℂ 505/758-4633.

Lo Fino   With a name meaning "the refined," you know that this expansive showroom is worth taking time to wander through. You'll find a variety of home furnishings, from driftwood lamps and finely painted *trasteros* (armoires) to hand-crafted traditional and contemporary Southwestern furniture. Lo Fino specializes in custom-built furniture. 201 Paseo del Pueblo Sur. ℂ 505/758-0298. lofino@newmex.com.

The Taos Company   This interior-design showroom specializes in unique Southwestern and contemporary furniture and decorative accessories. Especially look for graceful stone fountains, iron-and-wood furniture, and custom jewelry. 124K John Dunn Plaza, Bent St. ℂ 800/548-1141 or 505/758-1141.

GIFTS & SOUVENIRS

Chimayo Trading del Norte   Specializing in Navajo weavings, pueblo pot-tery, and other types of pottery, this is a fun spot to peruse on the Ranchos de Taos Plaza. Look especially for the Casas Grandes pottery from Mexico. #1 Ranchos de Taos Plaza. ℭ 505/758-0504.

El Rincón Trading Post *Finds*   This shop has a real trading-post feel. It's a wonderful place to find turquoise jewelry, whether you're looking for contem-porary or antique. In the back of the store is a museum full of Native American and Western artifacts. 114 Kit Carson Rd. ℭ 505/758-9188.

San Francisco de Asis Gift Shop   Local devotional art fills this funky little shop behind the San Francisco de Asis church. *Retablos* (altar paintings), rosary beads, and hand-carved wooden crosses appeal to a range of visitors, from the deeply religious to the pagan power shopper. Ranchos de Taos Plaza. ℭ 505/758-2754.

JEWELRY

Artwares Contemporary Jewelry   The gallery owners here call their con-temporary jewelry "a departure from the traditional." True to this slogan, each piece here offers a new twist on traditional Southwestern and Native American design, by artists such as John Hardy and Diane Malouf. 129 N. Plaza. ℭ 800/527-8850 or 505/758-8850.

Taos Gems & Minerals   In business for over 30 years, Taos Gems & Miner-als is a fine lapidary showroom. This is a great place to explore; you can buy jew-elry, carvings, and antique pieces at reasonable prices. 637 Paseo del Pueblo Sur. ℭ 505/758-3910.

MUSICAL INSTRUMENTS

Taos Drum Company   Drum-making is an age-old tradition to which local artisans give continued life in Taos. The drums are made of hollowed-out logs stretched with rawhide, and they come in all different shapes, sizes, and styles. Taos Drums has the largest selection of Native American log and hand drums in the world. In addition to drums, the showroom displays Southwestern and wrought-iron furniture, cowboy art, and more than 60 styles of rawhide lamp-shades, as well as a constantly changing selection of South American imports, primitive folk art, ethnic crafts, Native American music tapes, books, and other information on drumming. To find Taos Drum Company, look for the tepees and drums off NM 68. Ask about the tour that demonstrates the drum-making process. 5 miles south of Taos Plaza (off NM 68). ℭ 505/758-3796.

POTTERY & TILES

Stephen Kilborn Pottery   Visiting this shop in town is a treat, but for a real adventure, go 17 miles south of Taos toward Santa Fe to Stephen Kilborn's stu-dio in Pilar, open Monday to Saturday 10am to 5pm and noon to 4pm on Sun-day. There, you'll see where the pottery is made. 136A Paseo del Pueblo Norte. ℭ 800/758-0136 or 505/758-5760. www.kilbornpottery.com.

Vargas Tile Co.   Vargas Tile has a great little collection of hand-painted Mex-ican tiles at good prices. You'll find beautiful pots with sunflowers on them and colorful cabinet doorknobs, as well as inventive sinks. South end of town on NM 68. ℭ 505/758-5986.

7 Taos After Dark

For a small town, Taos has its share of top entertainment. The resort atmosphere and the arts community attract performers, and the city enjoys annual programs in music and literary arts. State troupes, such as the New Mexico Repertory Theater and New Mexico Symphony Orchestra, make regular visits.

Many events are scheduled by the **Taos Center for the Arts (TCA),** 133 Paseo del Pueblo Norte (✆ **505/758-2052;** www.taoscenterforthearts.org), at the **Taos Community Auditorium** (✆ **505/758-2052**). The TCA imports local, regional, and national performers in theater, dance, and concerts (Robert Mirabal among others, has performed here, and The Vagina Monologues has been presented). Also, look for a weekly film series offered year-round.

You can obtain information on current events in the *Taos News,* published every Thursday. The **Taos County Chamber of Commerce** (✆ **800/732-TAOS** or 505/758-3873; www.taoschamber.com) publishes semiannual listings of *Taos County Events,* as well as the annual *Taos Country Vacation Guide* that also lists events and happenings around town.

THE PERFORMING ARTS

Fort Burgwin   This historic site (of the 1,000-year-old Pot Creek Pueblo), located about 10 miles south of Taos, is a summer campus of Dallas's Southern Methodist University. From mid-May through mid-August, the SMU-in-Taos curriculum (including studio arts, humanities, and sciences) includes courses in music and theater. There are regularly scheduled orchestral concerts, guitar and harpsichord recitals, and theater performances available to the community, without charge, throughout the summer. 6580 NM 518, Ranchos de Taos. ✆ **505/758-8322.**

Music from Angel Fire   This acclaimed program of chamber music begins in mid-August, with weekend concerts, and continues up to Labor Day. Based in the small resort community of Angel Fire (located about 21 miles east of US 64), it also presents numerous concerts in Taos, Las Vegas, and Raton. P.O. Box 502, Angel Fire. ✆ **505/377-3233** or 505/989-4772.

Taos Poetry Circus   Aficionados of the literary arts appreciate this annual event, held during 8 days in mid-June. Billed as "a literary gathering and poetry showdown among nationally known writers," it includes readings, seminars, performances, public workshops, and a poetry video festival. The main event is the World Heavyweight Championship Poetry Bout, 10 rounds of hard-hitting readings—with the last round extemporaneous. Office mailing address: 5275 NDCBU. ✆ **505/758-1800.** Events take place at various venues around town.

> ## The Major Concert & Performance Halls
>
> **Taos Civic Plaza and Convention Center,** 121 Civic Plaza Dr. (✆ **505/ 758-4160**). This convention space has an exhibit center where presentations, lectures, and concerts are held.
>
> **Taos Community Auditorium,** Kit Carson Memorial State Park (✆ **505/ 758-4677**). A comfortable, small-town space, this community auditorium makes a nice venue for films, concerts, and lectures.

Taos School of Music   Founded in 1963, this music summer school offers excellent concerts by notable artists. The school is located at the Hotel St. Bernard in Taos Ski Valley. From mid-June to mid-August there is an intensive 8-week study and performance program for advanced students of violin, viola, cello, and piano. The 8-week **Chamber Music Festival,** an important adjunct of the school, offers 16 concerts and seminars for the public; performances are given by pianist Robert McDonald, the Chicago String Quartet, the Brentano String Quartet, Michael Tree, and the international young student artists. Performances are held at the Taos Community Auditorium and the Hotel St. Bernard. P.O. Box 1879. ℂ 505/776-2388. www.taosschoolofmusic.com. Tickets for chamber music concerts $15 for adults, $10 for children under 16.

THE CLUB & MUSIC SCENE

Adobe Bar   A favorite gathering place for locals and visitors, the Adobe Bar is known for its live music series (nights vary) devoted to the eclectic talents of Taos musicians. The schedule offers a little of everything—classical, jazz, folk, Hispanic, and acoustic. The Adobe Bar features a wide selection of international beers, wines by the glass, light New Mexican dining, desserts, and an espresso menu. In the Historic Taos Inn, 125 Paseo del Pueblo Norte. ℂ 505/758-2233. Noon–10:30pm.

Alley Cantina ★ *Moments*   This bar that touts its location as the oldest house in Taos has become the hot late-night spot. The focus is on interaction, as well as TV sports. Patrons playing shuffleboard, pool, chess, and backgammon listen to live music 4 to 5 nights a week. Burgers, fish and chips, and other informal dishes are served until 11pm. 121 Teresina Lane. ℂ 505/758-2121. Cover for live music only.

Anaconda Bar ★★   Set in the new eco-resort El Monte Sagrado, this is Taos's happening night spot, with live entertainment—jazz, blues, Native American flute, or country—playing nightly. An anaconda sculpture snaking across the ceiling and an 11,000-gallon fish tank set the contemporary tone of the place, where a variety of delectable tapas are served. In the El Monte Sagrado hotel, 317 Kit Carson Rd. ℂ 505/758-3502.

Hideaway Lounge   This hotel lounge, built around a large adobe fireplace, offers live entertainment and an extensive hors d'oeuvre buffet. Call for schedule. Don Fernando de Taos, 1005 Paseo del Pueblo Sur. ℂ 505/758-4444.

Momentitos de la Vida ★★   This low-lit, moody bar, with thick pine tables and comfortable chairs, serves up martinis and jazz in bluesy doses. Other drinks and music selections also play here, with live music on Friday and Saturday nights. The restaurant cum club serves a bistro menu with prices from $8.50 to $14. Nonsmoking. 4¾ miles north of the intersection of NM 150 and NM 522 (P.O. Box 505), Arroyo Seco. ℂ 505/776-3333. Tues–Sun 5–10:30pm or so (later on weekends).

Sagebrush Inn ★   This is a real hot spot for locals. The atmosphere is Old West, with a rustic wooden dance floor and plenty of smoke. Dancers generally two-step to country music nightly, year-round, starting at 9pm. Paseo del Pueblo Sur (P.O. Box 557). ℂ 505/758-2254.

Thunderbird Lodge   Throughout the winter, the Thunderbird offers a variety of nightly entertainment at the foot of the ski slopes. You'll also find wine tastings. Taos Ski Valley. ℂ 505/776-2280. Cover occasionally on holidays; then, the cost varies widely.

8 Exploring Beyond Taos: A Driving Tour of the Enchanted Circle

If you're in the mood to explore, take this 90-mile loop north of Taos, through the old Hispanic villages of Arroyo Hondo and Questa, into a pass that the Apaches, Kiowas, and Comanches once used to cross the mountains to trade with the Taos Indians. You'll come to the Wild West mining town of Red River, pass through the expansive Moreno Valley, and travel along the base of some of New Mexico's tallest peaks. Then, you'll skim the shores of a high mountain lake at Eagle Nest, pass through the resort village of Angel Fire, and head back to Taos along the meandering Rio Fernando de Taos. Although one can drive the entire loop in 2 hours from Taos, most folks prefer to take a full day, and many take several days.

ARROYO HONDO

Traveling north from Taos via NM 522, it's a 9-mile drive to this village, the remains of an 1815 land grant along the Rio Hondo. Along the dirt roads that lead off NM 522, you may find a windowless *morada* or two, marked by plain crosses in front—places of worship for the still-active Penitentes, a religious order known for self flagellation. This is also the turnoff point for trips to the Rio Grande Box, an awesome 1-day, 17-mile whitewater run for which you can book trips in Santa Fe, Taos, Red River, and Angel Fire. (See the "Outdoor Activities" sections in chapter 7 and earlier in this chapter for booking agents in Santa Fe and Taos, respectively.)

Arroyo Hondo was also the site of the New Buffalo commune in the 1960s. Hippies flocked here, looking to escape the mores of modern society. Over the years, the commune members have dispersed throughout northern New Mexico, bringing an interesting creative element to the food, architecture, and philosophy of the state. En route north, the highway passes near **San Cristobal,** where a side road turns off to the **D. H. Lawrence Ranch** (see "More Attractions," earlier in this chapter) and **Lama,** site of an isolated spiritual retreat.

QUESTA

Next, Highway 522 passes through Questa, most of whose residents are employed at a molybdenum mine about 5 miles east of town. Mining molybdenum (an ingredient in lightbulbs, television tubes, and missile systems) in the area has not been without controversy. The process has raked across hillsides along the Red River, and though Molycorp, the mine's owner, treats the water it uses before returning it to the river, studies show that it has adversely affected the fish life. Still, the mine is a major employer in the area, and locals are grateful for the income it generates.

If you turn west off NM 522 onto NM 378 about 3 miles north of Questa, you'll travel 8 miles on a paved road to the Bureau of Land Management–administered **Wild Rivers Recreation Area** (© **505/770-1600**). Here, where the Red River enters the gorge, you'll find 22 miles of trails, some suited for biking and some for hiking, a few trails traveling 800 feet down into the gorge to the banks of the Rio Grande. Forty-eight miles of the Rio Grande, which extend south from the Colorado border, are protected under the national Wild and Scenic River Act of 1968. Information on geology and wildlife, as well as hikers' trail maps, can be obtained at the visitor center here.

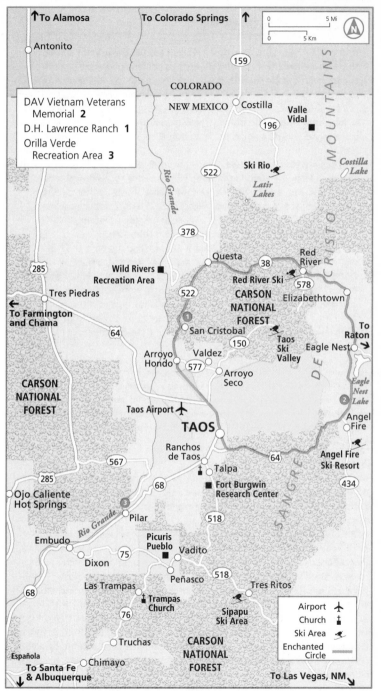

To Alamosa

To Colorado Springs

5 Mi

5 Km

Antonito

159

COLORADO

NEW MEXICO

Costilla

Valle
Vidal

196

DAV Vietnam Veterans
Memorial **2**
D.H. Lawrence Ranch **1**
Orilla Verde
Recreation Area **3**

Rio Grande

522

Ski Rio

*Latir
Lakes*

*Costilla
Lake*

378

285

Questa

38

Red
River

Wild Rivers
Recreation Area

522

Red River Ski

578

Tres Piedras

CARSON
NATIONAL
FOREST

Elizabethtown

To Farmington
and Chama

64

San Cristobal

150

Taos
Ski
Valley

Eagle Nest

To
Raton

Arroyo
Hondo

577

Valdez

Arroyo
Seco

*Eagle
Nest
Lake*

CARSON
NATIONAL
FOREST

Taos Airport

TAOS

2

Angel
Fire

Ranchos
de Taos

Talpa

64

Angel Fire
Ski Resort

567

285

68

Fort Burgwin
Research Center

434

Ojo Caliente
Hot Springs

Rio Grande

3

Pilar

518

Embudo

Picuris
Pueblo

Vadito

75

Dixon

518

Peñasco

68

Las Trampas

Tres Ritos

76

Trampas
Church

Sipapu
Ski Area

Airport

Church

Ski Area

Enchanted
Circle

Española

Truchas

CARSON
NATIONAL
FOREST

Chimayo

To Santa Fe
& Albuquerque

To Las Vegas, NM

A Sojourn on the Green Shore

A sweet spot en route to Taos from Santa Fe, the **Orilla Verde** (green shore) **Recreation Area,** offers just what its name implies: lovely green shores along the Rio Grande. It's an excellent place to camp or to simply have a picnic. If you're adventurous, the flat water in this section of the river makes for scenic canoeing, kayaking, rafting, and fishing. Hiking trails thread through the area as well. Along them, you may come across ancient cultural artifacts, but be sure to leave them as you find them.

While traveling to the area, you'll encounter two places of note. The village of **Pilar** is a charming farming village, home to apple orchards, corn fields, and artists. The **Rio Grande Gorge Visitor Center** (at the intersection of NM 570 and NM 68; ☎ **505/751-4899**) provides information about the gorge and has very clean restrooms. It's open daily during business hours from Memorial Day to Labor Day.

The day use fee for Orilla Verde is $3 per day; camping is $7 per night, and RV camping is $15 per night. All campsites have picnic tables, grills, and restrooms. For information contact the **Orilla Verde Visitor Station** (☎ **505/758-4060**; www.nm.blm.gov/tafo/rafting/rio_grande/ovra/ovra_info.html), at the campground. To reach the recreation area, travel north from Santa Fe 50 miles or southwest from Taos 15 miles on NM 68; turn north on NM 570 and travel 1 mile.

The village of **Costilla,** near the Colorado border, is 20 miles north of Questa. This is the turnoff point for four-wheel-drive jaunts and hiking trips into **Valle Vidal,** a huge U.S. Forest Service–administered reserve with 42 miles of roads and many hiking trails. A day hike in this area can bring you sightings of hundreds of elk.

RED RIVER

To continue on the Enchanted Circle loop, turn east at Questa onto NM 38 for a 12-mile climb to Red River, a rough-and-ready 1890s gold-mining town that has parlayed its Wild West ambience into a pleasant resort village that's especially popular with families from Texas and Oklahoma.

This community, at 8,750 feet, is a center for skiing, snowmobiling, fishing, hiking, off-road driving, horseback riding, mountain biking, river rafting, and other outdoor pursuits. Frontier-style celebrations, honky-tonk entertainment, and even staged shootouts on Main Street are held throughout the year.

Though it can be a charming and fun town, Red River's food and accommodations are mediocre at best. Its patrons are down-home folks, happy with a bed and a diner-style meal. If you decide to stay, try **The Lodge at Red River,** P.O. Box 189, Red River, NM 87558 (☎ **800/91-LODGE** or 505/754-6280; www.redrivernm.com/lodgeatrr), in the center of town. It offers hotel rooms ranging in price from $84 to $106. Knotty pine throughout, the accommodations are clean and comfortable. Downstairs, the restaurant serves three home-style meals daily.

If you're passing through and want a quick meal, the **Main Street Deli,** 316 E. Main St., Red River, NM 87558 (☎ **505/754-3400**), has brought some excellent flavors to the little village. You'll find tasty meat loaf and chicken-and-dumpling specials, as well as home-baked muffins, soups, and sub sandwiches under $9. Don't leave without trying a macadamia-nut white-chocolate chip cookie. Open Monday through Saturday 8am to 8pm, Sunday 8am to 2pm.

The **Red River Chamber of Commerce,** P.O. Box 870, Red River, NM 87558 (© **800/348-6444** or 505/754-2366; www.redrivernewmexico.com), lists more than 40 accommodations, including lodges and condominiums. Some are open winters or summers only.

EAGLE NEST

About 16 miles southeast of Red River, on the other side of 9,850-foot Bobcat Pass, is the village of Eagle Nest, resting on the shore of Eagle Nest Lake in the Moreno Valley. Gold was mined in this area as early as 1866, starting in what is now the ghost town of **Elizabethtown** about 5 miles north; Eagle Nest itself (pop. 200) wasn't incorporated until 1976. The 4-square-mile **Eagle Nest Lake** (© **888-NM-PARKS** or 505/476-3355; www.nmparks.com) recently became a New Mexico state park. At press time, work was under way to build a visitor center and upgrade facilities. The lake is considered one of the top trout producers in the United States and attracts ice fishermen in winter as well as summer anglers. It's too cold for swimming, but sailboaters and windsurfers ply the waters.

If you're heading to Cimarron or Denver, proceed east on US 64 from Eagle Nest. But if you're circling back to Taos, continue southwest on US 38 and US 64 to Agua Fría and Angel Fire.

Shortly before the Agua Fría junction, you'll see the **DAV Vietnam Veterans Memorial.** It's a stunning structure with curved white walls soaring high against the backdrop of the Sangre de Cristo Range. Consisting of a chapel and an underground visitor center, it was built by Dr. Victor Westphall in memory of his son, David, a marine lieutenant killed in Vietnam in 1968. The chapel has a changing gallery of photographs of Vietnam veterans who lost their lives in the Southeast Asian war, but no photo is as poignant as this inscription written by young David Westphall, a promising poet:

> *Greed plowed cities desolate.*
> *Lusts ran snorting through the streets.*
> *Pride reared up to desecrate*
> *Shrines, and there were no retreats.*
> *So man learned to shed the tears*
> *With which he measures out his years.*

ANGEL FIRE

If you like the clean efficiency of a resort complex, you may want to plan a night or two here—any time of year. Angel Fire is approximately 150 miles north of Albuquerque and 21 miles east of Taos. Opened in the late 1960s, this resort offers a hotel with spacious, comfortable rooms, as well as condominiums and cabins. Winter is the biggest season. This medium-size beginner and intermediate mountain is an excellent place for families to roam about (see "Skiing," earlier in this chapter). Two high-speed quad lifts zip skiers to the top quickly while allowing them a long ski down. The views of the Moreno Valley are awe inspiring. Fourteen miles of Nordic trail have been added at the top of the mountain; visitors can also snowmobile and take sleigh rides, including one out to a sheepherder's tent with a plank floor and a wood stove where you can eat dinner cooked over an open fire. Contact **Roadrunner Tours** (© **505/377-6416** or 505/377-1811).

Fun Fact **Ghosts of Elizabethtown**

Although only a few trodden clues remain, the gold-mining town Eliz-abethtown once boasted 7,000 residents and was the first seat of Col-fax county. It was called Virginia City when founded in 1865, but the name was changed to honor Elizabeth Moore, daughter of a leading citizen. What has become known as E-town had plenty of gold-town perks: five stores, two hotels, seven saloons, and three dance halls. By the early 1900s, much of the gold had run out, and in 1903 fire blazed through the town, leveling much of it. Today visitors can still see a few foundations and remnants of a cemetery. It's located on the west side of NM 38, about 10 miles east of Red River.

During spring, summer, and fall, **Angel Fire Resort** offers golf, tennis, hik-ing, mountain biking (you can take your bike up on the quad lift), fly-fishing, river rafting, and horseback riding. There are other fun family activities, such as the Human Maze, 5,200 square feet of wooden passageway within which you can let loose your inner rat. There are a video arcade, a miniature golf course, theater performances, and, throughout the year, a variety of festivals, including a hot-air balloon festival, Winterfest, and concerts of both classical and popular music.

The unofficial community center is the **Angel Fire Resort,** North Angel Fire Road (P.O. Drawer B), Angel Fire, NM 87710 (© **800/633-7463** or 505/377-6401; www.angelfireresort.com), a 155-unit hotel with spacious, comfortable rooms, some with fireplaces and some with balconies. Rates range from $85 to $199.

For more information on the Moreno Valley, including full accommodations listings, contact the **Angel Fire Chamber of Commerce,** P.O. Box 547, Angel Fire, NM 87710 (© **800/446-8117** or 505/377-6661; fax 505/377-3034; www.angelfirechamber.org).

A fascinating adventure you may want to try here is a 1-hour, 1-day, or overnight horseback trip with **Roadrunner Tours,** P.O. Box 274, Angel Fire, NM 87710 (© **505/377-6416;** www.rtours.com). One-hour rides run year-round for $30, but if you'd like a little more adventure, try an overnight. From Angel Fire, Nancy and Bill Burch guide adventurers on horseback through pri-vate ranchland of ponderosa forests and meadows of asters and sunflowers, often including wildlife sightings. Once at camp, riders bed down in an authentic mountain cowboy cabin. Call for prices.

15

Albuquerque

Albuquerque is the gateway to northern New Mexico, the portal through which most domestic and international visitors pass before traveling on to Santa Fe and Taos. But it's worth stopping in Albuquerque for a day or two in order to get a feel for the history of this area.

From the rocky crest of Sandia Peak at sunset, one can see the lights of this city of almost half a million people spread out across 16 miles of high desert grassland. As the sun drops beyond the western horizon, it reflects off the Rio Grande, flowing through Albuquerque more than a mile below.

This waterway is the bloodline for the area, what allowed a city to spring up in this vast desert, and it continues to be at the center of the area's growth. Farming villages that line its banks are being stampeded by expansion. As the west side of the city sprawls, more means for transporting traffic across the river have had to be built, breaking up the pastoral valley area.

The railroad, which set up a major stop here in 1880, prompted much of Albuquerque's initial growth, but that economic explosion was nothing compared with what has happened since World War II. Designated a major national center for military research and production, Albuquerque became a trading center for New Mexico, whose populace is spread widely across the land. That's why the city may strike visitors as nothing more than one big strip mall. Look closely, and you'll see ranchers, Native Americans, and Hispanic villagers stocking up on goods to take back to the New Mexico boot heel or the Texas panhandle.

Climbing out of the valley is **Route 66,** well worth a drive, if only to see the rust that time has left. Old court motels still line the street, many with their funky '50s signage. One enclave on this route is the **University of New Mexico and Nob Hill district,** with a number of hippie-ish cafes and shops.

Farther downhill, you come to **downtown Albuquerque.** During the day, this area is all suits and heels, but at night it boasts a hip nightlife scene. People from all over the state come to Albuquerque to check out the live music and dance clubs, most within walking distance from each other.

The section called **Old Town** is worth a visit. Though it's the most touristy part of town, it's also a unique Southwestern village with a beautiful and intact plaza. Also in this area are Albuquerque's aquarium and botanical gardens, as well as its zoo.

1 Orientation

ARRIVING

Albuquerque is the transportation hub for New Mexico, so getting in and out of town is easy. For more detailed information, see "Getting There," in chapter 2.

BY PLANE The **Albuquerque International Sunport** (© **505/842-4366**) is in the south-central part of the city, between I-25 on the west and Kirtland Air

Force Base on the east, just south of Gibson Boulevard. Sleek and efficient, the airport is served by most national airlines and two local ones.

Most hotels have courtesy vans to meet their guests and take them to their respective destinations. In addition, **Checker Airport Express** (℗ **505/765-1234**) runs services to and from city hotels. **ABQ Ride** (℗ **505/243-7433**), Albuquerque's public bus system, also makes airport stops. There is efficient taxi service to and from the airport, and there are numerous car-rental agencies.

BY TRAIN   **Amtrak**'s "Southwest Chief" arrives and departs daily to and from Los Angeles and Chicago. The station is at 214 First St. SW, 2 blocks south of Central Avenue (℗ **800/USA-RAIL** or 505/842-9650).

BY BUS   **Greyhound/Trailways** (℗ **800/231-2222** for schedules, fares, and information) and **TNM&O** (℗ **505/243-4435**) arrive and depart from the Albuquerque Bus Transportation Center, 300 Second St. SW (at the corner of Lead and Second, near the train station).

BY CAR   If you're driving, you'll probably arrive via either the east–west I-40 or the north–south I-25. Exits are well marked. For information and advice on driving in New Mexico, see "Getting There," in chapter 2.

VISITOR INFORMATION

The main office of the **Albuquerque Convention and Visitors Bureau** is at 20 First Plaza NW (℗ **800/284-2282** or 505/842-9918). It's open Monday to Friday 8am to 5pm. There are information centers at the airport, on the lower level at the bottom of the escalator, open daily 9:30am to 8pm; and in Old Town at 303 Romero St. NW (Suite 107), open daily 9am to 5pm. Tape-recorded information about current local events is available from the bureau after 5pm weekdays and all day Saturday and Sunday. Call ℗ **800/284-2282.**

CITY LAYOUT

The city's sprawl takes awhile to get used to. A visitor's first impression is of a grid of arteries lined with shopping malls and fast-food eateries, with residences tucked behind on side streets.

If you look at a map of Albuquerque, you'll notice that it lies at the crossroads of I-25 north–south and I-40 east–west. Focus your attention on the southwest quadrant: Here, you'll find both downtown Albuquerque and Old Town, site of many tourist attractions. Lomas Boulevard and Central Avenue, the old Route 66 (US 66), flank downtown on the north and south. They come together 2 miles west of downtown near Old Town Plaza, the historical and spiritual heart of the city. Lomas and Central continue east across I-25, staying about half a mile apart as they pass by the University of New Mexico and the New Mexico State Fairgrounds. The airport is directly south of the UNM campus, about 3 miles via Yale Boulevard. Kirtland Air Force Base—site of Sandia National Laboratories—is an equal distance south of the fairgrounds, on Louisiana Boulevard.

Roughly paralleling I-40 to the north is Menaul Boulevard, the focus of midtown and uptown shopping, as well as the hotel districts. As Albuquerque expands northward, the Journal Center business park area, about 4½ miles north of the freeway interchange, is getting more attention. East of Eubank Boulevard lie the Sandia Foothills, where the alluvial plain slants a bit more steeply toward the mountains.

When looking for an address, it is helpful to know that Central Avenue divides the city into north and south, and the railroad tracks—which run just

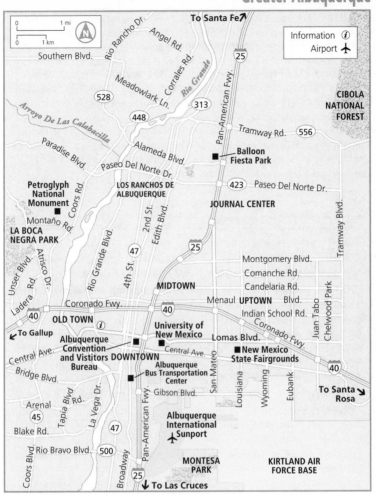

east of First Street downtown—comprise the dividing line between east and west. Street names are followed by a directional: NE, NW, SE, or SW.

MAPS The most comprehensive Albuquerque street map is distributed by the Convention and Visitors Bureau, 20 First Plaza NW (© **800/284-2282** or 505/842-9918).

2 Getting Around

Albuquerque is easy to get around, thanks to its wide thoroughfares and grid layout, combined with its efficient transportation systems.

BY PUBLIC TRANSPORTATION ABQ Ride (© **505/243-7433**) cloaks the arterials with its city bus network. Call for information on routes and fares.

BY TAXI Yellow Cab (© **505/247-8888**) serves the city and surrounding area 24 hours a day.

BY CAR   The Yellow Pages list more than 30 car-rental agencies in Albuquerque. Among them are the following well-known national firms: **Alamo,** 3400 University Blvd. SE (✆ **505/842-4057**); **Avis,** at the airport (✆ **505/842-4080**); **Budget,** at the airport (✆ **505/247-3443**); **Dollar,** at the airport (✆ **505/842-4224**); **Hertz,** at the airport (✆ **505/842-4235**); **Rent-A-Wreck,** 500 Yale Blvd. SE (✆ **505/232-7552**); and **Thrifty,** 2039 Yale Blvd. SE (✆ **505/842-8733**). Those not located at the airport itself are close by and can provide rapid airport pickup and delivery service.

Parking is generally not difficult in Albuquerque. Meters operate weekdays 8am to 6pm and are not monitored at other times. Only the large downtown hotels charge for parking. Traffic is a problem only at certain hours. Avoid I-25 and I-40 at the center of town around 5pm.

FAST FACTS: Albuquerque

Airport   See "Orientation," above.

Area Code   The telephone area code for all of New Mexico is **505,** though at press time plans were rumbling to add new ones in the state.

ATMs   You can find ATMs (also known as *cash pueblos*) all over town, at supermarkets, banks, and drive-throughs.

Business Hours   **Offices** and **stores** are generally open Monday to Friday, 9am to 5pm, with many stores also open Friday night, Saturday, and Sunday in the summer season. Most **banks** are also open Monday to Friday, 9am to 5pm. Some may be open Saturday morning. Most branches have ATMs available 24 hours. Call establishments for specific hours.

Car Rentals   See "Getting Around Northern New Mexico," in chapter 2, or "Getting Around," above.

Climate   See "When to Go," in chapter 2.

Currency Exchange   Foreign currency can be exchanged at any of the branches of **Bank of America** (its main office is at 303 Roma NW; ✆ **505/282-2450**).

Dentists   Call the **Albuquerque District Dental Society,** at ✆ **505/237-1412,** for emergency service.

Doctors   Call the **Greater Albuquerque Medical Association,** at ✆ **505/821-4583,** for information.

Embassies & Consulates   See "Fast Facts: For the International Traveler," in chapter 3.

Emergencies   For police, fire, or ambulance, dial ✆ **911.**

Hospitals   The major hospital facilities are **Presbyterian Hospital,** 1100 Central Ave. SE (✆ **505/841-1234,** or 505/841-1111 for emergency services); and **University of New Mexico Hospital,** 2211 Lomas Blvd. NE (✆ **505/272-2111,** or 505/272-2411 for emergency services).

Hot Lines   The following hot lines are available in Albuquerque: rape crises (✆ **505/266-7711**), poison control (✆ **800/432-6866**), suicide (✆ **505/247-1121**), and UNM Children's Hospital emergency crisis (✆ **505/272-2920**).

Information   See "Visitor Information," under "Orientation," above.

Internet Access **Fedex Kinko's** provides high-speed Internet access at five locations throughout the city. Two convenient ones are 6220 San Mateo Blvd. NE at Academy Boulevard (© **505/821-2222**) and 2706 Central Ave. SE at Princeton Boulevard (© **505/255-9673**).

Library The Albuquerque/Bernalillo County Public Library's **main branch** is at 501 Copper Ave. NW, between Fifth and Sixth streets (© **505/768-5140**). You can find the locations of the 17 other library facilities in the area by checking online at **www.cabq.gov/library**.

Liquor Laws The legal drinking age is 21 throughout New Mexico. Bars may remain open until 2am Monday to Saturday and until midnight on Sunday. Wine, beer, and spirits are sold at licensed supermarkets and liquor stores. It is illegal to transport liquor through most Native American reservations.

Lost Property Contact the city police at © **505/242-COPS**.

Newspapers & Magazines The two daily newspapers are the *Albuquerque Tribune* (© **505/823-7777**; www.abqtrib.com) and the *Albuquerque Journal* (© **505/823-7777**; www.abqjournal.com). You can pick up the *Alibi* (© **505/346-0660**; www.alibi.com), Albuquerque's alternative weekly, for free at newsstands all over town, especially around the University of New Mexico. It offers entertainment listings and alternative views on a variety of subjects.

Pharmacies **Walgreens** has many locations throughout Albuquerque. To find one near you, call © **800-WALGREENS**. Two centrally located ones that are open 24 hours are 8011 Harper Dr. NE at Wyoming (© **505/858-3134**) and 5001 Montgomery Blvd. NE at San Mateo (© **505/881-5210**).

Police For emergencies, call © **911**. For other business, contact the **Albuquerque City Police** (© **505/242-COPS**) or the **New Mexico State Police** (© **505/841-9256**).

Post Offices To find the nearest U.S. Post Office, dial © **800/275-8777**. The service will ask for your zip code and give you the closest post office address and hours.

Radio The local AM station **KKOB** (770) broadcasts news and events. FM band stations include **KUNM** (89.9), the University of New Mexico station, which broadcasts Public Radio programming and a variety of music; **KPEK** (100.3), which plays alternative rock music; and **KHFM** (95.5), which broadcasts classical music.

Taxes In Albuquerque, the sales tax is 5.8125%. An additional hotel tax of 5% will be added to your bill.

Taxis See "Getting Around," above.

Television There are five Albuquerque network affiliates: **KOB-TV** (Channel 4, NBC), **KOAT-TV** (Channel 7, ABC), **KQRE-TV** (Channel 13, CBS), **KASA TV** (Channel 2, FOX), and **KNME-TV** (Channel 5, PBS).

Time As is true throughout New Mexico, Albuquerque is on **Mountain Standard Time**. It's 2 hours earlier than New York, 1 hour earlier than Chicago, and 1 hour later than Los Angeles. Daylight saving time is in effect from early April to late October.

Transit Information **ABQ Ride** is the public bus system. Call ℂ **505/243-7433** for schedules and information.

Useful Telephone Numbers For **road information,** call ℂ **800/432-4269;** and for **emergency road service** (AAA), call ℂ **505/291-6600.**

Weather For **time** and **temperature,** call ℂ **505/247-1611.** To get **weather forecasts** on the Internet, check **www.accuweather.com** and use the Albuquerque zip code, 87104.

3 Where to Stay

Albuquerque's hotel glut is good news for travelers looking for quality rooms at a reasonable cost. Except during peak periods—specifically, the New Mexico Arts and Crafts Fair (late June), the New Mexico State Fair (Sept), and the Albuquerque International Balloon Fiesta (early Oct)—most of the city's hotels have vacant rooms, so guests can frequently request and get lower room rates than the ones posted.

A tax of nearly 11% is added to every hotel bill. All hotels and bed-and-breakfasts listed offer rooms for nonsmokers and travelers with disabilities.

HOTELS/MOTELS
EXPENSIVE

Albuquerque Marriott Pyramid North ✦   About a 15-minute drive from Old Town and downtown, this Aztec pyramid–shaped structure provides decent rooms in an interesting environment. The 10 guest floors are grouped around a hollow skylit atrium. Vines drape from planter boxes on the balconies, and water falls five stories to a pool between the two glass elevators. The rooms, remodeled in 2003, are spacious, though not extraordinary, all with picture windows and ample views. With lots of convention space at the hotel, you're likely to encounter name-tagged conventioneers here. Overall, the service seems to be good enough to handle the crowds, but there are only two elevators, so guests often must wait.

5151 San Francisco Rd. NE, Albuquerque, NM 87109. ℂ **800/228-9290** or 505/821-3333. Fax 505/822-8115. www.marriott.com. 310 units. $139–$184 double; $140–$275 suite. Ask about special weekend and package rates. AE, DC, DISC, MC, V. Free parking. **Amenities:** Restaurant; lounge; indoor/outdoor pool; medium-size health club; Jacuzzi; sauna; concierge; business center; room service; valet laundry. *In room:* A/C, TV, coffeemaker, hair dryer, iron.

Hyatt Regency Albuquerque ✦✦   If you're looking for luxury and want to be right downtown, this is the place to stay. This $60-million hotel, which opened in 1990, is pure shiny gloss and Art Deco. The lobby features a palm-shaded fountain beneath a pyramidal skylight, and throughout the hotel's public areas is an extensive art collection, including original Frederic Remington sculptures. The spacious guest rooms enhance the feeling of richness with mahogany furnishings, full-length mirrors, and views of the mountains. The hotel is located right next door to the Galeria, a shopping area, and has a number of shops itself. McGrath's serves three meals daily in a setting of forest-green upholstery and black-cherry furniture. Bolo Saloon is noted for its whimsical oil paintings depicting "where the deer and the antelope play."

330 Tijeras Ave. NW, Albuquerque, NM 87102. ℂ **800/233-1234** or 505/842-1234. Fax 505/766-6710. www.hyatt.com. 395 units. Weekdays $225 double, weekends $105 double; $335–$435 suite. AE, DC, DISC, MC, V.

Central Albuquerque Accommodations

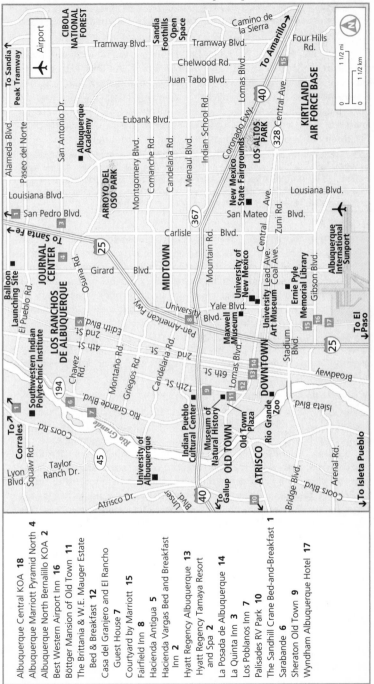

Albuquerque Central KOA **18**
Albuquerque Marriott Pyramid North **4**
Albuquerque North Bernalillo KOA **2**
Best Western Airport Inn **16**
Böttger Mansion of Old Town **11**
The Brittania & W.E. Mauger Estate Bed & Breakfast **12**
Casa del Granjero and El Rancho Guest House **7**
Courtyard by Marriott **15**
Fairfield Inn **8**
Hacienda Antigua **5**
Hacienda Vargas Bed and Breakfast Inn **2**
Hyatt Regency Albuquerque **13**
Hyatt Regency Tamaya Resort and Spa **2**
La Posada de Albuquerque **14**
La Quinta Inn **3**
Los Poblanos Inn **7**
Palisades RV Park **10**
The Sandhill Crane Bed-and-Breakfast **1**
Sarabande **6**
Sheraton Old Town **9**
Wyndham Albuquerque Hotel **17**

235

Self-parking $8, valet $11. **Amenities:** Restaurant; bar; outdoor pool; health club; sauna; concierge; car-rental desk; business center and secretarial services; salon; room service; babysitting; laundry service; dry cleaning. *In room:* A/C, TV, coffeemaker, hair dryer.

Sheraton Old Town ★   No Albuquerque hotel is closer to top tourist attractions than the Sheraton. It's only a 5-minute walk from Old Town Plaza and two important museums. Constructed in 1975, it has undergone an estimated $4-million renovation. The building has mezzanine-level windows lighting the adobe-toned lobby, creating an airiness that carries into the rooms. Request a south-side room, and you'll get a balcony overlooking Old Town and the pool. The medium-size rooms have handcrafted Southwestern furniture.

800 Rio Grande Blvd. NW, Albuquerque, NM 87104. ℂ **800/237-2133** reservations only, or 505/843-6300. Fax 505/842-9863. www.sheraton.com. 188 units. $119–$169 double; $189 suite. Children stay free in parent's room. AE, DC, DISC, MC, V. Free parking. **Amenities:** 2 restaurants; outdoor pool; Jacuzzi; concierge; business center; limited room service; babysitting; valet laundry; same-day dry cleaning; executive-level rooms. *In room:* A/C, TV, pay movies, dataport, minibar, coffeemaker, hair dryer, iron.

MODERATE

Courtyard by Marriott ★   If you don't like high-rises such as the Wyndham Albuquerque Hotel, this is the best selection for airport-area hotels. Opened in 1990, this four-story member of the Marriott family is built around an attractively landscaped courtyard. Families appreciate the security system—access is only by key card between 11pm and 6am—though most of the hotel's clients are business travelers. The units are roomy and comfortable, with walnut furniture and firm beds. Ask for a balcony room on the courtyard.

1920 Yale Blvd. SE, Albuquerque, NM 87106. ℂ **800/321-2211** or 505/843-6600. Fax 505/843-8740. www.marriott.com. 150 units. $71–$107 double. Weekend rates available. AE, DC, DISC, MC, V. Free parking. **Amenities:** Restaurant; lounge; indoor pool; exercise room; Jacuzzi; valet and coin-op laundry. *In room:* A/C, TV, hair dryer, iron.

La Posada de Albuquerque ★   Built in 1939 by Conrad Hilton as the famed hotelier's first inn in his home state of New Mexico, this hostelry on the National Register of Historic Places feels like old Spain. Though remodeled in 1996, it still maintains its historic atmosphere. An elaborate Moorish brass-and-mosaic fountain stands in the center of the tiled lobby, which is surrounded on all sides by high archways, creating the feel of a 19th-century hacienda courtyard. As in the lobby, all guest-room furniture is handcrafted, but here it's covered with Southwestern-style cushions. The more spacious rooms have big windows looking out across the city and toward the mountains. Though the rooms here are fine, they have some of the quirks of an older hotel. But if you want a feel for downtown Albuquerque as well as easy access to the Civic Plaza, nightclubs, and Old Town, this hotel will suit you well. Conrad's Downtown, La Posada's elegantly redesigned restaurant, features Southwestern cuisine from Jane Butel, who has a cooking school on the premises. The Lobby Bar is a favorite gathering place and has entertainment Wednesday through Saturday evenings.

125 Second St. NW (at Copper Ave.), Albuquerque, NM 87102. ℂ **800/777-5732** or 505/242-9090. Fax 505/242-8664. www.laposada-abq.com. 114 units. $89–$115 double; $195–$275 suite. AE, DISC, MC, V. Free parking. **Amenities:** Restaurant; bar; access to nearby health club; room service; dry cleaning/laundry. *In room:* A/C, TV, dataport, coffeemaker, hair dryer, iron.

Wyndham Albuquerque Hotel ★★   This 15-story hotel right at the airport provides spacious rooms with a touch of elegance. The lobby, grill, and lounge areas employ a lot of sandstone, wood, copper, and tile to lend an Anasazi feel, which carries into the rooms, each with a broad view from a balcony. Air travelers enjoy this hotel's location, but because it has good access to freeways and excellent views, it could also be a wise choice for a few days of browsing around Albuquerque. Of course, you will hear some jet noise. The Rojo Grill serves a variety of American and Southwestern dishes.

2910 Yale Blvd. SE, Albuquerque, NM 87106. ℭ **800/227-1117** or 505/843-7000. Fax 505/843-6307. www.wyndham.com. 276 units. $99–$179 double. AE, DC, DISC, MC, V. Free parking. Small pets welcome with prior approval. **Amenities:** Restaurant; outdoor pool; access to golf club; 2 tennis courts; concierge; business center; coin-op laundry. *In room:* A/C, TV, dataport, coffeemaker, hair dryer, iron.

INEXPENSIVE

Best Western Airport Inn   A good choice for a budget stay, the Best Western is just blocks from the airport. The average-size rooms are comfortable and have plenty of amenities. Some have balconies and patios, and deluxe units are equipped with refrigerators. A courtesy van is available 5am to midnight (the hotel will pay for a taxi during odd hours). The Rio Grande Yacht Club Restaurant and Lounge (p. 248) is adjacent to the inn.

2400 Yale Blvd. SE, Albuquerque, NM 87106. ℭ **800/528-1234** or 505/242-7022. Fax 505/243-0620. www.bestwestern.com. 101 units. $63–$102 double. Rates include hot breakfast. AE, DC, DISC, MC, V. Free parking. **Amenities:** Outdoor pool; Jacuzzi. *In room:* A/C, TV, hair dryer, iron.

Fairfield Inn *Value*   Owned by Marriott, this hotel has exceptionally clean rooms and a location with easy access to freeways that can quickly get you to Old Town, downtown, or the heights. Ask for an east-facing room to avoid the noise and a view of the highway. Rooms are medium-size and have medium-size bathrooms. Each has a balcony or terrace. You probably couldn't get more for your money (in a chain hotel) anywhere else.

1760 Menaul Blvd. NE, Albuquerque, NM 87102. ℭ **800/228-2800** or 505/889-4000. Fax 505/872-3094. www.fairfieldinn.com. 188 units. $69 double. Additional person $10. Children 18 and under stay free in parent's room. Free continental breakfast. AE, DC, DISC, MC, V. Free parking. **Amenities:** Indoor/outdoor pool; health club; Jacuzzi; sauna; laundry service. *In room:* A/C, TV.

La Quinta Inn   La Quinta offers reliable, clean rooms at a decent price. Rooms are tastefully decorated, fairly spacious, and comfortable, each with a table and chairs and a shower-only bathroom big enough to move around in. Each king room has a recliner, and two-room suites are available. If you're headed to the Balloon Fiesta, this is a good choice because it's not far from the launch site, though you'll have to reserve as much as a year in advance.

There's another La Quinta near the airport (La Quinta Airport Inn, 2116 Yale Blvd. SE); you can make reservations for either branch at the toll-free number.

5241 San Antonio Dr. NE, Albuquerque, NM 87109. ℭ **800/531-5900** or 505/821-9000. Fax 505/821-2399. www.lq.com. 130 units. $70–$76 double (higher during Balloon Fiesta). Children stay free in parent's room. AE, DC, DISC, MC, V. Free parking. Pets welcome. **Amenities:** Heated outdoor pool open May–Oct. *In room:* A/C, TV, coffeemaker, hair dryer, iron.

BED & BREAKFASTS

The Böttger Mansion of Old Town ★★   This Victorian inn situated right in Old Town offers a sweet taste of a past era. Decorated with antiques but not overdone with chintz, it's an excellent choice. My favorite room is the Carole Rose, with a canopy bed and lots of sun; also lovely is the Rebecca Leah, with pink marble tile and a Jacuzzi tub. All rooms are medium-size and have excellent beds; most have small bathrooms. The rooms facing south let in the most sun but pick up a bit of street noise from nearby Central Avenue and a nearby elementary school (both quiet down at night). Breakfast (such as green-chile quiche) is elaborate enough to keep you going through the day, at the end of which you can enjoy treats from the guest snack bar (try the chocolate cookies with a little chile in them). During warm months the patio is lovely.

110 San Felipe NW, Albuquerque, NM 87104. © **800/758-3639** or 505/243-3639. www.bottger.com. 8 units. $109–$179 double. Rates include full breakfast and snack bar. AE, MC, V. Free parking. **Amenities:** In-room massage. *In room:* A/C, TV/VCR, hair dryer.

The Brittania & W. E. Mauger Estate Bed & Breakfast ★   A restored Queen Anne–style home constructed in 1897, this former residence of wool baron William Mauger is listed on the National Register of Historic Places. Today, it is a wonderfully atmospheric bed-and-breakfast, with high ceilings and elegant decor that ranges from Tuscany to Africa in its sensibility. It's located close to downtown and Old Town, just 5 blocks from the convention center and only 5 miles from the airport. All rooms feature period furnishings and private bathrooms with showers, and one has a balcony. Treats of cheese, wine, and other beverages are offered in the evenings, and a full breakfast is served each morning in indoor and outdoor dining rooms.

701 Roma Ave. NW, Albuquerque, NM 87102. © **800/719-9189** or 505/242-8755. Fax 505/842-8835. www. maugerbb.com. 9 units. $89–$189 double. Additional person $25. Rates include full breakfast and evening refreshments. AE, DC, DISC, MC, V. Free parking. Dogs welcome with prior arrangement for a $30 fee. *In room:* A/C, TV/VCR, dataport, fridge, coffeemaker, hair dryer, iron.

Casa del Granjero and El Rancho Guest House ★   From the pygmy goats to the old restored wagon out front, Casa del Granjero (The Farmer's House) is true to its name. Located about a 15-minute drive north from Old Town, it's quiet and has a rich, homey feeling. Butch and Victoria Farmer have transformed this residence—the original part of which is 120 years old—into a fine bed-and-breakfast. The great room has an enormous sculptured adobe fireplace, comfortable *bancos* (benches) for lounging, a library, and many Southwestern artifacts. There's a 52-inch TV in the den. The guest rooms are beautifully furnished and decorated. Most have fireplaces. The Cuarto del Rey room features Mexican furnishings and handmade quilts and comforters. The Cuarto de Flores has French doors that open onto a portal. The newer guesthouse has comfortable rooms and access to a kitchen, but a less luxurious and Southwestern feel. A full breakfast is served every morning. Catered lunches and dinners are also available by arrangement. Smoking is permitted outdoors only.

414C de Baca Lane NW, Albuquerque, NM 87114. © **800/701-4144** or 505/897-4144. Fax 505/897-9788. www.innewmexico.com. 7 units. $79–$179 double. Additional person $20. Rates include full breakfast. DISC, MC, V. Free parking. Pets accepted with extra fee. **Amenities:** Jacuzzi; sauna; business center; in-room massage; babysitting; laundry service; all units nonsmoking. *In room:* A/C.

Hacienda Antigua ★★ *Finds*   This 200-year-old adobe home was once the first stagecoach stop out of Old Town in Albuquerque. Now, it's one of Albuquerque's most elegant inns. The artistically landscaped courtyard, with its large cottonwood tree and abundance of greenery, offers a welcome respite for tired travelers. The rooms are gracefully and comfortably furnished with antiques. La Capilla, the home's former chapel, is furnished with a queen-size bed, a fireplace, and a carving of St. Francis (the patron saint of the garden). La Sala has a king-size bed and a large Jacuzzi with a view of the Sandia Mountains. All the rooms are equipped with fireplaces and signature soaps. A gourmet breakfast is served in the garden during warm weather and by the fire in winter. The inn is a 20-minute drive from the airport. Light sleepers beware—the Santa Fe Railroad runs by this inn, with one to three trains passing by each night.

6708 Tierra Dr. NW, Albuquerque, NM 87107. ℂ **800/201-2986** or 505/345-5399. Fax 505/345-3855. www.
haciendantigua.com. 8 units. $129–$209 double. Additional person $25. Rates include gourmet breakfast. AE,
MC, V. Free parking. Pets welcome with $30 fee. **Amenities:** Outdoor pool; Jacuzzi. *In room:* A/C, TV/VCR, cof-
feemaker, hair dryer.

Los Poblanos Inn ⭐ Lushness in the desert city of Albuquerque? It's no
mirage. Nestled among century-old cottonwoods, this bed-and-breakfast sits on
25 acres of European-style gardens and peasantlike vegetable and lavender fields.
Notable architect John Gaw Meem built the structure in the 1930s. Each of the
six guest rooms, most arranged around a poetically planted courtyard, has
unique touches such as hand-carved doors, traditional tin fixtures, fireplaces,
and views across the lushly landscaped grounds. At breakfast, you might feast on
walnut-topped French toast and bacon while watching peacocks preen outside
the windows of the very Mexican-feeling, boldly decorated cantina. Light sleepers be aware that the peacocks can be noisy at night.

4803 Rio Grande Blvd. NW, Albuquerque, NM 87107. ℂ **866/344-9297** or 505/344-9297. Fax 505/342-
1302. www.lospoblanos.com. 6 units. $135–$250 double. Rates include full breakfast. AE, MC, V. Free parking. *In room:* A/C, dataport, hair dryer, iron.

Sarabande ⭐ You'll find home-style comfort mixed with elegance at this
bed-and-breakfast situated in the North Valley, a 10-minute drive from Old
Town. Once you pass through the front gate and into the well-tended courtyard
gardens with fountains, you'll forget that you're staying on the fringes of a big
city. With cut-glass windows, lots of pastels, traditional antiques, and thick carpet (in all but the pool-side room), you'll be well pampered here. Innkeepers
Janie and Scott Eggers have filled the home with fine art as well as comfortable
modern furniture. The Rose Room has a Japanese soaking tub and kiva fireplace.
The Iris Room has a stained-glass window depicting irises and a king-size bed.
Both rooms open onto a wisteria-shaded patio where you can eat breakfast in the
morning. Out back are a 50-foot lap pool and a Jacuzzi, and some great walking paths are accessible from the inn. There is a library stocked with magazines
and books, and a cookie jar always full of homemade cookies. Janie serves a full
breakfast either in the courtyard or the dining room.

5637 Rio Grande Blvd. NW, Albuquerque, NM 87107. ℂ **888/506-4923** or 505/345-4923. Fax 505/341-
0654. www.sarabandebb.com. 3 units. $99–$179 double. Rates include full breakfast. AE, DISC, MC, V. Free
parking. **Amenities:** Outdoor pool; Jacuzzi; bike rental; massage by appointment; library; walking paths.
In room: A/C, TV.

NEAR ALBUQUERQUE

Hacienda Vargas Bed and Breakfast Inn ⭐ Unassuming in its elegance,
this bed-and-breakfast feels like an old Mexican hacienda. It sits within the small
town of Algodones (about 20 miles from Albuquerque), a good place to stay if
you're planning to visit both Santa Fe and Albuquerque but don't want to stay
in one of the downtown hotels in either city. There's a real Mexican feel to the
decor, with brightly woven place mats in the breakfast room and Spanish suits
of armor hanging in the common area. Each guest room has a private entrance,
many opening onto a courtyard. All rooms are furnished with New Mexico
antiques, are individually decorated, and have handmade kiva fireplaces. Each of
the four suites has a Jacuzzi tub, fireplace, and private patio. A full breakfast is
served every morning in the dining room. Light sleepers take note: A train passes
near the inn a few times most nights.

El Camino Real (P.O. Box 307), Algodones/Santa Fe, NM 87001. ℂ **800/261-0006** or 505/867-9115. Fax 505/
867-0640. www.haciendavargas.com. 7 units. $89–$179 double. Additional person $15. Rates include full

---

Finds **Cruising Corrales**

If you'd like to travel along meadows and apple orchards into a place where life is a little slower and sweeter, head 15 minutes north of Albuquerque to the village of Corrales. Home to farmers, artists, and affluent land owners, this is a fun place to roam through shops and galleries, and, in the fall, sample vegetables from roadside vendors. Two excellent restaurants, both serving imaginative new American cuisine, sit on the main street. **Indigo Crow** ★★, 4515 Corrales Rd. (© 505/898-7000), serves lunch and dinner Tuesday to Saturday and brunch on Sunday, and Jim White's **Casa Vieja** ★★, 4541 Corrales Rd. (© 505/898-7489), serves dinner nightly.

The town also has a nature preserve and a historic church. In September, the Harvest Festival is well worth the trip. For more information about Corrales, contact Corrales Village (© 505/897-0502; www.corralesnm.org).

To get to the village, head north on either I-25 or Rio Grande Boulevard, turn west on Alameda Boulevard, cross the Rio Grande, and turn north on Corrales Road (NM 448). The village is just a few minutes up the road.

---

breakfast. AE, MC, V. Free parking. Some pets accepted with prior arrangement. **Amenities:** Jacuzzi; room service; in-room massage. *In room:* A/C, hair dryer, iron.

Hyatt Regency Tamaya Resort and Spa ★★★   This is the spot for a get-away-from-it-all luxury vacation. Set in the hills above the lush Rio Grande Valley on the Santa Ana Pueblo, this pueblo-style resort offers a 16,000-square-foot full-service spa and fitness center, an 18-hole Twin Warriors Championship Golf Course designed by Gary Panks, and views of the Sandia Mountains. Rooms are spacious, with large tile bathrooms. Request one that faces the mountains for one of the state's more spectacular vistas. Other rooms look out across a large courtyard, where the pools and hot tub are. Though the resort is surrounded by acres of quiet countryside, it's only 15 minutes from Albuquerque and 45 minutes from Santa Fe. The concierge offers trips to attractions daily, as well as on-site activities such as hot air balloon rides, horseback rides, and nature/cultural walks or carriage rides by the river. Plan at least one dinner at the innovative Corn Maiden (see "Where to Dine," below).

1300 Tuyuna Trail, Santa Ana Pueblo, NM 87004. © **800/55-HYATT** or 505/867-1234. www.hyatt.com. 350 units. May–Oct $200–$350; Nov–Apr $135–$250, depending on the type of room. Suite rates available upon request. Inquire about spa, horseback riding, golf, and family packages. AE, DC, DISC, MC, V. Free parking. From I-25 take exit 242, following US 550 west to Tamaya Blvd.; drive 1½ miles to the resort. **Amenities:** 2 restaurants (p. 249); 2 snack bars; lounge; 3 pools (heated year-round); golf course; 2 tennis courts; health club and spa; children's programs; concierge; tour desk; elaborate business center; room service; laundry; basketball court. *In room:* A/C, TV, dataport, fridge, coffeemaker, hair dryer, iron, safe.

The Sandhill Crane Bed-and-Breakfast ★   This lovely bed-and-breakfast about 20 minutes from Albuquerque in the sleepy little town of Corrales is a good choice if you want to explore the city but don't want to be right downtown. Wisteria-draped walls surround the renovated adobe hacienda, and each room is uniquely decorated in an elegant, traditional Southwestern style. For families or friends traveling together, the two-room suite with kitchenette and connecting bathroom works well. Be aware that this is a home, and with it comes close-quarters coziness; not necessarily the choice for those who like their own out-door entrance. In warmer weather, breakfast is served on the patio, where you're likely to see a roadrunner pass by.

389 Camino Hermosa, Corrales, NM 87048. ✆ **800/375-2445** or 505/898-2445. Fax 505/898-1189. www. sandhillcranebandb.com. 4 units. $90–$160. Rates include full breakfast. AE, MC, V. Free parking. *In room:* A/C, TV/VCR, hair dryer.

RV PARKS

Albuquerque Central KOA   This RV park in the foothills east of Albu-querque is a good choice for those who want to be close to town. It offers lots of amenities and convenient freeway access. Cabins are available.

12400 Skyline Rd. NE, Albuquerque, NM 87123. ✆ **800/562-7781** or 505/296-2729. www.koa.com. $19–$36 tent site; $33–$51 RV site, depending on hook-up; $38–$55 1-room cabin; $48–$65 2-room cabin. All prices valid for up to 2 people. Additional adult $5, child $3. AE, DISC, MC, V. Free parking. Pets welcome. **Amenities:** Outdoor pool (summer only); Jacuzzi; bike rentals; store; coin-op laundry; bathhouse; miniature golf; playground; accessible restroom.

Albuquerque North Bernalillo KOA ✰   More than 1,000 cottonwood and pine trees shade this park, and in the warm months there are many flowers. Located at the foot of the mountains, 14 miles from Albuquerque, this camp-ground has plenty of amenities. Guests enjoy a free pancake breakfast daily. Reservations are recommended. Six camping cabins are also available.

555 Hill Rd., Bernalillo, NM 87004. ✆ **800/562-3616** or 505/867-5227. www.koa.com. $20–$22 tent site; $30–$36 RV site, depending on hook-up; $35 1-bedroom cabin; $45 2-bedroom cabin. Rates include pancake breakfast and are valid for up to 2 people. Additional person $4. Children 5 and under free with parent. AE, DISC, MC, V. Free parking. Pets welcome. **Amenities:** Restaurant; outdoor pool (summer only); store; coin-op laundry; playground; free outdoor movies.

Palisades RV Park   Sitting out on the barren west mesa, this RV park has nice views of the Sandia Mountains and is the closest RV park to Old Town and the Biological Park (10-min. drive; see "Especially for Kids," later in this chap-ter); however, it is also in a fairly desolate setting, with only a few trees about. In midsummer it is hot.

9201 Central Ave. NW, Albuquerque, NM 87121. ✆ **888/922-9595** or 505/831-5000. Fax 505/352-9599. www.palisadesrvpark.com. 110 sites. $27 per day; $110 per week; $250 per month plus electricity. MC, V. Free parking. Pets welcome. **Amenities:** Store; coin-op laundry; reception room; bathhouse; propane.

4 Where to Dine

RESTAURANTS BY CUISINE

AMERICAN
La Hacienda (Old Town, $$, p. 244)
Range Café ✰ (Bernalillo, $$, p. 250)
66 Diner (University/Nob Hill, $, p. 248)

BAKERY
Flying Star Cafe (University/Nob Hill, $, p. 248)

BARBECUE
The County Line ✰ (Northeast, $$, p. 246)

CONTEMPORARY AMERICAN
Jennifer James ✰✰✰ (Northeast, $$$, p. 246)

CONTINENTAL
Artichoke Cafe ✰✰ (Downtown, $$, p. 245)

Key to Abbreviations: $$$$ = Very Expensive $$$ = Expensive $$ = Moderate $ = Inexpensive

High Finance Restaurant and
  Tavern ⭐ (Northeast, $$$,
  p. 245)

DELI/CAFE
Flying Star Cafe (University/Nob
  Hill, $, p. 248)

ECLECTIC
Chef du Jour ⭐ (Old Town, $,
  p. 244)

FRENCH
La Crêpe Michel ⭐⭐ (Old Town,
  $$, p. 242)

GREEK
Olympia Cafe (University/Nob
  Hill, $, p. 248)

INTERNATIONAL
Scalo ⭐ (University/Nob Hill, $$,
  p. 247)

ITALIAN
Scalo ⭐ (University/Nob Hill, $$,
  p. 247)

NEW AMERICAN
Corn Maiden ⭐⭐ (Santa Ana
  Pueblo, $$$, p. 249)
Graze ⭐⭐ (University/Nob Hill,
  $$, p. 247)
Prairie Star ⭐⭐ (Santa Ana
  Pueblo, $$$, p. 250)
Terra ⭐ (Old Town, $$$, p. 242)
Zinc Wine Bar and Bistro ⭐⭐
  (University/Nob Hill, $$$,
  p. 246)

NEW MEXICAN
Duran Central Pharmacy ⭐ (Old
  Town, $, p. 244)
La Hacienda (Old Town, $$,
  p. 244)
Range Café ⭐ (Bernalillo, $$,
  p. 250)
Sadie's ⭐ (Old Town, $, p. 245)

STEAK/SEAFOOD
The County Line ⭐ (Northeast,
  $$, p. 246)
Rio Grande Yacht Club Restaurant
  and Lounge ⭐ (Southeast/
  Airport, $$, p. 248)

IN OR NEAR OLD TOWN
EXPENSIVE
Terra ⭐ NEW AMERICAN   Those who live in Albuquerque's north valley
are overjoyed to finally have fine dining within their midst (at the end of Rio
Grande Blvd., about 15 min. from Old Town). Owner/chef Peter Lukes com-
bines thoughtful flavors with imaginative presentation. The setting is comfort-
able, quiet, and relaxed. An exposed kitchen allows diners to watch the chef in
action. During lunch you can select from sandwiches such as grilled jerk chicken
with Fontana cheese, as well as a variety of salads and heartier entrees. For din-
ner, you might try griddled crab and corn cakes with sweet-pepper sauce, then
move on to pan-seared pork loin with aromatic vegetables and dill corn bread.
Vegetarian entrees are available, as are beer and wine. For dessert try the choco-
late Appaloosa cake.

1119 Alameda NW. ⓒ 505/792-1700. Reservations recommended. Lunch $8–$11; dinner $14–$21. AE,
DISC, MC, V. Tues–Fri 11am–1:30pm; Tues–Sat 5:30–9 or 10pm.

MODERATE
La Crêpe Michel ⭐⭐ FRENCH   For years my father raved about the crepes
at this small cafe tucked away in a secluded walkway not far from the plaza.
Finally, he took me there, and now I understand what all the fuss was about.
Run by chef Claudie Zamet-Wilcox from France, it has a cozy, informal Euro-
pean feel, with checked table coverings and simple furnishings. Service is
friendly and calm, which makes this a good place for a romantic meal. You can't
miss with any of the crepes. The *crêpe aux fruits de mer* (blend of sea scallops,

Central Albuquerque Dining

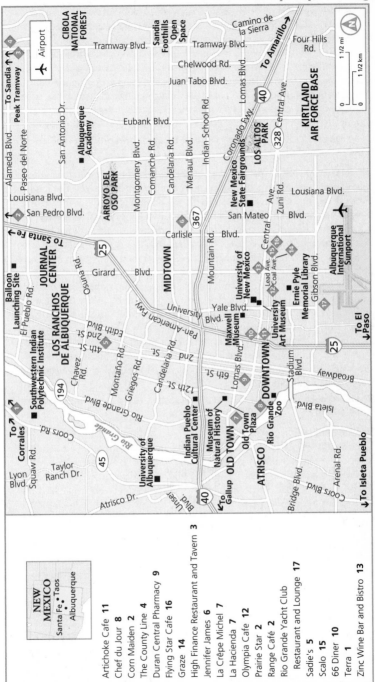

Artichoke Cafe **11**
Chef du Jour **8**
Corn Maiden **2**
The County Line **4**
Duran Central Pharmacy **9**
Flying Star Cafe **16**
Graze **14**
High Finance Restaurant and Tavern **3**
Jennifer James **6**
La Crêpe Michel **7**
La Hacienda **7**
Olympia Cafe **12**
Prairie Star **2**
Range Café **2**
Rio Grande Yacht Club
Restaurant and Lounge **17**
Sadie's **5**
Scalo **15**
66 Diner **10**
Terra **1**
Zinc Wine Bar and Bistro **13**

bay scallops, and shrimp in a velouté sauce with mushrooms) is especially nice, as is the *crêpe à la volaille* (chunks of chicken in a cream sauce with mushrooms and Madeira wine). For a heartier meal, try one of the specials listed on the board on the wall, such as the beef filet (tenderloin finished with either black peppercorn-brandy cream sauce or Roquefort-brandy cream sauce) or the *saumon au poivre vert* (filet of salmon with green peppercorn-brandy sauce). Both are served with vegetables cooked just enough to leave them crisp and tasty. For dessert, don't leave without having a *crêpe aux fraises* (strawberry crepe). To accompany your meal, choose from a carefully planned beer and wine menu.

400 San Felipe C2. ✆ 505/242-1251. Main courses $6–$24. MC, V. Tues–Sun 11:30am–2pm; Thurs–Sat 6–9pm.

La Hacienda NEW MEXICAN/AMERICAN This restaurant, which appeals mostly to tourist traffic, offers more atmosphere than flavor. The food is a muted version of real northern New Mexican cuisine. If you want the real thing, I suggest Duran Central Pharmacy or Sadie's (p. 244 and 245). Still, this place is full of history. It's set in a 100-year-old adobe structure and has been in business for over 70 years. A mural on La Hacienda's outer wall depicts the construction of this Villa de Albuquerque at the turn of the 18th century, and President Clinton ate here during a 1998 visit. Diners enter through a large gift shop. The interior, which has an intimate, laid-back atmosphere, has brightly painted tables and chairs set very close together. In summer, choose the sidewalk dining with a view of the plaza. Most like to start with one of the big margaritas in a variety of flavors, from strawberry to pineapple. The specialty here is the chimichanga, a fried burrito stuffed with *carne adovada* and topped with guacamole and sour cream, tasty but *muy rico* (very rich). The chicken enchilada is also a nice choice. Meals come with chips and salsa and good *sopaipillas*. The servers are friendly but elusive.

302 San Felipe St. NW (at N. Plaza). ✆ 505/243-3131. Reservations recommended for large parties. Lunch $5–$10; dinner $10–$16. AE, DC, DISC, MC, V. Daily 11am–9:30pm.

INEXPENSIVE

● **Chef du Jour** ✸ ECLECTIC This small, quiet, and informal one-room cafe (with a few outdoor tables) serves elegantly prepared food at very reasonable prices. There's an open kitchen along one side and oddly matched tables. Once you get a taste of what's on the menu (which changes every week), you'll be coming back for more. Take special note of the condiments, all of which—from the ketchup to the salsa—are homemade. Recent menu offerings included a smoked chicken quesadilla with barbecue drizzle and a garden burger with smoked gouda cheese. There is also a salad du jour. If you call in advance, the restaurant will fax you a copy of its current menu. Microbrewed beers and hard ciders are available. The restaurant is a little difficult to find; travel south from the plaza, cross Lomas, and find San Pasquale.

119 San Pasquale SW. ✆ 505/247-8998. Reservations recommended. Lunch $3–$9; dinner $6–$20. AE, DISC, MC, V. Mon–Fri 11am–2pm; Fri–Sat 5:30–10pm. Closed Christmas to New Year's Day.

Duran Central Pharmacy ✸ *Finds* NEW MEXICAN Sounds like an odd place to eat, I know. Although you could go to one of the touristy New Mexican restaurants in the middle of Old Town and have lots of atmosphere and mediocre food, you could instead come here, where locals eat, and feast on better, more authentic fare. It's a few blocks up Central, east of Old Town. On your way through the pharmacy, you may want to stock up on specialty soaps; there's a pretty good variety here. The restaurant itself is plain, with a red tile floor and small tables, as well as a counter. For years, I used to come here for a bowl of green-chile stew and a homemade tortilla, which is still an excellent choice. Now I go for the full meals, such as the blue-corn enchilada plate or the huevos rancheros (eggs over corn tortillas, smothered with chile). The menu is short, but you can count on authentic northern New Mexican food. No smoking is permitted.

1815 Central Ave. NW. © **505/247-4141.** Menu items $4.20–$8.10. No credit cards. Mon–Fri 9am–6:30pm; Sat 9am–2pm.

Sadie's ✪ *Kids* NEW MEXICAN   Many New Mexicans lament the lost days when this restaurant was in a bowling alley. In fact, much of my family has refused to go to its new, larger location, fearing that it has lost its good food. Well, it hasn't. Sure, you can no longer hear the pins fall, and the main dining room is a little too big and the atmosphere a little too bright, but something is still drawing crowds: It's the food—simply some of the best in New Mexico, with tasty sauces and large portions. I recommend the enchilada, either chicken or beef. The stuffed *sopaipilla* dinner is also delicious and is one of the signature dishes. All meals come with chips and salsa, beans, and *sopaipillas.* There's a full bar, with excellent margaritas (and TV screens for you sports lovers). A casual atmosphere where kids can be themselves makes this a nice spot for families.

6230 4th St. NW. © **505/345-5339.** Main courses $7–$14. AE, DC, DISC, MC, V. Mon–Sat 11am–10pm; Sun 11am–9pm.

DOWNTOWN
MODERATE
⊘ **Artichoke Cafe** ✪✪ CONTINENTAL   An art gallery as well as a restaurant, this popular spot has modern paintings and sculptures set against azure walls, a hint at the innovative dining experience offered here. Set in three rooms, with dim lighting, this is a nice romantic place. The staff is friendly and efficient, though a little slow on busy nights. I was impressed by the list of special drinks available: a variety of interesting waters that included my favorite, Ame, as well as ginger beer, Jamaican iced coffee, microbrews, and an excellent list of California and French wines. You might start with an artichoke, steamed with three dipping sauces, or have roasted garlic with montrachet goat cheese. For lunch, there are a number of salads and gourmet sandwiches, as well as dishes such as garlic and lime prawns with orzo. Check out the fresh fish specials; my favorite is wahoo on glass noodles with miso broth. From the menu, try the pumpkin ravioli with butternut squash, spinach, and ricotta filling with hazelnut-sage butter sauce.

424 Central Ave. SE. © **505/243-0200.** Reservations recommended. Main courses $7–$12 lunch, $13–$24 dinner. AE, DC, DISC, MC, V. Mon–Fri 11am–2:30pm; Mon 5:30–9pm; Tues–Sat 5:30–10pm; Sun 5–9 pm.

THE NORTHEAST HEIGHTS
EXPENSIVE
High Finance Restaurant and Tavern ✪ CONTINENTAL   People don't rave about the food at this restaurant, but they do rave about the experience of eating here. Set high above Albuquerque, at the top of the Sandia Peak Tramway, it offers a fun and romantic adventure. The decor includes lots of shiny brass and comfortable furniture, and the service is decent. You might start with the sesame-fried calamari, served with greens and Thai dipping sauce. There are a number of pasta dishes, or you can try skillet-roasted ahi tuna served with spicy curry glaze. For meat lovers, there's prime rib or a filet. High Finance has a full bar. The restaurant recommends that you arrive at the Tramway base 45 minutes before your reservation.

40 Tramway Rd. NE (atop Sandia Peak). ⓒ 505/243-9742. www.highfinancerestaurant.com. Reservations requested. Main courses $8–$13 lunch, $15–$45 dinner. Tramway $10 with dinner reservations ($15 without). AE, DC, DISC, MC, V. Summer daily 11am–9pm; winter daily 11am–8pm.

Jennifer James ⭐⭐⭐ CONTEMPORARY AMERICAN Between pale yellow walls accented with bright strokes of red, creating a French bistro feel, this restaurant's namesake serves excellent contemporary American cuisine, with even more panache than she once did in her little Chef du Jour near Old Town (now under new ownership, p. 244). Service is friendly, though not especially efficient, but the food makes up for that lack. Start with roasted butternut-squash soup with chipotle chiles and cilantro. For an entree, I recommend the pan-seared pork with apple bread pudding and herbed Brussels sprouts. The grilled quail over endive and radicchio with pomegranate date chutney is also delicious. A carefully selected wine list complements the menu.

2813 San Mateo NE ⓒ 505/884-3665. Reservations recommended. Main courses $16–$26. AE, DISC, MC, V. Tues–Sat 5–9pm.

MODERATE

The County Line ⭐ *Kids* BARBECUE/STEAKS After visiting the nearby ice-skating rink, my brother and his wife like to take their kids to this restaurant, which has great Southwestern barbecue at very reasonable prices. The place is popular and doesn't take reservations, but if you call before you leave your hotel, they'll put your name on the waiting list; by the time you get there, you'll probably be next in line. If not, you can always wait at the ever-crowded bar. The restaurant is loud and always busy, but it has a spectacular view of the city lights. Its decor is old Route 66, with wagon-wheel furniture, aged license plates, and cowboy-boot lamps. When you finally get a table, you'll be given a Big Chief Writing Tablet menu, then you'll likely get service so good it borders on pushy. We all like the garlic mashed potatoes, and most of us order the baby back ribs, but there's also a mixed platter that includes spicy sausage. The menu also includes grilled fish. A kid's menu, paper, markers, and take-home cups make it a treat for the little ones. If you're not very hungry, you should probably consider going somewhere else.

9600 Tramway Blvd. NE. ⓒ 505/856-7477. Reservations not accepted. Main courses $10–$20. AE, DC, DISC, MC, V. Mon–Thurs 5–8:30pm; Fri–Sat 5–9:30pm; Sun noon–9pm.

UNIVERSITY & NOB HILL
EXPENSIVE

Zinc Wine Bar and Bistro ⭐⭐ NEW AMERICAN In a moody, urban atmosphere with wood floors and a high ceiling, this newest in-place serves imaginative food meticulously prepared. The bi-level dining room with well-spaced tables can get crowded and noisy at peak hours (especially under the balcony, so avoid sitting there then). Service is congenial but inconsistent. Business people and others fill the seats here, dining on such treats as blackened flank steak, Greek salad at lunch (my favorite), or portobello-crusted Alaskan halibut with chorizo sausage polenta at dinner. The restaurant offers other inventive elements, such as "wine flights," in which diners may sample a variety of wines from a particular region for a set and fairly reasonable price. Or, you may simply opt for an excellent martini from the full bar. In the lower level, a lounge serves less formally in a wine cellar atmosphere with live music playing 2 to 3 nights a week (open Mon–Sat 4pm–1am; food served to midnight).

3009 Central Ave. NE. ⓒ 505/254-ZINC. Reservations recommended. Main courses $7.50–$12 lunch, $14–$25 dinner. AE, DC, DISC, MC, V. Sun–Fri 11am–2:30pm; Mon–Thurs 5–10pm; Fri–Sat 5–11pm.

Kids Family-Friendly Restaurants

The County Line (p. 246)   Kids enjoy their own menu and paper and markers at this casual, fun eatery.

Range Café (p. 250)   The fun and funky decor and Taos Cow Ice Cream make this a good spot for kids.

Sadie's (p. 245)   Kids like the quesadillas, tacos, and *sopaipillas* drizzled with honey; parents like the casual atmosphere where kid noise isn't scorned.

66 Diner (p. 248)   A full range of burgers and treats such as root beer floats and hot fudge sundaes will make any kid happy.

MODERATE

Graze ★★ *Finds* NEW AMERICAN   My first trip to this new restaurant not far from the university was with a relative from a small Texas town. The place offers a chance to sample the divine creations of chef Jennifer James without the higher costs at her namesake restaurant (p. 246). My relative looked at the menu and then looked at me with consternation. Be aware that this isn't a chicken-fried-steak kind of place, though I wouldn't be surprised to see some refined version of that on this inventive menu. Set in a minimalist room, with hardwood floors and sunny colored walls, it's a fun spot for a culinary adventure, even for a small-town Texas girl, it turned out. Service is excellent. The portion sizes here are intentionally small, with the notion that diners will order many and share, though they're larger than tapas, so will suffice for a meal for a medium-size appetite. You might try the "piccolo frito," flash-fried calamari, with baby tomatoes, garbanzo beans, and basil, or the grilled tuna, with nori, daikon salad, and nicely sweet ponzu sauce. My relative loved the penne tossed with sun-dried tomatoes, New Mexico goat cheese, and chorizo sausage. A nice selection of beers and wines accompanies the menu, and inventive desserts appear daily.

3128 Central Ave. SE. ✆ 505/268-4729. Reservations recommended on weekend nights. Individual plates $6–$20. AE, DISC, MC, V. Tues–Sat 11am–11pm.

Scalo ★ INTERNATIONAL/ITALIAN   This Italian restaurant is a local favorite, but over the years frequent chef turnover has made it less reliable than it once was, and the service varies greatly as well. The place has a simple, bistro-style elegance, with white-linen-clothed tables indoors, plus outdoor tables in a covered, temperature-controlled patio. The kitchen, which makes its own pasta and breads, has recently moved to a more international menu and offers meals in small, medium, and large portions. Seasonal menus focus on New Mexico–grown produce. One signature dish is a risotto-fried calamari with a spicy marinara sauce. A hearty main dish is the double-cut pork chop with champagne-roasted peaches, kale, and fried shallots. The daily specials are big hits. Dessert selections change daily. There's a good wine list, from which you can sample 30 wines by the glass; or you may order from the full bar.

3500 Central Ave. SE. ✆ 505/255-8781. Reservations recommended. Lunch $6–$12; dinner $8–$26. AE, DC, DISC, MC, V. Tues–Thurs 11:30am–10pm; Fri 11:30am–11pm; Sat 5–11pm; Sun 5–10pm.

INEXPENSIVE

Flying Star Cafe CAFE/BAKERY   The new Flying Star Cafe makes good on its promise of uptown food with down-home ingredients. This restaurant, with four locations, has actually been around Albuquerque awhile, under the moniker Double Rainbow, but it's been renamed and revamped into a more hip and urban restaurant with excellent contemporary international food. Beware: During meal-time the university location gets packed and rowdy. The selections range broadly, from 16 different breakfast options to homemade soups and salads to sandwiches and pasta (and pizza at the Juan Tabo and Rio Grande locations). Try the Rancher's melt (New Zealand sirloin sautéed with green chile, provolone, and horseradish on sourdough), or the Buddha's bowl (sautéed vegetables in ginger sauce with tofu over jasmine rice). Flying Star also has locations at 4501 Juan Tabo Blvd. NE (✆ **505/275-8311**); 8001 Menaul Blvd. NE (✆ **505/293-6911**); and 4026 Rio Grande Blvd. NW (✆ **505/344-6714**). They don't serve alcohol, but they do brew up plenty of espresso and cappuccino. Though hours vary for each location, they are all open daily for breakfast, lunch, and dinner.

3416 Central Ave. SE. ✆ **505/255-6633**. Reservations not accepted. All menu items under $10. AE, DISC, MC, V. Daily 6am–11pm.

Olympia Cafe GREEK   Ask any northern New Mexico resident where they go for Greek food, and the hands-down favorite is Olympia. It's very informal (you order at a counter), it's right across from the university, and diners eat there at all times of day. It has a lively atmosphere, with bursts of enthusiastic Greek chatter emanating from the kitchen. With a full carryout menu, it's also a great place to grab a meal on the run. I like to get the Greek salad, served with fresh pita bread, and white-bean soup. A standard is the falafel sandwich with tahini. The restaurant is well known for its gyros, and I hear the moussaka is excellent. For dessert try the baklava.

2210 Central Ave. SE. ✆ **505/266-5222**. Menu items $2–$12. DISC, MC, V. Mon–Fri 11am–10pm.

● **66 Diner** *Kids* AMERICAN   Like a trip back in time to the days when Martin Milner and George Maharis got "their kicks on Route 66," this thoroughly 1950s-style diner comes complete with Seeburg jukebox and full-service soda fountain. The white caps make great green-chile cheeseburgers, along with meatloaf sandwiches, grilled liver and onions, and chicken-fried steaks. Ham-and-egg and pancake breakfasts are served on weekends. Beer and wine are available. Comfy booths they can squirm around in and their own menu will please the kids.

1405 Central Ave. NE. ✆ **505/247-1421**. Menu items $3–$8. AE, DC, DISC, MC, V. Mon–Thurs 11am–11pm; Fri 11am–midnight; Sat 8am–midnight; Sun 8am–10pm.

SOUTHEAST, NEAR THE AIRPORT

Rio Grande Yacht Club Restaurant and Lounge ✿ SEAFOOD   This fes-tive restaurant serves decent seafood and steaks. Red, white, and blue sails hang beneath the skylight of a large room dominated by a tropical garden. The lunch menu features burgers, sandwiches, salads, and a few New Mexican specialties. At dinner, however, fresh fish is the main attraction. Snapper, sea scallops, ahi tuna, fresh oysters, and other denizens of the deep are prepared broiled, poached, black-ened, teriyaki, Vera Cruz, au gratin, mornay, stuffed, and more. You get to select how you want your fish prepared; however, I suggest asking the chef for the best cooking style to suit your fish. If you'd rather have something else, the chef also prepares certified Angus beef, shrimp, Alaskan king crab, several chicken dishes,

Moments Route 66 Revisited: Rediscovering New Mexico's Stretch of the Mother Road

As the old Bobby Troupe hit suggests: Get your kicks on Route 66. The highway that once stretched from Chicago to California was hailed as the road to freedom. During the Great Depression, it was the way west for farmers escaping Dust Bowl poverty out on the plains. If you found yourself in a rut in the late 1940s and 1950s, all you had to do was hop in the car and head west on Route 66.

Of course, the road existed long before it gained such widespread fascination. Built in the late 1920s and paved in 1937, it was the lifeblood of communities in eight states. Nowadays, however, US 66 is as elusive as the fantasies that once carried hundreds of thousands west in search of a better life. Replaced by other roads, covered up by interstates (mostly I-40), and just plain out of use, Route 66 still exists in New Mexico, but you'll have to do a little searching and take some extra time to find it.

Motorists driving west from Texas can take a spin (make that a slow spin) on a 20-mile gravel stretch of the original highway running from Glenrio (Texas) to San Jon. From San Jon to Tucumcari, you can enjoy nearly 24 continuous paved miles of vintage 66. In Tucumcari, the historic route sliced through the center of town along what is now Tucumcari Boulevard. Santa Rosa's Will Rogers Drive is that city's 4-mile claim to the Mother Road. In Albuquerque, US 66 follows Central Avenue for 18 miles, from the 1936 State Fairgrounds, past original 1930s motels and the historic Nob Hill district, on west through downtown.

One of the best spots to pretend you are a 1950s road warrior crossing the desert—whizzing past rattlesnakes, tepees, and tumbleweeds—is along NM 124, which winds 25 miles from Mesita to Acoma in northwestern New Mexico. You can next pick up old Route 66 in Grants, along the 6-mile Santa Fe Avenue. In Gallup, a 9-mile segment of US 66 is lined with restaurants and hotels reminiscent of the city's days as a western film capital from 1929 to 1964. Just outside Gallup, the historic route continues west to the Arizona border as NM 118.

For more information about Route 66, contact the **Grants/Cíbola County Chamber of Commerce** (② 800/748-2142) or the **New Mexico Department of Tourism** (② 800/545-2040).

and even barbecued baby back pork ribs. The bar here is a good place for evening drinks. You'll hobnob with flight crews and sample such delicacies as smoked trout and *lahvosh* (Armenian cracker bread covered with havarti and Parmesan, baked until bubbly). Don't leave without sharing an Aspen snowball (vanilla ice cream rolled in walnuts and covered in hot fudge).

2500 Yale Blvd. SE. ② 505/243-6111. Reservations recommended at dinner. Main courses $6–$12 lunch, $13–$41 dinner. AE, DC, DISC, MC, V. Mon–Fri 11am–2pm; Fri–Sat 5–11pm; Sun–Thurs 5–10pm.

OUTSIDE ALBUQUERQUE

Corn Maiden ☆☆ NEW AMERICAN   Plan a sunset dinner at this new restaurant at the Hyatt Tamaya, north of town. You'll feast not only on delicious innovative cuisine, but also on one of the best views in New Mexico. Set in the Rio Grande valley, with banks of windows looking out on the Sandia Mountains, this restaurant has a comfortably subdued decor wrapped around an open kitchen. The offerings will likely please conventional as well as adventurous palates. Served with your bread is a tasty Southwestern tapenade made with napolito cactus. For an appetizer you might try the seared blue lump crab cake. For an entree, the big favorite is the rotisserie—an interesting combination of meats and seafood. You'll also find an excellent filet mignon with sautéed mushrooms or a veal tenderloin with white asparagus. Dessert brings a dazzling display of confections as lively to look at as to taste. Wine lovers have their pick of a broad range of labels.

In the Hyatt Regency Tamaya Resort and Spa, 1300 Tuyana Trail, Santa Ana Pueblo. © 505/867-1234. Reservations recommended. Main courses $30–$40. AE, DC, DISC, MC, V. Tues–Sat 5:30–10pm. From I-25 take exit 242, following US 550 west to Tamaya Blvd.; drive 1½ miles to the resort.

Prairie Star ★★ NEW AMERICAN   Located on the Santa Ana Pueblo, about 30 minutes north of Albuquerque, and set in a sprawling adobe home with a marvelous view across the high plains and a golf course, this restaurant offers an interesting blend of old and new, both in terms of atmosphere and flavor. It was built in the 1940s in Mission architectural style. Exposed vigas and full *latilla* ceilings, as well as hand-carved fireplaces and *bancos,* complement the thick adobe walls. There is a lounge at the top of the circular stairway. Diners can start with wild-mushroom bruschetta, with kalamata-olive tampenade and goat chevre. Signature dishes include Chama Valley lamb chops with caramelized apple torte and white asparagus (delicious), and soy-grilled quail with wasabi potatoes and Asian shrimp mousse. An extensive wine list with more than 30 flavors by the glass tops out the menu, as do special desserts, which vary nightly.

288 Prairie Star Rd., Santa Ana Pueblo. © 505/867-3327. Reservations recommended. Main courses $17–$33. AE, DC, DISC, MC, V. Tues–Sun 5:30–9pm (lounge opens at 4:30pm).

Range Café ★ *Kids* NEW MEXICAN/AMERICAN   This cafe on the main drag of Bernalillo, about 15 minutes north of Albuquerque, is a perfect place to stop on your way out of town. Housed in what was once an old drugstore, the restaurant has a pressed tin ceiling and is decorated with Western touches, such as cowboy boots and whimsical art. The food ranges from enchiladas and burritos to chicken-fried steak to more elegantly prepared meals. The proprietors and chef here have come from such notable restaurants as Scalo in Albuquerque (p. 247) and Prairie Star at Santa Ana Pueblo (p. 250), so you can count on great food. For breakfast, try the pancakes or the breakfast burrito. For lunch or dinner, I recommend Tom's meatloaf, served with roasted-garlic mashed potatoes, mushroom gravy, and sautéed vegetables. For dinner, you might try pan-seared trout with sun-dried tomato and caper butter sauce. Taos Cow ice cream is the order for dessert, or try the baked goods and specialty drinks from the full bar. No smoking is permitted. In the same locale, the Range has opened the Lizard Rodeo Lounge, a smoke-free, hoppin' place with Wild West decor that offers live music many nights a week. There's also a retail space that sells local art and New Mexico wines. Two other branches of the restaurant in Albuquerque have similar food offerings (4200 Wyoming Blvd. NE, © **505/293-2633;** and 2200 Menaul Blvd. NE, © **505/888-1660**).

925 Camino del Pueblo (P.O. Box 1780), Bernalillo. © 505/867-1700. Reservations accepted for 8 or more. Breakfast and lunch $4–$9; dinner $9–$20. AE, DISC, MC, V. Summer Sun–Thurs 7:30am–10pm; winter Sun–Thurs 7:30am–9:30pm; a half-hour later on Fri and Sat. Closed Thanksgiving and Christmas.

5 What to See & Do

Albuquerque's original town site, known today as Old Town, is the central point of interest for visitors. Here, grouped around the plaza, are the venerable Church of San Felipe de Neri and numerous restaurants, art galleries, and crafts shops. Several important museums are situated close by. Within a few blocks are the 25,000-square-foot Albuquerque Aquarium and the 50-acre Rio Grande Botanic Garden (near Central Ave. and Tingley Dr. NW), both well worth a visit.

But don't get stuck in Old Town. Elsewhere you will find the Sandia Peak Tramway, the University of New Mexico with its museums, and a number of natural attractions. Within day-trip range are several pueblos and significant monuments (see "Exploring Nearby Pueblos & Monuments," later in this chapter).

THE TOP ATTRACTIONS

Albuquerque Museum of Art and History ★ *(Kids)* Take an interesting journey down into the caverns of New Mexico's past in this museum on the outskirts of Old Town. Drawing on the largest U.S. collection of Spanish colonial artifacts, displays here include Don Quixote–style helmets, swords, and horse armor. You can wander through an 18th-century house compound with adobe floor and walls, and see gear used by *vaqueros,* the original cowboys who came to the area in the 16th century. A weaving exhibition allows kids to try spinning wool, and a trapping section provides them with pelts to touch. In an old-style theater, two films on Albuquerque history are shown. In the History Hopscotch area, kids can explore an old trunk or play with antique blocks and other toys. An Old Town walking tour originates here at 11am Tuesday to Sunday during spring, summer, and fall. The upper floors house permanent art collections and, best of all, a huge exhibit space where you'll find some extraordinary shows. A gift shop sells books and jewelry and has a nice selection of Navajo dolls.

2000 Mountain Rd. NW. ⓒ 505/243-7255. www.albuquerquemuseum.com. Admission $4 adults, $2 seniors 65 and older and children 4–12. Tues–Sun 9am–5pm. Closed major holidays.

Indian Pueblo Cultural Center ★ *(Kids)* Owned and operated as a nonprofit organization by the 19 pueblos of New Mexico, this is a fine place to begin an exploration of Native American culture. Located about a mile northeast of Old Town, this museum—modeled after Pueblo Bonito, a spectacular 9th-century ruin in Chaco Culture National Historic Park—consists of several parts.

Begin your exploration in the basement, where a permanent exhibit depicts the **evolution of the various pueblos** from prehistory to present, including displays of the distinctive handcrafts of each community. Note especially how pottery differs in concept and design from pueblo to pueblo. You'll also find a small screening room where you can see films of some of New Mexico's most noted Native American artists making their wares, including San Ildefonso potter María Martinez (p. 147), firing her pottery with open flames.

The **Pueblo House Children's Museum,** located in a separate building, is a hands-on experience that gives children the opportunity to learn about and understand the evolution of Pueblo culture. There they can touch pot shards, play with *heishi* (shell) drills, and even don fox tails and dance.

Upstairs in the main building is an enormous (10,000-sq.-ft.) **gift shop** featuring fine pottery, rugs, sand paintings, kachinas, drums, and jewelry, among other things. Southwestern clothing and souvenirs are also available. Prices here are quite reasonable.

Every weekend throughout the year, **Native American dancers** perform at 11am and 2pm in an outdoor arena surrounded by original murals. Often, artisans demonstrate their crafts there as well. During certain weeks of the year, such as the Balloon Fiesta, dances are performed daily.

A restaurant serves traditional Native American foods. I wouldn't eat a full meal here, but it's a good place for some Indian fry bread and a bowl of *posole*.

2401 12th St. NW. ② 800/766-4405 or 505/843-7270. www.indianpueblo.org. Admission $4 adults, $3 seniors, $1 students, free for children 4 and under. AE, DISC, MC, V. Daily 9am–4:30pm; restaurant 8am–3pm. Closed New Year's Day, Memorial Day, July 4, Labor Day, Thanksgiving, and Christmas.

National Hispanic Cultural Center 🐝 Located in the historic Barelas neighborhood on the Camino Real, this gem of Albuquerque museums offers a rich cultural journey through hundreds of years of history and across the globe. It explores Hispanic arts and lifeways with visual arts, drama, music, dance, and other programs. I most enjoyed the 11,000-square-foot gallery space, which exhibits exciting contemporary and traditional works. Look for photographs by Miguel Gandert. An exciting 2004 exhibit was *Corridos Sin Fronteras*, which recreates the historical development of the *corrida* (a song portraying an adventure) in Mexico and the southwestern U.S. A restaurant offers New Mexican and American food. It's a good spot to sample authentic regional dishes such as tacos and enchiladas either from a buffet or by ordering from the menu. My favorite is the tortilla burger (a burger served in a flour tortilla, with all the fixin's). Plans are to incorporate a cultural cooking component into the center, which would allow visitors to sample Hispanic foods from all over the world.

1701 4th St. SW (Corner of 4th St. and Avenida Cesar Chavez). ② 505/246-2261. Fax 505/246-2613. www. nhccnm.org. Admission Tues–Sat $3 adults, $2 seniors 60 and over, free for children 16 and under; Sun $1 adults and seniors. AE, DISC, MC, V. Tues–Sun 10am–5pm; restaurant 8am–3pm. Closed New Year's Day, Easter, Memorial Day, Labor Day, and Christmas.

Old Town 🐝🐝 A maze of cobbled courtyard walkways leads to hidden patios and gardens, where many of Old Town's 150 galleries and shops are located. Adobe buildings, many refurbished in the pueblo revival style of the 1950s, are grouped around the tree-shaded plaza, created in 1780. Pueblo and Navajo artisans often display their pottery, blankets, and silver jewelry on the sidewalks lining the plaza.

The buildings of Old Town once served as mercantile shops, grocery stores, and government offices, but the importance of Old Town as Albuquerque's commercial center declined after 1880, when the railroad came through 1¼ miles east of the plaza and businesses relocated to be closer to the trains. Old Town clung to its historical and sentimental roots, but the quarter fell into disrepair until the 1930s and 1940s, when artisans and other shop owners rediscovered it and the tourism industry burgeoned.

When Albuquerque was established in 1706, the first building erected by the settlers was the **Church of San Felipe de Neri,** which faces the plaza on its north side. It's a cozy church with wonderful stained-glass windows and vivid *retablos* (religious paintings). This house of worship has been in almost continuous use for nearly 300 years.

Though you'll wade through a few trinket and T-shirt shops on the plaza, don't be fooled: Old Town is an excellent place to shop. Look for good buys from the Native Americans selling jewelry on the plaza, especially silver bracelets and strung turquoise. If you want to take something fun home and spend very little, buy a dyed corn necklace. Your best bet when wandering around Old

Central Albuquerque Attractions

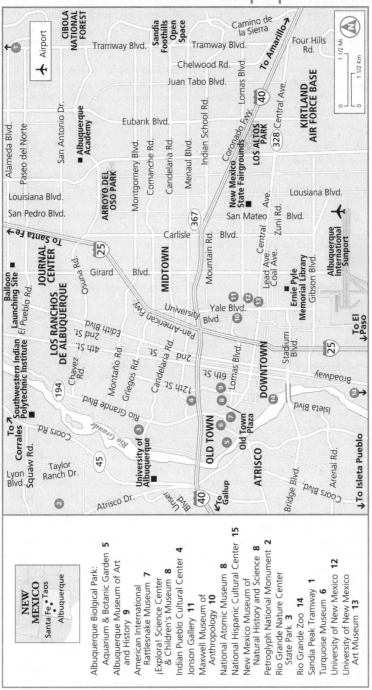

NEW MEXICO
Santa Fe • Taos
• Albuquerque

Albuquerque Biolgical Park:
  Aquarium & Botanic Garden **5**
Albuquerque Museum of Art
  and History **9**
American International
  Rattlesnake Museum **7**
¡Exploral Science Center
  & Children's Museum **8**
Indian Pueblo Cultural Center **4**
Jonson Gallery **11**
Maxwell Museum of
  Anthropology **10**
National Atomic Museum **8**
National Hispanic Cultural Center **15**
New Mexico Museum of
  Natural History and Science **8**
Petroglyph National Monument **2**
Rio Grande Nature Center
  State Park **3**
Rio Grande Zoo **14**
Sandia Peak Tramway **1**
Turquoise Museum **6**
University of New Mexico **12**
University of New Mexico
  Art Museum **13**

Town is to just peek into shops, but there are a few places you'll definitely want to spend time. See "Shopping," later in this chapter, for a list of recommendations. An excellent Old Town historic walking tour originates at the Albuquerque Museum of Art and History (see above) at 11am Tuesday to Sunday during spring, summer, and fall. Plan to spend 2 to 3 hours strolling around.

Northeast of Central Ave. and Rio Grande Blvd. NW. Old Town Visitor Center: 303 Romero St. NW, Albuquerque, NM 87104 (across the street from the Church of San Felipe de Neri). © **505/243-3215.** Visitor Center daily 9am–5pm summer; daily 9:30am–4:30pm rest of the year.

● **Sandia Peak Tramway** *(Kids)* ★★ This fun and exciting half-day or evening outing allows incredible views of the Albuquerque landscape and wildlife. The Sandia Peak Tram is a "jigback"; in other words, as one car approaches the top, the other nears the bottom. The two pass halfway through the trip, in the midst of a 1½-mile "clear span" of unsupported cable between the second tower and the upper terminal.

Several hiking trails are available on Sandia Peak, and one of them—La Luz Trail—takes you on a steep and rigorous trek from the base to the summit. The views in all directions are extraordinary. *Note:* The trails on Sandia may not be suitable for children. There is a popular and expensive restaurant, High Finance Restaurant and Tavern, at Sandia's summit (see "Where to Dine," earlier in this chapter). Special tram rates apply with dinner reservations. Be aware that the tram does not operate on very windy days.

10 Tramway Loop NE. © **505/856-7325.** Fax 505/856-6335. www.sandiapeak.com. Admission $15 adults, $12 seniors, $10 children 5–12, free for children under 5. Memorial Day to Labor Day daily 9am–9pm; spring and fall Thurs–Tues 9am–8pm, Wed 5–8pm; ski season Thurs–Tues 9am–8pm, Wed noon–8pm. Closed 2 weeks each spring and fall for maintenance; check the website for details. Parking $1 daily. AE, DISC, MC, V. To reach the base of the tram, take I-25 north to Tramway Rd. (exit 234), then proceed east about 5 miles on Tramway Rd. (NM 556); or take Tramway Blvd., exit 167 (NM 556), north of I-40 approximately 8½ miles.

OTHER ATTRACTIONS

National Atomic Museum   "I am become death, the shatterer of worlds." Shortly after the successful detonation of the first atomic bomb, Robert Oppenheimer, who headed the Manhattan Project, said this, quoting from ancient Hindu texts. This and other valuable information highlight the 51-minute film *Ten Seconds That Shook the World,* which is shown daily (throughout the day) at this museum, an experience worth fitting into a busy schedule. The museum itself offers the next-best introduction to the nuclear age after the Bradbury Science Museum in Los Alamos, making for an interesting 1- to 2-hour perusal. It traces the history of nuclear-weapons development, beginning with the top-secret Manhattan Project of the 1940s, including a copy of the letter Albert Einstein wrote to President Franklin D. Roosevelt suggesting the possible need to beat the Germans at creating an atomic bomb—a letter that surprisingly went ignored for nearly 2 years. You'll find a permanent Marie Curie exhibit in the lobby and full-scale models of the "Fat Man" and "Little Boy" bombs, as well as displays and films on the peaceful application of nuclear technology—including nuclear medicine—and other alternative energy sources.

1905 Mountain Rd. NW (P.O. Box 5800, MS1490). © **505/245-2137.** Fax 505/242-4537. www.atomicmuseum. com. Admission $4 adults, $3 seniors and children 7–18, free for children 6 and under. Children under 12 not admitted without adult. Group rates available. Daily 9am–5pm. Closed New Year's Day, Easter, Thanksgiving, and Christmas.

Petroglyph National Monument ★ *(Kids)*   These lava flows were once a hunting and gathering area for prehistoric Native Americans, who left a chronicle of their beliefs etched on the dark basalt boulders. Some 25,000 petroglyphs provide a nice outdoor adventure after a morning in a museum. You'll want to stop at the visitor center to get a map, check out the interactive computer, and, in summer, hook up with a ranger-led tour. From there, you can drive north to the Boca Negra area, where you'll have a choice of three trails. Take the Mesa Point Trail (30 min.) that climbs quickly up the side of a hill, offering many petroglyph sightings as well as an outstanding view of the Sandia Mountains. If you're traveling with your dog, you can bring her along on the Rinconada Trail. Hikers can have fun searching the rocks for more petroglyphs; there are many yet to be found. This trail (located a few miles south of the visitor center) runs for miles around a huge *rincon* (corner) at the base of the lava flow. Camping is not permitted in the park; it's strictly for day use, with picnic areas, drinking water, and restrooms provided.

6001 Unser Blvd. NW (3 miles north of I-40 at Unser and Western Trail). © 505/899-0205. Fax 505/899-0207. www.nps.gov/petr. Admission $1 per vehicle weekdays, $2 weekends. DISC, MC, V. Visitor Center and Boca Negra area daily 8am–5pm. Closed New Year's Day, Thanksgiving, and Christmas.

● **Turquoise Museum** *Kids*   Don't be put off by the setting of this little gem of a museum in a strip mall west of Old Town. For those with curiosity, it's a real find that's been featured in *Smithsonian Magazine* and on *60 Minutes*. The passion of father and son Joe P. Lowry and Joe Dan Lowry, it contains "the world's largest collection of turquoise"—from 60 mines around the world. You start through a tunnel, where turquoise is embedded in the walls, and move on to exhibits that present the blue stone's geology, history, and mythology. You'll see maps showing where turquoise is mined, ranging from Egypt to Kingman, Arizona, and find out how to determine whether the turquoise you're hoping to buy is quality or not. Lowry, Sr., will fill in any details and even tell you more about turquoise you're wearing. There's also a real lapidary shop; jewelry made there is sold in a gift shop that's open until 5pm. If you're lucky, one of Lowry's grandkids will tell a joke like this one she told me: What do you call a sleeping bull? A bulldozer. Plan to spend about 1 hour here.

2107 Central Ave. NW. © 505/247-8650. Admission $4 adults, $3 children 7–17 and seniors 60 and over, free for children 6 and under, $10 family rate. AE, DISC, MC, V. Mon–Sat 10am–4pm.

University of New Mexico   The state's largest institution of higher learning stretches across an attractive 70-acre campus about 2 miles east of downtown Albuquerque, north of Central Avenue and east of University Boulevard. The five campus museums, none of which charges admission, are constructed (like other UNM buildings) in a modified pueblo style. Popejoy Hall, in the south-central part of the campus, hosts many performing-arts presentations, including those of the New Mexico Symphony Orchestra; other public events are held in nearby Keller Hall and Woodward Hall.

I've found the best way to see the museums and campus is on a walking tour, which can make for a nice 2- to 3-hour morning or afternoon outing. Begin on the west side of campus at the Maxwell Museum of Anthropology. You'll find parking meters there, as well as Maxwell Museum parking, for which you can get a permit inside.

The **Maxwell Museum of Anthropology,** situated on the west side of the campus on Redondo Drive, south of Las Lomas Road (© **505/277-4404;** www.unm.edu/~maxwell), is an internationally acclaimed repository of Southwestern anthropological finds. What's really intriguing here is not just the ancient pottery, tools, and yucca weavings, but the anthropological context within which these items are set. You'll see a reconstruction of an archaeological site, complete with string markers, brushes, and field notes, as well as microscope lenses you can examine to see how archaeologists perform temper analysis to find out where pots were made, and pollen analysis to help reconstruct past environments. There are two permanent exhibits: *Ancestors,* which looks at human evolution, and *People of the Southwest,* a look at the history of the Southwest from 10,000 years ago to the 16th century from an archeological perspective. It's open Tuesday to Friday 9am to 4pm, and Saturday 10am to 4pm; the museum is closed Sundays, Mondays, and holidays. From the Maxwell, walk east into the campus until you come to the Duck Pond and pass Mitchell Hall; then turn south (right) and walk down a lane until you reach Northrup Hall.

In **Northrup Hall** (© 505/277-4204), about halfway between the Maxwell Museum and Popejoy Hall in the southern part of the campus, the adjacent **Geology Museum** (© 505/277-4204) and **Meteorite Museum** (© 505/277-1644) cover the gamut of recorded time from dinosaur bones to moon rocks. Within the Geology Museum, you'll see stones that create spectacular works of art, from black-on-white orbicular granite to brilliant blue dioptase. In the Meteorite Museum, 550 meteorite specimens comprise the sixth-largest collection in the United States. You'll see and touch a sink-size piece of a meteorite that weighs as much as a car, as well as samples of the many variations of stones that fall from the sky. Both museums are open Monday to Friday 9am to 4pm.

From here, you walk east, straight through a mall that takes you by the art building to the Fine Arts Center. The **University of New Mexico Art Museum** (© 505/277-4001; http://unmartmuseum.unm.edu) is located here, just north of Central Avenue and Cornell Street. The museum features changing exhibitions of 19th- and 20th-century art. Its permanent collection includes Old Masters paintings and sculpture, significant New Mexico artists, Spanish-colonial artwork, the Tamarind Lithography Archives, and one of the largest university-owned photography collections in the country. This is my favorite part. You'll see modern and contemporary works, and some striking images that you'll remember for years. It's open Tuesday to Friday 9am to 4pm, Tuesday evening 5 to 8pm, and Sunday 1 to 4pm; the museum is closed holidays. A gift shop offers a variety of gifts and posters. Admission is free.

Cooking School

If you've fallen in love with New Mexican and Southwestern cooking during your stay (or if you did even before you arrived), you might like to sign up for cooking classes with Jane Butel, a leading Southwest cooking authority, author of 14 cookbooks, and host of the national TV show *Jane Butel's Southwestern Kitchen.* At **Jane Butel Cooking School** ☆, 125 Second St. NW (La Posada de Albuquerque; © 800/472-8229 or 505/243-2622; fax 505/243-8296; www.janebutel.com), you'll learn the history and techniques of Southwestern cuisine and have ample opportunity for hands-on preparation. If you choose the week-long session, you'll start by learning about chiles and move on to native breads and dishes, appetizers, beverages, and desserts. Weekend sessions and special vegetarian sessions are also available, as are some sessions that include "culinary tours," including trips to Taos and Santa Fe. Call, fax, or check out Jane's website for current schedules and fees.

By now you'll probably want a break. Across the mall to the north is the Student Union Building, where you can get treats from muffins to pizza. Campus maps can be obtained here, along with directions. Once you're refreshed, head out the north door of the Student Union Building and walk west through Smith Plaza, then turn north by the bus stop and walk to Las Lomas Road, where you'll turn right and walk a half block to the intimate **Jonson Gallery,** at 1909 Las Lomas Rd. NE (𝄐 **505/277-4967;** www.unm.edu/~jonsong), on the north side of the central campus. This museum displays more than 2,000 works by the late Raymond Jonson, a leading modernist painter in early-20th-century New Mexico, as well as works by contemporary artists. This is my least favorite of the campus museums; if you're going to miss one, make it this one. The gallery is open Tuesday to Friday 9am to 4pm and Tuesday evening 5 to 8pm. From the Jonson you can walk west on Las Lomas Road to Redondo Road, where you'll turn south and arrive back at the Maxwell Museum, where your car is parked. Touring these museums takes a full morning or afternoon.

1 University Hill NE (north of Central Ave.). 𝄐 **505/277-0111.** www.unm.edu.

6 Especially for Kids

Albuquerque Biological Park: Aquarium and Botanic Garden ⚡ *Kids*
For those of us born and raised in the desert, this attraction quenches years of soul thirst. The self-guided aquarium tour begins with a beautifully produced 9-minute film that describes the course of the Rio Grande from its origin to the Gulf Coast. Then, you'll move on to the touch pool, where at certain times of day you can gently touch hermit crabs and starfish. You'll pass by a replica of a salt marsh, where a gentle tidal wave moves in and out, and you'll explore the eel tank, an arched aquarium you get to walk through. There's a colorful coral-reef exhibit, as well as the culminating show, in a 285,000-gallon shark tank, where many species of fish and 15 to 20 sand-tiger, brown, and nurse sharks swim around, looking ominous.

Within a state-of-the-art 10,000-square-foot conservatory, you'll find the botanical garden, split into two sections. The smaller one houses the desert collection and features plants from the lower Chihuahuan and Sonoran deserts, including unique species from Baja, California. The larger pavilion exhibits the Mediterranean collection and includes many exotic species native to the Mediterranean climates of southern California, South Africa, Australia, and the Mediterranean Basin. Allow at least 2 hours to see both parks. There is a restaurant on the premises.

In December, you can see the "River of Lights Holiday Light Display" Tuesday through Sunday; and June through August you can attend Thursday evening concerts.

2601 Central Ave. NW. 𝄐 **505/764-6200.** www.cabq.gov/biopark. Admission $7 adults ($10 with Rio Grande Zoo admission), $3 seniors 65 and over and children 12 and under ($5 with Rio Grande Zoo admission). Ticket sales stop a half-hour before closing. MC, V. Tues–Sun 9am–5pm (June–Aug Sat–Sun until 6pm) Closed New Year's Day, Thanksgiving, and Christmas.

American International Rattlesnake Museum *Finds* *Kids* This unique museum, located just off Old Town Plaza, has living specimens of common, uncommon, and very rare rattlesnakes of North, Central, and South America in naturally landscaped habitats. Oddities such as albino and patternless rattlesnakes are included, as is a display popular with youngsters: baby rattlesnakes. More than 30 species can be seen, followed by a 7-minute film on this contributor to

Kids   **In Search of Disneyland**

If you want to occupy the kids for a day, there are two decent options, though don't expect Disneyland. **Cliff's Amusement Park,** 4800 Osuna Rd. NE (© **505/881-9373;** www.cliffs.net), has roller coasters, including the daring "Galaxy," a waterpark with some fun get-wet rides, and an arcade. Gate entrance is $2.50; ride passes run $18 for kids 48 inches tall and under and $19 for those over 48 inches; individual ride tickets $2. **The Beach Waterpark,** 1600 Desert Surf Loop NE (© **505/345-6066;** www.beachwaterpark.com), offers a variety of attractions, including a 700,000-gallon wave pool, a quarter-mile "Lazy River," a children's play area, two inner-tube slides, and five body slides. Prices run $8 for those 4 years and older; $5 for seniors 62 and older; free for kids 3 and under. Both parks are open spring through fall, and both get crowded.

the ecological balance of our hemisphere. Throughout the museum are rattlesnake artifacts from early American history, Native American culture, medicine, the arts, and advertising. You'll also find a gift shop that specializes in Native American jewelry, T-shirts, and other memorabilia related to the natural world and the Southwest, all with an emphasis on rattlesnakes.

202 San Felipe St. NW. © **505/242-6569.** www.rattlesnakes.com. Admission $2.50 adults, $2 seniors, $1.50 children. AE, DISC, MC, V. Mon–Sat 10am–6pm; Sun noon–5pm.

¡Explora! Science Center and Children's Museum *Kids*   As a center for lifelong learning, ¡Explora! houses more than 250 hands-on scientific exhibits for visitors of all ages on topics as diverse as water, the Rio Grande, light and optics, biological perception, and energy. It features exhibits utilizing technology that is creatively accessible to the public and exhibits that engage visitors in creating all kinds of art.

1701 Mountain Rd. NW. © **505/224-8300.** Fax 505/224-8325. www.explora.mus.nm.us. Admission $7 adults ages 12–64, $5 seniors 65 and over and children 1–11, free for children under 1. Mon–Sat 10am–6pm; Sun noon–6pm.

New Mexico Museum of Natural History and Science ★★ *Kids*   A trip through this museum will take you through 12 billion years of natural history, from the formation of the universe to the present day. Begin by looking at a display of stones and gems, then stroll through the "Age of Giants" display, where you'll find dinosaur skeletons cast from the real bones. Moving along, you come into the Cretaceous Period and learn of the progression of flooding in the southwestern United States, beginning 100 million years ago and continuing until 66 million years ago, when New Mexico became dry. This exhibit takes you through a tropical oasis, with aquariums of alligator gars, fish that were here 100 million years ago and still exist today. Next, step into the Evolator (kids love this!), a simulated time-travel ride that moves and rumbles, taking you 1¼ miles (2km) up (or down) and through 38 million years of history. Then, you'll feel the air grow hot as you walk into a cave and see the inner workings of a volcano, including simulated magma flow. Soon, you'll find yourself in the age of the mammoths and moving through the ice age. Other stops along the way include the Naturalist Center, where kids can peek through microscopes and make their own bear or raccoon footprints in sand, and FossilWorks, where paleontologists work behind glass, excavating bones of a seismosaurus. Be sure to check out the newest addition to the museum, the LodeStar Astronomy Center, a sophisticated planetarium with the Virtual Voyages Simulation theater. Those exhibits, as well as the DynaTheater, which surrounds you with images and sound, cost an additional fee. A gift shop on the ground floor sells imaginative nature games and other curios. This museum has good access for people with disabilities, including scripts for people with impaired hearing and exhibit text written in Braille.

1801 Mountain Rd. NW. ✆ **505/841-2800.** www.nmmnh-abq.mus.nm.us/nmmnh. Admission $5 adults, $4 seniors, $2 children 3–12, free for children under 3. DynaTheater, Planetarium, and Virtual Voyages cost extra, with prices in the $6 range adults and $3 range children. Buying ticket combinations qualifies you for discounts. Daily 9am–5pm. Jan and Sept closed on Mon except major holidays, when it's open Mon; also closed Thanksgiving and Christmas.

Rio Grande Nature Center *Kids*   Whenever I'm in Albuquerque and want to get away from it all, I come here. The center, located just a few miles north of Old Town, spans 270 acres of riverside forest and meadows that include stands of 100-year-old cottonwoods and a 3-acre pond. Located on the Rio Grande Flyway, an important migratory route for many birds, it's an excellent place to see sandhill cranes, Canadian geese, and quail—more than 260 bird species have made this their temporary or permanent home. In a protected area where dogs aren't allowed (you can bring dogs on most of the 2 miles of trails), you'll find exhibits of native grasses, wildflowers, and herbs. Inside a building built half above and half below ground, you can sit next to the pond in a glassed-in viewing area and comfortably watch ducks and other birds in their avian antics. There are 21 self-guided interpretive exhibits as well as photo exhibits, a library, a small nature store, and a children's resource room. On Saturday mornings you can join a guided nature walk. Other weekend programs are available for adults and children, including nature photography and bird- and wildflower-identification classes. Call for a schedule.

2901 Candelaria Rd. NW. ✆ **505/344-7240.** Fax 505/344-4505. www.frgnc.org. Admission $1 adults, 50¢ children 6–16, free for children under 6. DISC, MC, V. Daily 10am–5pm; store Mon–Fri 11am–3pm, Sat–Sun 10am–4pm. Closed New Year's Day, Thanksgiving, and Christmas.

Rio Grande Zoo 🐾 *Kids*   More than 1,200 animals from 300 species live on 60 acres of riverside bosque among ancient cottonwoods. Open-moat exhibits with animals in naturalized habitats are a treat for zoo-goers. Major exhibits include polar bears, giraffes, sea lions (with underwater viewing), the cat walk, the bird show, and ape country, with gorillas and orangutans. The zoo has an especially fine collection of elephants, mountain lions, koalas, reptiles, and native Southwestern species. A children's petting zoo is open during the summer. There are numerous snack bars on the zoo grounds, and La Ventana Gift Shop carries film and souvenirs. Also check out the seal and sea lion feeding at 10:30am and 3:30pm daily and the summer Zoo Music Concert Series.

903 10th St. SW. ✆ **505/764-6200.** www.cabq.gov/biopark/zoo. Admission $7 adults ($10 with Aquarium and Botanic Garden admission), $3 seniors and children 3–12 ($5 with Aquarium and Botanic Garden admission), free for children 2 and under. Daily 9am–4:30pm (6pm summer weekends). Closed New Year's Day, Thanksgiving, and Christmas.

7 Outdoor Activities

BALLOONING

Visitors have a choice of several hot-air balloon operators; rates start at about $135 per person per hour. Call **Rainbow Ryders,** 11520 San Bernardino NE

(© 505/823-1111), or **World Balloon Corporation,** 1103 La Poblana NW (© 505/293-6800).

If you'd rather just watch, go to the annual **Albuquerque International Balloon Fiesta** 🎈🎈, which is held the first through second weekends of October (see "Frommer's Favorite Northern New Mexico Experiences," in chapter 1, and "Northern New Mexico Calendar of Events," in chapter 2, for details).

BIKING

Albuquerque is a major bicycling hub in the summer, for both road racers and mountain bikers. For an excellent map of Albuquerque bicycle routes, call the **Albuquerque Parks & Recreation Department** at © 505/768-3550 or visit **www.cabq.gov**, click on "Interactive Maps (GIS)," and then click on "Bike Paths." You can also find links to many recreation opportunities for adults and kids at **www.cabq.gov/visiting.htm**. A great place to bike is **Sandia Peak** (© 505/242-9133; www.sandiapeak.com) in Cíbola National Forest. You can't take your bike on the tram, but chairlift no. 1 is available for up- or downhill transportation with a bike. Bike rentals are available at the top and bottom of the chairlift. They cost $38 for adult bikes and $28 for junior ones. The lift costs $14 and runs on Saturday and Sunday, with Friday added in July and August, though you'll want to call to be sure. Helmets are mandatory. Bike maps are available; the clearly marked trails range from easy to very difficult.

Down in the valley, there's a **bosque trail** that runs along the Rio Grande, accessed through the Rio Grande Nature Center (see "Especially for Kids," above). To the east, the **Foothills Trail** runs along the base of the mountains. It's a fun 7-mile-long trail that offers excellent views. Access it by driving east from downtown on Montgomery Boulevard, past the intersection with Tramway Boulevard. Go left on Glenwood Hills Drive and head north about ½ mile before turning right onto a short road that leads to the Embudito trail head.

Northeast Cyclery, 8305 Menaul Blvd. NE (© 505/299-1210) rents bikes at the rate of $25 per day for front suspension mountain bikes and $35 per day for road bikes. Multiday discounts are available. Unfortunately, the shop doesn't rent children's bikes. Rentals come with helmets.

BIRD-WATCHING

Bosque del Apache National Wildlife Refuge 🐦🐦 (© 505/835-1828) is a haven for migratory waterfowl such as snow geese and cranes. It's located 90 miles south of Albuquerque on I-25, and it's well worth the drive. You'll find 7,000 acres of carefully managed riparian habitat, which include marshlands, meadows, agricultural fields, and old-growth cottonwood forests lining the Rio Grande. Particularly if you're here from November through March, the experience is thrilling, not only because of the variety of birds—more than 300 species—but for the sheer numbers of them. Huge clouds of snow geese and sandhill cranes take flight at dawn and dusk, the air filling with the sounds of their calls and wing flaps. In early December, the refuge may harbor as many as 45,000 snow geese, 57,000 ducks of many different species, and 18,000 sandhill cranes. You may even be fortunate enough—as I was on my last visit—to see a whooping crane or two. There are also plenty of raptors about, including numerous red-tailed hawks and northern harriers (or marsh hawks), Cooper's hawks and kestrels, and even bald and golden eagles. The refuge has a 15-mile auto-tour loop, which you should drive very slowly. Closer to town, check out the **Rio Grande Nature Center** (see "Especially for Kids," above).

FISHING

There are no real fishing opportunities in Albuquerque as such, but there is a nearby fishing area known as **Shady Lakes** (© 505/898-2568). Nestled among cottonwood trees, it's located near I-25 on Albuquerque's north side. The most common catches are rainbow trout, black bass, bluegill, and channel catfish. To reach Shady Lakes, take I-25 north to the Tramway exit. Follow Tramway Road west for a mile and then go right on NM 313 for ½ mile. **Sandia Lakes Recreational Area** (© 505/897-3971), also located on NM 313, is another popular fishing spot. There is a bait and tackle shop there.

GOLF

There are quite a few public courses in the Albuquerque area. The **Championship Golf Course at the University of New Mexico,** 3601 University Blvd. SE (© 505/277-4546), is one of the best in the Southwest and was rated one of the country's top 25 public links by *Golf Digest.* **Paradise Hills Golf Course,** 10035 Country Club Lane NW (© 505/898-7001), is a popular 18-hole golf course on the west side of town.

Other Albuquerque courses to check with for tee times are **Ladera,** 3401 Ladera Dr. NW (© 505/836-4449); **Los Altos,** 9717 Copper Ave. NE (© 505/298-1897); **Puerto del Sol,** 1800 Girard Blvd. SE (© 505/265-5636); and **Arroyo del Oso,** 7001 Osuna Rd. NE (© 505/884-7505).

If you're willing to drive a short distance just outside Albuquerque, you can play at the **Santa Ana Golf Club at Santa Ana Pueblo,** 288 Prairie Star Rd., Bernalillo, 87004 (© 505/867-9464), which was rated by the *New York Times* as one of the best public golf courses in the country. Club rentals are available (call for information). In addition, **Isleta Pueblo,** 4001 Hwy. 47 (© 505/869-0950), south of Albuquerque, has an 18-hole course.

HIKING

The 1½-million-acre **Cíbola National Forest** offers ample hiking opportunities. Within town, the best hike is the **Embudito Trail,** which heads up into the foothills, with spectacular views down across Albuquerque. The 5.5-mile one-way hike is moderate to difficult. Allow 1 to 8 hours, depending on how far you want to go. Access it by driving east from downtown on Montgomery Boulevard past the intersection with Tramway Boulevard. Go left on Glenwood Hills Drive and head north about .5 mile before turning right onto a short road that leads to the trail head. The premier Sandia Mountain hike is **La Luz Trail,** a very strenuous journey from the Sandia foothills to the top of the Crest. It's a 15-mile round-trip jaunt, and it's half that if you take the Sandia Peak Tramway (see "The Top Attractions," earlier in this chapter) either up or down. Allow a full day for this hike. Access is off Tramway Boulevard and Forest Service Road 333. For more details contact **Sandia Ranger Station,** Highway 337 south toward Tijeras (© 505/281-3304).

HORSEBACK RIDING

Sometimes I just have to get in a saddle and eat some trail dust. If you get similar hankerings, call the **Hyatt Regency Tamaya Resort and Spa,** 1300 Tuyuna Trail, Santa Ana Pueblo (© 505/771-6037). The resort offers 2½-hour-long rides near the Rio Grande for $60 per person. Children must be over 7 years of age and over 4 feet tall. The resort is located about 15 miles north of Albuquerque. From I-25 take exit 242, following US 550 west to Tamaya Boulevard, and drive 1½ miles to the resort.

Getting Pampered: The Spa Scene

If you're looking to get pampered, you have a few options. **Mark Prado Salon & Spa** (© 800/363-7115) offers treatments at four locations: 1100 Juan Tabo Blvd. NE (© 505/298-2983), 8001 Wyoming Blvd. NE (© 505/856-7700), 3500 Central Ave. SE 7-B (© 505/266-2400), and Cottonwood Mall, 10,000 Coors Blvd. NE (© 505/897-2288).

Albuquerque's most luxurious spa experience is at the **Hyatt Regency Tamaya Resort & Spa,** 1300 Tuyuna Trail, Santa Ana Pueblo (© 505/867-1234). A vast array of treatments, and a sauna and steam room, are available in a refined atmosphere set near the Rio Grande, 15 minutes north of Albuquerque, near the village of Bernalillo.

RIVER RAFTING

This sport is generally practiced farther north, in the area surrounding Santa Fe and Taos; however, Albuquerque is the home of **Wolf Whitewater,** 4626 Palo Alto SE (© 505/262-1099; www.wolfwhitewater.com), one of the best rafting companies in the region. (See chapter 7 for more details.)

SKIING

The **Sandia Peak Ski Area** is a good place for family skiing. There are plenty of beginner and intermediate runs. (However, if you're looking for more challenge or more variety, you'd better head north to Santa Fe or Taos.) The ski area has twin base-to-summit chairlifts to its upper slopes at 10,360 feet and a 1,700-foot vertical drop. There are 30 runs (35% beginner, 55% intermediate, 10% advanced) above the day lodge and ski-rental shop. Four chairs and two pomas accommodate 3,400 skiers an hour. All-day lift tickets are $38 for adults, $33 for teens ages 13 to 20, $29 for children ages 6 to 12 and seniors (ages 62–71), and free for children 46 inches tall or less in ski boots and seniors ages 72 and over; rental packages are available. The season runs mid-December to mid-March. Contact the ski area, 10 Tramway Loop NE (© 505/242-9133), for more information, or call the hot line for ski conditions (© 505/857-8977).

Cross-country skiers can enjoy the trails of the Sandia Wilderness from the ski area, or they can go an hour north to the remote Jemez Wilderness and its hot springs.

TENNIS

Albuquerque has 29 public parks with tennis courts. Because of the city's size, your best bet is to call the **Albuquerque Convention and Visitors Bureau** (© 800/284-2282) to find out which park is closest to your hotel.

8 Spectator Sports

BASEBALL

The **Albuquerque Isotopes** play 72 home games as part of the Pacific Coast League in their new stadium, Isotopes Park. Tickets range in price from $5 to $10. For information, contact © 505/924-2255; www.albuquerquebaseball. com. Isotopes Park is located at 1601 Avenida Cesar Chavez SE. Take I-25 south of town to Avenida Cesar Chavez and go east; the stadium is at the intersection of Avenida Cesar Chavez and University Boulevard.

BASKETBALL

The University of New Mexico team, **"The Lobos,"** plays an average of 16 home games from late November to early March. Capacity crowds cheer the team at the 17,121-seat University Arena (fondly called "The Pit") at University and Stadium boulevards. The arena was the site of the NCAA championship tournament in 1983. For tickets and information call ℭ **505/925-Lobo** (www. golobos.com).

FOOTBALL

The **UNM Lobos** football team plays a September-to-November season, usually with five home games, at the 30,000-seat University of New Mexico Stadium, opposite both Albuquerque Sports Stadium and University Arena at University and Stadium boulevards. For tickets and information call ℭ **505/925-Lobo** (www.golobos.com).

HOCKEY

The **New Mexico Scorpions** play in the Western Professional Hockey League. Their home is at **Tingley Coliseum,** New Mexico State Fairgrounds, Central Avenue and Louisiana Boulevard (ℭ **505/881-7825;** www.scorpions hockey.com).

HORSE RACING

The **Downs at Albuquerque Racetrack and Casino,** New Mexico State Fairgrounds (ℭ **505/266-5555** for post times; www.abqdowns.com), is near Lomas and Louisiana boulevards NE. Racing and betting—on thoroughbreds and quarter horses—take place on weekends from April to July and during the State Fair in September. The Downs has a glass-enclosed grandstand and exclusive club seating. General admission is free. Seasonal live horse racing takes place March through June and during the New Mexico State Fair. Simulcast racing happens year-round daily. The 300-slot casino is open daily noon to midnight, with a buffet for $5 to $8.

9 Shopping

Visitors seeking regional specialties will find many **local artists** and **galleries** of interest in Albuquerque, although not as many as in Santa Fe and Taos. The galleries and regional fashion designers around the plaza in Old Town comprise a kind of a shopping center for travelers, with more than 40 merchants represented. The Sandia Pueblo runs its own **crafts market** at the reservation, off I-25 at Tramway Road, just beyond Albuquerque's northern city limits.

Albuquerque has three of the largest **shopping malls** in New Mexico, two within 2 blocks of each other on Louisiana Boulevard just north of I-40— Coronado Center and Winrock Center. The other is the Cottonwood Mall on the west mesa, at 10000 Coors Blvd. NW (ℭ **505/899-SHOP**).

Business hours vary, but shops are generally open Monday to Saturday 10am to 6pm; many have extended hours; some have reduced hours; and a few, especially in shopping malls or during the high tourist season, are open on Sunday.

In Albuquerque the sales tax is 5.8125%.

BEST BUYS

The best buys in Albuquerque are Southwestern regional items, including **arts and crafts** of all kinds—traditional Native American and Hispanic as well as contemporary works. In local Native American art, look for silver and turquoise jewelry, pottery, weavings, baskets, sand paintings, and Hopi kachina dolls. Hispanic folk art—hand-crafted furniture, tinwork and *retablos,* and religious paintings—is worth seeking out. The best contemporary art is in paintings, sculpture, jewelry, ceramics, and fiber art, including weaving.

Other items of potential interest are Southwestern fashions, gourmet foods, and unique local Native American and Hispanic creations.

By far the most **galleries** are in Old Town; others are spread around the city, with smaller groupings in the university district and the northeast heights. Consult the brochure published by the **Albuquerque Gallery Association,** *A Select Guide to Albuquerque Galleries,* or Wingspread Communications's annual *The Collector's Guide to Albuquerque,* widely distributed at shops. Once a month, usually from 5 to 9pm on the third Friday, the **Albuquerque Art Business Association** (✆ **505/244-0362** for information) sponsors an ArtsCrawl to dozens of galleries and studios. It's a great way to meet the artists.

You'll find some interesting shops in the Nob Hill area, which is just west of the University of New Mexico and has an Art Deco feel.

Following are some shopping recommendations for the greater Albuquerque area.

ARTS & CRAFTS

● **Amapola Gallery** ⭐ Fifty artists and craftspeople show their talents at this lovely cooperative gallery off a cobbled courtyard. You'll find pottery, paintings, textiles, carvings, baskets, jewelry, and other items. 206 Romero St. ✆ **505/242-4311.**

● **Bien Mur Indian Market Center** ⭐ Sandia Pueblo's crafts market, on the reservation, sells turquoise and silver jewelry, pottery, baskets, kachina dolls, hand-woven rugs, sand paintings, and other arts and crafts. The market is open Monday through Saturday from 9am to 5:30pm and Sunday from 11am to 5pm. I-25 at Tramway Rd. NE. ✆ **800/365-5400** or 505/821-5400.

Dartmouth Street Gallery ⭐ This gallery features vapor mirage works of Larry Bell, tapestries by Nancy Kozikowski, and a variety of work by 40 other contemporary artists, most from New Mexico. 3011 Monte Vista NE. ✆ **800/474-7751** or 505/266-7751. www.dsg-art.com.

Gallery One This gallery features folk art, jewelry, contemporary crafts, cards and paper, and natural-fiber clothing. In the Nob Hill Shopping Center, 3500 Central Ave. SE. ✆ **505/268-7449.**

Hispaniae in Old Town ⭐ *Finds* Day of the Dead people and Frida Kahlo faces greet you at this wild shop with everything from kitschy Mexican tableware to fine Oaxacan woodcarvings. 410 Romero St. NW. ✆ **505/244-1533.**

La Piñata This shop features—what else?—piñatas, in shapes from dinosaurs to parrots to pigs, as well as paper flowers, puppets, toys, and crushable bolero hats decorated with ribbons. No. 2 Patio Market (Old Town). ✆ **505/242-2400.**

Outback Shopping

While cruising the remote desert lands between Albuquerque and Santa Fe, you may want to stop in at **Traditions! A Festival Marketplace,** on I-25, exit 257 (✆ **505/867-9700**). The open-air mall offers shoppers the chance to sample many forms of New Mexico culture, from art to jewelry to food to entertainment. It's open daily 10am to 8pm.

A Taste of the Grape

In addition to everything else New Mexico has to offer, wineries seem to be springing up all over the state. Call to find out about their wine-tasting hours. Wineries in Albuquerque or within a short driving distance of the city include **Anderson Valley Vineyards,** 4920 Rio Grande Blvd. NW, Albuquerque 87107 (© **505/344-7266**); **Sandia Shadows Vineyard and Winery,** 11704 Coronado NE, Albuquerque 87122 (© **505/ 856-1006;** www.sandiawines.com); and **Gruet Winery,** 8400 Pan-American Hwy. NE, Albuquerque 87113 (© **505/821-0055;** www.gruetwinery. com).

Mariposa Gallery ★★ *Value*   Eclectic contemporary art, jewelry, blown glass, and sculpture fill this Nob Hill shop, with prices that even a travel writer can afford. In the Nob Hill Shopping Center, 3500 Central Ave. SE. © **505/268-6828.**

Ortega's Indian Arts and Crafts   An institution in Gallup, adjacent to the Navajo Reservation, Ortega's now has this Albuquerque store. It sells, repairs, and appraises silver and turquoise jewelry. 6600 Menaul Blvd. NE, no. 359. © **505/881-1231.**

The Pueblo Loft (at Gallery One)   Owner Kitty Trask takes pride in the fact that all items featured at The Pueblo Loft are crafted by Native Americans. For almost 15 years, her slogan has been, "Every purchase is an American Indian work of art." In the Nob Hill Shopping Center, 3500 Central Ave. SE. © **505/268-8764.**

R. C. Gorman Nizhoni Gallery Old Town ★   The painting and sculpture of famed Navajo artist Gorman, a resident of Taos, are shown here. Most works are available in limited-edition lithographs. 323 Romero NW, Suite 1. © **505/843-7666.**

Schelu Gallery ★★   Inventive pottery you'll want to use in your kitchen as well as bold textiles present a sojourn in color in this Old Town shop. 306 San Felipe NW. © **800/234-7985** or 505/765-5869.

Skip Maisel's *Value*   If you want a real bargain in Native American arts and crafts, this is the place to shop. You'll find a broad range of quality and price here in goods such as pottery, weavings, and kachinas. *Take note:* Adorning the outside of the store are murals painted in 1933 by notable Navajo painter Harrison Begay and Pueblo painter Pablita Velarde. 510 Central Ave. SW. © **505/242-6526.**

Tanner Chaney Galleries ★   In business since 1875, this gallery has fine jewelry, pottery, rugs, and more. 323 Romero NW, no. 4 (Old Town). © **800/444-2242** or 505/247-2242.

Weyrich Gallery (Rare Vision Art Galerie)   Contemporary paintings, sculpture, textiles, jewelry, and ceramics by regional and non-regional artists are exhibited at this spacious midtown gallery. 2935-D Louisiana Blvd. at Candelaria Rd. © **505/883-7410.**

Wright's Collection of Indian Art   This gallery, first opened in 1907, features a free private museum and carries fine handmade Native American arts and crafts, both contemporary and traditional. 1100 San Mateo Blvd. NE. © **505/266-0120.**

BOOKS

Barnes & Noble   On the west side, just north of Cottonwood Mall, this huge bookstore offers plenty of browsing room and a Starbucks Cafe for lounging. The store is known for its large children's section and weekly story-time readings. 3701 Ellison Dr. NW #A. ✆ **505/792-4234.** Or at the Coronado Center, 6600 Menaul Blvd. NE. ✆ **505/883-8200.**

Bookworks ✯   This store, selling both new and used books, has one of the most complete Southwestern nonfiction and fiction sections in the region. A good place to linger, the store has a coffee bar and a stage area for readings. It also carries CDs, cassettes, and books on tape. 4022 Rio Grande Blvd. NW. ✆ **505/344-8139.**

Borders   This branch of the popular chain provides a broad range of books, music, and videos, and hosts in-store appearances by authors, musicians, and artists. Winrock Center, 2100 Louisiana Blvd. NE. ✆ **505/884-7711.**

FOOD

The Candy Lady   Having made chocolate for over 20 years, The Candy Lady is especially known for 21 varieties of fudge, including jalapeño flavor. 524 Romero NW (Old Town). ✆ **800/214-7731** or 505/243-6239.

La Mexicana   This is a great place to go shopping if you're a diehard fan of Mexican food. Many items at La Mexicana are imported directly from Mexico, and others, such as tortillas, tamales, and Mexican pastries, are made fresh daily. 423 Atlantic Ave. SW. ✆ **505/243-0391.**

Rocky Mountain Chocolate Factory   Old-fashioned candy is made right before your eyes. All chocolates are handmade. 380 Coronado Center. ✆ **800/658-6151** or 505/888-3399.

FURNITURE

Ernest Thompson Furniture ✯   Original-design, handcrafted furniture is exhibited in the factory showroom. Thompson is a fifth-generation furniture maker who still uses traditional production techniques. 4531 Osuna Rd. NE (¼ block west of I-25 and ½ block north of Osuna Rd.). ✆ **800/568-2344** or 505/344-1994.

Strictly Southwestern   You'll find nice, solid pine and oak Southwestern-style furniture here. Lighting, art, pottery, and other interior items are also available. 1321 Eubank Blvd. NE. ✆ **505/292-7337.**

GIFTS/SOUVENIRS

Jackalope International ✯✯   Wandering through this vast shopping area is like an adventure to another land—to many lands, really. You'll find Mexican *trasteros* (armoires) next to Balinese puppets. The store sells sculpture, pottery, and Christmas ornaments as well. 834 US 550, Bernalillo. ✆ **505/867-9813.**

MARKETS

Flea Market   Every Saturday and Sunday, year-round, the fairgrounds host this market from 8am to 5pm. It's a great place to browse for turquoise and silver jewelry and locally made crafts, as well as newly manufactured inexpensive goods such as socks and T-shirts. The place takes on a fair atmosphere, with the smell of cotton candy filling the air. There's no admission charge. New Mexico State Fairgrounds. For information call the Albuquerque Convention and Visitors Bureau, ✆ **800/284-2282.**

SOUTHWESTERN APPAREL

Albuquerque Pendleton   Cuddle up in a large selection of blankets and shawls, and haul them away in a handbag. 1100 San Mateo NE, Suites 2 and 4. © 505/255-6444.

Western Warehouse   Family Western wear, including an enormous collection of boots, is retailed here. This store claims to have the largest selection of work wear and work boots in New Mexico (8,000 pairs of boots altogether). 6210 San Mateo Blvd. NE. © 505/883-7161.

10 Albuquerque After Dark

Albuquerque has an active performing-arts and nightlife scene, as befits a city of half a million people. As also befits this area, the performing arts are multicultural, with Hispanic and (to a lesser extent) Native American productions sharing stage space with Anglo works, including theater, opera, symphony, and dance. Albuquerque also attracts many national touring companies. Nightclubs cover the gamut, with rock, jazz, and country predominant.

Complete information on all major cultural events can be obtained from the **Albuquerque Convention and Visitors Bureau** (© 800/284-2282 for recorded information after 5pm). Current listings appear in the two daily newspapers; detailed weekend arts calendars can be found in the Thursday evening *Tribune* and the Friday morning *Journal.* The monthly *On the Scene* also carries entertainment listings.

Tickets for nearly all major entertainment and sporting events can be obtained from **Ticketmaster,** 4004 Carlisle Blvd. NE (© 505/883-7800). Discount tickets are often available for midweek and matinee performances; check with individual theater or concert hall box offices.

THE PERFORMING ARTS
CLASSICAL MUSIC

Chamber Orchestra of Albuquerque   This 32-member professional orchestra performs from October to June, primarily at St. John's United Methodist Church, 2626 Arizona St. NE. There is a subscription series of seven classical concerts. The orchestra features guest artists of national and international renown. 2730 San Pedro Dr. NE, Suite H-23. © 505/881-0844. http://coa.aosys.com. Tickets $19–$28; $2 discount for students and seniors (62 and over).

The Major Concert & Performance Halls

Journal Pavilion, 5601 University Blvd. NE (© 505/452-5100).

Keller Hall, University of New Mexico, Cornell Street at Redondo Drive South NE (© 505/277-4569).

KiMo Theatre, 423 Central Ave. NW (© 505/768-3544).

Popejoy Hall, University of New Mexico, Cornell Street at Redondo Drive South NE (© 505/277-3824).

South Broadway Cultural Center, 1025 Broadway Blvd. SE (© 505/848-1320).

New Mexico Ballet Company   Founded in 1972, the state's oldest ballet company holds most of its performances at Popejoy Hall. Typically there is a fall production such as *Dracula,* a holiday one such as *The Nutcracker* or *A Christmas Carol,* and a contemporary spring production. 4200 Wyoming Blvd. NE, Suite B2 (P.O. Box 21518). ℭ 505/292-4245. www.nmballet.org. Tickets $20–$25 adults, $10–$20 children 12 and under.

New Mexico Symphony Orchestra ℛ   My first introduction to symphony was with the NMSO. Though I was so young I didn't quite understand the novelty of hearing live symphony, I loved picking out the distinct sounds and following as they melded together. The NMSO first played in 1932 (long before I attended, thank you) and has continued as a strong cultural force throughout the state. The symphony performs classics and pops, as well as family and neighborhood concerts. It plays for more than 20,000 grade-school students and visits communities throughout the state in its annual tour program. Concert venues are generally Popejoy Hall on the University of New Mexico campus and the Rio Grande Zoo, both of which are accessible to people with disabilities. Each season a few notable artists visit; recent years have included such guests as Yo Yo Ma and Guillermo and Ivonne Figueroa. I recommend going to one of the outdoor concerts at the band shell at the Rio Grande Zoo. 3301 Menaul Blvd. NE, Suite 4. ℭ 800/251-6676 for tickets and information, or 505/881-9590. www.nmso.org. Ticket prices vary with concert; call for details.

THEATER

Albuquerque Little Theatre   The Albuquerque Little Theatre has been offering a variety of productions ranging from comedies to dramas to musicals since 1930. Seven plays are presented here annually during an August-to-May season. Located across from Old Town, Albuquerque Little Theatre offers plenty of free parking. 224 San Pasquale Ave. SW. ℭ 505/242-4750. www.swcp.com/~alt. Tickets $18, $16 for students, $13 seniors. Box office Mon–Fri noon–6pm.

La Compañía de Teatro de Albuquerque *Finds*   Productions given by the company can provide a focused view into New Mexico culture. One of the few major professional Hispanic companies in the United States and Puerto Rico, La Compañía stages a series of bilingual productions (most original New Mexican works) every year, late September to May. Comedies, dramas, and musicals are offered, along with an occasional Spanish-language play. Performances take place in the National Hispanic Cultural Center, the South Broadway Cultural Center (1025 Broadway Blvd. SE), and other venues regionally. P.O. Box 884. ℭ 505/242-7929. Tickets $12 adults, $8 students ages 18 and above and seniors, $7 children under 18.

Musical Theatre Southwest   Formerly known as the Albuquerque Civic Light Opera Association, this successful company has now condensed its name and expanded its season. From February to January, six major Broadway musicals, in addition to several smaller productions, are presented each year at either Popejoy Hall or the MTS's own 890-seat Hiland Theater. Most productions are staged for three consecutive weekends, including some Sunday matinees. 4804 Central Ave. SE. ℭ 505/262-9301. www.hilandtheater.com. Tickets $15–$30 adults; students and seniors receive a $2 discount.

Vortex Theatre ℛ   A nearly 30-year-old community theater known for its innovative productions, the Vortex is Albuquerque's "Off-Broadway" theater, presenting a range of plays from classic to original. You'll see such plays as *One Flew Over the Cuckoo's Nest* and *Wait Until Dark* by Frederick Knott. Performances take place on Friday and Saturday at 8pm and on Sunday at 6pm. The black-box theater seats 90. 2004½ Central Ave. SE. ✆ 505/247-8600. Tickets $10 adults, $8 students and seniors, $8 for everyone on Sun.

THE CLUB & MUSIC SCENE
COMEDY CLUBS/DINNER THEATER
Laffs Comedy Cafe   Located on the west mesa, this club offers top acts from each coast, including comedians who have appeared on *The Late Show with David Letterman* and HBO. San Mateo Blvd. and Osuna Rd., in the Fiesta del Norte Shopping Center. ✆ 505/296-5653. www.laffscomedy.com. Shows Wed–Sun nights. $7 per person, with a two-drink and/or menu-item minimum purchase. Call for show times.

Mystery Cafe *Finds*   If you're in the mood for a little interactive dinner theater, the Mystery Cafe might be just the ticket. You'll help the characters in this ever-popular, delightfully funny show solve the mystery as they serve you a four-course meal. Reservations are a must. P.O. Box 11433. Performances held at Sheraton Uptown (at Menaul Blvd. and Louisiana Blvd.). ✆ 505/237-1385. www.abqmystery.com. Approximately $33. Performances Fri and Sat evenings at 7:30pm; doors open at 7pm.

COUNTRY MUSIC
Midnight Rodeo/Gotham   The Southwest's largest nightclub of any kind, this place has bars in all corners; it even has its own shopping arcade, including a boutique and gift shop. A DJ spins records nightly until closing; the hardwood dance floor is so big (5,500 sq. ft.) that it resembles an indoor horse track. There's also a hip-hop and techno dance bar called Gotham within Midnight Rodeo. 4901 McLeod Rd. NE (near San Mateo Blvd.). ✆ 505/888-0100. $4 cover Fri–Sat, closed Mon–Tues.

ROCK/JAZZ
Brewsters Pub   Tuesday to Sunday, this downtown hot spot offers live blues, jazz, folk, or light rock entertainment in a sports bar–type setting. Sports fans can enjoy the game on a big-screen TV. Barbecue and burgers are served at lunch and dinner. 312 Central Ave. SW (Downtown). ✆ 505/247-2533.

Burt's Tiki Lounge   This club won the weekly paper *Alibi's* award for the best variety of drinks. The club offers live music Thursday to Sunday and charges no cover. 313 Gold Ave. ✆ 505/243-BURT.

Kelly's BYOB   Near the university, Kelly's is a local brewpub, set in a renovated auto/body shop. The place has tasty pub fare, excellent brew specials, and live music Thursday to Saturday, usually with no cover. 3222 Central SE. ✆ 505/262-2739.

Martini Grille ★   On the eastern side of the Nob Hill district, this is the place for young professionals, who lush out on more than 30 flavors of martinis within a seductive Batman cave atmosphere. Live entertainment plays most weekends and some weeknights. 4200 Central SE. ✆ 505/255-4111.

O'niell's Pub   A favorite club in the University of New Mexico area, this Irish bar serves up good pub fare as well as live local music on Saturday nights and Celtic and bluegrass on Sunday evenings. 3211 Central NE. ✆ 505/256-0564.

MORE ENTERTAINMENT
Albuquerque's best nighttime attraction is the **Sandia Peak Tramway,** with the restaurant High Finance at the summit (see "What to See & Do" and "Where to Dine," earlier in this chapter). Here, you can enjoy a view nonpareil of the Rio Grande Valley and the city lights.

The best place to catch foreign films, art films, and limited-release productions is the **Guild Cinema,** 3405 Central Ave. NE (© **505/255-1848**). For film classics, check out the **Southwest Film Center,** on the UNM campus (© **505/ 277-5608**), which has double features, changing nightly (when classes are in session). In addition, Albuquerque has a number of first-run movie theaters whose numbers you can find in the local telephone directory.

Many travelers like to include a little dice throw and slot machine play in their trip to New Mexico. Those who do are in luck, with the expansive **Sandia Casino,** north of I-25 and a quarter-mile east on Tramway Boulevard (© **800/ 526-9366;** www.sandiacasino.com). The $80-million structure sits on Sandia Pueblo land and has outstanding views of the Sandia Mountains. Built in pueblo architectural style, the graceful casino has a 3,650-seat outdoor amphitheater, three restaurants (one, **Bien Shur,** has excellent food made by the same folks who operate the acclaimed Artichoke Cafe, p. 245), a lounge, more than 1,350 slot and video poker machines, the largest poker room in the state, and blackjack, roulette, and craps tables. It's open from 8am to 4pm Sunday to Wednesday and 24 hours Thursday to Saturday. The **Isleta Gaming Palace,** 11,000 Broadway SE (© **800/460-5686** or 505/724-3800; www.isletacasinoresort. com), is a luxurious, air-conditioned casino (featuring blackjack, poker, slots, bingo, and keno) with a full-service restaurant, nonsmoking section, and free bus transportation on request. Open Monday to Thursday 9am to 5am, Friday to Sunday 24 hours a day.

11 Exploring Nearby Pueblos & Monuments

Ten Native American pueblos are located within an hour's drive of central Albuquerque. One national and two state monuments preserve another five ancient pueblo ruins.

The active pueblos nearby include Acoma, Cochiti, Isleta, Jemez, Laguna, Sandia, San Felipe, Santa Ana, Santo Domingo, and Zia. Of these, Acoma is the most prominent.

ACOMA PUEBLO ✸✸✸

This spectacular "Sky City," a walled adobe village perched high atop a sheer rock mesa 365 feet above the 6,600-foot valley floor, is believed to have been inhabited at least since the 11th century—the longest continuously occupied community in the United States. Native legend claims that it has been inhabited since before the time of Christ. Both the pueblo and **San Estevan del Rey Mission** are National Historic Landmarks.

The Keresan-speaking Acoma (*Ack*-oo-mah) Pueblo boasts 6,005 inhabitants, but only about 50 people reside year-round on the 70-acre mesa top. They make their living from tourists who come to see the large church containing examples of Spanish colonial art and to purchase the pueblo's thin-walled white pottery with polychrome designs.

To reach Acoma from Albuquerque, drive west on I-40 approximately 52 miles to the Acoma–Sky City exit, then travel about 12 miles southwest.

You absolutely cannot wander freely around Acoma Pueblo, but you can start your tour of Acoma at the **visitor center** at the base of the mesa. While waiting, peruse the excellent little **museum** of Acoma history and crafts, or buy snacks at the nearby **concession stand.** Then board the **tour bus,** which climbs through a rock garden of 50-foot sandstone monoliths and past precipitously dangling outhouses to the mesa's summit. There's no running water or electricity in this

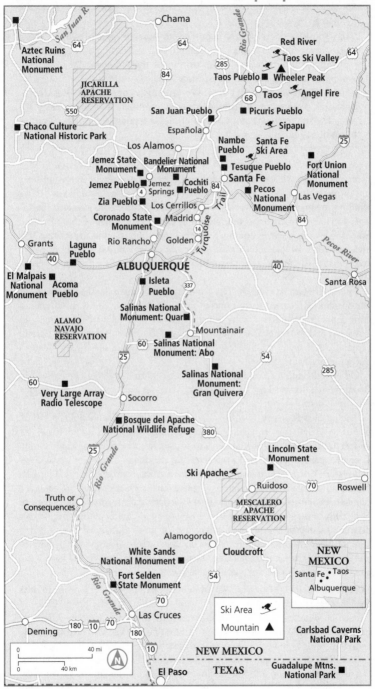

Aztec Ruins National Monument

Chama

San Juan R.

Rio Grande

64

64

64

285

Red River

Taos Ski Valley

Wheeler Peak

Taos Pueblo

84

JICARILLA APACHE RESERVATION

550

Chaco Culture National Historic Park

San Juan Pueblo

Española

68

Taos

Angel Fire

Picuris Pueblo

Sipapu

Los Alamos

Nambe Pueblo

Santa Fe Ski Area

25

Jemez State Monument

Bandelier National Monument

Tesuque Pueblo

Fort Union National Monument

Jemez Pueblo

Jemez Springs

Cochiti Pueblo

Santa Fe

4

84

Las Vegas

Zia Pueblo

Los Cerrillos

Pecos National Monument

Coronado State Monument

Madrid

84

14

Grants

Laguna Pueblo

Rio Rancho

Golden

Turquoise Trail

Pecos River

40

40

ALBUQUERQUE

40

El Malpais National Monument

Acoma Pueblo

Isleta Pueblo

337

Santa Rosa

ALAMO NAVAJO RESERVATION

Salinas National Monument: Quar

Mountainair

25

60

Salinas National Monument: Abo

54

285

60

Very Large Array Radio Telescope

Socorro

Salinas National Monument: Gran Quivera

Bosque del Apache National Wildlife Refuge

380

25

Lincoln State Monument

Ski Apache

Ruidoso

70

Roswell

Truth or Consequences

Rio Grande

MESCALERO APACHE RESERVATION

Alamogordo

White Sands National Monument

Cloudcroft

NEW MEXICO

Santa Fe • Taos

Albuquerque

Fort Selden State Monument

54

Rio Grande

70

Ski Area

Mountain

Deming

180

10

70

180

Las Cruces

10

0   40 mi

0   40 km

N

10

NEW MEXICO

Carlsbad Caverns National Park

El Paso

TEXAS

Guadalupe Mtns. National Park

Pueblo Etiquette

When you visit pueblos, it is important to observe certain rules of etiquette: Remember to respect the pueblos as people's homes; don't peek into doors and windows or climb on top of the buildings. Stay out of cemeteries and ceremonial rooms (such as kivas), since these are sacred grounds. Don't speak during dances or ceremonies or applaud after their conclusion; silence is mandatory. Most pueblos require a permit to carry a camera or to sketch or paint on location. Several pueblos prohibit picture taking at any time.

medieval-looking village; a small reservoir collects rainwater for most purposes, but drinking water is transported up from below. Wood-hole ladders and mica windows are prevalent among the 300-odd adobe structures. As you tour the village, you'll have many opportunities to buy pottery and other pueblo treasures. Pottery is expensive here, but you're not going to find it any cheaper anywhere else, and you'll be guaranteed that it's authentic if you buy it directly from the craftsperson. Along the way, be sure to sample some Indian fry bread topped with honey.

The annual San Esteban del Rey feast day is September 2, when the pueblo's patron saint is honored with a mid-morning Mass, a procession, an afternoon corn dance, and an arts-and-crafts fair. A Governor's Feast is held annually in February; and 4 days of Christmas festivals run from December 25 to 28. Still cameras are allowed for a $10 fee, and guided tours do not operate on the mesa during feast days.

Other celebrations are held in low-lying pueblo villages at Easter (in Acomita), the first weekend in May (Santa Maria feast at McCartys), and August 10 (San Lorenzo Day in Acomita).

The pueblo's address is P.O. Box 309, Acoma, NM 87034 (© **800/747-0181** or 505/ 552-6604; www.puebloofacoma.org). Admission is $8 for adults, $7 for seniors (60 and over), $6 for children 6 to 17, and free for children under 6. Group discounts apply to parties of 15 or more, and there's also a discount for students and Native American visitors. The charge to take still photographs is $10; digital cameras and tripods are prohibited, telephoto lenses are restricted, and no video cameras are allowed. Generally, the pueblo is open daily in the summer 8am to 6pm; daily in the spring, fall, and winter 8am to 4pm. One-hour tours begin every 30 minutes, depending on the demand; the last tour is scheduled 1 hour before closing. The pueblo is closed to visitors on Easter weekend (some years), June 24 and 29, July 10 to 13, and the first or second weekend in October. It's best to call ahead to make sure that the tour is available when you're visiting.

Coronado State Monument ✪   When the Spanish explorer Coronado traveled through this region in 1540–41 while searching for the Seven Cities of Cíbola, he wintered at a village on the west bank of the Rio Grande—probably one located on the ruins of the ancient Anasazi Pueblo known as Kuaua. Those excavated ruins have been preserved in this state monument.

Hundreds of rooms can be seen, and a kiva has been restored so that visitors can descend a ladder into the enclosed space, once the site of sacred rites. Unique multicolored murals, depicting human and animal forms, were found on successive layers of wall plaster in this and other kivas here; some examples are displayed in the monument's small archaeological museum.

485 Kuana Rd., Bernalillo. ✆ 505/867-5351. Admission $3 adults, free for children 16 and under. Wed–Mon 8am–5pm. Closed Easter, Thanksgiving, Christmas, New Year's. To get to the site (20 miles north of Albuquerque), take I-25 to Bernalillo and US 550 west for 1 mile.

Salinas Pueblo Missions National Monument ★ *Finds*   These rarely visited ruins provide a unique glimpse into history. The Spanish conquistadors' Salinas Jurisdiction, on the east side of the Manzano Mountains (southeast of Albuquerque), was an important 17th-century trade center because of the salt extracted by the Native Americans from the salt lakes. Franciscan priests, utilizing native labor, constructed missions of Abo red sandstone and blue-gray limestone for the native converts. The ruins of some of the most durable missions—along with evidence of preexisting Anasazi and Mogollon cultures—are the highlights of a visit to Salinas Pueblo Missions National Monument. The monument consists of three separate units: the ruins of Abo, Quarai, and Gran Quivira. They are situated around the quiet town of Mountainair, 75 miles southeast of Albuquerque at the junction of US 60 and NM 55.

Abo (✆ **505/847-2400**) boasts the 40-foot-high ruins of the **Mission of San Gregorio de Abo,** a rare example of medieval architecture in the United States. **Quarai** (✆ **505/847-2290**) preserves the largely intact remains of the **Mission of La Purísima Concepción de Cuarac** (1630). Its vast size, 100 feet long and 40 feet high, contrasts with the modest size of the pueblo mounds. A small museum in the visitor center has a scale model of the original church, along with a selection of artifacts found at the site. **Gran Quivira** (✆ **505/847-2770**) once had a population of 1,500. The pueblo has 300 rooms and seven kivas. Rooms dating back to 1300 can be seen. There are indications that an older village, dating to 800, may have previously stood here. Ruins of two churches (one almost 140 ft. long) and a *convento* (convent) have been preserved. The visitor center

Traditional Native American Bread Baking

While visiting the pueblos in New Mexico, you'll probably notice outdoor ovens (they look a bit like giant ant hills), known as *hornos,* which Native Americans have used to bake bread for hundreds of years. For Native Americans, making bread is a tradition that links them directly to their ancestors. The long process of mixing and baking also brings mothers and daughters together for what today we might call "quality time."

Usually, in the evening the bread dough (made of white flour, lard, salt, yeast, and water) is made and kneaded, and the loaves are shaped. They are then allowed to rise overnight. In the morning, the oven is stocked with wood and a fire lighted. After the fire burns down to ashes and embers, the oven is cleared, and the ashes are shoveled away. These primitive ovens don't have thermometers, so the baker has to rely on experience to judge when the temperature is right. At that point, the loaves are placed into the oven with a long-handled wooden paddle. They bake for about an hour.

If you would like to try a traditional loaf, you can buy one at the **Indian Pueblo Cultural Center** in Albuquerque (see "What to See & Do," earlier in the chapter), among other places.

Historic Culture with a Hint of Honey

Jemez Pueblo, home to more than 3,000, no longer welcomes visitors except on selected days. However, visitors can get a taste of the Jemez culture at the **Walatowa Visitor Center,** on NM 4, 8 miles north of the junction with US 550 (© **877/733-5687** or 505/834-7235; www.jemezpueblo. org). A museum and shop highlight the center, which also offers information about hiking and scenic tour routes. While in the area, you may encounter Jemez people sitting under *ramadas* (thatch-roofed lean-tos) selling home-baked bread, cookies, and pies. If you're lucky, they may also be making fry bread, which you can smother with honey for one of New Mexico's more delectable treats.

includes a museum with many artifacts from the site and shows a 40-minute movie about the excavation of some 200 rooms, plus a short history video of the pueblo.

All three pueblos and the churches that were constructed above them are believed to have been abandoned in the 1670s. Self-guided tour pamphlets can be obtained at the units' respective visitor centers and at the **Salinas Pueblo Missions National Monument Visitor Center** in Mountainair, on US 60, 1 block west of the intersection of US 60 and NM 55. The visitor center offers an audiovisual presentation on the region's history, a bookstore, and an art exhibit.

P.O. Box 517, Mountainair. © **505/847-2585.** www.nps.gov/sapu. Free admission. Sites summer daily 9am–6pm, rest of year 9am–5pm; visitor center in Mountainair daily 8am–5pm. Closed New Year's Day, Thanksgiving, and Christmas. Abo is 9 miles west of Mountainair on US 60. Quarai is 8 miles north of Mountainair on NM 55. Gran Quivira is 25 miles south of Mountainair on NM 55. All roads are paved.

JEMEZ SPRINGS

A visit to this village along the Jemez River can provide a relaxing retreat and/or an exhilarating adventure. In the area are historic sites and relaxing hot springs, as well as excellent stream fishing, hiking, and cross-country skiing. You may want to combine a drive through this area with a visit to Los Alamos and Bandelier National Monument (see chapter 10).

North of town you'll come to the **Soda Dam,** a strange and beautiful mineral mass formed by travertine deposits—minerals that precipitate out of geothermal springs. Considered a sacred site by Native Americans, it has a gushing waterfall and caves. During the warm months it's a popular swimming hole.

Jemez State Monument ⋒   A stop at this small monument takes you on a journey through the history of the Jemez people. The journey begins in the museum, which tells the tale of Giusewa, "place of boiling waters," the original Tewa name of the area. Then it moves out into the mission ruins, whose story is told on small plaques that juxtapose the first impressions of the missionaries against the reality of the Jemez life. The missionaries saw the Jemez people as barbaric and set out to settle them. Part of the process involved hauling up river stones and erecting 6-foot-thick walls of the Mission of San José de los Jemez (founded in 1621) in the early 17th century. Excavations in 1921–22 and 1935–37 unearthed this massive complex through which you may wander. You enter through a broad doorway to a room that once held elaborate fresco paintings, the room tapering back to the nave, with a giant bell tower above. The setting is startling next to a creek, with steep mountains rising behind.

18160 NM 4 (P.O. Box 143), Jemez Springs. ✆ 505/829-3530. Admission $3 adults, free for children 17 and under. Wed–Mon 8:30am–5pm. Closed New Year's Day, Easter, Thanksgiving, and Christmas. From Albuquerque, take NM 550 (NM 44) to NM 4 and then continue on NM 4 for about 18 miles.

WHERE TO STAY AND DINE

Cañon del Rio–Riverside Inn ⭐ "Eventually the watcher joined the river, and there was only one of us. I believe it was the river," wrote Norman Maclean in *A River Runs Through It.* That was my experience while sitting on a cottonwood-shaded bench at Cañon del Rio, on a long bow of the Jemez River, a small, fast-flowing stream lined with cottonwoods. Built in 1994, the inn has clean lines and comfortable rooms, each named after a Native American tribe. I stayed in the Hopi room, a queen room that wasn't large but was well planned, with built-in drawers and many amenities. Each room has a sliding glass door

---

Moments Sampling Nature's Nectars

When I was young, people often used to head out from Albuquerque to "the Jemez." That meant they were going to the hot springs. Back then, it was the place where the hippies hung out, naked, and it held a kind of foreboding allure for me. Today, the allure is one of comfort and beauty. My choice is to go to the naturally running springs (ask locally for directions), but if you prefer the more controlled environment of a bathhouse, that option is available, too. The waters running through the Jemez area are high in mineral content. In fact, the owner of **Jemez Springs Bath House,** 62 NM 4, on the Jemez Springs Plaza (✆ **505/829-3303;** www.jemezspringsbathhouse.com) says they are so healing, more than once she's had to run after visitors who walked off without their canes. This bathhouse was one of the first structures to be built in what is now Jemez Springs. Built in 1870 and 1878 of river rock and mud, it has thick walls and a richly herbal scent. You soak in individual tubs in either the men's side or the women's side. In back are a series of massage rooms, and outside is a hot tub within a wooden fence—not the most romantic setting. In front is a gift shop packed with interesting soaps and soulful gifts. Jemez Springs Bath House is open daily 10am to 8pm.

At **Ponderosa Valley Vineyard & Winery,** 3171 Hwy. 290, Ponderosa, 87044 (✆ **800/WINE-MAKER** or 505/834-7487; www.ponderosawinery. com), located 3 miles off NM 4 south of Jemez Springs, you'll find a quaint country store with some of New Mexico's best wines. If you're lucky, the vintners will be presiding over the small curved bar and will pour you delectable tastes while telling stories of the history of wine in New Mexico and of the Jemez area, where they have lived and grown grapes for 30 years. Be sure to try the dry Vidal Blanc and the full-bodied Cabernet Sauvignon, both excellent, and both award winners at the New Mexico State Fair. The fruity zinfandel is like nothing you've ever tasted. This is the oldest wine-growing region in the United States, and the product definitely has its own spirit. A 10- to 15-minute tour will take your through the cellar and vineyards. You'll likely want to take a bottle with you. They range in price from $8 to $20.

that opens out to a patio where there's a fountain. The beds are comfortably firm, with good reading lights. The suites have private Jacuzzis and kitchens. The Great Room has a cozy, welcoming feel, with a big-screen TV, as well as a large table where breakfast is served family-style. A separate house is available for rent, the only option for children at the inn. Also, smoking is not allowed.

16445 Scenic Hwy. 4, Jemez Springs, NM 87025. (📞 **505/829-4377.** www.canondelrio.com. 7 units. $99–$160 double, depending on the season; house $125–$150. Rates include full breakfast. AE, DISC, MC, V. **Amenities:** Jacuzzi; massage. *In room:* A/C, TV, hair dryer.

The Laughing Lizard Inn & Cafe 🌶 AMERICAN   This is the kind of small-town cafe that doesn't have to try to have a personality. It already has thick adobe walls, wood floors, and a wood-burning stove for its innate charm. Added touches are the brightly painted walls and funky old tables. If there were a Western version of the Whistle Stop Cafe, this would be it. The menu is somewhat eclectic—most dishes have a bit of an imaginative flair. The burritos come in a variety of types, such as fresh spinach with black beans, mushrooms, jack cheese, salsa, and guacamole. The pizzas feature ingredients such as pesto, sun-dried tomatoes, and feta, or more basic ones with red sauce as well. I had a Chinese stir-fry with tofu and peanut sauce that was a little overbearing but definitely sated my appetite. No alcohol is served, but there are daily dessert treats such as chocolate mousse and berry cobbler. The staff is friendly and accommodating. A small inn attached to the cafe provides inexpensive rooms that are clean but a bit timeworn.

17526 NM 4, Jemez Springs, NM 87025. (📞 **505/829-3108.** www.thelaughinglizard.com. Lunch or dinner $6.50–$8.50. DISC, MC, V. June–Oct Tues–Fri 11am–8pm, Sat 11am–8:30pm, Sun 11am–6pm; Nov–May Thurs–Fri 5–8pm, Sat 11am–8pm, Sun 9am–4pm.

THE TURQUOISE TRAIL

Known as "The Turquoise Trail," NM 14 begins about 16 miles east of downtown Albuquerque, at I-40's Cedar Crest exit, and winds some 46 miles to Santa Fe along the east side of the Sandia Mountains. This state-designated scenic and historic route traverses the revived ghost towns of Golden, Madrid, and Cerrillos, where gold, silver, coal, and turquoise were once mined in great quantities. Modern-day settlers, mostly artists and craftspeople, have brought a renewed frontier spirit to the old mining towns.

GOLDEN   Golden is approximately 10 miles north of the Sandia Park junction on NM 14. Its sagging houses, with their missing boards and the wind whistling through the broken eaves, make it a purist's ghost town. There's a general store widely known for its large selection of well-priced jewelry, as well as a bottle seller's "glass garden." Nearby are the ruins of a pueblo called **Paako,** abandoned around 1670. Such communities of mud huts were all that the Spaniards ever found during their avid quest for the gold of Cíbola.

MADRID   Madrid (pronounced *mah*-drid) is about 12 miles north of Golden. Madrid and neighboring Cerrillos were in a fabled turquoise-mining area dating back to prehistory. Gold and silver mines followed, and when they faltered, there was coal. The Turquoise Trail towns supplied fuel for the locomotives of the Santa Fe Railroad until the 1950s, when the railroad converted to diesel fuel. Madrid used to produce 100,000 tons of coal a year, but the mine closed in 1956. Today, this is a village of artists and craftspeople seemingly stuck in the 1960s: Its funky, ramshackle houses have many counterculture residents who operate several crafts stores and import shops.

The **Old Coal Mine Museum** (© 505/438-3780) invites visitors to go down into a real mine that was saved when the town was abandoned. You can see the old mine's offices, steam engines, machines, and tools. It's called a living museum because blacksmiths, metalworkers, and leatherworkers ply their trades here in restoring parts and tools found in the mine. It's open daily; admission is $4 for adults, $3 for seniors, $1 for children 6 to 12, and free for children under 6.

Next door, the **Mine Shaft Tavern** (© 505/473-0743) continues its colorful career by offering a variety of burgers and presenting live music Saturday nights and Sunday afternoons; it's open for dinner Friday to Sunday, and it attracts folks from Santa Fe and Albuquerque. Next door is the **Madrid Engine House Theater** (© 505/438-3780), possibly the only such establishment on earth with a built-in steam locomotive on its stage. (The structure had been an engine repair shed; the balcony is made of railroad track.) The place to eat is **Native Grill** (© 505/474-5555) on NM 14, in the center of town. You'll find food prepared with fresh ingredients, a broad range of choices, from pizza and burritos to a veggie bowl (steamed veggies with steak, chicken, or tofu). During the summer it's open from 11am to 6 or 7pm. In winter, it's open intermittently, so call ahead.

CERRILLOS   Cerrillos, about 3 miles north of Madrid, is a village of dirt roads that sprawls along Galisteo Creek. It appears to have changed very little since it was founded during a lead strike in 1879; the old hotel, the saloon, and even the sheriff's office look very much like parts of an Old West movie set. It's another 15 miles to Santa Fe and I-25. If, like me, you're enchanted by the Galisteo Basin, you might want to stay a night or two in nearby Galisteo at the **Galisteo Inn** (© 866/404-8200 or 505/466-4000; www.galisteoinn.com). Set on grassy grounds under towering cottonwood trees, this 250-year-old hacienda has thick adobe walls and all the quiet a person could want. Rooms, all remodeled in 2004, are decorated with brightly painted walls and fun, bold-colored art. Most rooms are not sunny, but this means they stay very cool in summer. The inn serves a full breakfast daily for guests, as well as a prix-fixe dinner (at an extra cost) for guests and others on some nights. (At press time plans were for Tues–Sat and Sun brunch, though inquire ahead.) There's a lovely pool large enough to swim laps, a hot tub, and guided horseback riding. The inn is located on NM 41, 15 miles from Cerrillos via the dirt County Road 42.

Appendix A:
Northern New Mexico in Depth

When I was a child in New Mexico, we'd sing a song while driving the dusty roads en route to such ruins as Chaco Canyon or Puye Cliff Dwellings. Sung to the tune of "Oh Christmas Tree," it went like this:

> *New Mexico, New Mexico*
> *Don't know why we love you so.*
> *It never rains*
> *It never snows*
> *The winds and sand*
> *They always blow.*
> *And how we live*
> *God only knows*
> *New Mexico, we love you so.*

Although this song exaggerates the conditions here, the truth remains that in many ways New Mexico has an inhospitable environment. So why are so many people drawn here, and why do so many of us stay?

Ironically, the very extremes that this song presents are the reason. From the moment you set foot in this 121,666-square-mile state, you are met with wildly varied terrain, temperature, and temperament. On a single day you might experience temperatures from 25° to 75°F (-4°–24°C). From the vast heat and dryness of White Sands in the summer to the 13,161-foot subzero, snow-encrusted Wheeler Peak in the winter, New Mexico's beauty is carved by extremes.

Culturally, this is also the case. Pueblo, Navajo, and Apache tribes occupy much of the state's lands, many of them still speaking their native languages and living within the traditions of their people. Some even live without running water and electricity. Meanwhile, the Hispanic culture remains deeply linked to its Spanish roots, practicing a devout Catholicism, and speaking a centuries-old Spanish dialect; some still living by subsistence farming in tiny mountain villages.

New Mexico has its very own sense of time and its own social mores. The pace is slower here, the objectives of life less defined. People rarely arrive on time for appointments, and businesses don't always hold to their posted hours. In most cases, people wear whatever they want here. You'll see men dressed for formal occasions wearing a buttoned collar with a bolo tie and women in cowboy boots and skirts. The other day I saw a man wearing a broad-brimmed bull-rider's hat and lemon-yellow cowboy boots.

All this leads to a certain lost-and-not-caring-to-be-found spell the place casts on visitors that's akin to some kind of voodoo magic. We find ourselves standing amid the dust or sparkling light, within the extreme heat or cold, not sure whether to speak Spanish or English. That's when we let go completely of society's common goals, its pace, and social mores. We slip into a kayak and let the river take us, or hike a peak and look at the world from a new perspective. Or we climb into a car and drive past ancient ruins being excavated at that instant, past ghost mining towns, and under hot-air balloons, by chile fields and around hand-smoothed *santuarios,* all on the road to nowhere, New Mexico's best destination.

At some point in your travels, you'll likely find yourself on this road, and you'll realize that there's no destination so fine.

And after that surrender, you may find yourself looking about with a new clarity. Having experienced the slower pace, you may question your own life's speediness. Having tasted New Mexico's relaxed style, you may look askance at those nylon stockings and heels or that suit and tie. And the next time you climb in the car in your own state or country, you might just head down a road you've never been on and hope that it goes nowhere.

1 How New Mexico Was Won—And Lost

The Pueblo tribes of the upper Rio Grande Valley are descendants of the Anasazi, better known today as the ancestral Puebloans, who from the mid-9th to the 13th centuries lived in the Four Corners Region—where the states of New Mexico, Arizona, Colorado, and Utah now meet. The ancestral Puebloans built spectacular structures; you get an idea of their scale and intricacy at the ruins at **Chaco Canyon** and **Mesa Verde.** It isn't known exactly why they abandoned their homes (some archaeologists suggest it was due to drought; others claim social unrest), but most theories suggest that they moved from these sites to areas like Frijoles Canyon **(Bandelier National Monument)** and **Puye,** where they built villages resembling the ones they had left. Then several hundred years later, for reasons not yet understood, they moved down from the canyons onto the high, flat plain next to the Rio Grande. By the time the Spaniards arrived in the 1500s, the Pueblo culture was well established throughout what would become northern and western New Mexico.

Architectural style was a unifying mark of the otherwise diverse ancestral Puebloan and today's Pueblo cultures. Both built condominium-style communities of stone and mud adobe bricks, three and four stories high. Grouped around central plazas, the villages they constructed incorporated circular spiritual chambers called kivas. As farmers, the ancestral Puebloan and Pueblo peoples used the waters of the Rio Grande and its tributaries to irrigate fields of corn, beans, and squash. They were also the creators of elaborate works of pottery.

THE SPANISH OCCUPATION

The Spanish ventured into the upper Rio Grande after conquering Mexico's Aztecs from 1519 to 1521. In 1540, Francisco Vásquez de Coronado led an expedition in search of the fabled Seven Cities of Cíbola, coincidentally introducing horses and sheep to the region. Neither Coronado nor a succession of fortune-seeking conquistadors could locate the legendary cities of gold, so the Spanish concentrated their efforts on exploiting the Native Americans.

Franciscan priests attempted to turn the Pueblo people into model peasants. Their churches became the focal points of every pueblo, with Catholic schools an essential adjunct. By 1625, there were approximately 50 churches in the Rio Grande Valley. (Two of the Pueblo missions, at Isleta and Acoma, are still in use today.) The Pueblos, however, weren't enthused about doing "God's work" for the Spanish—building new adobe missions, tilling fields, and weaving garments for export to Mexico—so Spanish soldiers came north to back the padres in extracting labor. In effect, the Pueblo people were forced into slavery.

Santa Fe was founded in 1610 as the seat of Spanish government in the upper Rio Grande. Governor Don Pedro de Peralta named the settlement La Villa Real de la Santa Fe de San Francisco de Asis (The Royal City of the Holy Faith of St. Francis of Assisi). The **Palace of the Governors** has been used continuously as a public building ever since—by the Spanish, Pueblos (1680–92), Mexicans, and Americans. Today it stands as the flagship of the state museum system.

Decades of resentment against the Spanish colonials culminated in the Pueblo occupation. Uprisings in the 1630s at Taos and Jemez left village priests dead and triggered even more repression. In 1680, a unified Pueblo rebellion, orchestrated from Taos, succeeded in driving the Spaniards from the upper Rio Grande. The leaders of the revolt defiled or destroyed the churches, just as the Spanish had destroyed the religious symbols of the native people. Revolutionaries took the Palace of the Governors, where they burned archives and prayer books, and converted the chapel into a kiva. They also burned much of the property in Santa Fe that had been built by the Europeans and laid siege to Spanish settlements up and down the Rio Grande Valley. Forced to retreat to Mexico, the colonists were not able to retake Santa Fe until 12 years later. Bloody battles raged for the next several years, but by the beginning of the 18th century, Nuevo Mexico was firmly in Spanish hands.

It remained so until Mexico gained its independence from Spain in 1821. The most notable event in the intervening years was the mid-1700s departure of the Franciscans, exasperated by their failure to wipe out all vestiges of traditional Pueblo religion. Throughout the Spanish occupation, eight generations of Pueblos had clung tenaciously to their way of life. However, by the 1750s, the number of Pueblo villages had shrunk by half.

THE ARRIVAL OF THE ANGLOS

The first Anglos to spend time in the upper Rio Grande Valley were mountain men: itinerant hunters, trappers, and traders. Trailblazers of the U.S. westward expansion, they began settling in New Mexico in the first decade of the 19th century. Many married into Pueblo or Hispanic families. Perhaps the best known was **Kit Carson,** a sometime federal agent, sometime scout, whose legend is inextricably interwoven with that of early Taos. Though he seldom stayed in one place for long, he considered the Taos area his home. He married Josepha Jaramillo, the daughter of a leading Taos citizen. Later he became a prime force in the final subjugation of the Plains Indians. The Taos home where he lived off and on for 40 years, until his death in 1868, is now a museum (though at this writing it is in ownership transition, with its future uncertain).

Wagon trains and eastern merchants followed Carson and the other early settlers. Santa Fe, Taos, and Albuquerque, already major trading and commercial centers at the end of the **Chihuahua Trail** (the Camino Real from Veracruz, Mexico, 1,000 miles south), became the western terminals of the new **Santa Fe Trail** (from Independence, Missouri, 800 miles east).

Even though independent Mexico granted the Pueblo people full citizenship and abandoned restrictive trade laws instituted by their former Spanish rulers, the subsequent 25 years of direct rule from Mexico City were not peaceful in the upper Rio Grande. Instead, they were marked by ongoing rebellion against severe taxation, especially in Taos. Neither did things quiet down when the United States assumed control of the territory during the U.S.–Mexican War. Shortly after General Stephen Kearney occupied Santa Fe (in a bloodless takeover) on orders of President James Polk in 1846, a revolt in Taos in 1847 led to the slaying of the new governor of New Mexico, Charles Bent. In 1848, the Treaty of Guadalupe Hidalgo officially transferred title of New Mexico, along with Texas, Arizona, and California, to the United States.

Aside from Kit Carson, perhaps the two most notable personalities of 19th-century New Mexico were priests. **Father José Martinez** (1793–1867) was one

Spots of Regional Historic Interest

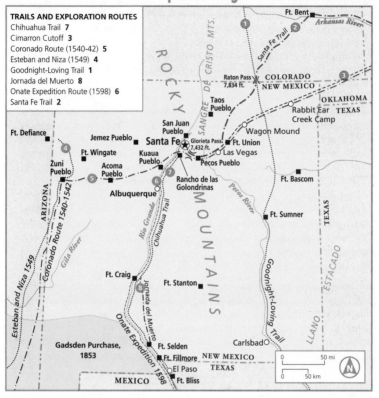

TRAILS AND EXPLORATION ROUTES
Chihuahua Trail **7**
Cimarron Cutoff **3**
Coronado Route (1540-42) **5**
Esteban and Niza (1549) **4**
Goodnight-Loving Trail **1**
Jornada del Muerto **8**
Onate Expedition Route (1598) **6**
Santa Fe Trail **2**

of the first native-born priests to serve his people. Ordained in Durango, Mexico, he jolted the Catholic church after assuming control of the Taos parish: Martinez abolished the obligatory church tithe because it was a hardship on poor parishioners, published the first newspaper in the territory (in 1835), and fought large land acquisitions by Anglos after the United States annexed the territory.

On all these issues Martinez was at loggerheads with **Bishop Jean-Baptiste Lamy** (1814–88), a Frenchman appointed in 1851 to supervise the affairs of the first independent New Mexican diocese. Lamy, on whose life Willa Cather based her novel *Death Comes for the Archbishop,* served the diocese for 37 years. Lamy didn't take kindly to Martinez's independent streak and, after repeated conflicts, excommunicated the maverick priest in 1857. But Martinez was steadfast in his preaching. He established an independent church and continued as northern New Mexico's spiritual leader until his death.

Nevertheless, Lamy made many positive contributions to New Mexico, especially in the fields of education and architecture. Santa Fe's Romanesque **Cathedral of St. Francis** and the nearby Gothic-style **Loretto Chapel,** for instance, were constructed under his aegis. But he was adamant about adhering to strict Catholic religious tenets. Martinez, on the other hand, embraced the folk tradition, including the craft of *santero* (religious icon) carving and a tolerance of the

Penitentes, a flagellant sect that flourished after the departure of the Franciscans in the mid–18th century.

With the advent of the **Atchison, Topeka & Santa Fe Railway** in 1879, New Mexico began to boom. Albuquerque in particular blossomed in the wake of a series of major gold strikes in the Madrid Valley, close to ancient Native American turquoise mines. By the time the gold lodes began to shrink in the 1890s, cattle and sheep ranching had become well entrenched. The territory's growth culminated in statehood in 1912.

Territorial governor Lew Wallace, who served from 1878 to 1881, was instrumental in promoting interest in the arts, which today flourish in northern New Mexico. While occupying the Palace of the Governors, Wallace penned the great biblical novel *Ben-Hur.* In the 1890s, Ernest Blumenschein, Bert Phillips, and Joseph Sharp launched the Taos art colony; it boomed in the decade following World War I when Mabel Dodge Luhan, D. H. Lawrence, Georgia O'Keeffe, Willa Cather, and many others visited or established residence in the area.

During World War II, the federal government purchased an isolated boys' camp west of Santa Fe and turned it into the **Los Alamos National Laboratory,** where the Manhattan Project and other top-secret atomic experiments were developed and perfected. The science and military legacies continue today; Albuquerque is among the nation's leaders in attracting defense contracts and high technology.

2 Life Today—From Flamenco to Craps

On rock faces throughout northern New Mexico, you'll find circular symbols carved in sandstone, the wavy mark of Avanu the river serpent, or the ubiquitous Kokopelli playing his magic flute. These petroglyphs are constant reminders of the enigmatic history of the ancestral Puebloans (Anasazi), the Indians who inhabited this area from A.D. 1100 until the arrival of the Spanish conquistadors, around 1550.

The Spanish conquistadors, in their inimitable fashion, imposed a new, foreign order on the resident Native Americans and their land. As an inevitable component of conquest, they changed most Native American names—today, you'll find a number of Native Americans with Hispanic names—and renamed the villages "pueblos." The Spaniards' most far-reaching legacy, however, was the forceful conversion of Indian populations to Catholicism, a religion that many Indians still practice today. In each of the pueblos you'll see a large, often beautiful, Catholic church, usually made with sculpted adobe; during the holiday seasons, Pueblo people perform ritual dances outside their local Catholic churches. The churches, set against the ancient adobe dwellings, are symbolic of the melding of two cultures.

This mix of cultures is apparent in today's northern New Mexican cuisine. When the Spaniards came to the New World, they brought cows and sheep. They quickly learned to appreciate the indigenous foods here, most notably corn, beans, squash, and chiles. Look also for such Pueblo dishes as the thin-layered blue *piki* bread, or *chauquehue,* a thick corn pudding similar to polenta.

GROWING PAINS

Northern New Mexico is experiencing a reconquest of sorts, as the Anglo population soars and outside money and values again make their way in. The process continues to transform New Mexico's three distinct cultures and their unique ways of life, albeit in a less violent manner than during the Spanish conquest.

Certainly, the Anglos—many of them from large cities—add a cosmopolitan flavor to life here. The variety of restaurants has greatly improved, as have entertainment options. For their small size, towns such as Taos and Santa Fe offer a broad variety of restaurants and cultural events. Santa Fe has developed a strong dance and drama scene, with treats such as flamenco and opera that you'd expect to find in New York or Los Angeles. And Albuquerque has an exciting nightlife scene downtown; you can walk from club to club and hear a wealth of jazz, rock, country, and alternative music.

Yet many newcomers, attracted by the adobe houses and exotic feel of the place, often bring only a loose appreciation for the area. Some tend to romanticize the lifestyle of the other cultures and trivialize their beliefs. Native American symbology, for example, is employed in ever-popular Southwestern decorative motifs; New Age groups appropriate valued rituals, such as sweats (in which believers sit encamped in a very hot, enclosed space to cleanse their spirits). The effects of cultural and economic change are even apparent throughout the countryside, where land is being developed at an alarming rate.

Transformation of the local way of life and landscape is also apparent in the stores continually springing up in the area. For some of us, these are a welcome relief from Western clothing stores and provincial dress shops. The downside is that city plazas, which once contained pharmacies and grocery stores frequented by residents, are now crowded with T-shirt shops and galleries appealing to tourists. Many locals in these cities now rarely visit their plazas except during special events such as fiestas.

Environmental threats are another regional reality. Nuclear-waste issues form part of an ongoing conflict affecting the entire Southwest, and a section of southern New Mexico has been designated a nuclear-waste site. Because much of the waste must pass through Santa Fe, the U.S. government, along with the New Mexico state government, constructed a bypass that directs some transit traffic around the west side of the city.

Still, new ways of thinking have also brought positive changes to the life here, and many locals have directly benefited from New Mexico's influx of wealthy newcomers and popularity as a tourist destination. Businesses and industries large and small have come to the area. In Albuquerque, Intel Corporation now employs more than 5,500 workers, and in Santa Fe, the nationally renowned *Outside* magazine publishes monthly. Local artists and artisans also benefit from growth. Many craftspeople—furniture makers, tin workers, and weavers—have expanded their businesses. The influx of people has broadened the sensibility of a fairly provincial state. The area has become a refuge for many gays and lesbians, as well as for political exiles, such as Tibetans. With them has developed a level of creativity and tolerance you would generally find only in very large cities.

CULTURAL QUESTIONS

Faced with new challenges to their ways of life, both Native Americans and Hispanics are marshaling forces to protect their cultural identities. A prime concern is language. Through the years, many Pueblo people have begun to speak more and more English, with their children getting little exposure to their native tongue. In a number of the pueblos, elders are working with school children in language classes. Some of the pueblos have even developed written dictionaries, the first time their languages have been presented in this form.

Many pueblos have introduced programs to conserve the environment, preserve ancient seed strains, and protect religious rites. Because their religion is tied closely to nature, a loss of natural resources would threaten the entire culture. Certain rituals have been closed off to outsiders, the most notable being some of the rituals of Shalako at Zuni, a popular and elaborate series of year-end ceremonies.

Hispanics, through art and observance of cultural traditions, are also embracing their roots. In northern New Mexico, murals depicting important historic events, such as the Treaty of Guadalupe Hidalgo of 1848, adorn many walls. The **Spanish Market** in Santa Fe has expanded into a grand celebration of traditional arts—from tin working to *santo* carving. Public schools in the area have bilingual education programs, allowing students to embrace their Spanish-speaking roots.

Hispanics are also making their voices heard, insisting on more conscientious development of their neighborhoods and rising to positions of power in government. When she was in office, former Santa Fe Mayor Debbie Jaramillo made national news as an advocate of the Hispanic people, and Congressman Bill Richardson, Hispanic despite his Anglo surname, was appointed U.S. ambassador to the United Nations and then left that post to become energy secretary in President Clinton's cabinet. Currently, he is governor of New Mexico.

GAMBLING WINS & LOSSES

Gambling, a fact of life and source of much-needed revenue for Native American populations across the country, has been a center of controversy in northern New Mexico for a number of years. In 1994, Governor Gary Johnson signed a compact with tribes in New Mexico, ratified by the U.S. Department of the Interior, to allow full-scale gambling. **Tesuque Pueblo** was one of the first to begin a massive expansion, and many other pueblos followed suit.

Many New Mexicans are concerned about the tone gambling sets in the state. The casinos are for the most part large, neon-bedecked buildings that stand out sorely on some of New Mexico's most picturesque land. Though most residents appreciate the boost that gambling can ultimately bring to the Native American economies, many critics wonder where gambling profits actually go—and if the casinos can possibly be a good thing for the pueblos and tribes. Some detractors suspect that profits go directly into the pockets of outside backers.

A number of pueblos and tribes, however, are showing signs of prosperity, and they are using newfound revenues to buy firefighting and medical equipment and to invest in local schools. Isleta Pueblo built a $3½-million youth center, and the lieutenant governor says the money for it came from gambling revenues. Sandia Pueblo built a $2-million medical and dental clinic and, most recently, provided a computer for every tribal home. Its governor said these projects were "totally funded by gaming revenues." Some of the pueblos have built hotels on their property, most notable of them the Hyatt Regency Tamaya Resort at Santa Ana.

SANTA FE

Santa Fe is where the splendor of diverse cultures really shines, and it does so in a setting that's unsurpassed. There's a magic in Santa Fe that's difficult to explain, but you'll sense it when you glimpse an old adobe building set against blue mountains and giant billowing thunderheads, or when you hear a ranchero song come from a low-rider's radio and you smell chicken and chile grilling at a roadside vending booth. Although it's quickening, the pace of life here is still a few steps slower than that in the rest of the country. We use the word *mañana* to describe the pace—which doesn't mean "tomorrow" exactly, it just means "not today." There's also a level of creativity here that you'll find in few other places in the world. Artists who have fled big-city jobs are here to follow their passions, as are locals who grew up making crafts and continue to do so. Conversations often center on how to structure one's day so as to take advantage of the incredible outdoors while still making enough money to survive.

Meanwhile, Santa Fe's precipitous growth and enduring popularity with tourists have been a source of conflict and squabbling. Outsiders have bought up land in the hills around the city, building housing developments and sprawling single-family homes. The hills that local populations claimed for centuries as their own are being overrun, while property taxes for all have skyrocketed. Local outcry has prompted the city to implement zoning restrictions on where and how development can proceed. Some of the restrictions include banning building on ridge tops and on steep slopes and limiting the size of homes built.

Only in recent years have Santa Fe's politicians become conscientious about the city's growth. Mayor Debbie Jaramillo was one of the first local politicians to take a strong stand against growth. A fiery native of Santa Fe, she came into office as a representative of *la gente* (the people) and set about discouraging tourism and rapid development. The subsequent mayor, Larry Delgado, took a middle-of-the-road approach to the issue, which resulted in a calmer community and an increase in tourism and development.

TAOS

A funky town in the middle of a beautiful, sage-covered valley, Taos is full of narrow streets dotted with galleries and artisan shops. You might find an artist's studio tucked into a century-old church or a furniture maker working at the back of his own small shop.

More than any other major northern New Mexico community, Taos has successfully opposed much of the heavy development slated for the area. In the 1980s, locals stalled indefinitely plans to expand their airport; in the 1990s, they blocked plans for a $40-million golf course and housing development; and in 2003, they prevented a Super Wal-Mart from opening. It's hard to say where Taos gets its rebellious strength; the roots may lie in the hippie community that settled here in the '60s, or possibly the Pueblo community around which the city formed. After all, Taos Pueblo was at the center of the 17th-century Pueblo revolt.

Still, changes are upon Taoseños. The blinking light that for years residents used as a reference point has given way to a real traffic light. You'll also see the main route through town becoming more and more like Cerrillos Road in Santa Fe, as fast-food restaurants and service businesses set up shop. Though the town is working on alternate routes to channel through-traffic around downtown, there's no feasible way of widening the main drag because the street—which started out as a wagon trail—is bordered closely by historic buildings.

ALBUQUERQUE

The largest city in New Mexico, Albuquerque has borne the brunt of the state's most massive growth. Currently, the city sprawls more than 16 miles, from the lava-crested mesas on the west side of the Rio Grande to the steep alluvial slopes of the Sandia Mountains on the east, and north and south through the Rio Grande Valley. New subdivisions sprout up constantly.

Despite the growth, this town is most prized by New Mexicans for its genuineness. You'll find none of the self-conscious artsy atmosphere of Santa Fe here. Instead, there's a traditional New Mexico feel that's evident when you spend some time in the heart of the city. It centers around downtown, a place of shiny skyscrapers built around the original Route 66, which still maintains some of its 1950s charm.

The most emblematic growth problem concerns the **Petroglyph National Monument** on the west side. The area is characterized by five extinct volcanoes. Adjacent lava flows became a hunting and gathering place for prehistoric Native Americans, who left a chronicle of their beliefs etched in the dark basalt boulders. Over 25,000 petroglyphs have been found in the preserve. Now, there's a push to carve out a highway corridor through the center of the monument. Opponents have fought the extension for more than a decade, with Native American groups likening the highway to building a road through a church.

At press time, 8½ acres had been taken out of the national monument's jurisdiction, opening the way for the paving process; however, funding is not yet in place, and opponents are still fighting the project.

Northern New Mexico's extreme popularity as a tourist destination has leveled out in the 21st century. Though many artists and other businesspeople lament the loss of the crowds we had back in the '80s, most people are glad that the wave has subsided. It's good news for travelers, too; they longer have to compete so heavily for restaurant seats or space when hiking through ruins. Though parts of northern New Mexico have lost some of the unique charm that attracted so many to the area, the overall feeling is still one of mystery and a cultural depth unmatched in the world.

3 Land of Art

It's all in the light—or at least that's what many artists claim drew them to northern New Mexico. In truth, the light is only part of the attraction: Nature in this part of the country, with its awe-inspiring thunderheads, endless expanse of blue skies, and rugged desert, is itself a canvas. To record the wonders of earth and sky, the Anasazi imprinted images—in the form of **petroglyphs** and **pictographs**—on the sides of caves and on stones, as well as on the sides of pots they shaped from clay dug in the hills.

Today's Native American tribes carry on that legacy, as do the other cultures that have settled here. Life in northern New Mexico is shaped by the arts. Everywhere you turn, you see pottery, paintings, jewelry, and weavings. You're liable to meet an artist whether you're having coffee in a Taos cafe or walking along Canyon Road in Santa Fe.

The area is full of little villages that maintain their own artistic specialties. Each Indian pueblo has a trademark design, such as Santa Clara's and San Ildefonso's black pottery and Zuni's needlepoint silver work. Bear in mind that the images used often have deep symbolic meaning. When purchasing art or an artifact, you may want to talk to its maker about what the symbols mean.

Hispanic villages are also distinguished by their artistic identities. Chimayo has become a center for Hispanic weaving, while the village of Cordova is known for its *santo* (icon) carving. *Santos, retablos* (paintings), and *bultos* (sculptures), as well as works in tin, are traditional devotional arts tied to the Roman Catholic faith. Often, these works are sold out of artists' homes in these villages, allowing you to glimpse the lives of the artists and the surroundings that inspire them.

Hispanic and Native American villagers take their goods to the cities, where for centuries people have bought and traded. Under the portals along the plazas of Santa Fe, Taos, and Albuquerque, you'll find a variety of works in silver, stone, and pottery for sale. In the cities, you'll find streets lined with galleries, some very slick, some more modest. At major markets, such as the Spanish Market and Indian Market in Santa Fe, some of the top artists from the area sell their works. Smaller shows at the pueblos also attract artists and artisans. The **Northern Pueblo Artists and Craftsman Show,** revolving each July to a different pueblo, continues to grow.

Drawn by the beauty of the local landscape and respect for indigenous art, artists from all over have flocked here, particularly during the 20th and 21st centuries. They have established locally important art societies; one of the most notable is the **Taos Society of Artists.** An oft-repeated tale explains the roots of this society. The artists **Bert Phillips** and **Ernest L. Blumenschein** were traveling through the area from Colorado on a mission to sketch the Southwest when their wagon broke down north of Taos. The scenery so overwhelmed them that they abandoned their journey and stayed. Joseph Sharp joined them, and still later came Oscar Berninghaus, Walter Ufner, Herbert Dunton, and others. You can see a brilliant collection of some of their romantically lit portraits and landscapes at the **Van Vechten Lineberry Museum** in Taos. The 100th anniversary marking the artists' broken wheel was celebrated in 1998.

A major player in the development of Taos as an artists' community was the arts patron **Mabel Dodge Luhan.** A writer who financed the work of many an artist, in the 1920s Luhan held court for many notables, including Georgia O'Keeffe, Willa Cather, and D. H. Lawrence. This illustrious history goes a long way to explaining how it is that Taos—a town of about 5,000 inhabitants—has more than 100 arts-and-crafts galleries and many resident painters.

Santa Fe has its own art society, begun in the 1920s by a nucleus of five painters who became known as **Los Cinco Pintores.** Jozef Bakos, Fremont Ellis, Walter Mruk, Willard Nash, and Will Shuster lived in the area of dusty Canyon Road (now the arts center of Santa Fe, with countless artists, approximately 100 galleries, and many museums). Despite its small size, Santa Fe is, remarkably, considered one of the top three art markets in the United States.

Perhaps the most celebrated artist associated with northern New Mexico is **Georgia O'Keeffe** (1887–1986), a painter who worked and lived most of her later years in the region. O'Keeffe's first sojourn to New Mexico in 1929 inspired her sensuous paintings of the area's desert landscape and bleached animal skulls. The house where she lived in Abiquiu (42 miles northwest of Santa Fe on US 84) is now open for limited public tours (see "Along the High Road to Taos," in chapter 10 for details). The **Georgia O'Keeffe Museum,** the largest museum in the United States dedicated entirely to a woman artist, opened in Santa Fe in 1997.

Santa Fe is also home to the **Institute of American Indian Arts,** where many of today's leading Native American artists have studied, including the Apache sculptor Allan Houser (whose works you can see near the State Capitol building and in other public areas in Santa Fe). The best-known Native American painter is R. C. Gorman, an Arizona Navajo who has made his home in Taos for more than 2 decades. Now in his 70s, Gorman is internationally acclaimed for his bright, somewhat surrealistic depictions of Navajo women. A relative newcomer to national fame is Dan Namingha, a Hopi artist who weaves native symbology into contemporary concerns.

If you look closely, you'll find notable works from a number of local artists. There's Tammy Garcia, a young Taos potter who year after year continues to sweep the awards at Indian Market with her intricately shaped and carved pots. Cippy Crazyhorse, a Cochiti, has acquired a steady following of patrons for his silver jewelry. All around the area you'll see the frescoes of Frederico Vigil, a noted muralist and Santa Fe native. From the village of Santa Cruz comes a new rising star named Andrés Martinez, noted for his Picasso-esque portraits of Hispanic village life.

For the visitor interested in art, however, some caution should be exercised; there's a lot of schlock out there, targeting the tourist trade. Yet if you persist, you're likely to find much inspiring work as well. The museums and many of the galleries are excellent repositories of local art. Their offerings range from small-town folk art to works by major artists who show internationally.

4 Architecture: A Rich Melting Pot

Northern New Mexico's distinctive architecture reflects the diversity of cultures that have left their imprint on the region. The first people in the area were the ancestral Puebloans or Anasazi, who built stone and mud homes at the bottom of canyons and inside caves (which look rather like condominiums to the modern urban eye). **Pueblo-style adobe architecture** evolved and became the basis for traditional New Mexican homes: sun-dried clay bricks mixed with grass for strength, mud-mortared, and covered with additional protective layers of mud. Roofs are supported by a network of vigas—long beams whose ends protrude through the outer facades—and *latillas,* smaller stripped branches layered between the vigas. Other adapted Pueblo architectural elements include plastered adobe-brick kiva fireplaces, *bancos* (adobe benches that protrude from walls), and *nichos* (small indentations within a wall in which religious icons are placed). These adobe homes are characterized by flat roofs and soft, rounded contours.

Spaniards wedded many elements to Pueblo style, such as portals (porches held up with posts, often running the length of a home) and enclosed patios, as well as the simple, dramatic sculptural shapes of Spanish mission arches and bell towers. They also brought elements from the Moorish architecture found in southern Spain: heavy wooden doors and elaborate *corbels*—carved wooden supports for the vertical posts.

With the opening of the Santa Fe Trail in 1821 and later the 1860s gold boom, both of which brought more Anglo settlers, came the next wave of building. New arrivals contributed architectural elements such as neo-Grecian and Victorian influences popular in the middle part of the United States at the time. Distinguishing features of what came to be known as **Territorial-style** architecture can be seen today; they include brick facades and cornices as well as porches, often placed on the second story. You'll also note millwork on doors and wood trim around windows and doorways, double-hung windows, and Victorian bric-a-brac.

Santa Fe Plaza is an excellent example of the convergence of these early architectural styles. On the west side is a Territorial-style balcony, while the Palace of the Governors is marked by Pueblo-style vigas and oversize Spanish/Moorish doors.

Nowhere else in the United States are you likely to see such extremes of architectural style as in northern New Mexico. In Santa Fe, you'll see the Romanesque architecture of the **St. Francis Cathedral** and the Gothic-style **Loretto Chapel,** brought by Archbishop Lamy from France, as well as the railroad station built in the **Spanish Mission style**—popular in the early part of this century.

Since 1957, strict city building codes have required that all new structures within the circumference of the Paseo de Peralta conform to one of two revival styles: Pueblo or Territorial. The regulation also limits the height of the buildings and restricts the types of signs permitted, and it requires buildings to be topped by flat roofs.

Albuquerque also has a broad array of styles, most evident in a visit to **Old Town.** There, you'll find the large Italianate brick house known as the **Herman Blueher home,** built in 1898; throughout Old Town you'll find little *placitas,* homes, and haciendas built around courtyards, a strategy developed not only for defense purposes but also as a way to accommodate several generations of the same family in different wings of a single dwelling. **The Church of San Felipe de Neri** at the center of Old Town is centered between two folk Gothic towers. This building was begun in a cruciform plan in 1793; subsequent architectural changes resulted in an interesting mixture of styles.

Most notable architecturally in Taos is the **Taos Pueblo,** the site of two structures emulated in homes and business buildings throughout the Southwest. Built to resemble Taos Mountain, which stands behind it, the two structures are pyramidal in form, with the different levels reached by ladders. Also quite prevalent is architecture echoing colonial hacienda style. What's nice about Taos is that you can see historic homes inside and out. You can wander through artist **Ernest Blumenschein's home.** Built in 1797 and restored by Blumenschein in 1919, it represents another New Mexico architectural phenomenon: homes that were added onto year after year. Doorways are typically low, and floors rise and fall at the whim of the earth beneath them. The **Martinez Hacienda** is an example of a hacienda stronghold. Built without windows facing outward, it originally had 20 small rooms, many with doors opening out to the courtyard. One of the few refurbished examples of colonial New Mexico architecture and life, the hacienda is on the National Historic Registry.

As you head into villages in the north, you'll see steep pitched roofs on most homes. This is because the common flat-roof style doesn't shed snow; the water builds up and causes roof problems. In just about any town in northern New Mexico, you may detect the strong smell of tar, a sure sign that another resident is laying out thousands to fix his enchanting but frustratingly flat roof.

Today, very few new homes are built of adobe. Instead, most are constructed with wood frames and plasterboard, and then stuccoed over. Several local architects are currently employing innovative architecture to create a Pueblo-style feel. They incorporate straw bails, pumice-crete, rammed earth, old tires, even aluminum cans in the construction of homes. Most of these elements are used in the same way bricks are used, stacked and layered, and then covered over with plaster and made to look like adobe. Often it's difficult to distinguish homes built with these materials from those built with wood-frame construction. West of Taos, a number of "earthships" have been built. Many of these homes are constructed with alternative materials, most bermed into the sides of hills, utilizing the earth as insulation and the sun as an energy source.

A visitor could spend an entire trip to New Mexico focusing on the architecture. As well as relishing the wealth of architectural styles, you'll find more subtle elements everywhere. You may encounter an ox-blood floor, for example. An old Spanish tradition, ox blood is spread in layers and left to dry, hardening into a glossy finish that's known to last centuries. You're also likely to see coyote fences—narrow cedar posts lined up side by side—a system early settlers devised to ensure safety of their animals. Winding around homes and buildings you'll see *acequias,* ancient irrigation canals still maintained by locals for watering crops and trees. Throughout the area you'll notice that old walls are whimsically bowed, and windows and floors are often crooked, constant reminders of the effects time has had on even these stalwart structures.

5 Anthropology 101: Beliefs & Rituals

Religion has always been a central, defining element in the life of the Pueblo people. Within the cosmos, which they view as a single whole, all living creatures are mutually dependent. Thus, every relationship a human being may have, whether with a person, an animal, or a plant, has spiritual significance. A hunter prays before killing a deer, asking the creature to sacrifice itself to the tribe. A slain deer is treated as a guest of honor, and the hunter performs a ritual in which he sends the animal's soul back to its community, so that it may be reborn. Even the harvesting of plants requires prayer, thanks, and ritual.

The Pueblo people believe that their ancestors originally lived under the ground, which, as the place from which plants spring, is the source of all life. According to their beliefs, the original Pueblos, encouraged by burrowing animals, entered the world of humans—the so-called "fourth" world—through a hole, a *sipapu*. The ways in which this came about and the deities that the Pueblo people revere vary from tribe to tribe. Most, however, believe this world is enclosed by four sacred mountains, where four sacred colors—coral, black, turquoise, and yellow or white—predominate.

Moments   **Danse Macabre**
_____

The **Dance of the Matachines,** a ritualistic dance performed at northern New Mexico pueblos and in many Hispanic communities, reveals the cultural miscegenation, identities, and conflicts that characterize northern New Mexico. It's a dark and vivid ritual in which a little girl, Malinche, is wedded to the church. The dance, depicting the taming of the native spirit, is difficult even for historians to decipher.

Brought to the New World by the Spaniards, the dance has its roots in the painful period during which the Moors were driven out of Spain. However, some symbols seem obvious: At one point, men bearing whips tame "El Toro," a small boy dressed as a bull who has been charging about rebelliously. The whip-men symbolically castrate him and then stroll through the crowd, pretending to display the dismembered body parts, as if to warn villagers of the consequences of disobedience. At another point, a hunched woman-figure births a small troll-like doll, perhaps representative of the union between Indian and Hispanic cultures.

The Dance of the Matachines ends when two *abuelo* (grandparent) figures dance across the dirt, holding up the just-born baby, while the Matachines, adorned with bishop-like headdresses, follow them away in a recessional march. The Matachines' dance, often performed in the early mornings, is so dark and mystical that every time I see it, my passion for this area deepens. The image of that baby always stays with me, and in a way represents New Mexico itself: a place born of disparate beliefs that have melded with the sand, sage, and sun and produced incredible richness.

There is no single great spirit ruling over this world; instead, it is watched over by a number of spiritual elements. Most common are Mother Earth and Father Sun. In this desert land, the sun is an element of both life and death. The tribes watch the skies closely, tracking solstices and planetary movements, to determine the optimal time for crop planting.

Ritualistic dances are occasions of great symbolic importance. Usually held in conjunction with the feast days of Catholic saints (including Christmas Eve), Pueblo ceremonies demonstrate the parallel absorption of Christian elements without the surrendering of traditional beliefs. To this day, communities enact medicine dances, fertility rites, and prayers for rain and for good harvests. The spring and summer corn, or *tablita,* dances are among the most impressive. Ceremonies begin with an early-morning Mass and procession to the plaza; the image of the saint is honored at the forefront. The rest of the day is devoted to song, dance, and feasting, with performers masked and clad as deer, buffalo, eagles, or other creatures.

Visitors are usually welcome to attend Pueblo dances, but they should respect the tribe's requests not to be photographed or recorded. It was exactly this lack of respect that led the Zunis to ban outsiders from attending many of their famous Shalako ceremonies.

Catholicism, imposed by the Spaniards, has infused northern New Mexico with an elaborate set of beliefs. This is a Catholicism heavy with iconography, expressed in carved *santos* (statues) and beautiful *retablos* (paintings) that adorn the altars of many cathedrals. Catholic churches are the focal points of most northern New Mexico villages. If you take the high road to Taos, be sure to note the church in **Las Trampas,** as well as the one in **Ranchos de Taos;** both have 3- to 4-foot-thick walls sculpted from adobe and inside have old-world charm, with beautiful *retablos* decorating the walls and vigas supporting the ceiling.

Hispanics in northern New Mexico, in particular, maintain strong family and Catholic ties, and they continue to honor traditions associated with both. Communities plan elaborate celebrations such as the *quinciniera* for young girls reaching womanhood, and weddings with big feasts and dances in which well-wishers pin money to the bride's elaborately laced gown.

If you happen to be in the area during a holiday, you may even get to see a religious procession or pilgrimage. Most notable is the **pilgrimage to the Santuario de Chimayo,** an hour's drive north of the state capital. Constructed in 1816, the sanctuary has long been a pilgrimage site for Catholics who attribute miraculous healing powers to the earth found in the chapel's anteroom. Several days before Easter, fervent believers begin walking the highway headed north or south to Chimayo, some carrying large crosses, others carrying nothing but small bottles of water, most praying for a miracle.

In recent years, New Mexico has become known (and in some circles, ridiculed) for **New Age pilgrims and celebrations.** The roots of the local movement are hard to trace. It may have something to do with northern New Mexico's centuries-old reputation as a place where rebel thinkers come to enjoy the freedom to believe what they want. Pueblo spirituality and deeply felt connection to the land are also factors that have drawn New Agers. At any rate, the liberated atmosphere here has given rise to a thriving New Age network, one that now includes alternative churches, healing centers, and healing schools. You'll find all sorts of alternative medicine and fringe practices here, from aromatherapy to rolfing (a form of massage that realigns the muscles and bones in the body) and chelation therapy (in which an IV drips ethylene diamine tetra-acetic acid into the blood to remove heavy metals). If those sound too invasive, you can always try psychic surgery.

New Age practices and beliefs have given rise to a great deal of local humor targeting their supposed psychobabble. One pointed joke asks: "How many New Agers does it take to change a light bulb?" Answer: "None. They just form a support group and learn to live in the dark." For many, however, there's much good to be found in the movement. The Dalai Lama visited Santa Fe because the city is seen as a healing center and has become a refuge for Tibetans. Notable speakers such as Ram Dass and Thomas Moore have also come to the area. Many practitioners find the alternatives—healing resources and spiritual paths—they are looking for in the receptive northern New Mexico desert and mountains.

6 Chiles, *Sopaipillas* & Other New Mexican Specialties

Northern New Mexicans are serious about eating, and the area's cuisine reflects the amalgam of cultural influences found here. Locals have given their unique blend of Hispanic and Pueblo recipes a rather prosaic, but direct, label: "Northern New Mexico Cuisine."

Food here isn't the same as Mexican cuisine or even variations like Tex-Mex and Cal-Mex. New Mexican cooking is a product of Southwestern history: Native Americans taught the Spanish conquerors about corn—how to roast it and how to make corn pudding, stewed corn, cornbread, cornmeal, and *posole* (hominy)—and they also taught the Spanish how to use chile peppers, a crop indigenous to the New World, having been first harvested in the Andean highlands as early as 4000 B.C. The Spaniards brought the practice of eating beef to the area.

Waves of newcomers have introduced other elements to the food here. From Mexico came the interest in seafood. You'll find fish tacos on many menus as well as shrimp enchiladas and ceviche (or seviche; chilled fish marinated in lime juice). New Southwestern cuisine combines elements from various parts of Mexico, such as sauces from the Yucatán Peninsula, and fried bananas served with bean dishes, typical of Costa Rica and other Central American locales. You'll also find Asian elements mixed in, such as pot stickers in a tortilla soup.

The basic ingredients of northern New Mexican cooking are three indispensable, locally grown foods: **chile, beans,** and **corn.** Of these, perhaps the most crucial is the chile, whether brilliant red or green and with various levels of spicy bite. Chiles form the base for the red and green sauces that top most northern New Mexico dishes such as enchiladas and burritos. One is not necessarily hotter than the other; spiciness depends on the type and where and during what kind of season (dry or wet) the chiles were grown. You'll also find salsas, generally made with jalapeños, tomatoes, onions, and garlic, used for chip dipping and as a spice on tacos.

Beans—spotted or painted pinto beans with a nutty taste—are simmered with garlic, onion, cumin, and red chile powder and served as a side dish. When mashed and refried in oil, they become *frijoles refritos.* **Corn** supplies the vital dough for tortillas and tamales called *masa.* New Mexican corn comes in six colors, of which yellow, white, and blue are the most common.

Even if you're familiar with Mexican cooking, the dishes you know and love are likely to be prepared differently here. The following is a rundown of some regional dishes, a number of which aren't widely known outside the Southwest:

> **(Fun Fact** **You Say Chili, We Say Chile**
>
> You'll never see "chili" on a menu in New Mexico. New Mexicans are adamant that chile, the Spanish spelling of the word, is the only way to spell it—no matter what your dictionary might say.
>
> In fact, we have such a personal attachment to this small agricultural gem that in 1983, we directed our senior U.S. senator Pete Domenici to enter New Mexico's official position on the spelling of chile into the Congressional Record. That's taking your chiles seriously.
>
> Chiles are grown throughout the state, in a perfect climate for cultivating and drying the small but powerful red and green varieties. But it is the town of Hatch, in southern New Mexico, that bills itself as the "Chile Capital of the World." Regardless of where you travel in the state, chiles appear on the menu. Usually you'll be asked whether you prefer red or green. Your best bet is to inquire which, on that particular day in that particular restaurant, is hottest and tastiest and make your decision based on the answer. If you can't decide, just say, "Christmas," and you'll get both.
>
> Virtually anything you order in a restaurant is likely to be topped with a chile sauce. If you're not accustomed to spicy foods, certain varieties will make your eyes water, your sinuses drain, and your palate feel as if it's on fire—all after just one forkful. *Warning:* No amount of water or beer will alleviate the sting. (Drink milk or eat a *sopaipilla* drizzled with honey.)
>
> But don't let these words of caution scare you away from genuine New Mexico chiles. The pleasure of eating them far outweighs the pain. Start slow, with salsas and chile sauces first, perhaps rellenos (stuffed peppers) next. Before long, you'll be buying chile ristras (chiles strung on rope) and hanging them up for decoration. Perhaps you'll be so smitten that you'll purchase bags of chile powder or a chile plant to take home.
>
> If you happen to be in New Mexico in the fall, you'll find fresh roasted green chile sold in the parking lots of most grocery stores and at some roadside stands. If you have a means of freezing the chile before transporting it home, you can sample the delicacy throughout the year. This will certainly make you an expert on the difference between chile and chili.

biscochito   A cookie made with anise.

carne adovada   Tender pork marinated in red chile sauce, herbs, and spices, and then baked.

chile rellenos   Peppers stuffed with cheese, deep-fried, then covered with green chile sauce.

chorizo burrito (also called a "breakfast burrito")   Mexican sausage, scrambled eggs, potatoes, and scallions wrapped in a flour tortilla with red or green chile sauce and melted Jack cheese.

empañada   A fried pie with nuts and currants.

enchiladas   Tortillas either rolled or layered with chicken, beef, or cheese, topped with chile sauce.

fajitas   Strips of beef or chicken sautéed with onions, green peppers, and other vegetables and served on a sizzling platter.

green chile stew   Locally grown chiles cooked in a stew with chunks of meat, beans, and potatoes.

huevos rancheros   Fried eggs on corn tortillas, topped with cheese and red or green chile, served with pinto beans.

pan dulce   A sweet Native American bread.

posole   A corn soup or stew (called *hominy* in other parts of the south), sometimes prepared with pork and chile.

sopaipilla   A lightly fried puff pastry served with honey as a dessert or stuffed with meat and vegetables as a main dish. *Sopaipillas* with honey have a cooling effect on your palate after you've eaten a spicy dish.

tacos   Spiced chicken or beef served either in soft tortillas or crispy shells.

tamales   A dish made from cornmeal mush, wrapped in husks and steamed.

vegetables and nuts   Unusual local ingredients, such as piñon nuts, jicama, and prickly pear cactus, will often be a part of your meals.

Appendix B:
Useful Toll-Free Numbers & Websites

AIRLINES

Air Canada
© 888/247-2262
www.aircanada.ca

American Airlines
© 800/433-7300
www.aa.com

America West Airlines
© 800/235-9292
www.americawest.com

British Airways
© 800/247-9297
© 0345/222-111 or
© 0845/77-333-77 in Britain
www.british-airways.com

Continental Airlines
© 800/525-0280
www.continental.com

Delta Air Lines
© 800/221-1212
www.delta.com

Frontier Airlines
© 800/432-1359
www.frontierairlines.com

Northwest Airlines
© 800/225-2525
www.nwa.com

Southwest Airlines
© 800/435-9792
www.southwest.com

United Airlines
© 800/241-6522
www.united.com

US Airways
© 800/428-4322
www.usairways.com

Virgin Atlantic Airways
© 800/862-8621 in Continental U.S.
© 0293/747-747 in Britain
www.virgin-atlantic.com

CAR-RENTAL AGENCIES

Advantage
© 800/777-5500
www.advantagerentacar.com

Alamo
© 800/327-9633
www.goalamo.com

Avis
© 800/331-1212 in Continental U.S.
© 800/TRY-AVIS in Canada
www.avis.com

Budget
© 800/527-0700
www.budget.com

Dollar
© 800/800-4000
www.dollar.com

Enterprise
© 800/325-8007
www.enterprise.com

Hertz
© 800/654-3131
www.hertz.com

National
© 800/CAR-RENT
www.nationalcar.com

Rent-A-Wreck
© 800/535-1391
www.rentawreck.com

Thrifty
© 800/367-2277
www.thrifty.com

MAJOR HOTEL & MOTEL CHAINS

Best Western International
© 800/528-1234
www.bestwestern.com

Clarion Hotels
© 800/CLARION
www.clarionhotel.com or
www.hotelchoice.com

Comfort Inns
© 800/228-5150
www.hotelchoice.com

Courtyard by Marriott
© 800/321-2211
www.courtyard.com or
www.marriott.com

Days Inn
© 800/325-2525
www.daysinn.com

Doubletree Hotels
© 800/222-TREE
www.doubletree.com

Econo Lodges
© 800/55-ECONO
www.hotelchoice.com

Fairfield Inn by Marriott
© 800/228-2800
www.marriott.com

Hampton Inn
© 800/HAMPTON
www.hampton-inn.com

Hilton Hotels
© 800/HILTONS
www.hilton.com

Holiday Inn
© 800/HOLIDAY
www.basshotels.com

Howard Johnson
© 800/654-2000
www.hojo.com

Hyatt Hotels & Resorts
© 800/228-9000
www.hyatt.com

ITT Sheraton
© 800/325-3535
www.starwood.com

La Quinta Motor Inns
© 800/531-5900
www.laquinta.com

Marriott Hotels
© 800/228-9290
www.marriott.com

Motel 6
© 800/4-MOTEL6
www.motel6.com

Quality Inns
© 800/228-5151
www.hotelchoice.com

Radisson Hotels International
© 800/333-3333
www.radisson.com

Ramada Inns
© 800/2-RAMADA
www.ramada.com

Red Roof Inns
© 800/843-7663
www.redroof.com

Residence Inn by Marriott
© 800/331-3131
www.marriott.com

Rodeway Inns
© 800/228-2000
www.hotelchoice.com

Sheraton Hotels & Resorts
© 800/325-3535
www.sheraton.com

Super 8 Motels
© 800/800-8000
www.super8.com

Travelodge
© 800/255-3050
www.travelodge.com

Westin Hotels & Resorts
© 800/937-8461
www.westin.com

Wyndham Hotels and Resorts
© 800/822-4200
www.wyndham.com

Index

See also Accommodations and Restaurant indexes, below.

ACCOMMODATIONS

RESTAURANTS

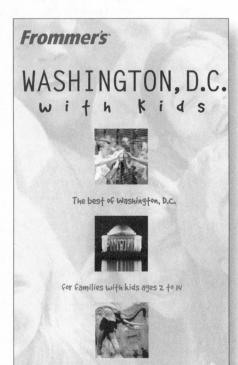

FROMMER'S® COMPLETE TRAVEL GUIDES

Alaska
Alaska Cruises & Ports of Call
American Southwest
Amsterdam
Argentina & Chile
Arizona
Atlanta
Australia
Austria
Bahamas
Barcelona, Madrid & Seville
Beijing
Belgium, Holland & Luxembourg
Bermuda
Boston
Brazil
British Columbia & the Canadian
  Rockies
Brussels & Bruges
Budapest & the Best of Hungary
Calgary
California
Canada
Cancún, Cozumel & the Yucatán
Cape Cod, Nantucket & Martha's
  Vineyard
Caribbean
Caribbean Ports of Call
Carolinas & Georgia
Chicago
China
Colorado
Costa Rica
Cruises & Ports of Call
Cuba
Denmark
Denver, Boulder & Colorado
  Springs
England
Europe
Europe by Rail
European Cruises & Ports of Call

Florence, Tuscany & Umbria
Florida
France
Germany
Great Britain
Greece
Greek Islands
Halifax
Hawaii
Hong Kong
Honolulu, Waikiki & Oahu
India
Ireland
Italy
Jamaica
Japan
Kauai
Las Vegas
London
Los Angeles
Maryland & Delaware
Maui
Mexico
Montana & Wyoming
Montréal & Québec City
Munich & the Bavarian Alps
Nashville & Memphis
New England
Newfoundland & Labrador
New Mexico
New Orleans
New York City
New York State
New Zealand
Northern Italy
Norway
Nova Scotia, New Brunswick &
  Prince Edward Island
Oregon
Ottawa
Paris
Peru

Philadelphia & the Amish
  Country
Portugal
Prague & the Best of the Czech
  Republic
Provence & the Riviera
Puerto Rico
Rome
San Antonio & Austin
San Diego
San Francisco
Santa Fe, Taos & Albuquerque
Scandinavia
Scotland
Seattle
Shanghai
Sicily
Singapore & Malaysia
South Africa
South America
South Florida
South Pacific
Southeast Asia
Spain
Sweden
Switzerland
Texas
Thailand
Tokyo
Toronto
Turkey
USA
Utah
Vancouver & Victoria
Vermont, New Hampshire &
  Maine
Vienna & the Danube Valley
Virgin Islands
Virginia
Walt Disney World® & Orlando
Washington, D.C.
Washington State

FROMMER'S® DOLLAR-A-DAY GUIDES

Australia from $50 a Day
California from $70 a Day
England from $75 a Day
Europe from $85 a Day
Florida from $70 a Day
Hawaii from $80 a Day

Ireland from $80 a Day
Italy from $70 a Day
London from $90 a Day
New York City from $90 a Day
Paris from $90 a Day
San Francisco from $70 a Day

Washington, D.C. from $80 a
  Day
Portable London from $90 a Day
Portable New York City from $90
  a Day
Portable Paris from $90 a Day

FROMMER'S® PORTABLE GUIDES

Acapulco, Ixtapa & Zihuatanejo
Amsterdam
Aruba
Australia's Great Barrier Reef
Bahamas
Berlin
Big Island of Hawaii
Boston
California Wine Country
Cancún
Cayman Islands
Charleston
Chicago
Disneyland®
Dominican Republic
Dublin

Florence
Frankfurt
Hong Kong
Las Vegas
Las Vegas for Non-Gamblers
London
Los Angeles
Los Cabos & Baja
Maine Coast
Maui
Miami
Nantucket & Martha's Vineyard
New Orleans
New York City
Paris

Phoenix & Scottsdale
Portland
Puerto Rico
Puerto Vallarta, Manzanillo &
  Guadalajara
Rio de Janeiro
San Diego
San Francisco
Savannah
Vancouver
Vancouver Island
Venice
Virgin Islands
Washington, D.C.
Whistler

FROMMER'S® NATIONAL PARK GUIDES

Algonquin Provincial Park
Banff & Jasper
Family Vacations in the National
  Parks

Grand Canyon
National Parks of the American
  West
Rocky Mountain

Yellowstone & Grand Teton
Yosemite & Sequoia/Kings
  Canyon
Zion & Bryce Canyon

FROMMER'S® MEMORABLE WALKS

Chicago
London

New York
Paris

San Francisco

FROMMER'S® WITH KIDS GUIDES

Chicago
Las Vegas
New York City

Ottawa
San Francisco
Toronto

Vancouver
Walt Disney World® & Orlando
Washington, D.C.

SUZY GERSHMAN'S BORN TO SHOP GUIDES

Born to Shop: France
Born to Shop: Hong Kong,
  Shanghai & Beijing

Born to Shop: Italy
Born to Shop: London

Born to Shop: New York
Born to Shop: Paris

FROMMER'S® IRREVERENT GUIDES

Amsterdam
Boston
Chicago
Las Vegas
London

Los Angeles
Manhattan
New Orleans
Paris
Rome

San Francisco
Seattle & Portland
Vancouver
Walt Disney World®
Washington, D.C.

FROMMER'S® BEST-LOVED DRIVING TOURS

Austria
Britain
California
France

Germany
Ireland
Italy
New England

Northern Italy
Scotland
Spain
Tuscany & Umbria

THE UNOFFICIAL GUIDES®

Beyond Disney
California with Kids
Central Italy
Chicago
Cruises
Disneyland®
England
Florida
Florida with Kids
Inside Disney

Hawaii
Las Vegas
London
Maui
Mexico's Best Beach Resorts
Mini Las Vegas
Mini Mickey
New Orleans
New York City
Paris

San Francisco
Skiing & Snowboarding in the
  West
South Florida including Miami &
  the Keys
Walt Disney World®
Walt Disney World® for
  Grown-ups
Walt Disney World® with Kids
Washington, D.C.

SPECIAL-INTEREST TITLES

Athens Past & Present
Cities Ranked & Rated
Frommer's Best Day Trips from London
Frommer's Best RV & Tent Campgrounds
  in the U.S.A.
Frommer's Caribbean Hideaways
Frommer's China: The 50 Most Memorable Trips
Frommer's Exploring America by RV
Frommer's Gay & Lesbian Europe
Frommer's NYC Free & Dirt Cheap

Frommer's Road Atlas Europe
Frommer's Road Atlas France
Frommer's Road Atlas Ireland
Frommer's Wonderful Weekends from
  New York City
The New York Times' Guide to Unforgettable
  Weekends
Retirement Places Rated
Rome Past & Present

Travel Tip: He who finds the best hotel deal has more to spend on facials involving knobbly vegetables.

Hello, the Roaming Gnome here. I've been nabbed from the garden and taken round the world. The people who took me are so terribly clever. They find the best offerings on Travelocity. For very little cha-ching. And that means I get to be pampered and exfoliated till I'm pink as a bunny's doodah.

travelocity®

1-888-TRAVELOCITY | travelocity.com | America Online Keyword: Travel

Travel Tip: Make sure there's customer service for any change of plans — involving friendly natives, for example.

One can plan and plan, but if you don't book with the right people you can't seize le moment and canoodle with the poodle named Pansy. I, for one, am all for fraternizing with the locals. Better yet, if I need to extend my stay and my gnome nappers are willing, it can all be arranged through the 800 number at, oh look, how convenient, the lovely company coat of arms.

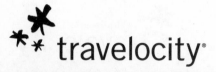

travelocity®

1-888-TRAVELOCITY / travelocity.com / America Online Keyword: Travel